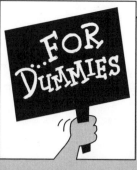

® FOR DUMMIES

References for the Rest of Us!®

COMPUTER BOOK SERIES FROM IDG

Are you intimidated and confused by computers? Do you find that traditional manuals are overloaded with technical details you'll never use? Do your friends and family always call you to fix simple problems on their PCs? Then the *. . . For Dummies®* computer book series from IDG Books Worldwide is for you.

. . . For Dummies books are written for those frustrated computer users who know they aren't really dumb but find that PC hardware, software, and indeed the unique vocabulary of computing make them feel helpless. *. . . For Dummies* books use a lighthearted approach, a down-to-earth style, and even cartoons and humorous icons to diffuse computer novices' fears and build their confidence. Lighthearted but not lightweight, these books are a perfect survival guide for anyone forced to use a computer.

Already, hundreds of thousands of satisfied readers agree. They have made *. . . For Dummies* books the #1 introductory level computer book series and have written asking for more. So, if you're looking for the most fun and easy way to learn about computers, look to *. . . For Dummies* books to give you a helping hand.

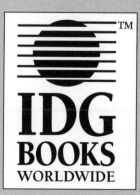

IDG BOOKS WORLDWIDE ™

P9-EMK-146

EXCEL
FOR
WINDOWS® 95
FOR
DUMMIES®

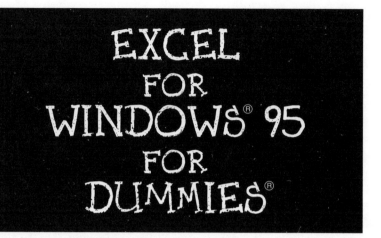

EXCEL FOR WINDOWS® 95 FOR DUMMIES®

by Greg Harvey

IDG Books Worldwide, Inc.
An International Data Group Company

Foster City, CA ◆ Chicago, IL ◆ Indianapolis, IN ◆ Braintree, MA ◆ Dallas, TX

Excel for Windows® 95 For Dummies®

Published by
IDG Books Worldwide, Inc.
An International Data Group Company
919 E. Hillsdale Blvd.
Suite 400
Foster City, CA 94404

Library of Congress Catalog Card No.: 95-79929

ISBN: 1-56884-930-3

Printed in the United States of America

10 9 8 7 6 5 4 3 2 1

1A/QW/RQ/ZV

Distributed in the United States by IDG Books Worldwide, Inc.

Distributed by Macmillan Canada for Canada; by Computer and Technical Books for the Caribbean Basin; by Contemporanea de Ediciones for Venezuela; by Distribuidora Cuspide for Argentina; by CITEC for Brazil; by Ediciones ZETA S.C.R. Ltda. for Peru; by Editorial Limusa SA for Mexico; by Transworld Publishers Limited in the United Kingdom and Europe; by Al-Maiman Publishers & Distributors for Saudi Arabia; by Simron Pty. Ltd. for South Africa; by IDG Communications (HK) Ltd. for Hong Kong; by Toppan Company Ltd. for Japan; by Addison Wesley Publishing Company for Korea; by Longman Singapore Publishers Ltd. for Singapore, Malaysia, Thailand, and Indonesia; by Unalis Corporation for Taiwan; by WS Computer Publishing Company, Inc., for the Philippines; by WoodsLane Pty. Ltd. for Australia; by WoodsLane Enterprises Ltd. for New Zealand.

For general information on IDG Books Worldwide's books in the U.S., please call our Consumer Customer Service department at 800-762-2974. For reseller information, including discounts and premium sales, please call our Reseller Customer Service department at 800-434-3422.

For information on where to purchase IDG Books Worldwide's books outside the U.S., contact IDG Books Worldwide at 415-655-3021 or fax 415-655-3295.

For information on translations, contact Marc Jeffrey Mikulich, Director, Foreign & Subsidiary Rights, at IDG Books Worldwide, 415-655-3018 or fax 415-655-3295.

For sales inquiries and special prices for bulk quantities, write to the address above or call IDG Books Worldwide at 415-655-3200.

For information on using IDG Books Worldwide's books in the classroom, or ordering examination copies, contact Jim Kelly at 800-434-2086.

For authorization to photocopy items for corporate, personal, or educational use, please contact Copyright Clearance Center, 222 Rosewood Drive, Danvers, MA 01923, or fax 508-750-4470.

 is a trademark under exclusive license to IDG Books Worldwide, Inc., from International Data Group, Inc.

About the Author

Greg Harvey, the author of over 30 computer books, has been training business people in the use of IBM PC, DOS, and software application programs such as WordPerfect, Lotus 1-2-3, and dBASE since 1983. He has written numerous training manuals, user guides, and books for business users of software, including IDG's *PC World WordPerfect 6 Handbook, 1-2-3 For Dummies, Windows For Dummies Quick Reference, WordPerfect For DOS For Dummies Quick Reference, DOS For Dummies Quick Reference, WordPerfect For Windows For Dummies Quick Reference, and Windows 95 For Dummies Quick Reference.* He currently teaches courses in Lotus 1-2-3 and dBASE in the Department of Information Systems at Golden Gate University in San Francisco.

ABOUT IDG BOOKS WORLDWIDE

Welcome to the world of IDG Books Worldwide.

IDG Books Worldwide, Inc., is a subsidiary of International Data Group, the world's largest publisher of computer-related information and the leading global provider of information services on information technology. IDG was founded more than 25 years ago and now employs more than 7,500 people worldwide. IDG publishes more than 235 computer publications in 67 countries (see listing below). More than 70 million people read one or more IDG publications each month.

Launched in 1990, IDG Books Worldwide is today the #1 publisher of best-selling computer books in the United States. We are proud to have received 8 awards from the Computer Press Association in recognition of editorial excellence, and our best-selling ...For Dummies® series has more than 19 million copies in print with translations in 28 languages. IDG Books Worldwide, through a recent joint venture with IDG's Hi-Tech Beijing, became the first U.S. publisher to publish a computer book in the People's Republic of China. In record time, IDG Books Worldwide has become the first choice for millions of readers around the world who want to learn how to better manage their businesses.

Our mission is simple: Every one of our books is designed to bring extra value and skill-building instructions to the reader. Our books are written by experts who understand and care about our readers. The knowledge base of our editorial staff comes from years of experience in publishing, education, and journalism — experience which we use to produce books for the '90s. In short, we care about books, so we attract the best people. We devote special attention to details such as audience, interior design, use of icons, and illustrations. And because we use an efficient process of authoring, editing, and desktop publishing our books electronically, we can spend more time ensuring superior content and spend less time on the technicalities of making books.

You can count on our commitment to deliver high-quality books at competitive prices on topics consumers want to read about. At IDG Books Worldwide, we value quality, and we have been delivering quality for more than 25 years. You'll find no better book on a subject than an IDG book.

John Kilcullen
President and CEO
IDG Books Worldwide, Inc.

WINNER
Eighth Annual
Computer Press
Awards 1992

WINNER
Ninth Annual
Computer Press
Awards 1993

IDG Books Worldwide, Inc., is a subsidiary of International Data Group, the world's largest publisher of computer-related information and the leading global provider of information services on information technology. International Data Group publishes over 235 computer publications in 67 countries. More than seventy million people read one or more International Data Group publications each month. The officers are Patrick J. McGovern, Founder and Board Chairman; Kelly Conlin, President; Jim Casella, Chief Operating Officer. International Data Group's publications include: **ARGENTINA'S** Computerworld Argentina, Infoworld Argentina; **AUSTRALIA'S** Computerworld Australia, Computer Living, Australian PC World, Australian Macworld, Network World, Mobile Business Australia, Publish!, Reseller, IDG Sources; **AUSTRIA'S** Computerwelt Oesterreich, PC Test; **BELGIUM'S** Data News (CW); **BOLIVIA'S** Computerworld; **BRAZIL'S** Computerworld, Connections, Game Power, Mundo Unix, PC World, Publish, Super Game; **BULGARIA'S** Computerworld Bulgaria, PC & Mac World Bulgaria, Network World Bulgaria; **CANADA'S** CIO Canada, Computerworld Canada, InfoCanada, Network World Canada, Reseller; **CHILE'S** Computerworld Chile, Informatica; **COLOMBIA'S** Computerworld Colombia, PC World; **COSTA RICA'S** PC World; **CZECH REPUBLIC'S** Computerworld, Elektronika, PC World; **DENMARK'S** Communications World, Computerworld Denmark, Computerworld Focus, Macintosh Produktkatalog, Macworld Danmark, PC World Danmark, PC Produktguide, Tech World, Windows World; **ECUADOR'S** PC World Ecuador; **EGYPT'S** Computerworld (CW) Middle East, PC World Middle East; **FINLAND'S** MikroPC, Tietoviikko, Tietoverkko; **FRANCE'S** Distributique, GOLDEN MAC, InfoPC, Le Guide du Monde Informatique, Le Monde Informatique, Telecoms & Reseaux; **GERMANY'S** Computerwoche, Computerwoche Focus, Computerwoche Extra, Electronic Entertainment, Gamepro, Information Management, Macwelt, Netzwelt, PC Welt, Publish, Publish; **GREECE'S** Publish & Macworld; **HONG KONG'S** Computerworld Hong Kong, PC World Hong Kong; **HUNGARY'S** Computerworld SZT, PC World; **INDIA'S** Computers & Communications; **INDONESIA'S** Info Komputer; **IRELAND'S** ComputerScope; **ISRAEL'S** Beyond Windows, Computerworld Israel, Multimedia, PC World Israel; **ITALY'S** Computerworld Italia, Lotus Magazine, Macworld Italia, Networking Italia, PC Shopping Italy, PC World Italia; **JAPAN'S** Computerworld Today, Information Systems World, Macworld Japan, Nikkei Personal Computing, SunWorld Japan, Windows World; **KENYA'S** East African Computer News; **KOREA'S** Computerworld Korea, Macworld Korea, PC World Korea; **LATIN AMERICA'S** GamePro; **MALAYSIA'S** Computerworld Malaysia, PC World Malaysia; **MEXICO'S** Compu Edicion, Compu Manufactura, Computacion/Punto de Venta, Computerworld Mexico, MacWorld, Mundo Unix, PC World, Windows; **THE NETHERLANDS'** Computer! Totaal, Computable (CW), LAN Magazine, Lotus Magazine, MacWorld; **NEW ZEALAND'S** Computer Buyer, Computerworld New Zealand, Network World, New Zealand PC World; **NIGERIA'S** PC World Africa; **NORWAY'S** Computerworld Norge, Lotusworld Norge, Macworld Norge, Maxi Data, Networld, PC World Ekspress, PC World Nettvork, PC World Norge, PC World's Produktguide, Publish& Multimedia World, Student Data, Unix World, Windowsworld; **PAKISTAN'S** PC World Pakistan; **PANAMA'S** PC World Panama; **PERU'S** Computerworld Peru, PC World; **PEOPLE'S REPUBLIC OF CHINA'S** China Computerworld, China Infoworld, China PC Info Magazine, Computer Fan, PC World China, Electronics International, Electronics Today/Multimedia World, Electronic Product World, China Network World, Software World Magazine, Telecom Product World; **PHILIPPINES'** Computerworld Philippines, PC Digest (PCW); **POLAND'S** Computerworld Poland, Computerworld Special Report, Networld, PC World/Komputer, Sunworld; **PORTUGAL'S** Cerebro/PC World, Correio Informatico/Computerworld, MacIn; **ROMANIA'S** Computerworld, PC World, Telecom Romania; **RUSSIA'S** Computerworld-Moscow, Mir - PK (PCW), Sety (Networks); **SINGAPORE'S** Computerworld Southeast Asia, PC World Singapore; **SLOVENIA'S** Monitor Magazine; **SOUTH AFRICA'S** Computer Mail (CIO), Computing S.A., Network World S.A., Software World; **SPAIN'S** Advanced Systems, Amiga World, Computerworld Espana, Communicaciones World, Macworld Espana, NeXTWORLD, Super Juegos Magazine (GamePro), PC World Espana, Publish; **SWEDEN'S** Attack, ComputerSweden, Corporate Computing, Macworld, Mikrodatorn, Natverk & Kommunikation, PC World, CAP & Design, DataIngenjoren, Maxi Data, Windows World; **SWITZERLAND'S** Computerworld Schweiz, Macworld Schweiz, PC Tip; **TAIWAN'S** Computerworld Taiwan, PC World Taiwan; **THAILAND'S** Thai Computerworld; **TURKEY'S** Computerworld Monitor, Macworld Turkiye, PC World Turkiye; **UKRAINE'S** Computerworld, Computers+Software Magazine; **UNITED KINGDOM'S** Computing/Computerworld, Connexion/Network World, Lotus Magazine, Macworld, Open Computing/Sunworld; **UNITED STATES'** Advanced Systems, AmigaWorld, Cable in the Classroom, CD Review, CIO, Computerworld, Computerworld Client/Server Journal, Digital Video, DOS World, Electronic Entertainment Magazine (E2), Federal Computer Week, Game Hits, GamePro, IDG Books Worldwide, Infoworld, Laser Event, Macworld, Maximize, Multimedia World, Network World, PC Letter, PC World, Publish, SWATPro, Video Event; **URUGUAY'S** PC World Uruguay; **VENEZUELA'S** Computerworld Venezuela, PC World; **VIETNAM'S** PC World Vietnam.
08/30/95

Dedication

To Shane, my partner in business and life and truly the best friend a person could have.

Acknowledgments

Let me take this opportunity to thank all of the wonderful people, both at IDG Books Worldwide and at Harvey & Associates, whose dedication and talent combined to get this book out and into your hands in such great shape.

At IDG Books, I want to thank Jennifer Wallis for making this project run as smooth as silk (and for being so much fun to work with), Milissa Koloski and Diane Steele for their unceasing support, both personal and professional, and Beth Jenkins, Cindy Phipps, Sherry Gomoll, Kathie Schnorr, Steve Peake, Paul Belcastro, Gina Scott, Dwight Ramsey, Cameron Booker, and Linda Boyer on the production team.

At Harvey & Associates, thanks to Carol Beebe for meticulously (is that right, Carol?) copy editing the raw manuscript as well as for taking care of the myriad details related to getting this thing done and out the door. Also thanks to Shane Gearing for his great work on the example files (Mother Goose would be proud).

(The Publisher would like to give special thanks to Patrick J. McGovern, without whom this book would not have been possible.)

Credits

Senior Vice President and Publisher
Milissa L. Koloski

Associate Publisher
Diane Graves Steele

Brand Manager
Judith A. Taylor

Product Development Manager
Mary Bednarek

Editorial Managers
Kristin A. Cocks
Mary C. Corder

Editorial Executive Assistant
Richard Graves

Editorial Assistants
Chris Collins
Stacey Holden Prince
Kevin Spencer

Acquisitions Assistant
Suki Gear

Production Director
Beth Jenkins

Supervisor of Project Coordination
Cindy L. Phipps

Supervisor of Page Layout
Kathie S. Schnorr

Pre-Press Coordination
Steve Peake
Tony Augsburger
Patricia R. Reynolds
Theresa Sánchez-Baker
Elizabeth Cárdenas-Nelson

Media/Archive Coordinator
Paul Belcastro
Leslie Popplewell

Associate Project Editor
Jennifer Wallis

Copy Editors
Shannon Lesley Ross
Diana R. Conover
Suzanne Packer

Technical Reviewers
Jim McCarter
Kevin Spencer

Associate Project Coordinator
Sherry Gomoll

Graphics Coordination
Shelley Lea
Gina Scott
Carla C. Radzikinas

Production Staff
Shawn Aylsworth
Cameron Booker
Linda M. Boyer
Todd Klemme
Jane Martin
Alicia Shimer
Michael Sullivan

Proofreader
Henry Lazarek
Melissa D. Buddendeck
Gwenette Gaddis
Dwight Ramsey
Robert Springer

Indexer
Richard T. Evans

Cover Design
Kavish + Kavish

Contents at a Glance

• •

Introduction *1*

Part I: Getting In on the Ground Floor *9*

Chapter 1: What Is All This Stuff? 11

Chapter 2: Creating a Spreadsheet from Scratch 55

Part II: Editing without Tears *95*

Chapter 3: Making It All Look Pretty 97

Chapter 4: Going through Changes 139

Chapter 5: Printing the Masterpiece 169

Part III: Getting Organized and Staying That Way *193*

Chapter 6: Oh What a Tangled Worksheet We Weave! 195

Chapter 7: Maintaining Multiple Worksheets 217

Part IV: Life beyond the Spreadsheet *239*

Chapter 8: The Simple Art of Making Charts 241

Chapter 9: How to Face a Database 267

Part V: Doing a Custom Job *289*

Chapter 10: Tearing Up the Town with Templates 291

Chapter 11: Stating Your Preferences 315

Chapter 12: Macros Like Your Mom Used to Make 327

Chapter 13: Button Up That Toolbar! 339

Part VI: From the Home Office in Foster City 353

Chapter 14: Top Ten New Features in Excel for Windows 95 355

Chapter 15: Top Ten Beginner Basics 357

Chapter 16: The Ten Commandments of Excel for Windows 95 359

Chapter 17: Top Ten Things in Excel That Can Trip You Up 361

Chapter 18: Top Ten Ways to Impress the Boss 363

Chapter 19: Top Ten Fun Things to Do with Excel for Windows 95
on a Network 365

Chapter 20: Top Ten Thousand Keystroke Shortcuts 367

Glossary 373

Index 385

Reader Response Card... Back of Book

Cartoons at a Glance

By Rich Tennant

page 1

page 9

page 54

page 95

page 193

page 216

page 239

page 289

page 326

page 353

Table of Contents

Introduction 1

About This Book 2
How to Use This Book 2
What You Can Safely Ignore 3
Foolish Assumptions 3
How This Book Is Organized 4
    Part I: Getting In on the Ground Floor 4
    Part II: Editing without Tears 5
    Part III: Getting Organized and Staying That Way 5
    Part IV: Life beyond the Spreadsheet 5
    Part V: Doing a Custom Job 5
    Part VI: From the Home Office in Foster City 6
Conventions Used in This Book 6
    Parts of the screen 6
    Keyboard and mouse 6
    Special icons 8
Where to Go from Here 8

Part I: Getting In on the Ground Floor 9

Chapter 1: What Is All This Stuff? 11

What the Hell Would I Do with Excel? 12
    "Little boxes, little boxes . . ." 12
    Send it to my cell address 13
    So, just how many cells are we talking about here? 14
    Assigning 26 letters to 256 columns 16
    What you should know about Excel at this point 16
    What you still need to know about Excel 17
Getting the Darn Thing Started 18
    Starting Excel from the Microsoft Office shortcut bar .. 18
    Starting Excel from the Windows 95 Start Menu 19
    Starting Excel from the Windows Explorer 19
    Creating an Excel shortcut 20
    Automatically opening Excel every time you turn on
        your computer 21
Mousing Around 23
    Minding your mouse manners 23
    Getting your mouse pointer in shape 23

So What Do All These Buttons Do? 25
    Turning on to the title bar 25
    Meandering through the menu bar 25
    Scrutinizing the Standard toolbar 27
    Finding your way around the Formatting toolbar 28
    Fumbling around the formula bar 30
    Winding your way through the workbook window 31
        When a workbook sheet is not a worksheet 31
        Manually manipulating the workbook window 31
        Slipping through the sheets 33
    Scoping out the status bar 34
        You AutoCalculate my totals 34
        The Num Lock indicator and the numeric keypad 35
You Gotta Get Me out of This Cell! 35
    The secrets of scrolling 36
        Calling up new columns with the horizontal scroll bar 36
        Raising up new rows with the vertical scroll bar 36
        Scrolling from screen to screen 37
    The keys to moving the cell pointer 37
    Block moves 39
    When you gotta go to that cell now! 40
    Lotsa luck with Scroll Lock 40
Ordering Directly from the Menus 40
    Penetrating the pull-down menus 41
    A word to you Lotus 1-2-3 converts 42
        Parlez-vous 1-2-3? 42
        Those old-fashioned formulas 43
    Comprehending context menus 44
Digging Those Dialog Boxes 46
Ogling the Online Help 49
    Handling the Help tool 50
    Asking the Answer Wizard 51
    Tending to the Tip Wizard 53
When It's Time to Make Your Exit 53

Chapter 2: Creating a Spreadsheet from Scratch **55**
So, What Ya Gonna Put in That New Workbook of Yours? 56
    The ins and outs of data entry 56
    "You must remember this . . ." 57
Doing the Data Entry Thing 57
It Takes All Types 60
    The telltale signs of text 60

How Excel evaluates its values 62
    Making sure that Excel's got your number 62
    How to get your decimal places fixed (when you don't
      even know if they're broken) 64
    Tapping on the old ten-key 65
    Entering dates with no debate 67
Fabricating those fabulous formulas! 68
If you want it, just point it out 69
Altering the natural order of operations 71
Formula flub-ups 72
Fixing Up Those Data Entry Flub-ups 73
    You really AutoCorrect that for me 74
    Cell editing etiquette 75
Taking the Drudgery out of Data Entry 77
    I'm just not complete without you 77
    Fill 'er up with AutoFill 78
      Working with a spaced series 80
      Copying with AutoFill 81
      Creating custom lists for AutoFill 82
    Entries all around the block 83
    Data entry express 84
How to Make Your Formulas Function Even Better 85
    Conjuring up formulas with the Function Wizard 86
    I'd be totally lost without AutoSum 88
Making Sure the Data's Safe and Sound 91

Part II: Editing without Tears 95

Chapter 3: Making It All Look Pretty 97

Choosing a Select Group of Cells 98
    Point-and-click cell selections 99
    Keyboard cell selections 103
Trimming Your Tables with AutoFormat 105
Festooning Your Cells with the Formatting Toolbar 108
    Transient toolbars 108
    Toolbar docking maneuvers 109
Using the Format Cells Dialog Box 111
    Getting to know the number formats 112
    The values behind the formatting 118
    Ogling the other number formats 120
Calibrating Columns 122
    Rambling rows 124
    Now you see it, now you don't 124
Futzing with the Fonts 126

Altering the Alignment 128
　　From top to bottom 128
　　Tampering with how the text wraps 130
　　Reordering the orientation 132
　　Bring on the borders! 132
　　Putting on new patterns 134
Showing Off in Styles 136
Fooling Around with the Format Painter 137

Chapter 4: Going through Changes **139**

Opening the Darned Thing Up for Editing 140
　　Opening more than one workbook at a time 140
　　Opening recently edited workbooks from the File menu 141
　　When you don't know where to find them 142
　　　　Searching the wide disk over 142
　　　　File hide-and-seek 143
　　　　Advanced hide-and-seek 144
　　　　Making a positive ID 145
　　Doing stuff besides opening files 148
Much Ado about Undo. 149
　　Undo is Redo the second time around 150
　　What ya gonna do when you can't Undo? 150
Doing the Old Drag-and-Drop Thing 151
　　Copies drag-and-drop style 152
　　Insertions courtesy of drag-and-drop 154
Formulas on AutoFill 156
　　Relatively speaking 158
　　Some things are absolutes! 158
　　Cut and Paste, digital style 161
　　"Paste it again Sam . . ." 162
　　So what's so special about Paste Special? 163
Let's Be Clear about Deleting Stuff 164
　　Sounding the all clear! 165
　　Get these cells outta here! 165
Kindly Step Aside 166
Stamping Out Your Spelling Errors 167

Chapter 5: Printing the Masterpiece **169**

Starting the Show with Print Preview 170
"The Page Stops Here . . ." 173
　　Printing it right away 173
　　Printing it your way 174
　　Printing in particular 175

My Page Was Setup! 176
    Getting the lay of the landscape 177
    Packing it all on one page 178
    Massaging the margins 179
    From header to footer 181
        Getting a standard job 181
        Getting a custom job 183
    Sorting out the sheet settings 184
    Putting out the print titles 186
When Ya Gonna Give Your Page a Break? 188
Letting Your Formulas All Hang Out 191

Part III: Getting Organized and Staying That Way 193

Chapter 6: Oh What a Tangled Worksheet We Weave! 195
Zeroing In with Zoom 196
Splitting the Difference 198
Fixed Headings Courtesy of Freeze Panes 200
Electronic Sticky Notes 204
    Singing cells (or "Do you hear what I hear?. . .") 205
    Dancing from note to note 206
The Cell Name Game 206
    If I only had a name 207
    Name that formula! 208
"Seek and Ye Shall Find . . ." 210
You Can Be Replaced! 212
You Can Be So Calculating! 213
Putting On the Protection 214

Chapter 7: Maintaining Multiple Worksheets 217
Juggling Worksheets 218
    Sliding between the sheets 218
    Editing en masse 221
Don't Short-Sheet Me! 222
    A sheet by any other name 223
    Getting your sheets in order 225
Opening Windows on Your Worksheets 227
Passing Sheets in the Night 231
To Sum Up 235

Part IV: Life beyond the Spreadsheet 239

Chapter 8: The Simple Art of Making Charts 241

Conjuring Up Charts with the ChartWizard 242
When a Chart's Just Not Your Type! 250
    The fine art of spiffing up your charts 252
    Telling all with a text box 254
    Formatting the x- or y-axis 256
    Vacillating values mean changing charts 256
    Changing perspectives 256
Picture This! 258
    One on top of the other 260
    When you need to ditch the graphics 261
Map Madness 262
Printing Charts Only 266

Chapter 9: How to Face a Database 267

Designing the Data Form 268
    Adding records to the database 269
    Locating, changing, and deleting records 273
    Scrolling the night away! 273
    Finders keepers 274
Sorting It All Out 277
You AutoFilter the Database to See the Records You Want 282
    Viewing the top ten records 284
    Getting creative with custom AutoFilters 284

Part V: Doing a Custom Job 289

Chapter 10: Tearing Up the Town with Templates 291

Templates at Your Fingertips 291
Customizing the Ready-Made Templates 295
    Tailored timecards thanks to the customized Timecard template 299
    Culling employee info from the Common database 301
    Saving timecard data in a database 302
        Creating a new database for the timecard data 304
        Saving the timecard workbook and updating the database ... 304
Turning Workbooks into Templates 304
Conjuring Up Templates with the Template Wizard 308

Chapter 11: Stating Your Preferences **315**

Varying the View Options 315
Fooling Around with the General Options 318
Changing Those Crazy Color Palettes 320
Editing the Edit Options 323
The Very Model of a Module General 325

Chapter 12: Macros Like Your Mom Used to Make **327**

Recording Macros 328
Personally Speaking 329
A Macro a Day 330
It's playback time! 334
A macro for all months 335
Relative macro recording 337
Re-recording a macro 338

Chapter 13: Button Up That Toolbar! **339**

Toolbars — Now You See 'em, Now You Don't 340
Customizing the built-in toolbars 341
Adding buttons from the Customize dialog box 342
Removing buttons from a toolbar 343
Playing musical chairs with buttons 343
What a bunch of spaced-out buttons! 343
It's not my default! 344
Designing Your Own Toolbars 344
Adding buttons that play macros 347
Cute as a button 348

Part VI: From the Home Office in Foster City *353*

Chapter 14: Top Ten New Features in Excel for Windows 95 .... **355**

Chapter 15: Top Ten Beginner Basics **357**

Chapter 16: The Ten Commandments of Excel for Windows 95 .... **359**

Chapter 17: Top Ten Things in Excel That Can Trip You Up **361**

Chapter 18: Top Ten Ways to Impress the Boss **363**

Chapter 19: Top Ten Fun Things to Do with Excel for Windows 95 on a Network 365

Chapter 20: Top Ten Thousand Keystroke Shortcuts 367

Glossary 373

Index 385

Reader Response Card .... *Back of Book*

Introduction

Welcome to *Excel For Windows 95 For Dummies*, the definitive work on Excel for Windows 95 for those of you who have no intention of ever becoming a spreadsheet guru. In this book, you find all the information that you need to keep your head above water as you accomplish the everyday tasks that people do with Excel. The intention of this book is to keep things simple and not bore you with a lot of technical details that you neither need nor care anything about. As much as possible, this book attempts to cut to the chase by telling you in plain terms just what it is that you need to do to accomplish a task using Excel.

The 5th Wave   By Rich Tennant

Determined to help Wanda find her lost database, Del connects his "Royco 100 Fish Finder" to her hard drive.

Excel For Windows 95 For Dummies covers all the fundamental techniques that you need to know in order to create, edit, format, and print your own worksheets. In addition to showing you around the worksheet, this book also exposes you to the basics of charting and creating databases. Keep in mind, though, that this book just touches on the easiest ways to get a few things done with these features — I make no attempt to cover charting and databases in a definitive way. In the main, this book concentrates on spreadsheets because spreadsheets are what most people need to create with Excel.

About This Book

This book is not meant to be read from cover to cover. Although its chapters are loosely organized in a logical order (progressing as you might when learning Excel in a classroom situation), each topic covered in a chapter is really meant to stand on its own.

Each discussion of a topic briefly addresses the question of what a particular feature is good for before launching into how to use it. In Excel, as with most other sophisticated programs, there is usually more than one way to do a task. For the sake of your sanity, I have purposely limited the choices by usually giving you only the most efficient ways to do a particular task. Later on, if you're so tempted, you can experiment with alternative ways of doing a task. For now, just concentrate on performing the task as described.

As much as possible, I've tried to make it unnecessary for you to remember anything covered in another section of the book. From time to time, however, you come across a cross-reference to another section or chapter in the book. For the most part, such cross-references are meant to help you get more complete information on a subject, should you have the time and interest. If you have neither, no problem; just ignore the cross-references as if they never existed.

How to Use This Book

This book is like a reference where you start out by looking up the topic you need information about (either in the table of contents or the index) and then refer directly to the section of interest. Most topics are explained conversationally (as though you were sitting in the back of a classroom where you can safely nap). Sometimes, however, my regiment-commander mentality takes over, and I list the steps you need to take to accomplish a particular task in a particular section.

What You Can Safely Ignore

When you come across a section that contains the steps you take to get something done, you can safely ignore all text accompanying the steps (the text that isn't in bold) if you have neither the time nor the inclination to wade through more material.

Whenever possible, I have also tried to separate background or footnote-type information from the essential facts by exiling this kind of junk to a sidebar. These sections are often flagged with icons that let you know what type of information you will encounter there. You can easily disregard text marked this way.

Information that only techie-types are likely to enjoy is flagged with a Technical Stuff icon. Unless you're a glutton for punishment, you may want to bypass this information, too.

Note, too, that the information you find flagged with a Tip icon, although designed to help you become more efficient with the program, is also usually extraneous and can be safely skipped over until you're ready for it.

When you see the bomb that signifies the Warning icon, however, it might be a good idea to linger awhile and take some time to read about what might happen if you do something that Excel doesn't like.

Foolish Assumptions

I'm going to make only one assumption about you (let's see how close I get): You have access to a PC (at least some of the time) that has Windows 95 and Excel for Windows 95 installed on it (and I'll bet there isn't much room on your hard disk for anything more!). However, having said that, I make no assumption that you've ever opened Excel for Windows 95, let alone done anything with it.

This book is written expressly for users of Excel for Windows 95. If you have a previous version of Excel for Windows (like Excel 5.0) running under the previous version of Windows (Version 3.1), please put this book down and, instead, pick up a copy of *Excel For Dummies,* 2nd Edition, or *MORE Excel 5 For Windows For Dummies,* both published by IDG Books. If you have an earlier version of Excel for the Macintosh, you also need to put this book down, walk over to the Macintosh section of the store, and pick up a copy of *Excel 5 For Macs For Dummies.*

If you happen to be using Excel 5.0 under Windows 95 (either because you just haven't seen the need for upgrading yet, you're just too cheap to purchase the upgrade, or after installing Windows 95 you simply don't have enough disk space left for Excel for Windows 95), you can use this book to learn Excel 5.0, provided that you promise me two things:

- ✔ First, you won't try to use long filenames when naming your Excel documents. This is because even though the brand-new Windows 95 recognizes filenames longer than eight characters and filenames with spaces, the older Excel 5.0 does not. This means that if you name your documents with long filenames — as I do in the examples you see in the figures in the book — their filenames will all appear horribly truncated in your Excel dialog boxes (although they're just fine in the Excel for Windows 95 dialog boxes).

- ✔ Second, you'll pay strict attention to the icon shown in the left margin. Anytime you see this baby, it means that I'm talking about a feature or set of features that are brand-new in Excel for Windows 95 (which means that they weren't yet invented in your version of Excel). I don't want any flame mail from you saying how the book's all wrong about some feature that doesn't appear in your copy of Excel. If that happens, I'll have to write you back and tell you that you weren't paying attention to the New-in-Excel-for-Windows-95 icon. Shame on you.

How This Book Is Organized

This book is organized in six parts (which gives you a chance to see at least six of those great Rich Tennant cartoons!). Each part contains two or more chapters (to keep the editors happy) that more or less go together (to keep you happy). Each chapter is further divided into loosely related sections that cover the basics of the topic at hand. You should not, however, get too hung up about following along with the structure of the book; ultimately, it doesn't matter at all if you learn how to edit the worksheet before you learn how to format it, or you learn printing before you learn editing. The important thing is that you find the information — and understand it when you find it — when you need to perform a particular task.

Just in case you're interested, a brief synopsis of what you find in each part follows.

Part I: Getting In on the Ground Floor

As the name implies, Part I covers such fundamentals as how to start the program, identify the parts of the screen, enter information in the worksheet, save a document, and so on. If you're starting with absolutely no background in using spreadsheets, you definitely want to glance at the information in Chapter 1 to learn what this program is good for before you move on to how create new worksheets in Chapter 2.

Part II: Editing without Tears

Part II gives you the skinny on how to edit spreadsheets to make them look good as well as how to make major editing changes to them without courting disaster. Refer to Chapter 3 when you need information on formatting the data to improve the way it appears in the worksheet. Refer to Chapter 4 when you need information on rearranging, deleting, or inserting new information in the worksheet. And refer to Chapter 5 when you need information on how to print out your finished product.

Part III: Getting Organized and Staying That Way

Part III gives you all kinds of information on how to stay on top of the data that you've entered in your spreadsheets. Chapter 6 is full of good ideas on how to keep track of and organize the data in a single worksheet. Chapter 7 gives you the ins and outs of working with data in different worksheets in the same workbook, and gives you information on transferring data between the sheets of different workbooks.

Part IV: Life beyond the Spreadsheet

Part IV explores some of the other aspects of Excel besides the spreadsheet. In Chapter 8, you find out just how ridiculously easy it is to create a chart using the data in a worksheet. In Chapter 9, you learn just how useful Excel's database capabilities can be when you have to track and organize a large amount of information.

Part V: Doing a Custom Job

Part V gives you ideas about how to customize the way you work with Excel. In Chapter 10, you learn how to create special form-type workbooks (called templates) from which you can quickly and easily generate all sorts of particular spreadsheets. In Chapter 11, you learn how to change the display options in Excel. In Chapter 12, you learn how to record and play back macros to automate tasks. In Chapter 13, you learn how to customize the built-in toolbars and create new toolbars of your own.

Part VI: From the Home Office in Foster City . . .

As is the tradition in these . . . *For Dummies* books, the last part contains lists of the top ten most useful and useless facts, tips, and suggestions. Don't worry, you won't have to read ten more chapters when you flip to this Part.

Conventions Used in This Book

The following information gives you the lowdown on how things look in this book — publishers call these the book's *conventions* (no campaigning, flag-waving, name-calling, or finger-pointing is involved, however).

Parts of the screen

In this book, I often refer to specific parts of the Excel for Windows 95 screen. So that you know exactly what I'm talking about, the following figure points out the names for all the different parts.

Keyboard and mouse

Excel for Windows 95 is a sophisticated program with lots of fancy boxes, plenty of bars, and more menus than you can count. In Chapter 1, I explain all about these features and how to use them. Be sure to review Chapter 1 if you have any questions about how to get around the program.

Although you use the mouse and keyboard shortcut keys to move your way in, out, and around the Excel worksheet, you do have to take some time to enter the data so that you can eventually mouse around with it. Therefore, this book occasionally encourages you to type something specific into a specific cell in the worksheet. Of course, you can always choose not to follow the instructions. When I tell you to enter a specific function, the part you should type generally appears in **bold** type. For example, **=SUM(A2:B2)** means that you should type exactly what you see: an equal sign, the word **SUM**, a left parenthesis, the text **A2:B2** (complete with a colon between the letter-number combos), and a right parenthesis. You then, of course, have to press Enter to make the entry stick.

When Excel isn't talking to you by popping up message boxes, it displays highly informative messages in the status bar at the bottom of the screen. This book renders many messages that you see on-screen like this:

```
=SUM(A2:B2)
```

Formula Bar   Workbook Title bar   Office 95 toolbar   Close button

Formatting toolbar   Restore button

Standard toolbar   Title bar   Menu bar   Minimize button

Sheet Tab scrolling buttons   Status Bar   AutoCalculate   Horizontal scroll bar

Workbook window   Sheet tabs   Windows 95 taskbar   Vertical scroll bar

Occasionally I may ask you to press a *key combination* in order to perform a certain task. Key combinations are written like this: Ctrl+S. That plus sign in between means that you should hold down both the Ctrl key and the S key at the same time before releasing them. This (sometimes cruel) type of finger aerobics may take some practice for you novices, but don't worry, you'll soon be a key-combo pro!

When you need to wade through one or more menus to get to the selection you want, I sometimes use *command arrows* to lead you from the initial menu to the submenu and so on to the command you ultimately want. For example, if you need to first open the File menu to get to the Open menu, I may write that instruction like this: File⇨Open.

Notice those underlined letters in the preceding paragraph? Those letters — given the racy name *hot keys* — represent commands that you can activate simply by first pressing the Alt key, and then pressing the underlined keys in succession. In the example of File⇨Open, you'd press Alt, and then F, and then O.

Special icons

The following icons are strategically placed in the margins to point out stuff you may or may not want to read.

This icon alerts you to nerdy discussions that you may well want to skip (or read when no one else is around).

This icon alerts you to shortcuts or other valuable hints related to the topic at hand.

This icon alerts you to information to keep in mind if you want to meet with a modicum of success.

This icon alerts you to information to keep in mind if you want to avert complete disaster.

This icon alerts you to brand-new features never before seen in Excel.

Where to Go from Here

If you've never worked with a computer spreadsheet, I suggest you go first to Chapter 1 and find out what you're dealing with. If you're already familiar with the ins and outs of electronic spreadsheets but don't know anything about creating worksheets with Excel, jump into Chapter 2 where you find out how to get started entering data and formulas. Then, as specific needs arise (like "How do I copy a formula?" or "How do I print just a particular section of my worksheet?"), you can go to the table of contents or the index to find the appropriate section and go right to that section for answers.

Part I

Getting In on the Ground Floor

The 5th Wave   By Rich Tennant

SOFTWARE APPLICATION
TESTING CENTER

EXIT

"WE TEST FOR COMPATIBILITY, PERFORMANCE, SERVICE AND FORMATTING. IF IT FAILS THESE, THEN IT'S TESTED FOR THE DISTANCE IT CAN BE SAILED ACROSS THE PARKING LOT AND ONTO THE EXPRESSWAY."

In this part . . .

One look at the Excel for Windows 95 screen (with all its boxes, buttons, and tabs), and you realize that there's a whole lot of stuff going on here. This is no doubt due to the addition of the Windows 95 taskbar to the (already rather over-designed) Excel 5.0 for Windows 3.1 screen and then throwing in the Office toolbar to boot! Well, not to worry: Chapter 1's only reason for being is to break down the parts of the Excel for Windows 95 screen and make some sense out of the rash of icons, buttons, and boxes that you're going to be facing day after day after day.

Of course, it's not enough to just sit back and have someone like me explain what's what on the screen. To get any good out of Excel, you've got to start learning how to use all these bells and whistles (or buttons and boxes, in this case). That's where Chapter 2 comes in, giving you the lowdown on how to use some of the screen's more prominent buttons and boxes to get your spreadsheet data entered and keep it there. From this humble beginning, it's a quick trip to total screen mastery.

Chapter 1

What Is All This Stuff?

. . . .

In This Chapter

▶ Deciding how you can use Excel

▶ Looking at cell basics

▶ Starting Excel in lots of cool ways

▶ Making sense of the Excel for Windows 95 screen

▶ Getting the lowdown on the Excel toolbars

▶ Surfing an Excel workbook

▶ Selecting commands from the pull-down menus

▶ Selecting commands from the context menus

▶ Telling the Answer Wizard all your problems

▶ Getting the hell out of Excel

. . . .

*J*ust because electronic spreadsheets like Excel for Windows 95 have become almost as commonplace on today's personal computers as word processors and games doesn't mean that they're either well understood or well used. In fact, I've encountered scads of users, even those who are reasonably well versed in the art of writing and editing in Microsoft Word, who have little or no idea of what they could or should do with Excel.

This is really a shame, especially in this day and age when Microsoft Office seems to be the only software found on the majority of machines (probably because Windows 95 and Microsoft Office for Windows 95 hog so much hard disk space, there's no room left to install anybody else's software). If you're one of the folks who has Office on your computer but doesn't know a spreadsheet from a bedsheet, this means that Excel for Windows 95 is just sitting there taking up a lot of space. Well, it's high time to change all that.

What the Hell Would I Do with Excel?

Excel is a great organizer for all types of data, be they numeric, textual, or otherwise. Because the program has loads of built-in calculating capabilities, most people turn to Excel when they need to set up financial spreadsheets. These spreadsheets tend to be filled to the gills with formulas for computing stuff like total sales, net profits and losses, growth percentages, and that sort of thing.

Also popular are Excel's charting capabilities that enable you to create all types of charts and graphs from the numbers you crunch in your financial worksheets. Excel makes it really easy to turn columns and rows of boring, black-and-white numbers into colorful and snappy charts and graphs. You can then use these charts to add some pizazz to written reports (like those created with Microsoft Word) or to punch up overheads used in formal business presentations (like those created with Microsoft PowerPoint).

Now, even if your job doesn't involve creating worksheets with a lot of fancy-Dan financial calculations or la-di-da charts, you probably have plenty of things for which you could and should be using Excel. For instance, you may have to keep lists of information or maybe even put together tables of information for your job. Excel is a great list keeper (even though we tend to refer to such lists as *databases* in Excel) and one heck of a table maker. Therefore, you can use Excel anytime you need to keep track of the products you sell, clients you service, employees you oversee, or you name it.

"Little boxes, little boxes . . ."

There's a really good reason why Excel is such a whiz at doing financial calculations by formula and keeping lists and tables of information organized. Look at any blank Excel worksheet (the one in Figure 1-1 will do fine) and just what do you see? Boxes, lots of little boxes, that's what! These little boxes (and there are millions of them in each worksheet you encounter) are called *cells* in spreadsheet jargon. And each piece of information (like a name, address, monthly sales figure, even your Aunt Sally's birthdate) goes into its own box (cell) in the worksheet you're building.

If you're used to word processing, this idea of entering different types of information in little, bitty cells can be somewhat strange to get used to. If you're thinking in word-processing terms, you need to think of the process of building an Excel worksheet as being more like setting up a table of information in a Word document than writing a letter or report.

Figure 1-1:
"Little boxes,
little boxes,
and they all
look just the
same!"

Send it to my cell address

As you can see in Figure 1-1, the Excel worksheet contains a frame used to label the columns and rows. Columns are given letters of the alphabet, while the rows are numbered. The columns and rows must be labeled because the Excel worksheet is humongous (Figure 1-1 shows only a tiny part of the total worksheet). The column and row labels act like street signs in a city — they can help you identify your current location, even if they don't prevent you from becoming lost.

TECHNICAL STUFF

Why spreadsheet programs produce nothing but worksheets

Spreadsheet programs like Excel for Windows 95 refer to their electronic sheets as *worksheets* rather than *spreadsheets*. And, although it is perfectly acceptable (even preferable) to call one of its electronic sheets a worksheet, you never, never refer to Excel as a worksheet program — it is always referred to as a spreadsheet program. Therefore, you can think of Excel as a spreadsheet program that produces worksheets, but *not* as a worksheet program that produces spreadsheets.

Cells: the building blocks of all worksheets

The cells in an Excel worksheet are formed by the intersection of the column and row grid. Technically, such an arrangement is known as an *array*. An array keeps track of different pieces of information stored in it by referring to its row position and its column position (something you'll see more clearly when the subject of the R1C1 cell referencing system is discussed in the sidebar called "Cell A1 aka Cell R1C1," later in this chapter). This means that to display your worksheet data in its grid and tabular format, Excel just reads off the row and column position associated with the data you entered there.

In Figure 1-2, Excel constantly shows you your current position in the worksheet in two different ways:

- ✔ Above the worksheet display at the beginning of what's called the *formula bar,* Excel lists the current cell location by its column and row reference as D5 when the cell at the intersection of column D and row 5 is current (the so-called *A1 cell reference system*).
- ✔ In the worksheet itself, the *cell pointer* (see the callout in Figure 1-2), shown by a heavy border, appears in the cell that's currently selected.

You wonder why Excel makes such a big deal about telling you which cell is current in the worksheet? That's a good question, and the answer is important:

In the worksheet, you can only enter or edit information in the cell that's current.

The repercussions of this seemingly innocuous little statement are enormous. It means that if you're paying more attention to what you need to enter in your spreadsheet than to which cell is current, you can end up replacing something you've already entered. It also means that you'll never be able to edit a particular cell entry if you haven't first selected the cell to make it current.

So, just how many cells are we talking about here?

It's no exaggeration to say that each worksheet contains millions of cells, any of which can be filled with information. Each worksheet has 256 columns (of which, only the first 9 [A through I] are normally visible in a new worksheet) and 16,384 rows (of which, only the first 16 or 17 are normally visible in a new worksheet). If you multiply 256 by 16,384, you come up with a total of 4,194,304 empty cells in each worksheet you use (that's over 4 million of those suckers)!

Current cell reference   Cell pointer

Cell A1 aka Cell R1C1

The A1 cell reference system is a holdover from the VisiCalc days (VisiCalc being the granddaddy of spreadsheet programs for personal computers). In addition to the A1 system, Excel for Windows 95 supports a much older, technically more correct system of cell references called the *R1C1* cell reference system. In this system, both the columns and rows in the worksheet are numbered, and the row number precedes the column number. For example, in this system, cell A1 is called R1C1 (row 1, column 1); cell A2 is R2C1 (row 2, column 1); and cell B1 is R1C2 (row 1, column 2).

And, as if that weren't enough, each new workbook that you start comes equipped with 16 of these worksheets, each with its own 4,194,304 blank cells. This gives you a grand total 46,108,864 cells at your disposal in any one Excel file you happen to have open. And, should that prove to be too few (yeah, right!), you can add more worksheets (each with its 4,194,304 cells) to the workbook.

Assigning 26 letters to 256 columns

When it comes to labeling the 256 columns in a worksheet, our alphabet — with its measly 26 letters — is not up to the task. To make up the difference, Excel doubles up the cell letters in the column reference so that column AA immediately follows column Z. This is followed by column AB, AC, and so on to AZ. After column AZ, you find column BA, and then BB, BC, and so on. According to this system for doubling the column letters, the 256th (and last) column of the worksheet is column IV. This, in turn, gives the very last cell of any worksheet the cell reference IV16384.

What you should know about Excel at this point

Thus far, you know (or should know) the following things about Excel:

✔ Each Excel file is referred to as a *workbook*.

✔ Each new workbook you open contains 16 blank worksheets.

✔ Each worksheet in a workbook is divided into about 4 million cells (4,194,304 actually) made by the intersection of the 256 columns and 16,384 rows.

More worksheet size trivia

If you were to produce the entire worksheet grid on paper, you would need a sheet that was approximately 21 feet wide by 341 feet long to do it! On a 13-inch computer screen, you can normally see no more than 9 complete columns and 17 complete rows of the entire worksheet. With columns being about 1 inch wide and rows about ¼ inch high, 9 columns represent a scant 3.5 percent of the total width of the worksheet, while 17 rows fill only about 0.1 percent of its total length. This should give you some idea of how little of the total worksheet is visible on the screen as well as just how much area is available.

✔ Each worksheet is surrounded on the left and the top with a frame that labels the columns with letters of the alphabet and rows with numbers. Columns beyond column Z have a double-letter designation such as AA, AB, and so on.

✔ All spreadsheet information is stored in the individual cells of the worksheet. You can, however, only enter information into the cell that is current.

✔ Excel indicates which of the 4 million cells in the worksheet is the current one by displaying its cell reference on the formula bar and displaying the cell pointer in the worksheet itself. (Refer to Figure 1-2.)

✔ The system for referencing cells in a worksheet — the so-called A1 cell reference system — combines the column letter (or letters) with the row number.

What you still need to know about Excel

Armed with the preceding information alone, however, you could easily get the mistaken idea that a spreadsheet program like Excel is little more than a quirky word processor with a gridlock that forces you to enter your information in tiny, individual cells instead of offering you the spaciousness of full pages.

Well, I'm here to say that Bill Gates didn't become a billionaire several times over by selling a quirky word processor (all you Microsoft Word users out there, please hold your tongues!). The big difference between the cell of a worksheet and the pages of a word processor is that each cell offers computing power along with text-editing and formatting capabilities. This computing power takes the form of formulas that you create in various cells of the worksheet.

Quite unlike a paper spreadsheet, which contains only values computed somewhere else, an electronic worksheet can store both the formulas and the computed values returned by these formulas. Even better, your formulas can use values stored in other cells of the worksheet, and, as explained later, Excel automatically updates the computed answer returned by such a formula anytime you change these values in the worksheet.

Excel's computational capabilities, combined with its editing and formatting capabilities, make the program perfect for generating any kind of document that uses textual and numeric entries and requires you to perform calculations on the values. Because you can make your formulas dynamic — so that their calculations are automatically updated when you change referenced values stored in other cells of the worksheet — you will find it much easier to keep the calculated values in a worksheet document both current and correct.

Getting the Darn Thing Started

If you're at all familiar with using Windows 95, it will come as no shock to find out that there about a zillion ways to get Excel up and running (actually, there are only about five, and I'm only going to talk about four of them). Suffice it to say at this point that all the various and sundry methods for starting Excel require that you have Windows 95 installed on your personal computer. After that, you have only to turn on the computer before you can use any of the following methods to get Excel started.

Starting Excel from the Microsoft Office shortcut bar

Starting Excel from the Microsoft Office shortcut bar is the easiest way to get the program up and running. The only problem with this method is that you can't use it unless you have Microsoft Office for Windows 95 installed on your computer and, further, have the shortcut bar open. Supposing that both these preconditions are met, to start Excel you have merely to click the Microsoft Excel button on this shortcut bar to start the program (use Figure 1-3 to identify the Microsoft Excel button on this bar).

Figure 1-3: To start Excel from the Microsoft Office shortcut bar, click the Microsoft Excel button as shown in the upper-right corner.

Starting Excel from the Windows 95 Start Menu

Even if you don't have the luxury of starting Excel from the Microsoft Office shortcut bar (because you don't have Microsoft Office), you can still start the program from Windows 95's Start menu. And if you only use Excel and don't own Microsoft Office for Windows 95, the Start menu is definitely the way to go.

To start Excel from the Start menu, follow these simple steps:

1. **Click the Start button on the Windows 95 taskbar to open the Windows 95 Start menu.**

2. **Select ⎯Programs at the top of the Start menu.**

3. **Select Microsoft Excel on the continuation menu.**

As soon as you get through step 3, Windows 95 opens Excel. As the program loads, you see the opening screen for Microsoft Excel for Windows 95. When Excel finishes loading, you are presented with a screen like the one shown in Figure 1-1 and Figure 1-2, containing a new workbook where you can begin working.

Starting Excel from the Windows Explorer

Not content with just two ways for starting Excel for Windows 95? Well, how about another — this time using the Windows Explorer! The reason this start-up method is so valuable is that, with a slight variation, you can use it to open the Excel workbook you need to work on at the same time you start the program.

First, here are the steps for starting Excel from the Explorer with a new, empty workbook:

1. **Open the Windows 95 Explorer.**

   Click the Start button on the taskbar, select ⎯Programs on the Start menu, and then click Windows Explorer.

2. **Locate the Microsoft Excel folder or the Office 95 folder in the All Folders list box of the Exploring - C:\ window.**

   If you don't have Microsoft Office, go to step 3a; if you do have it, go to step 3b.

3a. **Click the Microsoft Excel folder icon in the All Folders list box, and then double-click the Excel program icon (appearing as the word "Excel" preceded by the XL icon) in the Contents of list box.**

3b. Click the Microsoft Office folder icon in the All Folders list box, and then double-click the Excel folder icon in the Contents of list box before finally double-clicking the Excel program icon.

Now this is a lot of stuff to go through if all you need to do is to start Excel for Windows 95 with a new workbook. But it's a great way to start the program if you happen to be using the Windows Explorer to find the Excel file you want to work with. In such a case, you have only to locate the Excel workbook file in the Contents of list box in the Exploring window and then double-click its file icon. Windows starts Excel for Windows 95 and then immediately opens the workbook file you just double-clicked.

Creating an Excel shortcut

If you don't own Excel for Windows 95 as part of Microsoft Office, and therefore don't have the option of starting the program with the Microsoft Office shortcut bar, I highly recommend that you create a shortcut for Excel so that you can start the program simply by double-clicking the shortcut icon on the desktop. To create a shortcut for Excel, you follow these steps:

1. **Click the Start button on the taskbar.**

2. **Select Find on the Start menu and click Files or Folders on the Find continuation menu.**

3. **Type excel in the Named edit box of the Find: All Files dialog box, and then press Enter or click the Find Now button.**

4. **When Windows 95 finishes locating all files named Excel on your hard disk, scroll down until you find a file named EXCEL.EXE whose Type is listed as Application (this is the program file that Windows uses to open Excel).**

5. **Click the EXCEL.EXE file icon.**

   This opens its context menu.

6. **Click Create Shortcut on the context menu.**

   Windows 95 displays the alert dialog box warning you that Windows cannot create a shortcut in the Find dialog box and asking whether you want the shortcut placed on the desktop instead.

7. **Press Enter or click the Yes button.**

8. **Click the Close button (the one with the X) on the Find dialog box to get rid of it.**

   When Windows 95 closes the Find dialog box, you find a new icon on your desktop called "Shortcut to Excel." If you want, you can rename this icon to something a little less obvious like **Excel**, or words to that effect, by following step 9. Otherwise, if you're satisfied with the default shortcut name, you're done!

9. **Click the Shortcut to Excel icon with the secondary mouse button, and then click Rename on the context menu.**

   You can then replace the original name by typing a new name beneath the icon and pressing Enter when you're finished.

To start Excel for Windows 95 with your new shortcut on the desktop, double-click the icon. Excel then opens with a new workbook as it does when you start the program from the Microsoft Office shortcut bar or the Start menu.

Automatically opening Excel every time you turn on your computer

This last technique for starting Excel for Windows 95 is only for those few of you who need to use Excel almost every single time you use your computer. If you fall into this class of Excel users, you can have Windows automatically start Excel as soon as Windows 95 finishes loading, every time you turn on your computer. This way, all you have to do is turn on the power to your computer (you do know where the computer's power switch is, don't you?), and in just a little while, you're set to get down to work in Excel.

To get Windows 95 to automatically start Excel every time you turn on the computer, you need to put a copy of the Microsoft Excel shortcut in the Startup folder. You accomplish this little trick with these steps:

1. **Click the Start button on the taskbar, and then select Settings on the Start menu and click Taskbar on the Settings continuation menu.**

2. **Click the Start Menu Programs tab in the Taskbar Properties dialog box.**

3. **Click the A̲dvanced button (don't be afraid of the name) on the Start Menu Programs tab.**

4. **Click the little plus sign (+) in front of the Programs icon.**

   You can find the Programs icon beneath the Start Menu folder icon in the All Folders list box to open the Programs folder.

5. **Locate Microsoft Excel in the Contents of list box.**

   It's the one with the XL icon in front of it.

6. **Use the scroll bar for the All Folders list box to scroll down until the Startup folder icon is displayed in this list box.**

7. **Hold down the Ctrl key, and then click and drag the Microsoft Excel icon from the Contents of list box to the Startup folder in the All Folders list box.**

   When doing this step, be sure that you hold down the Ctrl key the whole time you drag (if you're doing it right, you should see a little plus sign in a box beneath your mouse pointer). Don't release the mouse button until you see that the Startup folder name is highlighted. Then, release first the mouse button before you let up on the Ctrl key.

8. **Make sure that you've copied the Microsoft Excel shortcut to the Startup folder by clicking the Startup folder icon in the All Folders list box to open it.**

   You should see the Microsoft Excel shortcut icon in the Contents of list box of the Exploring window, along with any other utilities or programs that you run each time you start Windows 95. If you don't see this shortcut icon, sorry, but you need to repeat steps 6 through 8 before proceeding to step 9.

9. **Click the Close button in the Exploring window to get rid of it.**

   The Close button is the one with an X.

10. **Click the OK button in the Taskbar Properties dialog box to close it.**

After placing a copy of the Microsoft Excel shortcut in the Startup folder, Excel will now automatically open the next time you start Windows. You can test this by clicking the Start button, and then clicking Shut Down on the Start menu. Next, click the Restart the computer radio button in the Shut Down windows dialog box before you choose the Yes button or press Enter.

If you later decide that you don't want or need Excel staring you in the face each time you start your computer, you can stop all this automated start-up nonsense by removing the Microsoft Excel shortcut from the Startup folder. To do this, follow the first four steps of the preceding list and then switch to these steps:

5. **Locate the Startup folder in the All Folders list box; then click its icon to open it.**

6. **Click the Microsoft Excel shortcut icon in the Contents of list box.**

7. **Press the Delete key.**

8. **Click the Yes button.**

   Or you can press Enter in response to the message in the Confirm File Delete dialog box asking you if you are sure that you want to send 'Microsoft Excel' to the Recycle Bin.

9. **Click the Close button in the Exploring window to get rid of it.**

   The Close button is the one with the X.

10. **Click the OK button in the Taskbar Properties dialog box to close it.**

Mousing Around

Although most of Excel's capabilities are accessible from the keyboard, in most cases the mouse is the most efficient way to select a command or perform a particular procedure. For that reason alone, if you need to use Excel regularly in getting your work done, it is well worth your time to master the program's various mouse techniques.

Minding your mouse manners

Windows programs such as Excel use three basic mouse techniques to select and manipulate various objects in the program and workbook windows:

- **Clicking an object:** positioning the pointer on something and then pressing and immediately releasing the primary (left for right-handers or right for lefties) or, more rarely, the secondary (right for right-handers and left for southpaws) mouse button.

- **Double-clicking an object:** positioning the pointer on something and then pressing and immediately releasing the primary mouse button rapidly twice in a row.

- **Dragging an object:** positioning the pointer on something and then pressing and holding down the primary mouse button as you move the mouse in the direction you wish to drag the object. When you have positioned the object in the desired location on the screen, you then release the primary mouse button to place it.

When clicking an object to select it, you must make sure that the point of the arrowhead is touching the object you want to select before you click. To avoid moving the pointer slightly before you click, grasp the sides of the mouse between your thumb (on one side) and your ring and little fingers (on the other side), and then click the primary button with your index finger. If you run out of room on your desktop for moving the mouse, just pick up the mouse and reposition it on the desk (this does not move the pointer).

Getting your mouse pointer in shape

The shape of the mouse pointer is anything but static in the Excel program. As you move the mouse pointer to different parts of the Excel screen, the pointer changes shape to indicate a change in function. Table 1-1 shows you the various faces of the mouse pointer as well as the use of each shape. (This is such important information, you will also find it repeated on the cheat sheet located at the very beginning of the book — unless someone has already torn the darn thing out!)

Table 1-1	Minding the shape of the mouse pointer in Excel
Mouse Pointer Shape	*What It Means*
⊕	This thick, white cross pointer appears as you move the pointer around the cells of the current worksheet. You use this pointer to select the cells you need to work with.
↖	The arrowhead pointer appears when you position the pointer on the toolbar, Excel menu bar, or on one of the edges of the block of cells that you've selected. You use the arrowhead pointer to choose Excel commands or to move or copy a cell selection with the drag-and-drop technique.
I	The I-beam pointer appears when you click the entry in the formula bar, double-click a cell, or press F2 to edit a cell entry. You use this pointer to locate your place when editing a cell entry either in the cell itself or on the formula bar.
+	The fill handle (the thin, black cross) appears only when you position the pointer on the lower-right corner of the cell that contains the cell pointer. You use this pointer to create a series of sequential entries in a block or to copy an entry or formula in a block of cells.
↖?	The help pointer appears when you click the Help tool in the Standard toolbar. You use this pointer to click the menu command or tool on a toolbar for which you want help information.
↔	The double-headed arrow pointer appears when you've moved over the side of some object that can be sized. You use this pointer to increase or decrease the size of the object (be it a column, row, or text box).
╫	The split double-headed arrow pointer appears when you position the pointer over the horizontal or vertical split box or the tab split bar. You use this pointer to split the workbook window into different panes or to increase or decrease the size of the horizontal scroll bar.
✥	The crossed double-headed arrow pointer appears when you choose Move on the workbook Control menu or press Ctrl+F7. You use this pointer to drag the workbook window into a new position in the area between the formula and status bar.

Don't confuse the cell pointer with the mouse pointer. The mouse pointer changes shape as you move it around the screen. The cell pointer always maintains its shape as an outline around the current cell or cell selection (whereupon it expands to include all the selected cells). The mouse pointer responds to any movement of your mouse on the desk and always moves independently of the cell pointer. You can use the mouse pointer to reposition the cell pointer, however. You do this by positioning the thick, white cross pointer in the cell that you want to hold the cell pointer and then clicking the primary mouse button.

So What Do All These Buttons Do?

Figure 1-4 identifies the different parts of the Excel program window that appear when you first start the program (assuming that you haven't selected an existing workbook to open at the same time the program starts and that you don't have the Microsoft Office shortcut bar open). As you can see, the Excel window, upon opening, is chock-full of all kinds of useful, though potentially confusing, stuff!

Turning on to the title bar

The first bar in the Excel window is called the *title bar* because it shows you the name of the program that is running in the window (Microsoft Excel). When the workbook window is maxed out (as it is in Figure 1-4), the name of the workbook file follows Microsoft Excel, as in

```
Microsoft Excel - Book1
```

To the left of the program and filename on the title bar, you see the XL icon. If you click this icon, the program Control menu opens with all the commands that let you size and move the Excel program window. If you choose the Close command on this menu (or press the shortcut keys, Alt+F4), you exit from Excel and are returned to the desktop.

The buttons on the right side of the title bar are sizing buttons. If you click the Minimize button (the one with the underscore), the Excel window shrinks down to a button on the Windows 95 taskbar. If you click the Restore button (the one with the image of two smaller, tiled windows), the Excel window assumes a somewhat smaller size on the desktop and the Restore button changes to the Maximize button (the one with a single, full-size window), which you can use to restore the window to its original full size. If you click the Close button (the one with an X), you exit Excel (just as though you had chosen Close on the Control menu or pressed Alt+F4).

Meandering through the menu bar

The second bar in the Excel window is the menu bar. This bar contains the Excel pull-down menus, File through Help, that you use to select the Excel commands you need to use (jump ahead to the section "Ordering Directly from the Menus" for more information on how to select commands).

Formula bar

Formatting toolbar

Standard toolbar   Title bar   Menu bar

Close button

Restore button

Minimize button

Figure 1-4:
The Excel
program
window
contains as
many
buttons and
bars as a
general's
lapel.

Workbook window
with new workbook

Status bar

Horizontal scroll bar with sheet tabs

Windows 95 taskbar

Vertical scroll bar

To the left of the pull-down menus, you see an Excel file icon. If you click this icon, the file Control menu (much like the program Control menu) opens, showing all the commands that let you size and move the Excel workbook window (which fits within the Excel program window). If you choose the Close command on this menu (or press the shortcut keys, Ctrl+W or Ctrl+F4), you close the current Excel workbook without exiting the Excel program.

The sizing buttons on the right side of the menu bar do the same thing to the current workbook window as the sizing buttons on the title bar do to the Excel program window. If you click the Minimize button, the Excel workbook window shrinks down to a tiny workbook title bar at the bottom of the workbook area. If you click the Restore button, the current workbook window assumes a some-what smaller size on the workbook area; the XL workbook icon, filename, and file-sizing buttons move to the title bar of this somewhat smaller workbook window; and the Restore button changes to the Maximize button, which you can use to restore the window to its original full size. If you click the Close button (the one with the X), you close the current workbook file (just as though you had chosen Close on the file Control menu or pressed Ctrl+W or Ctrl+F4).

Tiptoe through the tooltips

To display the name of a tool on any toolbar shown on the screen, simply position the mouse pointer on the tool. Excel then displays the name of the tool in a little box below the pointer and a brief description of what the tool does on the Status bar. (Microsoft refers to this feature as "tooltips" — I'm not making this up!)

Scrutinizing the Standard toolbar

The Standard toolbar occupies the third bar of the Excel program window. Each button (more commonly called a *tool*) in this bar performs a particular function when you click it with the mouse. For example, you can use the first tool to open a new workbook, the second one to open an existing workbook file, the third one to save the current workbook, and the fourth one to print the workbook. Table 1-2 shows you the name and function of each tool on the Standard toolbar. Rest assured, you will come to know each one intimately as your experience with Excel grows.

Table 1-2	The cool tools on the Standard toolbar	
Tool in Question	*Tool Name*	*What the Tool Does When You Click It*
	New Workbook	Opens a new workbook with 16 blank worksheets
	Open	Opens an existing Excel workbook
	Save	Saves changes in the active workbook
	Print	Prints the workbook
	Print Preview	Previews how the worksheet will appear when printed
	Spelling	Checks the spelling of text in your worksheet
	Cut	Cuts the current selection to the Clipboard
	Copy	Copies the current selection to the Clipboard
	Paste	Pastes the contents of the Clipboard in the current worksheet
	Format Painter	Applies all the formatting used in the current cell to any cell selection you choose

(continued)

Table 1-2 *(continued)*

Tool in Question	Tool Name	What the Tool Does When You Click It
	Undo	Undoes your last action
	Repeat	Repeats your last action
	AutoSum	Adds a list of values with the SUM function
	Function Wizard	Steps you through creating a formula using one of Excel's many built-in functions (see Chapter 2 for details)
	Sort Ascending	Sorts data in a cell selection in alphabetical and/or numerical order, depending upon the type of data in the cell
	Sort Descending	Sorts data in a cell selection in reverse alphabetical and/or numerical order, depending upon the type of data in the cells
	ChartWizard	Steps you through the creation of a new chart in the active worksheet (see Chapter 8 for details)
	Map	Creates a map from worksheet data that analyzes the info by geographic region (see Chapter 8 for details)
	Drawing	Displays the Drawing toolbar, which lets you draw various shapes and arrows (see Chapter 8 for details)
100%	Zoom Control	Changes the screen magnification to zoom in or out on your worksheet data
	TipWizard	Gives you tips on how to do things faster and quicker in Excel based on whatever actions you've just been performing
	Help	Gives you help information on the command or region of the screen that you click with the question-mark pointer

Finding your way around the Formatting toolbar

Beneath the Standard toolbar, you see the Formatting toolbar, so called because its buttons are mainly used to format cells in your worksheet. Table 1-3 shows you the name of each tool on this toolbar along with a brief description of its function.

Table 1-3	The cool tools on the Formatting toolbar	
Tool	*Tool Name*	*What the Tool Does When You Click It*
`Arial` ▾	Font	Applies a new font to the entries in the cell selection
`10` ▾	Font Size	Applies a new font size to the entries in the cell selection
B	Bold	Applies bold to the cell selection
I	Italic	Applies italics to the cell selection
U	Underline	Underlines the *entries* in the cell selection (not the cells); if the entries are already underlined, clicking this tool removes the underlining
▤	Align Left	Left-aligns the entries in the cell selection
▤	Center	Centers the entries in the cell selection
▤	Align Right	Right-aligns the entries in the cell selection
⊞	Center Across Columns	Centers the entry in the active cell across selected columns
$	Currency Style	Applies a Currency number format to the cell selection to display all values with a dollar sign, with commas between thousands, and two decimal places
%	Percent Style	Applies a Percentage number format to the cell selection; the values are multiplied by 100 and displayed with a percent sign and no decimal places
,	Comma Style	Applies a Comma number format to the cell selection to display commas separating thousands and adds two decimal places
⁺⁰⁰	Increase Decimal	Adds one decimal place to the number format in the cell selection each time you click the tool; reverses direction and reduces the number of decimal places when you hold the Shift key as you click this tool
⁰⁰₊	Decrease Decimal	Reduces one decimal place from the number format in the cell selection each time you click the tool; reverses direction and adds one decimal place when you hold the Shift key as you click this tool

(continued)

Table 1-3 *(continued)*

Tool	Tool Name	What the Tool Does When You Click It
	Borders	Selects a border for the cell selection from the pop-up palette of border styles
	Color	Selects a new color for the background of the cells in the cell selection from the pop-up color palette
	Font Color	Selects a new color for the text in the cells in the cell selection from the pop-up color palette

The Standard and Formatting toolbars contain the most commonly used tools and are the ones that are automatically displayed in the Excel window when you first start the program. Excel does, however, include several other toolbars that you can display as your work requires their special tools. As you soon discover, Excel's toolbars are a real boon to productivity because they make the program's standard routines so much more accessible than the pull-down menus.

Fumbling around the formula bar

The formula bar displays the cell address and the contents of the current cell. This bar is divided into three sections by two vertical lines. If the current cell is empty (as is cell A1 in Figure 1-4), the third section of the formula bar is blank. As soon as you begin typing an entry or building a worksheet formula, the second and third sections of the formula bar come alive.

As soon as you press a key, a drop-down list button (designed to show you a list of range names that you've created for the workbook — see Chapter 6 for details on using range names), followed by the Cancel, Enter, and Function Wizard buttons (see Chapter 2 to learn how you use these), appears in the second section.

After this string of buttons, you see the characters that you've typed in the third section of the bar, mirroring the characters that appear in the worksheet cell itself. After you complete the entry in the cell — either by clicking the Enter button on the formula bar or by pressing Enter or an arrow key — Excel displays the entire entry or formula in the formula bar, and the string of buttons disappears from the center section of the formula bar. The contents of that cell thereafter appear in the formula bar whenever that cell contains the cell pointer.

Winding your way through the workbook window

A blank Excel workbook appears in a workbook window right below the formula bar when you first start the program (assuming that you don't start it by double-clicking an Excel workbook icon). As you can see in Figure 1-5, when the workbook window is less than full size and larger than a minimized workbook title bar, the window has its own Control menu (accessed by clicking the XL file icon), title bar, and sizing buttons. Its title bar also displays the workbook filename (this appears as a temporary filename like Book1, and then Book2 when you open your next new workbook, and so on, until you save the file the first time).

On the bottom of the workbook window, you see sheet-tab scrolling buttons, the sheet tabs for activating the various worksheets in your workbook (remember that there are 16 new sheets to start), followed by the horizontal scroll bar that you can use to bring new columns of the current worksheet into view. On the right side of the workbook window, you see a vertical scroll that you can use to bring new rows of the current worksheet into view (keeping in mind that you are only viewing a small percentage of the total columns and rows in each worksheet). At the intersection of the horizontal and vertical scroll bars, in the lower-right corner, you find a size box, which you can use to manually modify the size and shape of the less-than-maximized workbook window.

As soon as you start Excel, you can immediately begin creating a new spreadsheet in Sheet1 of the Book1 workbook that appears in the maximized workbook window. If you separate the workbook title bar, Control menu, and sizing buttons from the Excel menu bar, click the Restore button on the menu bar. Doing this will reduce the workbook window just enough to get all this stuff off the menu (as it's shown in Figure 1-5).

When a workbook sheet is not a worksheet

Worksheets are not the only type of sheet that you can have in an Excel workbook. In addition to worksheets, your workbook can contain *chart sheets,* which contain charts (see Chapter 8) created from data in one of the worksheets, and/or *macro sheets* (see Chapter 12), which in turn contain the code for macros that automate various tasks that you perform on your worksheets or charts.

Manually manipulating the workbook window

As I mention in the preceding section, when you're working with a less-than-maximized workbook window (like the one shown in Figure 1-5), you can manually size and move the window with the sizing box that appears in the lower-right corner at the intersection of the horizontal and vertical scroll bars.

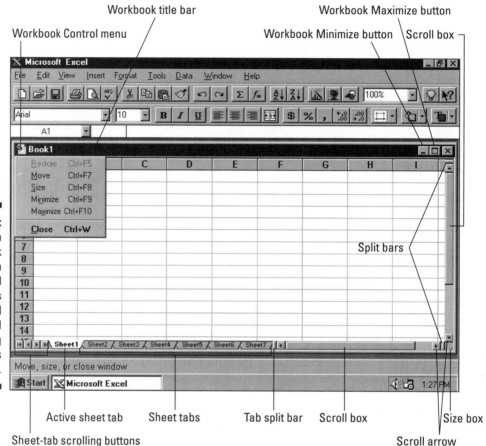

Workbook Control menu

Workbook title bar

Workbook Maximize button

Workbook Minimize button · Scroll box

Split bars

Figure 1-5:
Each
workbook
window in
Excel
contains its
own Control
menu and
sizing
buttons as
shown here.

Active sheet tab   Sheet tabs   Tab split bar   Scroll box   Size box

Sheet-tab scrolling buttons   Scroll arrow

To manipulate the size of a workbook window, position the mouse pointer on this sizing box, and then, when the mouse pointer changes shape to a double-headed arrow, drag the mouse as needed to adjust the size of the side or sides of the window. Note that the mouse pointer does not change to a double-headed arrow unless you position it on the edge of the window (that is, somewhere on the corner). While the pointer is positioned within the box, it retains its arrowhead shape.

✔ If you position the pointer on the bottom side of the window, and then drag the pointer straight up, the workbook window becomes shorter. If you drag the pointer straight down, the window becomes longer.

✔ If you position the pointer on the right side of the window, and then drag the pointer straight to the left, the workbook window becomes narrower; if you drag straight to the right, the window becomes wider.

✔ If you position the pointer on the lower-right corner of the window, and then drag the pointer diagonally toward the upper-left corner, the workbook window becomes both shorter and narrower; if you drag diagonally away from the upper-left corner, it becomes longer and wider.

When the outline of the workbook window reaches the desired size, you then release the primary mouse button and Excel redraws the workbook window to your new size.

After using the size button to change the size and shape of a workbook window, you must use the size button again and manually restore the window to its original shape and dimensions. There is, unfortunately, no magic Restore button available that you can click to automatically restore the workbook window that you changed back to its original shape and size.

Besides resizing workbook windows, you can also move them around within the area between the formula bar and status bar in the Excel program window. To move a workbook window

1. **Simply pick it up by the scruff of its neck — which, in this case, corresponds to the window's title bar.**

2. **After you've got it by the title bar, drag it to the desired position and release the primary mouse button.**

If you are experiencing any difficulty in dragging objects with the mouse, you can also move a workbook window by following these steps:

1. **Click the XL file icon on the workbook window's title bar to open its Control menu and then select the <u>M</u>ove command or press Ctrl+F7.**

    The mouse pointer will change shape from the normal thick, white-cross pointer to a pointer with crossed, double-headed arrows.

2. **Drag the window with the arrowheads' cross-hair pointer or press the arrow keys on the cursor keypad (←, ↑, →, or ↓) to move the workbook window into the desired position.**

3. **Press Enter to set the workbook window into position.**

    The mouse pointer resumes its normal thick, white-cross shape.

Slipping through the sheets

At the very bottom of the Excel workbook window that contains the horizontal scroll bar, you see the sheet-tab scrolling buttons followed by the sheet tabs for the first six to seven worksheets in the workbook. Excel shows which worksheet is active by displaying its sheet tab on top in white as part of the displayed worksheet (rather than belonging to unseen worksheets below). To activate a new worksheet (thus bringing it to the top and displaying its information in the workbook window), you click its sheet tab.

If the sheet tab for the worksheet you want to work with is not displayed, you can use the sheet-tab scrolling buttons to bring the worksheet into view. Click the buttons with the triangles pointing left and right to scroll one worksheet at a time in either direction (left to scroll left and right to scroll right). Click the buttons with the triangles pointing left and right to the vertical lines to scroll the sheets so that the tabs for the very first or very last worksheets are displayed at the bottom.

Scoping out the status bar

The bar at the very bottom of the Excel program window is called the status bar because it displays information that keeps you informed of the current state of Excel. The left part of the status bar displays messages indicating the current activity you're undertaking or the current command you've selected from the Excel menu bar. When you first start Excel, the message Ready is displayed in this area (as shown in Figure 1-6), telling you that the program is ready to accept your next entry or command.

The right side of the status bar contains various boxes that display different indicators telling you when you've placed Excel in a particular state that somehow affects how you work with the program. For example, normally, when you first start Excel, the AutoCalculate indicator shows SUM=0 and the Num Lock indicator shows NUM in this part of the status bar.

You AutoCalculate my totals

The SUM=0 in the AutoCalculate indicator tells you that currently no cells containing values are selected. Should you, however, select a range of cells containing values (be they numbers you've entered there or values calculated by formulas that you created), the AutoCalculate indicator automatically shows their total.

You can use the AutoCalculate indicator to get a running total of any group of values in your worksheet (see the beginning of Chapter 3 if you need information on how to select groups of cells in a worksheet). For example, Figure 1-6 shows you a typical spreadsheet after selecting part of a column of cells, many of which contain values. The total of all the values in the cells that are currently selected in this worksheet automatically appears in the AutoCalculate indicator on the status bar.

Not only does the AutoCalculate indicator on the status bar give you the sum of the values in the cells you currently have selected, but it can also give you the count or the average of these values. To get the count of all the cells that contain values (cells containing text entries are not counted), you click the AutoCalculate indicator with the secondary mouse button and select COUNT on this indicator's context menu. To get the average of the values in the current

Figure 1-6:
The
AutoCalculate
indicator
on the
status bar
automatically
shows you
the total of
any values
in the cells
that are
selected.

cell selection, you click the AutoCalculate indicator with the secondary mouse button and select AVERAGE on this indicator's context menu. To return the AutoCalculate indicator to its normal totaling function, you click it with the secondary mouse button and choose SUM on the indicator's context menu.

The Num Lock indicator and the numeric keypad

The NUM in the Num Lock indicator tells you that you can use the numbers on the numeric keypad to enter values in the worksheet. When you press the Num Lock key, NUM disappears from the Num Lock indicator. This is your signal that the cursor-movement functions that are also assigned to this keypad are now in effect. This means, for instance, that pressing 6 will move the cell pointer one cell to the right instead of entering this value in the formula bar!

You Gotta Get Me Out of This Cell!

Excel provides several methods for getting around each of the huge worksheets in your workbook. One the easiest ways is to click the tab for the sheet you want to work with, and then use the scroll bars in the workbook window to bring new parts of this worksheet into view. In addition, the program provides a wide range of keystrokes that you can use not only to move a new part of the worksheet into view but also to make a new cell active by placing the cell pointer in it.

The secrets of scrolling

To understand how scrolling works in Excel, imagine the worksheet as a humongous papyrus scroll attached to rollers on the left and right. To bring into view a new section of a papyrus worksheet that is hidden on the right, you crank the left roller until the section with the cells you want to see appears. Likewise, to scroll into view a new section of the worksheet that is hidden on the left, you would crank the right roller until the section of cells appears.

Calling up new columns with the horizontal scroll bar

You can use the *horizontal scroll bar* to scroll back and forth through the columns of a worksheet. To scroll new columns into view from the right, you click the right-arrow scroll button on the horizontal scroll bar. To scroll new columns into view from the left (anytime except when column A is the first column displayed), you click the left-arrow scroll button.

To scroll very quickly through columns in one direction or the other, you click the appropriate arrow scroll button in the scroll bar and *continue to hold down* the primary mouse button until the columns you want to see are displayed on the screen. As you scroll to the right in this manner, the *horizontal scroll box* (that big shaded box between the left- and right-arrow scroll buttons in the scroll bar) becomes increasingly smaller — it gets really teeny if you scroll really far right to columns in the hinterland such as BA. If you then click and hold down the left-arrow scroll button to scroll quickly back through columns to the left, you will notice that the horizontal scroll box becomes increasingly larger, until it takes up most of the scroll bar when you finally display column A again.

You can use the scroll box in the horizontal scroll bar to make big jumps to the left and right in the columns of the worksheet. Simply drag the scroll box in the appropriate direction along the bar. As you drag, the letter of the column that would appear as the leftmost column in the worksheet (should you then release the mouse button) is displayed above the horizontal scroll bar. You can use the column letter display to gauge when to release the mouse button to stop the horizontal scrolling.

Raising up new rows with the vertical scroll bar

You can use the *vertical scroll bar* to scroll up and down through the rows of a worksheet. To scroll to new rows below those currently in view, you click the down-arrow scroll button on the vertical scroll bar. To scroll back up to rows above that are no longer in view (anytime except when row 1 is the first one displayed), you click the up-arrow scroll button.

To scroll very quickly through rows in one direction or the other, you click and hold down the appropriate arrow scroll button in the vertical scroll bar just as you do in the horizontal scroll bar. As you scroll down the rows with the down-arrow scroll button, the *vertical scroll box* (that big shaded box between the up- and down-arrow scroll buttons in the scroll bar) becomes increasingly smaller and smaller — it gets really teeny if you scroll way down to rows like 100 and higher. If you then click and hold down the up-arrow scroll button to scroll quickly back up through the rows, you will notice that the vertical scroll box becomes increasingly larger, until it takes up most of the scroll bar when you finally display row 1 again.

You can use the vertical scroll box to make big jumps up and down the rows of the worksheet by dragging the vertical scroll box in the appropriate direction along the bar. As you drag, the number of the row that would appear at the very top of the worksheet area (should you release the mouse button at that very moment) is displayed to the left of the vertical scroll bar. You can use this row number display to tell when you should release the mouse button to stop the vertical scrolling.

Scrolling from screen to screen

You can also use the horizontal and vertical scroll bars to scroll through the columns and rows of your worksheet a screenful at a time. To do this, you click the light gray area of the scroll bar *not* occupied by the scroll box or the arrow scroll buttons. For example, to scroll to the right by a screenful of columns when the scroll box is snug against the left-arrow scroll button, you simply click the light gray area of the scroll bar behind the scroll box, between it and the right-arrow scroll button. Then, to scroll back to the left by a screenful of columns, you click the light gray area in front of the scroll box, between it and the left-arrow scroll button.

Likewise, to scroll up and down the rows of the worksheet a screenful at a time, you click the light gray area either above or below the vertical scroll, between it and the appropriate arrow scroll button.

The keys to moving the cell pointer

The only disadvantage to using the scroll bars to move around is that the scrolls only bring new parts of the worksheet into view — they don't actually change the position of the cell pointer. This means that, if you want to start making entries in the cells in a new area of the worksheet, you still have to re-member to select the cell (by clicking it) or the group of cells (by dragging through them) where you want the data to appear before you begin entering the data.

Excel offers a wide variety of keystrokes for moving the cell pointer to a new cell. When you use one of these keystrokes, the program automatically scrolls a new part of the worksheet in view, if this is required in moving the cell pointer. Table 1-4 summarizes these keystrokes and how far each one moves the cell pointer from its starting position.

Note that, in the case of those keystrokes listed in Table 1-4 that use arrow keys, you must either use the arrows on the cursor keypad or else have the Num Lock disengaged on the numeric keypad of your keyboard. If you try to use these arrow keys to move around the worksheet when Num Lock is on (indicated by the appearance of NUM on the status bar), you'll either get num-bers in the current cell or nothing will happen at all (and then you'll blame me)!

Table 1-4	Keystrokes for moving the cell pointer
Keystroke in Question	*Where the Cell Pointer Moves*
→ or Tab	Cell to the immediate right
← or Shift+Tab	Cell to the immediate left
↑	Cell up one row
↓	Cell down one row
Home	Cell in Column A of the current row
Ctrl+Home	First cell (A1) of the worksheet
Ctrl+End or End, Home	Cell in the worksheet at the intersection of the last column that has any data in it and the last row that has any data in it (that is, the last cell of the so-called *active area* of the worksheet)
PgUp	Cell one screenful up in the same column
PgDn	Cell one screenful down in the same column
Ctrl+→ or End, →	First occupied cell to the right in the same row that is either preceded or followed by a blank cell
Ctrl+← or End, ←	First occupied cell to the left in the same row that is either preceded or followed by a blank cell
Ctrl+↑ or End, ↑	First occupied cell above in the same column that is either preceded or followed by a blank cell
Ctrl+↓ or End, ↓	First occupied cell below in the same column that is either preceded or followed by a blank cell
Ctrl+PgDn	Last occupied cell in the next worksheet of that workbook
Ctrl+PgUp	Last occupied cell in the previous worksheet of that workbook

Block moves

The keystrokes that combine the Ctrl or End key with an arrow key listed in Table 1-4 are among the most helpful for moving quickly from one edge to the other in large tables of cell entries or in moving from table to table in a section of the worksheet that contains many blocks of cells.

- ✔ If the cell pointer is positioned on a blank cell somewhere to the left of a table of cell entries that you want to view, pressing Ctrl+→ moves the cell pointer to the first cell entry at the leftmost edge of the table (in the same row, of course).

- ✔ When you then press Ctrl+→ a second time, the cell pointer moves to the last cell entry at the rightmost edge (assuming that there are no blank cells in that row of the table).

- ✔ If you switch direction and press Ctrl+↓, Excel moves right to the last cell entry at the bottom edge of the table (again assuming that there are no blank cells below in that column of the table).

- ✔ If, when the cell pointer is at the bottom of the table, you press Ctrl+↓ again, Excel moves the pointer to the first entry at the top of the next table located below (assuming that there are no other cell entries above this table in the same column).

    If you press Ctrl or End and arrow key combinations and there are no more occupied cells in the direction of the arrow key you selected, Excel advances the cell pointer right to the cell at the very edge of the worksheet in that direction.

- ✔ If the cell pointer is located in cell C15 and there are no more occupied cells in row 15, when you press Ctrl+→, Excel moves the cell pointer to cell IV at the rightmost edge of the worksheet.

- ✔ If you are in cell C15 and there are no more entries below in Column C and you press Ctrl+↓, Excel moves the pointer to cell C16,384 at the very bottom edge of the worksheet.

When you use Ctrl and an arrow key to move from edge to edge in a table or between tables in a worksheet, you hold down Ctrl while you press one of the four arrow keys (indicated by the + symbol in keystrokes such as Ctrl+→).

When you use End and an arrow-key alternative, you must press and then release the End key *before* you press the arrow key (indicated by the comma in keystrokes such as End,→). Pressing and releasing the End key causes the END indicator to appear on the status bar. This is your sign that Excel is ready for you to press one of the four arrow keys.

Because you can keep the Ctrl key depressed as you press the different arrow keys you need to use, the Ctrl-plus-arrow-key method provides a more fluid method for navigating blocks of cells than the End-then-arrow-key method.

When you gotta go to that cell now!

Excel's Go To feature provides an easy method for moving directly to a distant cell in the worksheet. To use this feature, you display the Go To dialog box by selecting the Go To command on the Edit pull-down menu or by pressing Ctrl+G or the function key, F5. Then, in the Go To dialog box, you type the address of the cell you want to go to in the Reference edit box and select OK or press Enter. When typing in the cell address in the Reference text box, you can type the column letter or letters in upper- or lowercase letters.

When you use the Go To feature to move the cell pointer, Excel remembers the references of the last four cells that you visited. These cell references then appear in the Go To list box. Notice that the address of the cell you last came from is also listed in the Reference box. This makes it possible to move quickly from your present location to your previous location in a worksheet by pressing F5 and Enter (provided that you used the Go To feature to move to your present position).

Lotsa luck with Scroll Lock

You can use the Scroll Lock key to "freeze" the position of the cell pointer in the worksheet so that you can scroll new areas of the worksheet in view with keystrokes such as PgUp and PgDn without changing the cell pointer's original position (in essence, making these keystrokes work in the same manner as the scroll bars).

After engaging Scroll Lock, when you scroll the worksheet with the keyboard, Excel does not select a new cell as it brings a new section of the worksheet into view. To "unfreeze" the cell pointer when scrolling the worksheet via the keyboard, you just press the Scroll Lock key again.

Ordering Directly from the Menus

For those occasions when the Excel Standard and Formatting toolbars don't provide you with a ready-made tool for getting a particular task done, you have to turn to the program's system of menu commands. Excel exhibits a little bit of menu overkill in that, in addition to the regular pull-down menus found in nearly all Windows applications, the program also offers a secondary system of *context* (or shortcut) *menus*.

Context menus are so called because they offer just those menu commands that are normally used to manipulate the particular screen object that the menu is attached to (such as a toolbar, workbook window, or worksheet cell). As a result, context menus often bring together commands that are otherwise found on several individual pull-down menus on the menu bar.

Penetrating the pull-down menus

As when moving the cell pointer in the worksheet, Excel offers you a choice between using the mouse or the keyboard to select commands from the pull-down menu bars. To open a pull-down menu with the mouse, you simply click the menu name on the menu bar. To open a pull-down menu with the keyboard, you hold down the Alt key as you type the letter that is underlined in the menu name (also known as the *command letter*). For instance, if you press Alt and then E, Excel opens the Edit menu because the *E* in "Edit" is underlined.

Alternately, you can press and release the Alt key or function key F10 to access the menu bar, and then press the → key until you highlight the menu you want to open. Then, to open the menu, you press the ↓ key.

After you've opened your pull-down menu, you can select any of its commands by clicking the command with the mouse, pressing the underlined letter in the command name, or by pressing the ↓ key until you highlight the command and then pressing the Enter key.

As you learn the Excel commands, you can combine the opening of a menu and selecting one of its menu commands. With the mouse, you click the menu, and then drag the pointer down the open menu until you highlight the desired command, whereupon you release the mouse button. You can accomplish the same thing with the keyboard by holding down the Alt key as you type the command letters for both the pull-down menu and its command. So that, to close the active workbook window by choosing the Close command on the File menu, you simply press Alt, and then type **FC**.

Some commands on the Excel pull-down menus have shortcut keystrokes assigned to them (shown after the command on the pull-down menu). You can use the shortcut keystrokes to select the desired command instead of having to access the pull-down menus. For example, to save changes to your workbook, you press the shortcut keys Ctrl+S instead of having to select the Save command from the File pull-down menu.

Many commands on the pull-down menus lead to the display of a dialog box, which contains further commands and options (see "Digging Those Dialog Boxes" later in this chapter). You can tell which commands on a pull-down menu lead to dialog boxes because the command name is followed by three periods (known as an *ellipsis*). For example, you know that selecting the Save As command on the File menu opens a dialog box because the command is listed as Save As on the File menu.

Also, note that pull-down menu commands are not always available to you. You can tell when a command is not currently available because the command name is in light gray (or *dimmed*) on the pull-down menu. A command on a pull-down menu remains dimmed until the conditions under which it operates exist in your document. For example, the Paste command on the Edit menu remains dimmed as long as the Clipboard is empty. But as soon as you move or copy some information into the Clipboard with the Cut or Copy commands on the Edit menu, the Paste option is no longer dimmed and appears in normal bold type when you open the Edit menu — indicating, of course, that this command is now available for your use.

A word to you Lotus 1-2-3 converts

If you ever used (or tried to use) Lotus 1-2-3 for DOS, you may remember that, in that spreadsheet program, you press the slash key (/ — the key that does double duty with the ? key) to activate the 1-2-3 menus. In deference to the millions of 1-2-3 users out there who have converted to Excel, this program also recognizes and responds appropriately (that is, it activates the menu bar) when you press the / key. It is only right that Excel borrows this keystroke from Lotus 1-2-3, since 1-2-3 borrowed it from its predecessor, VisiCalc, which actually originated its usage.

Because the slash key activates the menus, you can combine its use instead of that of the Alt key with the command letters when you wish to select Excel commands with the keyboard. For example, instead of pressing Alt+FS to save changes to the active document, you can just as well press /FS (almost takes you home, doesn't it?).

Parlez-vous 1-2-3?

If you're a Lotus 1-2-3 user who's just starting to use Excel with this current version, Excel for Windows 95, you'll be pleased to know that Excel also offers a couple of ways to make your transition from the 1-2-3 commands and keystroke shortcuts to the Excel commands and keystrokes a lot smoother:

- ✔ You can make it so that when you select the 1-2-3 command, Excel tells you what menu and menu commands you use to do the same thing in Excel (kind of like saying something in English and having the computer give you the French equivalent).

- ✔ Or you can set it up so that you select the 1-2-3 command and the program demonstrates what menu and menu commands you choose to do the same thing in Excel (kind of like saying something in English and having the computer actually translate it into French).

To set up Excel so that the program shows or tells you what to do in Excel via the 1-2-3 equivalents, you follow these steps:

1. **Choose Options on the Tools menu to open the Options dialog box.**
2. **Click the tab marked Transition in the Options dialog box.**

   This displays the options for changing the Transition settings.
3. **Choose the Lotus 1-2-3 Help radio button.**
4. **Choose the OK button or press Enter.**

After switching from the default Microsoft Excel Menus setting to Lotus 1-2-3 Help in the Options dialog box, whenever you type the almighty / key, instead of activating the Excel menu bar, the program displays the Help for Lotus 1-2-3 Users dialog box. This dialog box contains a Menu list box that shows all the old, familiar 1-2-3 menus (from Worksheet through Quit).

If you want the program to simply indicate the Excel command sequence when you finish selecting the 1-2-3 commands in the Menu list box, you select the Instructions radio button (under Help options on the right side). If you would prefer to have the program demonstrate the Excel command (meaning that the program will actually select the Excel commands and thereby make real changes to your worksheet), you choose the Demo radio button instead.

Then, to choose the 1-2-3 command you need Excel help on (either in instruction or demonstration form), you type the first letter of each menu command. For example, to learn how to format a range of cells with the Currency format in Excel, you type **RFC** to select the Range menu followed by the Format and Currency commands (just as you would normally do to select these commands within 1-2-3 itself).

If you have the Instruction radio button selected when you type **RFC**, Excel displays a small text box with the step-by-step instructions for selecting the Currency number format in Excel (something you can otherwise learn in Chapter 3). If you have the Demo radio button selected instead, Excel displays a dialog box asking you to select the number of decimal places you want the Currency format to show (two is the default, as in Lotus 1-2-3) as well as the range of cells to which this number format is to be applied. After selecting these settings and choosing OK, the program then demonstrates the procedure for choosing the Cells command on the Format menu and then selecting the $#,##0.00_);($#,##0.00) format codes (Excel's user-friendly way of representing the Currency format) in the Format Cells dialog box (something else you can learn about in Chapter 3).

Those old-fashioned formulas

As one of the 1-2-3 faithful, you'll also be pleased to learn that although Excel prefers you type an equal sign (=) to start a formula, it will accept the plus sign (+) that you're used to entering in Lotus 1-2-3.

The same goes when using a built-in function. Although Excel does not require anything other than the = sign followed by the function name, the program will accept the @ symbol that 1-2-3 requires when using its functions. (So, for example, Excel will accept **@SUM** but will then convert it to the preferred **=SUM**).

Finally, although Excel uses a colon between the first and last cell address when designating a cell range, the program will accept the 1-2-3 method of placing two periods between the cell addresses (meaning that Excel will accept the range address **A1..A4** but convert it to the preferred **A1:A4**).

The program has also worked it all out so that 1-2-3 converts like yourself can have almost all of your old favorite navigation keys back the way Lotus intended them. For example, you know how the Tab and Shift+Tab in Excel only move the cell pointer one cell left or right, instead of scrolling the worksheet left or right by a screenful as they do in 1-2-3? Well, you can restore the so-called Big Right and Big Left scrolling functions (as well as moving to the first cell with Home key instead of to the beginning of the row) by choosing Options on the Tools menu, selecting the Transition tab, and then choosing the Transition Navigation Keys check box in the Settings area of the Options dialog box.

Comprehending context menus

Unlike the pull-down menus, which you can access either with the mouse or the keyboard, you must use the mouse to open context menus and select their commands. Because context menus are attached to particular objects on the screen — like a workbook window, toolbar, or worksheet cell — Excel uses the *secondary* mouse button (that is, the right button for right-handers and the left button for lefties) to open context menus. (Clicking a screen object, such as a cell, with whatever button is the *primary* button on your mouse simply selects that object).

Figure 1-7 shows you the context menu attached to the Excel toolbars. To open this menu, you position the mouse pointer somewhere on the toolbar and click the secondary mouse button. Be sure that you don't click the primary button, or you will end up activating the tool that the pointer is on!

Once you open the Toolbar context menu, you can use its commands to display or hide any of the built-in toolbars or to customize the toolbars (see Chapter 13 for details).

Figure 1-8 shows you the context menu attached to any of the cells in a worksheet. To open this menu, you position the pointer on any one of the cells and click the secondary mouse button. Note that you can also open this context menu and apply its commands to the group of cells that you have selected. (You can learn how to make cell selections in Chapter 3.)

Figure 1-7:
The toolbar
context
menu.

Figure 1-8:
The
worksheet
cell context
menu.

Because the commands on context menus do not contain command letters (although some of them do display shortcut keystrokes), to select one of their commands you must drag down to the command and then click it either with the primary or secondary mouse button to select it. Otherwise, you can press the ↓ or ↑ key until you highlight the command and press Enter to select it.

The one context menu that you can open with the keyboard is the context menu attached to cells in a worksheet. To open this context menu in the very upper-right corner of the workbook window, you press Shift+F10. Note that this keystroke works for any type of Excel sheet except a chart, which doesn't have this type of context menu attached to it.

Digging Those Dialog Boxes

Many an Excel command is attached to a dialog box that presents you with a variety of options that you can apply to the command. Figures 1-9 and 1-10 show you the Save As and Options dialog boxes. Between these two dialog boxes, you can find almost all of the different types of buttons, tabs, and boxes used by Excel in Table 1-5.

Drop-down list boxes · List box · Command buttons

Figure 1-9: The Save As dialog box contains text boxes, list boxes, and drop-down list boxes, along with command buttons.

Text box

Figure 1-10:
The Options
dialog box
contains a
variety of
tabs, check
boxes, radio
buttons, and
command
buttons.

Table 1-5	The parts of a dialog box
Button or Box in Question	*What It's Good For*
Tab	Provides a means of displaying a certain set of options in a complex dialog box like the Options dialog box (shown in Figure 1-10) bringing together a whole mess of different types of program settings that you can change.
Edit box (or Text box)	Provides a place for typing a new entry. Many edit boxes contain default entries that you can alter or replace entirely.
List box	Provides a list of options from which you choose. If the list box contains more options than can be displayed in its box, the list box contains a scroll bar that you can use to bring new options into view. Some list boxes are attached to a text box, allowing you to make a new entry in the text box either by typing it or by selecting it in the related list box.
Drop-down list box	Provides a condensed version of a standard list box that, instead of displaying several options in its list, shows only the current option (which originally is also the default option). To open the list box and display the other options, you click the drop-down button that accompanies the box. Once the list is displayed, you can select a new option from it as you would in any standard list box.

(continued)

Table 1-5 *(continued)*

Button or Box in Question	What It's Good For
Check box	Presents a dialog box option that you can turn on or off. When the check box is selected, you know that its option is selected. When a check box is blank, you know that its option is not selected.
Radio button	Presents items that have mutually exclusive options. The option button consists of a circle followed by the named option. Radio buttons are always arranged in groups and only one of the buttons in the group can be selected at one time. Excel lets you know which option is currently selected by placing a dot in the middle of its circle (when an option button is selected, it looks like a knob on an old-fashioned radio, thus the name radio button).
Spinner buttons	Spinner buttons appear as a pair of small boxes one on top of the other. The spinner button on the top has an upward-pointing arrowhead on it, whereas the spinner button on the bottom has a downward-pointing arrowhead on it. You use the spinner buttons to scroll up and down through a series of preset options as you select the one you want.
Command button	Initiates an action. The command button is rectangular in shape, and the name of the command is displayed within the button. If a name in a command button is followed by an ellipsis (...), Excel displays another dialog box containing even more options when you select the button.

Note: Although you can move a dialog box out of the way of some data in your worksheet, you cannot change the box's size or shape — these dimensions are permanently fixed by the program.

Many dialog boxes contain default options or entries that are automatically selected unless you make new choices before you close the dialog box.

✔ To close a dialog box and put your selections into effect, you choose the OK button or the Close button (some boxes lack an OK button).

If the OK button is surrounded by a dark border, which is very often the case, you can also press Enter to put your selections into effect.

✔ To close a dialog box without putting your selections into effect, you can either select the Cancel or Close button (the one with the X) in the dialog box, or simply press Esc.

Most dialog boxes group related options together as an item (often, this is done by placing a box around the options). When making selections in a dialog box with the mouse, you simply click the selection you want to use or, in the case of text entries, click the pointer in the entry to set the insertion point and then modify the entry.

When making selections with the keyboard, however, you must sometimes first activate the item before you can select any of its options.

- ✔ Press the Tab key until you activate one of the options in the item. (Shift+Tab activates the previous item.)

- ✔ When you press Tab (or Shift+Tab), Excel indicates which option is activated either by highlighting the default entry or placing a dotted line around the name of the option.

- ✔ After activating an option, you can change its setting either by pressing ↑ or ↓ (this works with sets of radio buttons or options in a list or drop-down list boxes), pressing the space bar (this works to select and deselect check boxes), or by typing a new entry (used in text boxes).

You can also select an option by pressing Alt and then typing the underlined (command) letter in the option or item name.

- ✔ By pressing Alt and typing the command letter of a text box option, you select the entry in that text box (which you can then replace by typing the new entry).

- ✔ By pressing Alt and typing the command letter of a check box option, you can turn the option on and off (by adding or removing its X).

- ✔ By pressing Alt and typing the command letter of a radio button, you can select the option while at the same time deselecting whatever radio button was previously current.

- ✔ By pressing Alt and typing the command letter of a command button, you either initiate the command or display another dialog box.

You can also select an item in the current list box option by typing the first few characters of its name — as soon as you begin typing, Excel opens an edit box to contain your characters and jumps to the first option in the list box whose name begins with the characters you enter.

In addition to the more elaborate dialog boxes shown in Figures 1-9 and 1-10, you also encounter a simpler type of dialog box used to display messages and warnings (these dialog boxes are appropriately known as *alert boxes*). Many dialog boxes of this type contain just an OK button that you must select to close the dialog box after reading the message.

Ogling the Online Help

You can get online help with Excel anytime you need it while using the program. The only problem with the traditional online Help system is that it is only truly helpful when you are familiar with the Excel jargon. If you don't know what

Excel calls a particular feature, you will have trouble locating it in the Help topics (just like trying to look up in a dictionary a word that you have no idea how to spell). To help alleviate this problem, Excel has added a new Answer Wizard that lets you type in a question about how to do something in Excel in your own words. The Answer Wizard then attempts to translate your question, phrased in perfectly good English, into its horrible Excel-technobabble so that it can then display the Help topics that give you the information you need.

Handling the Help tool

Beyond using the Answer Wizard, the easiest way to avoid the frustration of having to use the Help topics when you don't know what anything is called is to use the Help tool on the Standard toolbar (the one with the question mark to the right of the arrowhead at the very end of the toolbar). The Help tool lets you get help information that is specific to the particular menu command or toolbar button you want to use.

When you click the Help tool, Excel changes the mouse pointer shape by adding a question mark to it. To get help on a particular command or a part of the Excel window, you use this question-mark pointer to select it. For example, say that you want to refresh your memory on how you use the AutoSum tool on the Standard toolbar to total a column of numbers. You simply click the Help tool, and then click the AutoSum tool with the arrowhead/question-mark pointer. When you do this, the program displays the Microsoft Excel Help window with a brief paragraph of information on using the AutoSum tool.

You can also use the Help tool to get information on any of the commands on the pull-down menus. Suppose, for instance, that you are curious about the purpose of the Full Screen command on the View pull-down menu. To obtain information on what this command does and how you use it, you click the Help tool and then click the View menu with the arrowhead/question-mark pointer and, once this menu opens, click the Full Screen command. Doing this opens the Microsoft Excel Help window with a screenful of information on displaying the maximum number of worksheet cells on the screen.

When reading a help topic in the Microsoft Help system, you may notice that certain terms are underlined (and in a different color on a color monitor).

  ✔ A term that is underlined with a solid underline is called a *jump term* because, when you click it, the Help system immediately "jumps" you to a related help topic.

  ✔ A term that is underlined with a dotted line is a *glossary term,* meaning that it is attached to a brief definition. When you click a glossary term, the Help system displays the definition of that term in a small pop-up dialog box for as long as you hold down the mouse button.

If you come upon a help topic that you want to print out, you can select the Print Topic command on the Options pull-down menu or the Help context menu.

You can also copy information from an Excel Help topic to your word processor or even to an Excel document. To copy Help information, choose the Copy command on the Options pull-down menu or Help context menu.

Once you've copied the Help topic in this manner, you can copy the Help information into a word-processing document or worksheet by starting the program and opening the document (if necessary) and then choosing the Paste command on the program's Edit menu.

Asking the Answer Wizard

The Answer Wizard gives you a chance to ask questions about doing stuff in Excel without knowing any of the commands involved or special Excel jargon. To get to the Answer Wizard, you either choose Answer Wizard on the Help pull-down menu or press the function key, F1. You can also get to Answer Wizard by choosing the Answer Wizard tab in the Help Topics dialog box (which you open using the Microsoft Help Topics command on the Help menu).

To use the Answer Wizard, follow these steps:

1. **Type your question in the editing area of the 1. Type your request.**

2. **Click the Search drop-down list box.**

3. **Press Enter or click the Search button to have the Answer Wizard attempt to find Help topics that can answer your question.**

   When the Help Wizard finishes searching, it returns what it thinks are helpful Help topics in the 2. Select a topic.

4. **Click Display list box.**

   These topics are organized into three different areas: How Do I, Tell Me About, and Programming and Language Reference.

5. **To peruse any one of the Help topics displayed in this list box, click it.**

6. **Either press Enter or click the Display button.**

If the Answer Wizard can't even figure out where to look for Help topics because you asked a completely zany question, at least as it relates to using Excel, such as, "When will I win the lottery?", Excel beeps and then displays an alert box stating

```
Sorry, but I don't know what you mean. Please rephrase your
              question.
```

which is the Answer Wizard's way of saying, "I don't have a clue as to what you're talking about!"

If the Answer Wizard doesn't find any related topics, maybe because you asked a really ambiguous question, at least according to its limited, technical vocabulary, Excel beeps and then displays an alert box stating

```
There are several Help topics that may be related to your
        request. If you don't see a topic that looks
            helpful, please rephrase your question.
```

Most of the time, however, the Answer Wizard will fetch a bunch of Help topics (whether they're helpful or not) no matter how irrelevant or stupid your question. For example, I asked the Tip Wizard

```
Why is Excel so hard to use?
```

and, as you can see in Figure 1-11, its reply was to go and get a whole bunch of general How Do I and Tell Me About topics along with a bunch of general topics on Programming (not visible in this figure). When you think about it, I guess this screen is a pretty good answer to the question, "Why is Excel so hard to use?"

To reduce the number of times that the Answer Wizard gives you almost all the general Help topics at its disposal, you should try to get as much specific information in your question as possible. If you want to know whether Excel can figure compound interest on an investment, be sure to include key words such as

Figure 1-11:
Asking the
Answer
Wizard why
Excel is so
hard to use.

compound interest and *investment* in the body of the question (unlike your grade school English teacher or Alex Trebek on *Jeopardy,* the Answer Wizard could care less if your request is in the form of a question or demonstrates anything close to good grammar).

Sometimes, you may think that the Help topics returned by the Answer Wizard have nothing to do with your question, only later to discover that the weird topics listed under Tell Me About were exactly what you needed to know. A lot of this is just the result of not yet being familiar with the bulk of Excel's technobabble.

Tending to the Tip Wizard

As you go about building and editing your worksheets in Excel, the Tip Wizard, like some spy in the background, is silently analyzing everything you do. As you select commands and push buttons, the Tip Wizard is busy trying to amass a list of tips and tricks related to the tasks that you just did. You can always tell when the Tip Wizard has come up with some new tips because the lightbulb icon displayed on the TipWizard button on the Standard toolbar lights up — actually, it just changes from white to yellow (or light gray, if you have a monochrome monitor) with little, tiny light rays emanating from it.

To see all the tips that the Tip Wizard has dug up for you, just click the TipWizard button on the Standard toolbar. Excel then displays the last tip (these things are automatically numbered) in between the Formatting toolbar and the formula bar. To see earlier tips, click the spinner button with the up arrowhead. To return to later tips, click the spinner button with the down arrowhead. When you're finished looking at the tips and want to put them away, just click the TipWizard button on the Standard toolbar again.

When It's Time to Make Your Exit

When you're ready to call it a day and quit Excel, you have several choices for shutting down the program. One way to exit Excel is by choosing the Exit command on the File menu. You can accomplish the same thing by double-clicking the Control menu button on the Excel program window (the one with the XL icon in the very upper-left corner of the screen), or by pressing Alt+F4.

If you try to exit Excel after working on a workbook, and you haven't saved your latest changes, the program beeps at you and displays an alert box asking you if want to save your changes. To save your changes before exiting, choose the Yes command button (for detailed information on saving documents, see Chapter 2). If you've just been playing around in the worksheet and don't want to save your changes, you can abandon the document by choosing the No button.

The 5th Wave

By Rich Tennant

"...AND FOR THE HI-TECH MAN IN YOUR LIFE, WE HAVE THIS LOVELY PC-ON-A-ROPE."

Chapter 2

Creating a Spreadsheet from Scratch

● ●

In This Chapter

▶ Starting a new workbook

▶ Entering the three different types of data in a worksheet

▶ Getting Excel to put in your decimal point for you

▶ Creating simple formulas by hand

▶ Fixing your data-entry boo-boos

▶ Using the new AutoCorrect feature

▶ Understanding the new AutoComplete feature

▶ Using the AutoFill feature to complete a series of entries

▶ Restricting data entry to a particular group of cells

▶ Entering the same thing in a bunch of cells in one operation

▶ Entering built-in functions in your formulas with the Function Wizard

▶ Totaling columns and rows of numbers with AutoSum

▶ Saving your precious work

● ●

*O*nce you know how to get into Excel, it's time to find out how to get yourself into trouble by actually using it! In this chapter, you're gonna find out how to put all kinds of information into all those little, blank worksheet cells you learned about in Chapter 1. Here, you learn about Excel's new AutoCorrect and AutoComplete features, and how they can help cut down on errors and speed up your work. You also get some basic pointers on other smart ways to minimize the drudgery of data entry, such as filling out a series of entries with the AutoFill feature and entering the same thing in a bunch of cells all at the same time.

And after learning how to fill up a worksheet with all this raw data, you find out what has to be the most important lesson of all: how to save all the information on disk so that you don't ever have to enter the stuff again!

So, What Ya Gonna Put in That New Workbook of Yours?

When you start Excel without specifying a document to open, as happens if you start the program by clicking the Microsoft Excel button on the Office 95 shortcut bar (see Chapter 1), you get a blank workbook in a new workbook window. This workbook, temporarily named Book1, contains 16 blank worksheets (Sheet1 through Sheet16, although you can only see the sheet tabs of the first six or seven sheets). To begin to work on a new spreadsheet, you simply start entering information in the first sheet of the Book1 workbook window.

The ins and outs of data entry

Here are a few simple guidelines (a kind of data-entry etiquette, if you will) that you should keep in mind when you start creating a spreadsheet in Sheet1 of your new workbook:

✔ Whenever you can, organize your information in tables of data that use adjacent (neighboring) columns and rows. Start the tables in the upper-left corner of the worksheet and work your way down the sheet, rather than across the sheet, whenever possible. When it's practical, separate each table by no more than a single column or row.

✔ When you set up these tables, don't skip columns and rows just to "space out" the information. In Chapter 3, you see how to place as much white space as you want between information in adjacent columns and rows by widening columns, heightening rows, and changing the alignment.

✔ Reserve a single column at the left edge of the table for the table's row headings.

✔ Reserve a single row at the top of the table for the table's column headings.

✔ If your table requires a title, put the title in the row above the column headings. Put the title in the same column as the row headings. You see how to center this title across the columns of the entire table in Chapter 3.

You may wonder why, after making such a big stinking deal about how big each of the worksheets in a workbook is back in Chapter 1, I'm now on your case about not using that space to spread out the data you enter into it. After all, given all the real estate that comes with each and every Excel worksheet, you'd think conserving space would be one of the last things you'd have to worry about.

And you'd be 100 percent correct . . . except for one little, itty-bitty thing: Space conservation in the worksheet equals memory conservation. You see, as a table of data grows and expands into columns and rows in new areas of the worksheet, Excel decides that it had better reserve a certain amount of computer memory and hold it open just in case you might go crazy and fill that area full of cell entries. This means that if you skip columns and rows that you really don't need to skip (just to cut down on all that cluttered data), you end up wasting computer memory that could otherwise be used to store more information in the worksheet.

"You must remember this . . ."

So now you know: It's the amount of computer memory available to Excel that determines the ultimate size of the spreadsheet you can build, not the total number of cells in the worksheets of your workbook. When you run out of memory, you've effectively run out of space — no matter how many columns and rows are still left to fill. To maximize the information you can get into a worksheet, always adopt the "covered wagon" approach to worksheet design by keeping your data close together.

To check out how much computer memory is available to Excel at any given time, choose the About Microsoft Excel command from the Help menu, and then click the System Info button in the About Microsoft Excel dialog box. The Microsoft System Information dialog box then appears, displaying the Total memory as well as the Available Memory in *kilobytes* (thousands of bytes), along with a bunch of operating system factoids. When you finish viewing this information, click the Close box in both the Microsoft System Information and About Microsoft Excel dialog boxes.

Doing the Data-Entry Thing

Let's start by reciting (in unison) the basic rule of worksheet data entry. All together now:

> To enter data in a worksheet, position the cell pointer in the cell where you want the data, and then begin typing the entry.

Note that, before you can position the cell pointer in the cell where you want the entry, Excel must be in Ready mode (as evidenced by the Ready indicator on the status bar). When you start typing the entry, however, Excel goes through a mode change from Ready to Enter mode (and "Enter" replaces "Ready" on the status bar).

If you're not in Ready mode, try pressing Esc.

As soon as you begin typing in Enter mode, the characters you type appear both in a cell in the worksheet area and on the formula bar near the top of the screen. Starting to type something that's ultimately destined to go into the current cell also triggers a change to the formula bar because, in front of the characters that you type, you now see three new boxes: the Cancel, Enter, and Function Wizard (marked with *fx*) boxes.

As you continue to type, Excel displays your progress both on the formula bar and in the active cell in the worksheet (see Figure 2-1). However, the insertion point (the flashing vertical bar that acts as your cursor) is displayed only at the end of the characters displayed in the cell.

After you finish typing your cell entry, you still have to get it into the cell so that it stays put. In doing this, you also change the program from Enter mode back to Ready mode so that you can move the cell pointer to another cell and, perhaps, enter or edit the data there.

To complete your cell entry and, at the same time, get Excel out of Enter mode and back into Ready mode, you can click the Enter box on the formula bar, press Enter, or press one of the arrow keys like ↓ or → to move to another cell.

Now, even though each of these alternatives gets your text into the cell, each does something a little different afterwards, so please take note:

- ✔ If you click the Enter box on the formula bar, the text goes into the cell and the cell pointer just stays in the cell containing the brand new entry.

- ✔ If you press Enter, the text goes into the cell and the cell pointer moves down to the cell below in the next row.

Figure 2-1:
The stuff you type to go into a cell appears in both the cell and on the formula bar.

✔ If you press one of the arrow keys, the text goes into the cell, and the cell pointer moves the next cell in the direction of the arrow. If you press ↓, the cell pointer moves below in the next row just as when you finish off a cell entry with the Enter key. However, if you press →, the cell pointer moves right to the cell in the next column; if you press ←, the cell pointer moves left to the cell in the previous column; and if you press ↑, the cell pointer moves up to the cell in the next row above.

No matter which of the methods you choose when putting an entry in its place, as soon as you complete your entry in the current cell, Excel deactivates the formula bar by removing the Cancel, Enter, and Function Wizard boxes. Thereafter, the data you entered continues to appear in the cell in the worksheet (with certain exceptions I discuss later in this chapter), and every time you put the cell pointer into that cell, the data will reappear on the formula bar as well.

If, while still typing an entry or after finishing typing but prior to completing the entry, you realize that you're just about to stick it in the wrong cell, you can clear and deactivate the formula bar by clicking the Cancel box (the one with the X in it) or by pressing Esc. If, however, you don't realize that you had the wrong cell current until after you've entered your data there, you have to either move the entry to the correct cell (something you can learn to do in Chapter 4) or delete the entry (see Chapter 4) and then re-enter the data in the correct cell.

Getting the Enter key to put the cell pointer where you want it

Excel automatically advances the cell pointer to the next cell down in the column every time you press Enter to complete the cell entry. If you want to customize Excel so that pressing Enter doesn't move the cell pointer as the program enters your data, or to have it move the cell pointer to the next cell up, left, or right, choose Options on the Tools menu and select the Edit tab in the Options dialog box.

To prevent the cell pointer from moving at all, choose the Move Selection after Enter option in the Settings section to remove the check from its check box. To have the cell pointer move in another direction, choose the Direction drop-down list box right below the Move Selection after Enter check box and then select the new direction you want to use (Right, Up, or Left). When you're finished changing this Edit setting, click the OK button or press Enter.

It Takes All Types

Unbeknownst to you as you go about happily entering data in your spreadsheet, Excel is constantly analyzing the stuff you type and classifying it into one of three possible data types: a piece of *text,* a *value,* or a *formula.*

If Excel finds that the entry is a formula, the program automatically calculates the formula and displays the computed result in the worksheet cell (you continue to see the formula itself, however, on the formula bar). If Excel is satisfied that the entry does not qualify as a formula (I give you the qualifications for an honest-to-goodness formula a little later in this chapter), the program then determines whether the entry should be classified as text or as a value.

Excel makes this distinction between text and values so that it knows how to align the entry in the worksheet. It aligns text entries with the left edge of the cell and values with the right edge. Also, because most formulas work properly only when they are fed values, by differentiating text from values, the program knows which will and will not work in the formulas you build. Suffice to say, you can foul up your formulas good if they refer to any cells containing text where Excel expects values to be.

The telltale signs of text

A text entry is simply an entry that Excel can't pigeonhole as either a formula or value. This makes text the catchall category of Excel data types. As a practical rule of thumb, most text entries (also known as *labels*) are a combination of letters and punctuation or letters and numbers. Text is used mostly for titles, headings, and notes in the worksheet.

You can tell right away whether Excel has accepted a cell entry as text because text entries are automatically aligned at the left edge of their cells. If the text entry is wider than the cell can display, the data spills over into the neighboring cell or cells on the right, *as long as those cells remain blank* (see Figure 2-2).

This means that if, sometime later, you enter information in a cell that contains spill-over text from a cell to its left, Excel cuts off the spillover of the long text entry (see Figure 2-3). Not to worry: Excel doesn't actually lop these characters off the cell entry — it simply shaves the display to make room for the new entry. To redisplay the suddenly "missing" portion of the long text entry, you have to widen the column that contains the cell where the text is entered (to find out how to do this, skip ahead to Chapter 3).

Figure 2-2:
Long text
entries spill
over into
neighboring
blank cells.

Figure 2-3:
Cell entries
in the cells
to the right
cut off the
spillover
text.

How Excel evaluates its values

Values are the building blocks of most of the formulas that you create in Excel. As such, they come in two flavors: numbers that represent quantities (such as 14 stores or 140,000 dollars) and numbers that represent dates (such as July 30, 1995) or times (such as 2:00 PM).

You can tell whether Excel has accepted your entry as a value because values are aligned at the right edge of their cells, and the AutoCalculate SUM=0 indicator on the status bar changes to display the value the cell now contains. For example, if you enter the number **102** in cell E4 of the worksheet, the AutoCalculate indicator reads

```
SUM=102
```

whenever the cell pointer is in cell E4. If, however, you enter a date like **11/30/96** in this cell, the AutoCalculate indicator reads

```
SUM=11/30/96
```

whenever the cell pointer is in cell E4.

If the value you enter is wider than the column containing the cell can display, Excel automatically converts the value to (of all things) *scientific notation* (for example, 6E+08 indicates that the 6 is followed by eight zeros for a grand total of six hundred million!). To restore a value that's been converted into that weird scientific notation stuff back to a regular number, simply widen the column for that cell (Chapter 3 shows you how).

Making sure that Excel's got your number

In building a new worksheet, you'll probably spend a lot of your time entering numbers, representing all types of quantities from money you made (or lost) to the percentage of the office budget that went to coffee and donuts (you mean you don't get donuts?).

To Excel, text is nothing but a big zero

You can use the AutoCalculate indicator to prove to yourself that Excel gives all text entries the value of 0 (zero). Simply enter some stupid piece of text, like "Excel is a like a box of chocolates," in a cell. When you put the cell pointer in the cell that contains this bit of wisdom, take a gander at the AutoCalculate indicator on the status bar, and you see that it reads SUM=0 (although maybe, for this example, it would be more appropriate if it read GUMP=0).

To enter a numeric value that represents a positive quantity, like the amount of money you made last year, just select a cell, type the numbers — for example, **459600** — and complete the entry in the cell by clicking the Enter box, pressing the Enter key, and so on. To enter a numeric value that represents a negative quantity, like the amount of money the office spent on coffee and donuts last year, begin the entry with the minus sign or hyphen (–) before typing the numbers — for example, **–175** (that's not too much to spend on coffee and donuts when you just made $459,600) — and then complete the entry.

If you're trained in Accounting, you can enclose the negative number (that's *expense* to you) in parentheses — **(175)**. Just note that, if you go to all the trouble to use parentheses for your negatives (expenses), Excel goes ahead and automatically converts the number so that it begins with a minus sign; meaning that you enter **(175)** in the Coffee and Donut expense cell, if Excel spits back **–175** (relax, you can find out how to get your beloved parentheses back for the expenses in your spreadsheet in Chapter 3).

With numeric values that represent dollar amounts, like the amount of money you made last year, you can include dollar signs ($) and commas (,) just as they appear in the printed or handwritten numbers you are working from. Just be aware that when you enter a number with commas, Excel assigns a number format to the value that matches your use of commas (for more information on number formats and how they are used, see Chapter 3). Likewise, when you preface a financial figure with a dollar sign, Excel assigns an appropriate dollar-number format to the value (one that automatically inserts commas between the thousands).

When entering numeric values with decimal places, use the period as the decimal point. When you enter decimal values, the program automatically adds a zero before the decimal point (Excel inserts **0.34** in a cell when you enter **.34**) and drops trailing zeros entered after the decimal point (Excel inserts **12.5** in a cell when you enter **12.50**).

If you don't know the decimal equivalent for a value that contains a fraction, you can just go ahead and enter the value with its fraction. For example, if you don't know that 2.1875 is the decimal equivalent for $2\,^3/_{16}$, just type **$2\,^3/_{16}$** (making sure to add a space between the 2 and 3) in the cell. After completing the entry, when you put the cell pointer in that cell, you see $2\,^3/_{16}$ in the cell of the worksheet, but 2.1875 appears on the formula bar. As you see in Chapter 3, it's then a simple trick to format the display of $2\,^3/_{16}$ in the cell so that it matches the 2.1875 on the formula bar.

Note that, if you need to enter simple fractions such as $^3/_4$ or $^5/_8$, you must enter them as a mixed number preceded by zero; for example, enter **0 3/4** or **0 5/8** (be sure to include a space between the zero and the fraction). Otherwise, Excel gets mixed up and thinks that you're entering the dates March 4th (3/4) and May 8 (5/8).

When entering in a cell a numeric value that represents a percentage (so much out of a hundred), you have a choice:

- You can either divide the number by 100 and enter the decimal equivalent (by moving the decimal point two places to the left like your teacher taught you; for example, enter **.12** for 12 percent).
- You can enter the number with the percent sign (for example, enter **12%**).

Either way, Excel stores the decimal value in the cell (0.12 in this example). If you use the percent sign, Excel assigns a percentage-number format to the value in the worksheet so that it appears as 12%.

How to get your decimal places fixed (when you don't even know if they're broken)

If you find that you need to enter a whole slew of numbers that use the same number of decimal places, you can turn on Excel's Fixed Decimal setting and have the program enter the decimals for you. This feature really comes in handy when you have to enter hundreds of financial figures that all use two decimal places (for example, for the number of cents).

To *fix* the number of decimal places in a numeric entry, follow these steps:

1. **Choose Tools, and then choose Options.**

   The Options dialog box appears.

2. **Choose the Edit tab in the Options dialog box.**

3. **Choose Fixed Decimal in the Settings section to select its check box.**

   By default, Excel fixes the decimal place two places to the left of the last number you type. To change the default Places setting, go to step 4, otherwise move to step 5.

4. **Type a new number in the Places text box or use the spinner buttons to change the value.**

   For example, you could change the Places setting to 3 to enter numbers with the following decimal placement: 00.000.

5. **Choose OK or press Enter.**

   Excel displays the FIX status indicator on the status bar to let you know that the Fixed Decimal feature is active.

After fixing the decimal place in numeric values, Excel automatically adds the decimal point to any numeric value you enter — all you do is type the digits and complete the entry in the cell. For example, to enter the numeric value 100.99 in

Don't get in a fix over your decimal places!

While the Fixed Decimal setting is turned on, Excel adds a decimal point to all the numeric values you enter. However, if you want to enter a number without a decimal point, or one with a decimal point in a position different from the one called for by this feature, you have to remember to type the decimal point (period) yourself. For example, to enter the number 1099 instead of 10.99

when the decimal point is fixed at 2 places, type **1099.** in the cell.

And, for Heaven's sake, please don't forget to turn off the Fixed Decimal feature before you start work on another worksheet or exit Excel. Otherwise, when you intend to enter values like 20, you'll end up 0.2 instead, and you won't have a clue what's going on!

a cell after fixing the decimal point to 2 places, type the digits **10099**. When you complete the cell entry, Excel automatically inserts a decimal point two places from the right in the number you typed, leaving 100.99 in the cell.

When you're ready to return to normal data entry for numerical values (where you enter any decimal points yourself), open the Options dialog box and choose the Edit tab again, and then deselect the Fixed Decimal check box and choose OK or press Enter. Excel removes the FIX indicator from the status bar.

Tapping on the old ten-key

You can make the Fixed Decimal feature work even better by selecting the block of the cells where you want to enter the numbers (see "Entries all around the block," later in this chapter) and then pressing Num Lock so that you can do all the data entry for this cell selection from the numeric keypad (à la ten-key adding machine).

Using this approach, all you have to do to enter the range of values in each cell is type the number's digits and press Enter on the numeric keypad — Excel inserts the decimal point in the proper place as it moves the cell pointer down to the next cell. Even better, when you finish entering the last value in a column, pressing Enter automatically moves the cell pointer to the cell at the top of the next column in the selection.

Figures 2-4 and 2-5 illustrate how you can make the ten-key method work for you. In Figure 2-4, the Fixed Decimal feature has been turned on (using the default of two decimal places), and the block of cells from B3 through D9 has been selected. You also see that six entries have already been made in cells B3 through B8 and a seventh, 30834.63, is about to be completed in cell B9. To make this entry when the Fixed Decimal feature is turned on, you simply type **3083463** from the numeric keypad.

Figure 2-4:
To enter the value 30834.63 in cell B9, you simply type **3083463** and press Enter.

Figure 2-5:
When you press Enter to enter 30834.63 in cell B9, the program automatically moves the cell pointer to cell C3.

Figure 2-5 shows you what happens when you press Enter (either on the regular keyboard or the numeric keypad). As you can see, not only does Excel automatically add the decimal point to the value in cell B9, but it also moves the cell pointer up and over to cell C3 where you can continue entering the values for this column.

Entering dates with no debate

At first look, it may strike you as a bit odd that dates and times are entered as values in the cells of a worksheet rather than as text. The reason for this is simple, really: Dates and times entered as values can be used in formula calculations, whereas dates and times entered as text cannot. For example, if you enter two dates as values, you can then set up a formula that subtracts the more recent date from the older date and returns the number of days between them. This kind of thing just couldn't happen if you were to enter the two dates as text entries.

Excel determines whether the date or time you type is entered as a value or as text by the format you follow. If you follow one of Excel's built-in date and time formats, the program recognizes the date or time as a value. If you don't follow one of the built-in formats, the program enters the date or time as a text entry — it's as simple as that.

Excel recognizes the following time formats:

3:21 PM

3:21:04 PM

15:21

15:21:04

The dating game

Dates are stored as serial numbers that indicate how many days have elapsed from a particular starting date; times are stored as decimal fractions indicating the elapsed part of the 24-hour period. Excel supports two date systems: the 1900 date system used by Excel for Windows 95, where January 1, 1900 is the starting date (serial number 1) and the 1904 system used by Excel for the Macintosh, where January 2, 1904 is the starting date.

If you ever get a hold of a workbook created with Excel for the Macintosh that contains dates that seem all screwed up when you open the file, you can rectify this problem by choosing Options on the Tools menu, selecting the Calculation tab in the Options dialog box, and then selecting the 1904 Date System check box under Workbook Options before you choose OK.

Excel knows the following date formats (Note that month abbreviations always use the first three letters of the name of the month, as in Jan, Feb . . .):

November 24, 1996 or November 24, 96

11/24/96 or 11-24-96

25-Nov-96

25-Nov

Nov-96

Fabricating those fabulous formulas!

As entries go in Excel, formulas are the real workhorses of the worksheet. If you set up a formula properly, it computes the right answer when you first enter it into a cell. From then on, it keeps itself up-to-date, recalculating the results whenever you change any of the values that the formula uses.

You let Excel know that you're about to enter a formula, rather than some text or a value, in the current cell by starting the formula with the equal sign (=). Most simple formulas follow the equal sign with a built-in function such as SUM or AVERAGE (see "Conjuring up formulas with the Function Wizard," later in this chapter, for more information on using functions in formulas). Other simple formulas use a series of values or cell references that contain values separated by one or more of the following mathematical operators:

+ (plus sign) for addition

– (minus sign or hyphen) for subtraction

* (asterisk) for multiplication

/ (slash) for division

^ (caret) for raising a number to a power

For example, to create a formula in cell C2 that multiplies a value entered in cell A2 by value in cell B2, enter the following formula in cell C2:

```
=A2*B2
```

To enter this formula in cell C2, follow these steps:

1. Select cell C2.

2. Type the entire formula =A2*B2 **in the cell.**

3. Press Enter.

Or

1. **Select Cell C2.**

2. **Type = (equal sign).**

3. **Select cell A2 in the worksheet by using the mouse or the keyboard.**

   This action places the cell reference A2 in the formula in the cell (as shown in Figure 2-6).

4. **Type *.**

   The asterisk is used for multiplication rather than the × you used in school.

5. **Select cell B2 in the worksheet by using the mouse or the keyboard.**

   This action places the cell reference B2 in the formula (as shown in Figure 2-7).

6. **Click the Enter box to complete the formula entry, while at the same time keeping the cell pointer in cell C2.**

   Excel displays the calculated answer in cell C2 and the formula =A2*B2 in the formula bar (as shown in Figure 2-8).

When you're finished entering the formula =A2*B2 in cell C2 of the worksheet, Excel displays the calculated result depending on the values currently entered in cells A2 and B2. The major strength of the electronic spreadsheet is the capability of formulas to automatically change their calculated results to match changes in the cells referenced by the formulas.

Now comes the fun part: After creating a formula like the preceding one that refers to the values in certain cells (rather than containing those values itself), you can change the values in those cells, and Excel automatically recalculates the formula, using these new values and displaying the updated answer in the worksheet! Using the example shown in Figure 2-8, say that you change the value in cell B2 from 100 to 50. The moment you complete this change in cell B2, Excel recalculates the formula and displays the new answer, 1000, in cell C2.

If you want it, just point it out

The method of selecting the cells you use in a formula, rather than typing their cell references, is known as *pointing*. Pointing is not only quicker than typing cell references, it also reduces the risk that you might type the wrong cell reference. When you type a cell reference, you can easily type the wrong column letter or row number and not realize your mistake just by looking at the calculated result returned in the cell.

Figure 2-6: To start the formula, type = and then select cell A2.

Figure 2-7: To complete the second part of the formula, type * and select cell B2.

Figure 2-8: When you click the Enter box on the formula bar, Excel displays the answer in cell C2 (you can still see the formula in formula bar above).

If you select the cell you want to use in a formula, either by clicking it or moving the cell pointer to it, there is less chance that you'll enter the wrong cell reference.

Altering the natural order of operations

Many formulas you create perform more than one mathematical operation. Excel performs each operation, moving from left to right, according to a strict pecking order (the natural order of arithmetic operations). In this order, multiplication and division pull more weight than addition and subtraction and are, therefore, performed first, even if these operations don't come first in the formula (when reading from left to right).

Consider the series of operations in the following formula:

```
=A2+B2*C2
```

If cell A2 contains the number 5, B2 contains the number 10, and C2 contains the number 2, Excel evaluates the following formula:

```
=5+10*2
```

In this formula, Excel multiplies 10 times 2 to equal 20 and then adds this result to 5 to produce the result 25.

If you want Excel to perform the addition between the values in cells A2 and B2 before the program multiplies the result by the value in cell C2, enclose the addition operation in parentheses as follows:

```
=(A2+B2)*C2
```

The parentheses around the addition tell Excel you want this operation performed before the multiplication. If cell A2 contains the number 5, B2 contains the number 10, and C2 contains the number 2, Excel adds 5 and 10 to equal 15 and then multiplies this result by 2 to produce the result 30.

In fancier formulas, you may need to add more than one set of parentheses, one within another (like the wooden Russian dolls that nest within each other) to indicate the order in which you want the calculations to take place. When nesting parentheses, Excel first performs the calculation contained in the most inside pair of parentheses, and then uses that result in further calculations as the program works its way outward. For example, consider the following formula:

```
=(A4+(B4-C4))*D4
```

Excel first subtracts the value in cell C4 from the value in cell B4, then adds the difference to the value in cell A4, and, finally, multiplies that sum by the value in D4.

Without the additions of the two sets of nested parentheses, left to its own devices, Excel would first multiply the value in cell C4 by that in D4, add the value in A4 to that in B4, and then perform the subtraction.

When nesting parentheses in a formula, pair them properly so that you have a right parenthesis for every left parenthesis in the formula. If you do not include a right parenthesis for every left one, Excel displays an alert dialog box with the message "Parentheses do not match" or "Error in Formula" when you try to enter the formula. After you close this dialog box, Excel goes right back to the formula bar, where you can insert the missing parenthesis and press Enter to correct the unbalanced condition. By the way, Excel tries to show you where the unbalanced condition exists by highlighting the closest cell reference.

Formula flub-ups

Under certain circumstances, even the best formulas can appear to have freaked out once you get them in your worksheet. You can tell right away that a formula's gone haywire because instead of the nice calculated value you expected to see in the cell, you get a strange, incomprehensible message in all uppercase letters beginning with the number sign (#) and ending with an exclamation point (!) or, in one case, a question mark (?). This weirdness is known, in the parlance of spreadsheets, as an *error value*. Its purpose is to let you know that some element — either in the formula itself or in a cell referred to by the formula — is preventing Excel from returning the anticipated calculated value.

The worst thing about error values is that they can contaminate other formulas in the worksheet. If a formula returns an error value to a cell, and a second formula in another cell refers to the value calculated by the first formula, the second formula returns the same error value, and so on down the line.

Once an error value shows up in a cell, you have to discover what caused the error and edit the formula in the worksheet. Table 2-1 lists some error values that you might run into in a worksheet and explains the most common causes.

Table 2-1 Error values that you can encounter from faulty formulas	
What Shows Up in the Cell	*What's Going On Here?*
#DIV/0!	Appears when the formula calls for division by a cell that either contains the value 0 or, as is more often the case, is empty. Division by zero is a no-no according to our math.
#NAME?	Appears when the formula refers to a *range name* (see Chapter 6 for info on naming ranges) that doesn't exist in the worksheet. This error value appears when you type the wrong range name or fail to enclose in quotation marks some text used in the formula, causing Excel to think that the text refers to a range name.
#NULL!	Appears most often when you insert a space, where you should have used a comma, to separate cell references used as arguments for functions.
#NUM!	Appears when Excel encounters a problem with a number in the formula, such as the wrong type of argument in an Excel function or a calculation that produces a number too large or too small to be represented in the worksheet.
#REF!	Appears when Excel encounters an invalid cell reference, such as when you delete a cell referred to in a formula or paste cells over the cells referred to in a formula.
#VALUE!	Appears when you use the wrong type of argument in a function, the wrong type of operator, or when you call for a mathematical operation that refers to cells that contain text entries.

Fixing Up Those Data Entry Flub-ups

We all wish we were perfect, but, alas, since so few of us are, we are best off preparing for those inevitable times when we mess up. When entering vast quantities of data, it's really easy for those nasty little typos to creep into your work. In your pursuit of the perfect spreadsheet, there are things you can do: First, get Excel to automatically correct certain typos right as they happen with its AutoCorrect feature; second, manually correct any of the disgusting little errors that get through, either while you're still in the process of making the entry in the cell or after the entry has gone in.

You really AutoCorrect that for me

The new AutoCorrect feature is a godsend for those of us who tend to make the same stupid typos over and over again. With AutoCorrect, you can alert Excel to your own particular typing gaffes and tell the program how it should automatically fix them for you.

When you first install Excel, the AutoCorrect feature already knows to automatically correct two initial capital letters in an entry (by lowercasing the second capital letter), capitalize the name of the days of the week, and to replace a set number of text entries and typos with particular substitute text.

You can add to the list of text replacements at any time when using Excel. These text replacements can be of two types: typos that you routinely make along with the correct spellings, and abbreviations or acronyms that you type all the time along with their full forms. To add to the replacements

1. **Choose <u>A</u>utoCorrect on the <u>T</u>ools menu.**

2. **Enter the typo or abbreviation in the <u>R</u>eplace edit box.**

3. **Enter the correction or full form in the <u>W</u>ith text box.**

Figure 2-9 shows the AutoCorrect dialog box after I entered my favorite typo "h-t-e" along with the correct spelling "t-h-e" (AutoCorrect already knows to replace "t-e-h" with "t-h-e," but that's not one I tend to make). Figure 2-10 shows the AutoCorrect dialog box another time after I entered the abbreviation "m-g-e" for "Mother Goose Enterprises." That way, I don't have to take the time to spell out Mother Goose Enterprises in any of the spreadsheets that I create because AutoCorrect will be there, ready to convert my "mge" as soon as I type it.

Figure 2-9:
Entering my
favorite typo
and the
automatic
correction
that Excel is
to replace
it with.

Figure 2-10:
Entering my
favorite
acronym
and the
automatic
correction
that Excel is
to replace
it with.

Cell editing etiquette

Despite the help of AutoCorrect, some mistakes are bound to get you. How you correct them really depends upon whether you notice before or after you complete the cell entry.

✔ If you catch the mistake before you complete an entry, you can delete it by pressing Backspace (the key immediately above the Enter key) until you remove all the incorrect characters from the cell. Then you can retype the rest of the entry or the formula before you complete the entry in the cell.

✔ If you don't discover the mistake until after you've completed the cell entry, you have a choice between replacing the whole thing or editing just the mistakes.

- When dealing with short entries, you'll probably want to go the replacement route. To replace a cell entry, you have only to position the cell pointer in that cell, type your replacement entry, and then complete the replacement entry by clicking the Enter box, or pressing Enter or one of the arrow keys.

- When the error in an entry is relatively easy to fix and the entry is on the long side, you'll probably want to edit the cell entry rather than replace it. To edit the entry in the cell, simply double-click the cell or select the cell and then press F2.

- Doing either one reactivates the formula bar by once again displaying the Enter, Cancel, and Function Wizard boxes, while at the same time placing the insertion point in the cell entry in the worksheet (if you double-click, the insertion point is positioned wherever you click; if you press F2, the insertion point is positioned after the last character in the entry).

- Notice also that the mode indicator changes to Edit. While in this mode, you can use the mouse or the arrow keys to position the insertion point at the place in the cell entry that needs fixing.

Table 2-2 lists the keystrokes you can use to reposition the insertion point in the cell entry and delete unwanted characters. If you want to insert new characters at the insertion point, simply start typing. If you want to delete existing characters at the insertion point as you type new ones, press Ins to switch from the normal insert mode to overtype mode. To return to normal insert mode, press Ins a second time. When you finish making corrections to the cell entry, you must re-enter the edited entry before Excel updates the contents of the cell.

While Excel is in Edit mode, you must re-enter the edited cell contents by either clicking the Enter box or pressing Enter. You can only use the arrow keys as a way to complete an entry when the program is in Enter mode. When the program is in Edit mode, the arrow keys only move the insertion point through the entry that you're editing, not to a new cell.

Table 2-2	Keystrokes for fixing those cell entry flub-ups
Keystroke	*What the Keystroke Does*
Del	Deletes the character to the right of the insertion point
Backspace	Deletes the character to the left of the insertion point
→	Positions the insertion point one character to the right
←	Positions the insertion point one character to the left
↑	Positions the insertion point, when it is at the end of the cell entry, to its preceding position to the left
End or ↓	Moves the insertion point after the last character in the cell entry
Home	Moves the insertion point in front of the first character of the cell entry
Ctrl+→	Positions the insertion point in front of the next word in the cell entry
Ctrl+←	Positions the insertion in front of the preceding word in the cell entry
Ins	Switches between insert and overtype mode

The Tale of Two Edits: cell versus formula bar editing

Excel gives you a choice between editing a cell's contents either in the cell (as discussed earlier) or on the formula bar. Whereas, most the time, editing right in the cell is just fine, when dealing with really, really long entries (like humongous formulas that seem to go on forever or text entries that take up paragraphs and paragraphs), you may prefer to do your editing on the formula bar. This is because Excel expands the formula bar to as many rows as are necessary to display the entire cell contents; whereas, in the worksheet display, the cell contents may be running right off the screen.

To edit the contents in the formula bar rather than in the cell itself, you must position the cell pointer in the cell and then double-click somewhere (probably the first place that needs changing) in the cell contents on the formula bar.

Taking the Drudgery out of Data Entry

Before leaving the topic of data entry, I feel duty bound to cover some of the shortcuts that really help to cut down on the drudgery of this task. These data-entry tips include using the AutoComplete and AutoFill features as well as doing data entry in a preselected block of cells and entering the same things in a bunch of cells all at the same time.

I'm just not complete without you

The new AutoComplete feature in Excel for Windows 95 is not something you can do anything about; it's just something to be aware of as you enter data. In an attempt to cut down on your typing load, our friendly software engineers at Microsoft came up with the AutoComplete feature.

AutoComplete is kinda like a moronic mind reader who anticipates what you might want to enter next based upon what you just entered earlier. This feature only comes into play when you're entering a column of text entries (it does not come into play when entering values or formulas or when entering a row of text entries). When entering a column of text entries, AutoComplete looks at the kinds of entries you make in that column and automatically duplicates them in subsequent rows whenever you start a new entry that begins with the same letter as an existing entry.

For example, say I enter **Jack Sprat Diet Centers** (one of the companies owned and operated by Mother Goose Enterprises) in cell A3, and then move the cell pointer down to cell A4 in the row below and press J (lowercase or uppercase, it doesn't matter), AutoComplete immediately inserts "ack Sprat Diet Centers" in this cell after the J, as shown in Figure 2-11.

Now this is great if I happen to need Jack Sprat Diet Centers as the row heading in both cells A3 and A4. Anticipating that I might be typing a different entry that just happens to start with the same letter as the one above, AutoComplete automatically selects everything after the first letter in the duplicated entry it inserted (from "ack" on, in this example). This enables me to replace the duplicate supplied by AutoComplete just by continuing to type (which is what I did after shooting Figure 2-11 since I needed to enter Jack and Jill Trauma Centers — another of Mother's companies — in cell A4).

If you override a duplicate supplied by AutoComplete in a column by typing one of your own (as in my example with changing Jack Sprat Diet Centers to Jack and Jill Trauma Centers in cell A4), you effectively shut down its ability to supply any more duplicates for that particular letter. So, for instance, in my example, after changing Jack Sprat Diet Centers to Jack and Jill Trauma Centers in cell A4, AutoComplete doesn't do anything if I then type **J** in cell A5. In other words, you're on your own if you don't continue to accept Auto-Complete's typing suggestions.

Fill 'er up with AutoFill

Many of the worksheets you create with Excel require the entry of a series of sequential dates or numbers. For example, a worksheet may require you to title the columns with the 12 months, from January through December, or to number the rows from 1 to 100.

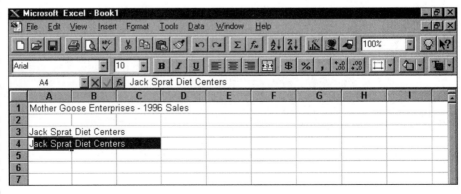

Excel's AutoFill feature makes short work of this kind of repetitive task. All you have to enter is the starting values for the series. In most cases, AutoFill is smart enough to figure out how to extend the series for you when you drag the fill handle to the right (to take the series across columns to the right) or down (to extend the series to the rows below).

Remember that the AutoFill handle looks like this **+** and appears only when you position the mouse pointer on the lower-right corner of the cell (or the last cell, when you've selected a block of cells). Keep in mind that if you drag a cell selection with the white-cross mouse pointer rather than the AutoFill handle, Excel simply extends the cell selection to those cells you drag through (see Chapter 3). If you drag a cell selection with the arrowhead pointer, Excel moves the cell selection (see Chapter 4).

When creating a series with the fill handle, you can only drag in one direction at a time. For example, you can extend the series or fill the range to the left or right of the cell range that contains the initial values, or you can extend the series or fill the range above or below the cell range that contains the initial values. You can't, however, extend the series or fill the range in two directions at the same time (such as down and to the right by dragging the fill handle diagonally).

When you release the mouse button after extending the range with the fill handle, Excel either creates a series in all of the cells you selected or fills the entire range with the initial value.

Figures 2-12 and 2-13 illustrate how to use AutoFill to enter a row of months, starting with January in cell B2 and ending with June in cell G2. To do this, you simply enter **January** in cell B2, and then position the mouse pointer on the fill handle in the lower-right corner of this cell before you drag through to cell G2 on the right (as shown in Figure 2-12). When you release the mouse button, Excel fills in the names of the rest of the months (February through June) in the selected cells (as shown in Figure 2-13). Note that Excel keeps the cells with the series of months selected, giving you another chance to modify the series (if you went too far, you can drag the fill handle to the left to cut back on the list of months; if you didn't go far enough, you can drag it to the right to extend the list of months further).

Table 2-3 shows some of the different initial values that AutoFill can use and the types of series that Excel can create from them.

Figure 2-12:
To create a series of months, type **January** in the first cell, and then use the AutoFill handle to select the range of cells where the rest of the months will be.

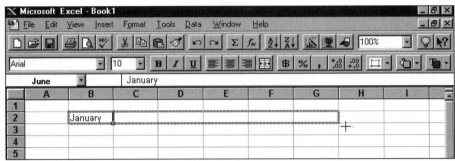

Figure 2-13:
As soon as you release the mouse button, Excel fills the cell selection with the rest of the months.

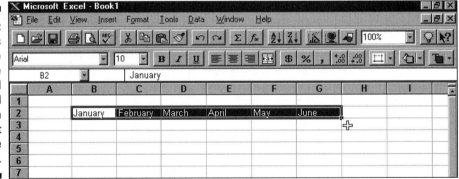

Working with a spaced series

AutoFill uses the initial value you select (date, time, day, year, and so on) to "design" the series. All of the sample series shown in Table 2-3 change by a factor of one (one day, one month, or one number). You can tell AutoFill to create a series that changes by some other value: Enter two sample values in neighboring cells that describe the amount of change you want between each value in the series. Make these two values the initial selection that you extend with the fill handle.

For example, to start a series with Saturday and enter every other day across a row, enter **Saturday** in the first cell and **Monday** in the cell next-door. After selecting both cells, drag the fill handle across the cells to the right as far you need to extend the series. When you release the mouse button, Excel follows the example set in the first two cells by entering every other day (Wednesday to the right of Monday, Friday to the right of Wednesday, and so on).

Table 2-3	Samples of series you can create with AutoFill
Value Entered in First Cell	*Extended Series Created by AutoFill in the Next Three Cells*
June	July, August, September
Jun	Jul, Aug, Sep
Tuesday	Wednesday, Thursday, Friday
Tue	Wed, Thu, Fri
4/1/96	4/2/96, 4/3/96, 4/4/96
Jan-96	Feb-96, Mar-96, Apr-96
15-Feb	16-Feb, 17-Feb, 18-Feb
10:00 PM	11:00 PM, 12:00 AM, 1:00 AM
8:01	9:01, 10:01, 11:01
Quarter 1	Quarter 2, Quarter 3, Quarter 4
Qtr2	Qtr3, Qtr4, Qtr1
Q3	Q4, Q1, Q2
Product 1	Product 2, Product 3, Product 4
1st Product	2nd Product, 3rd Product, 4th Product

Copying with AutoFill

You can use AutoFill to copy a text entry throughout a cell range (rather than fill in a series of related entries). To copy a text entry to a cell range, you must hold down the Ctrl key as you click the thin black-cross pointer on the lower-right corner of the cell and drag the fill handle. When you hold down the Ctrl key as you click the fill handle, a plus sign appears to the right of the thin black-cross pointer — your sign that AutoFill will *copy* the entry in the active cell instead of create a series using it.

Although holding down Ctrl as you drag the fill handle copies a text entry, just the opposite is true when it comes to values! If you enter a number like 17 in a cell and then drag the fill handle across the row, Excel just copies the number 17 in all the cells you select. If, however, you hold down Ctrl as you drag the fill handle, Excel then fills out the series (17, 18, 19, and so on).

Creating custom lists for AutoFill

In addition to varying the increment in a series created with AutoFill, you can also create your own custom series. For example, in the bosom of the Mother Goose Enterprises, you will find the following companies:

- ✔ Jack Sprat Diet Centers
- ✔ Jack and Jill Trauma Centers
- ✔ Mother Hubbard Dog Goodies
- ✔ Rub-a-Dub-Dub Hot Tubs and Spas
- ✔ Georgie Porgie Pudding Pies
- ✔ Hickory, Dickory, & Dock Clock Repair
- ✔ Little Bo-Peep Pet Detectives

Rather than have to type this list of companies in the cells of each new worksheet (or even copy them from an existing worksheet), you can create a custom series that will produce the whole list of companies simply by entering Jack Sprat Diet Centers in the first cell and then dragging the fill handle to the blank cells where the rest of the companies should appear.

To create this kind of custom series, follow these steps:

1. **Choose Tools, and then choose Options to open the Options dialog box.**

2. **Choose the Custom Lists tab to display the Custom Lists and List Entries boxes.**

   If you've already gone to the time and trouble of typing the custom list in a range of cells, go to 3a. If you haven't yet typed the series in an open worksheet, go to 3b instead.

3a. **Click in the Import List from the Cells edit box, and then drag the dialog box out of the way so that you can see your list and select the range of cells (see Chapter 3 for details). After selecting the cells, choose the Import button to copy this list into the List Entries list box and skip to step 5 (as shown in Figure 2-14).**

3b. **Choose the List Entries list box, and then type each entry (in the desired order), being sure to press Enter after typing each one.**

   When all of the entries in the custom list appear in the List Entries list box in the order you're going to want them, proceed to step 4.

Figure 2-14:
Creating a
custom
company list
from
existing
worksheet
entries.

4. **Choose the Add button to add the list of entries to the Custom Lists box.**

   Finish creating all the custom lists you need using the preceding steps.
   When you are done, move on to step 5.

5. **Choose OK or press Enter to close the Options dialog box and return to
   the current worksheet in the active workbook.**

After adding a custom list to Excel, from then on you need only enter the first
entry in a cell and then use the fill handle to extend it to the cells below or to
the right.

Entries all around the block

When you want to enter a table of information in a new worksheet, you can
simplify the job of entering the data if you select all the empty cells in which
you want to make entries before you begin entering any information. Just
position the cell pointer in the first cell of what is to become the data table and
then select all the cells in the subsequent columns and rows (for information on
the ways to select a range of cells, see Chapter 3). After you select the block of
cells, you can begin entering the first entry.

When you select a block of cells (also known as a *range*) before you start entering information, Excel restricts data entry to that range as follows:

- ✔ The program automatically advances the cell pointer to the next cell in the range when you click the Enter box or press Enter to complete each cell entry.

- ✔ In a cell range that contains several different rows and columns, Excel advances the cell pointer down each row of the column as you make your entries. When the cell pointer reaches the cell in the last row of the column, the cell pointer advances to the first selected row in the next column to the right. If the cell range uses only one row, Excel advances the cell pointer from left to right across the row.

- ✔ When you finish entering information in the last cell in the selected range, Excel positions the cell pointer in the first cell of the now-completed data table. To deselect the cell range, click the mouse pointer on one of the cells in the worksheet (inside or outside the selected range — it doesn't matter) or press one of the arrow keys.

Be sure that you don't press one of the arrow keys to complete a cell entry within a preselected cell range instead of clicking the Enter box or pressing Enter. Pressing an arrow key deselects the range of cells when Excel moves the cell pointer. To move the cell pointer around a cell range without deselecting the range, try these methods:

- ✔ Press Enter to advance to the next cell down each row and then across each column in the range. Press Shift+Enter to move up to the previous cell.

- ✔ Press Tab to advance to the next cell in the column on the right and then down each row of the range. Press Shift+Tab to move left to the previous cell.

- ✔ Press Ctrl+. (period) to move from one corner of the range to another.

Data entry express

You can save a lot of time and energy when you want the same entry (text, value, or formula) to appear in many cells of the worksheet; you can enter the information in all the cells in one operation. You first select the cell ranges to hold the information (Excel lets you select more than one cell range for this kind of thing — see Chapter 3 for details). Then you construct the entry on the formula bar and press Ctrl+Enter to put the entry into all the selected ranges.

The key to making this operation a success is to hold the Ctrl key as you press Enter so that Excel inserts the entry on the formula bar into all the selected cells. If you forget to hold Ctrl, and you just press Enter, Excel only places the entry in the first cell of the selected cell range.

How to Make Your Formulas Function Even Better

Earlier in this chapter, I showed you how to create formulas that perform a series of simple mathematical operations such as addition, subtraction, multiplication, and division. Instead of creating more complex formulas from scratch out of an intricate combination of these operations, you can find an Excel function to get the job done.

A *function* is a predefined formula that performs a particular type of computation. All you have to do to use a function is supply the values that the function uses when performing its calculations (in the parlance of the Spreadsheet Guru, such values are known as the *arguments of the function*). As with simple formulas, you can enter the arguments for most functions either as a numerical value (for example, **22** or **–4.56**) or, as is more common, as a cell reference (for example, **B10**), or as a cell range (for example, **C3:F3**).

Just as with a formula you build yourself, each function you use must start with an equal sign (=) so that Excel knows to enter the function as a formula rather than as text. Following the equal sign, you enter the name of the function (in uppercase or lowercase — it doesn't matter, as long as you don't misspell the name). Following the name of the function, you enter the arguments required to perform the calculations. All function arguments are enclosed in a pair of parentheses.

If you type the function directly in a cell, remember not to insert spaces between the equal sign, function name, and the arguments enclosed in parentheses. Some functions use more than one value when performing their designated calculations. When this is the case, you separate each function with a comma (not a space).

After you type the equal sign, function name, and the left parenthesis that marks the beginning of the arguments for the function, you can point to any cell or cell range you want to use as the first argument instead of typing the cell references. When the function uses more than one argument, you can point to the cells or cell ranges you want to use for the second argument right after you type the **,** (comma) to complete the first argument.

After you finish entering the last argument, type a right parenthesis to mark the end of the argument list, and then click the Enter box or press Enter or an arrow key to insert the function in the cell and have Excel calculate the answer.

Conjuring up formulas with the Function Wizard

Although you can enter a function by typing it directly in a cell, Excel provides a Function Wizard whose magic allows you not only to select the function but also to specify the function arguments. This is a real boon when you're fooling with an unfamiliar function or one that's kind of complex (some of these puppies can be really hairy). The Function Wizard keeps track of all the arguments you need to use and sees to it that you don't mess up on your parentheses or commas separating the argument list.

To dial up the Function Wizard after selecting the cell that needs the formula, you click the Function Wizard button (the one marked *fx*) on the Standard toolbar or, if you've already typed = (equal sign), you can click the Function Wizard button on the formula bar (the one with *fx* right next to the Enter button). When you click the Function Wizard button, the Function Wizard — Step 1 of 2 dialog box appears, similar to the one shown in Figure 2-15.

The Function Wizard — Step 1 of 2 dialog box contains two list boxes: Function Category and Function Name. When you open this dialog box, Excel automatically selects Most Recently Used as the category in the Function Category list box and displays the functions you usually use in the Function Name list box.

If your function isn't among the most recently used, you must then select the appropriate category of your function in the Function Category list box (if you don't know the category, choose All). After that, of course, you still need to choose the particular function in the Function Name list box.

When you select a function in the Function Name list box, Excel displays the required arguments for the function at the bottom of this dialog box and inserts the function name (along with the obligatory parentheses) in the current cell. For example, suppose that you select the SUM function (the "crown jewel" of the Most Recently Used function category) in the Function Name list box. As soon as you do, the program puts

```
=SUM( )
```

in the cell (and on the formula bar) and shows the arguments as

```
SUM(number1,number2,...)
```

at the bottom of the first Function Wizard dialog box.

Figure 2-15:
Select the
function to
use in the
Function
Wizard —
Step 1 of 2
dialog box.

To continue and fill in the number arguments for the SUM function, you then
choose the Next button in the Function Wizard — Step 1 of 2 dialog box. This
takes you (surprise, surprise) to the Function Wizard — Step 2 of 2 dialog box
(like the one shown in Figure 2-16) where you can add the arguments for the
SUM function.

As the Function Wizard — Step 2 of 2 dialog box points out, you can select up
to 30 numbers to be summed. What it doesn't tell you, however (there's always
some trick, huh?), is that these numbers don't have to be in single cells. In fact,
most of the time you will be selecting a whole slew of numbers in nearby cells
(in a multiple cell selection — that range thing) that you want to total.

To select your first number argument in the Function Wizard — Step 2 of 2
dialog box, you click the cell (or drag through the block of cells) in the
worksheet while the insertion point is in the number1 text box. Excel then
displays the cell address (or range address) in the number1 text box while, at
the same time, showing the value in the cell (or values, if you've selected a
bunch of cells) in the box to the right and the total so far in the Value text box
at the top.

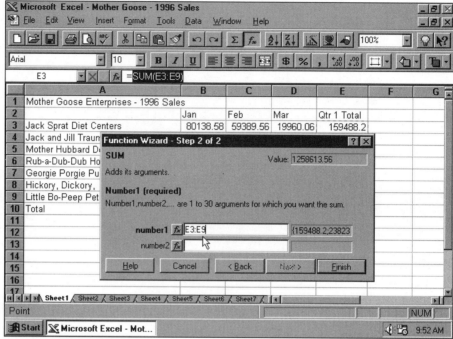

Figure 2-16:
Specify the
arguments
to use in the
Function
Wizard —
Step 2 of 2
dialog box.

If you're adding more than one cell (or bunch of cells) in a worksheet, you press the Tab key or click the number2 text box to move the insertion point there (Excel responds by extending the argument list with a number3 text box). Here is where you specify the second cell (or cell range) that is to be added to the one now showing in the number1 text box. After you click the cell or drag through the second cell range, the program displays the cell address(es), with the numbers in the cell(s) to the right, and the running total in the Value text box (as shown in Figure 2-17).

When you've finished pointing out the cells or bunches of cells to be summed, you then click the Finish button to close the Function Wizard — Step 2 of 2 dialog box and put the SUM function in the current cell.

I'd be totally lost without AutoSum

Before leaving this fascinating discussion on entering functions, I want you to get to the AutoSum tool on the Standard toolbar (the one with the Σ). This little tool is worth its weight in gold, as it not only enters the SUM function but also selects the most likely range of cells in the current column or row that you want

Figure 2-17:
To specify
additional
arguments
for a
function,
press Tab to
extend the
argument
list.

totaled and automatically enters them as the function's argument. And nine times out of ten, Excel selects (by highlighting) the correct cell range to be totaled. For that tenth case, you can manually correct the range by simply dragging the cell pointer through the block of cells that need to be summed.

Figure 2-18 shows how to use the AutoSum tool to total the sales of Jack Sprat Diet Centers in row 3. To total the sales in this row, position the cell pointer in cell E3, where the first-quarter total is to appear, and click the AutoSum tool. Excel inserts the SUM function (equal sign and all) onto the formula bar; places a *marquee* (the moving dotted line) around the cells B3, C3, and D3; and uses the cell range B3:D3 as the argument of the SUM function.

Figure 2-19 shows the worksheet after you insert the function in cell E3. The calculated total appears in cell E3 while the following SUM formula appears in the formula bar:

```
=SUM(B3:D3)
```

After entering the function to total the sales of Jack Sprat Diet Centers, you can copy this formula to total sales for the rest of the companies by dragging the fill handle down column E until the cell range E3:E9 is highlighted.

Figure 2-18:
Using
AutoSum to
total the
sales of
Jack Sprat
Diet Centers
in row 3.

Figure 2-19:
The work-
sheet with
the first
quarter total
for Jack
Sprat Diet
Centers.

Figure 2-20 illustrates how you can use the AutoSum tool to total the January sales for all the Mother Goose Enterprises in column B. Position the cell pointer in cell B10 where you want the total to appear. When you click the AutoSum tool, Excel places the marquee around cells B3 through B9 and correctly enters the cell range B3:B9 as the argument of the SUM function.

Figure 2-21 shows the worksheet after inserting the function in cell B10 and using the AutoFill feature to copy the formula to cells C10, D10, and E10 to the right. (To use AutoFill, drag the fill handle through the cells to the right until you reach cell E10 before you release the mouse button.)

Figure 2-20: Using the AutoSum tool to add the January sales in column B.

Figure 2-21: The worksheet after copying the SUM formula.

Making Sure the Data's Safe and Sound

All the work you do in any of the worksheets in your workbook is at risk until you save the workbook as a disk file. Should you lose power or should your computer crash for any reason before you save the workbook, you're out of luck. You have to recreate each and every keystroke — a painful task, made all the worse because it's so unnecessary. To avoid this unpleasantness altogether, adopt this rule of thumb: Save your work any time you've entered more information than you could possibly bear to lose.

To encourage frequent saving on your part, Excel even provides you with a Save button on the Standard toolbar (the one with the picture of the disk, third from the left). You don't even have to take the time and trouble to choose the Save command from the File menu (or even press Ctrl+S); you can simply click this tool whenever you want to save new work on disk.

The first time you click the Save tool, Excel displays the Save As dialog box (similar to the one shown in Figure 2-22). You can use this dialog box to replace the temporary document name (Book1, Book2, and the like) with a more descriptive filename and to select a new drive and folder before you save the workbook as a disk file. It's just this easy:

✔ To rename the workbook, type the filename in the File name edit box. When you first open the Save As dialog box, the suggested Book1-type filename is selected; you can just start typing the new filename to replace it.

✔ To change the drive on which the workbook is stored, click the Save in drop-down list button, and then click the appropriate drive name, such as Hard disk (C:) or 3 $^1/_2$ Floppy (A:) in the drop-down list box.

✔ To change the folder in which the workbook is saved, select the drive, if necessary (as described above), and then click the desired folder. If you want to save the workbook in a folder that's inside one of the folders shown in the list box, just double-click that folder. When all is said and done, the name of the folder where the workbook file will be saved should appear in the Save in edit box. If you want to save the file in a brand-new folder, click the Create new folder button (see Figure 2-22) and enter the folder name in the New Folder dialog box before choosing OK or pressing Enter.

Remember that, under Windows 95, your filenames can contain spaces and be a maximum of 255 characters long (you do want to name your a file with an entire paragraph, don't you?). This is great news, especially if you were a DOS or Windows 3.1 user who suffered under that eight-dot-three filename restriction for so long. Just be aware when naming your workbooks that if you transfer it to a machine that doesn't use Windows 95, the Excel filenames will appear severely abbreviated, and they will all be followed with the .XLS Excel filename extension (which, by the way, is stuck onto workbook files created in Excel for Windows 95: It's just that Windows 95 has enough sense to hide this filename extension from you).

Create new folder   Properties

Look in favorites   Details

Up one level   List   Commands and settings

Figure 2-22:
The Save As
dialog box.

When you finish making changes in the Save As dialog box, choose the Save button or press Enter. Excel may display the Summary tab of the file's Properties dialog box, like the one shown in Figure 2-23, where you can add information that may help you identify this file later in the Open dialog box. If you don't see this dialog box when you first save your workbook, you can make it appear by selecting the Prompt for File Properties check box on the General tab of the Options dialog box (See "Fooling Around with the General Options" in Chapter 11.).

When filling out the Summary information (which you can skip, of course, if you're in a hurry and are sure you'll never, ever forget what kind of stuff you put in the workbook file), you can specify the Title, Subject, Author, Manager, Company, Category, Keywords, and Comments about the workbook and its worksheets. Just keep in mind that, later on, you'll be able to display this summary information in the Open dialog box (see Chapter 4) to help you identify whether or not this is the file you want to work with.

After filling in the Summary information in the Properties dialog box (or just moving on, if you think it best), choose OK or press Enter to close this dialog box and save the workbook file (with all its worksheets) on disk. After saving a workbook the first time, Excel displays the filename you assigned in the workbook title bar (or after Microsoft Excel on the program title bar when the workbook is maximized). You'll never be bothered by the Summary information unless you deliberately choose Properties on the File pull-down menu and select the Summary tab.

Figure 2-23:
Adding
summary
information
when first
saving a
workbook
file.

When Excel saves your workbook file, the program saves all the information in every worksheet in your workbook (including the last position of the cell pointer) in the designated folder and disk. You don't have to fool with the Save As dialog box again unless you want to rename the workbook or save a copy of it in a different directory. If you want to do either of these things, you must choose the Save As command from the File menu rather than click the Save tool or press Ctrl+S.

Part II
Editing without Tears

The 5th Wave   By Rich Tennant

"HOW'S THAT FOR FAST SCROLLING?"

In this part . . .

The business world wouldn't be half bad if it just weren't for the fact that right around the time you master your job, somebody goes and changes it on you. When your life must always be flexible, changing gears and "going with the flow" can really grate on a person! The sad truth is that a big part of the work that you do with Excel for Windows 95 is changing the stuff you slaved so hard to enter into the spreadsheet in the first place.

Part II breaks this editing stuff down into three phases: formatting the raw data, rearranging the formatting data and/or in some cases deleting it, and, finally, spitting the final formatted and edited data out in printed form. Take it from me, once you know your way around editing your spreadsheets (as presented in this part of the book), you're more than half way home with Excel for Windows 95.

Chapter 3

Making It All Look Pretty

In This Chapter

▶ Selecting the cells to be formatted

▶ Formatting a table of data with AutoFormat

▶ Using number formats on cells containing values

▶ Creating custom number formats for your worksheet

▶ Adjusting the widths of columns in a worksheet

▶ Adjusting the height of rows in a worksheet

▶ Hiding columns and rows in the worksheet

▶ Changing the font and font size

▶ Changing the alignment of the entries in a cell selection

▶ Adding borders, shading, and colors to a cell selection

▶ Formatting cells with styles

*I*n spreadsheet programs like Excel, you don't normally worry about how the stuff looks until after you've entered all the data in the worksheets of your workbook and saved it all safe and sound (see Chapters 1 and 2). Only then is it time to pretty up the information so that it's clearer and easy to read.

After you decide on the types of formatting you want to apply to a portion of the worksheet, you select all the cells to be beautified and then click the appropriate tool or choose the menu command to apply those formats to the cells. This means that, before you learn about all the fabulous formatting features you can use to dress up cells, you first need to know how to pick out the group of cells that you want to apply the formatting to — a process formally known as *selecting the cells* or, alternately, *making a cell selection*.

Be aware, also, that entering data into a cell and formatting that data are two completely different things in Excel. Because they're separate, you can change the entry in a formatted cell and the new entry will assume the cell's formatting. This enables you to format blank cells in a worksheet, knowing that, when you get around to making entries in those cells, those entries will automatically assume the formatting assigned to those cells.

Choosing a Select Group of Cells

Given the monotonously rectangular nature of the worksheet and its components, it shouldn't come as a surprise to find that all the cell selections you make in the worksheet have the same kind of cubist feel to them. After all, worksheets are just blocks of cells of varying numbers of columns and rows.

A *cell selection* (also known as a *cell range*) is whatever collection of neighboring cells you pick out for formatting or editing. The smallest possible cell selection in a worksheet is just one cell (the so-called *active cell;* the cell with the cell pointer is really just a single cell selection). The largest possible cell selection in a worksheet is all of the cells in that worksheet (the whole enchilada, so to speak). Most of the cell selections you need for formatting a worksheet will probably be somewhere in between, consisting of cells in several adjacent columns and rows.

Excel shows a cell selection in the worksheet by highlighting the block (Figure 3-1 shows several cell selections of different sizes and shapes).

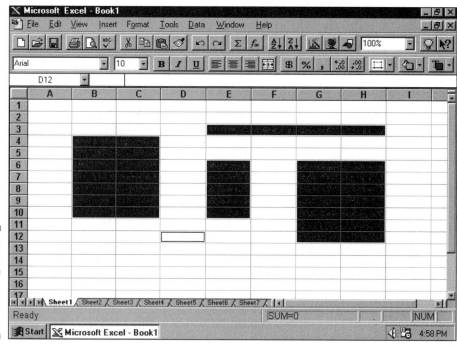

Figure 3-1:
Several cell selections of various shapes and sizes.

In Excel, you can select more than one cell range at a time (a phenomenon somewhat ingloriously called a *discontiguous* or *nonadjacent selection*). In fact, although I billed Figure 3-1 as having several cell selections, it is really just one big, nonadjacent cell selection with cell D12 (the active one), the cell that was selected last.

Point-and-click cell selections

The mouse is a natural for selecting a range of cells. Just position the mouse pointer (in its thick, white-cross form) on the first cell and drag in the direction that you want to extend the selection.

- ✔ To extend the cell selection to columns to the right, drag right, highlighting neighboring cells as you go.
- ✔ To extend the selection to rows to the bottom, drag down.
- ✔ To extend the selection down and to the right at the same time, drag diagonally toward the cell in the lower-right corner of the block you are highlighting.

Shifty cell selections

To speed up the old cell-selection procedure, you can use the old Shift-click method, which goes as follows:

1. **Click the first cell in the selection.**

   This selects that cell.

2. **Position the mouse pointer in the last cell in the selection.**

   This would be kitty-corner from the first cell if you're selecting a rectangular block.

3. **Press the Shift key and hold it down as you click the mouse button again.**

   When you click the mouse button the second time, Excel selects all the cells in the columns and rows between the first cell and last cell.

The Shift key works with the mouse like an *extend* key to extend a selection from the first object you select through to, and including, the second object you select (see "Extend that cell selection," later in this chapter). Shift enables you to select the first and last cells as well as all the intervening cells in a worksheet or all the document names in a dialog list box.

If, when making a cell selection with the mouse, you notice that you have included the wrong cells before you release the mouse button, you can deselect the cells and resize the selection by moving the pointer in the opposite direction. If you've already released the mouse button, click the first cell in the highlighted range to select just that cell (and deselect all the others) and then start the whole selection process again.

Nonadjacent cell selections

To select a nonadjacent cell selection made up of more than one discontiguous block of cells, drag through the first cell range and then hold down the Ctrl key as you click the first cell of the second range and drag the pointer through the cells in this range. As long as you hold down Ctrl while you select the subsequent ranges, Excel doesn't deselect any of the previously selected cell ranges.

The Ctrl key works with the mouse like an *add* key to include non-neighboring objects in Excel (see "Nonadjacent cell selections with the keyboard," later in this chapter). With Ctrl, you can add to the selection of cells in a worksheet or to the document names in a dialog list box without having to deselect those already selected.

Going for the "big" cell selections

You can select the cells in entire columns or rows or even all the cells in the worksheet by applying the following clicking-and-dragging techniques to the worksheet frame:

- ✔ To select every single cell in a particular column, click its column letter on the frame at the top of the worksheet document window.

- ✔ To select every cell in a particular row, click its row number on the frame at the left edge of the document window.

- ✔ To select a range of entire columns or rows, drag through the column letters or row numbers on the frame surrounding the workbook.

- ✔ To select more than entire columns or rows that are not right next to each other (that old discontiguous stuff, again), press and hold down the Ctrl key while you click the column letters or row numbers of the columns and rows that you want to add to the selection.

- ✔ To select each and every cell in the worksheet, click the unmarked button in the upper-left corner of the workbook frame formed by the intersection of the row with the column letters and the column with the row numbers.

Selecting the cells in a table of data, courtesy of AutoSelect

Excel provides a really quick way (called AutoSelect) to select all the cells in a table of data entered as a solid block. (Don't try this when you need to select empty cells or on a table of data that has blanks in the first column or top row.) To use AutoSelect, simply follow these steps:

1. **Click the first cell of the table to select it.**

   That's the one in the table's upper-left corner.

2. **Hold down the Shift key as you double-click either the right or bottom edge of the selected cell with the arrowhead mouse pointer (see Figure 3-2).**

   If you double-click the bottom edge of the cell, the cell selection expands to that cell in the last row of the first column (as shown in Figure 3-3). If you double-click the right edge of the cell, the cell selection expands to the cell in the last column of the first row.

3a. **Double-click somewhere on the right edge of the cell selection (see Figure 3-3) if the cell selection now consists of the first column of the table.**

   This selects all the remaining rows of the table of data (as shown in Figure 3-4).

3b. **Double-click somewhere on the bottom edge of the current cell selection if the cell selection now consists of the first row of the table.**

   This selects all the rest of the rows in the table.

Figure 3-2:
Position the mouse pointer on the bottom edge of the first cell to select the cells in the first column of the data table with AutoSelect.

	A	B	C	D	E	F	G	H	I	
1	Mother Goose Enterprises - 1996 Sales									
2		Jan	Feb	Mar	Qtr 1 Total					
3	Jack Sprat	80138.58	59389.56	19960.06	159488.2					
4	Jack and J	123456.2	89345.7	25436.84	238238.74					
5	Mother Hu	12657.05	60593.56	42300.28	115550.89					
6	Rub-a-Dub	17619.79	40635	42814.99	101069.78					
7	Georgie P	57133.56	62926.31	12408.73	132468.6					
8	Hickory, D	168291	124718.1	41916.13	334925.23					
9	Little Bo-P	30834.63	71111.25	74926.24	176872.12					
10	Total	490130.8	508719.5	259763.3	1258613.6					
11										
12										

Figure 3-3: Double-clicking the bottom edge of the selected cell with Shift depressed selects the first column of the data table.

Figure 3-4: Double-clicking the right edge of the current column selection with Shift depressed selects the rest of the columns in the table.

Although the preceding steps make it sound like you have to select the first cell of the table when you use AutoSelect, you can actually select any of the cells in the four corners of the table. Then, when expanding the cell selection in the table with the Shift key depressed, you can choose whatever direction you like (left by clicking the left edge, right by clicking the right edge, up by clicking the top edge, or down by clicking the bottom edge) to select either the first or last row of the table or the first or last column. After expanding the cell selection to include either the first or last row or first or last column, you need to click whichever edge of that current cell selection will expand it so that it includes all the remaining table rows or columns.

Keyboard cell selections

If you're not really keen on using the mouse, you can use the keyboard to select the cells you want. In keeping with the Shift-click method of selecting cells, the easiest way to select cells with the keyboard is to combine the Shift key with other keystrokes that move the cell pointer. (Chapter 1 lists these keystrokes.)

Start by positioning the cell pointer in the first cell of the selection and then hold the Shift key as you press the appropriate cell-pointer movement keys. When you hold the Shift key as you press direction keys such as the arrow keys ($\uparrow$, $\leftarrow$, $\downarrow$, $\rightarrow$), PgUp, or PgDn, Excel anchors the selection on the current cell and not only moves the cell pointer as usual but also highlights cells as it goes.

When making a cell selection this way, you can continue to alter the size and shape of the cell range with the cell-pointer movement keys as long as you don't release the Shift key. Once you let up on the Shift key, pressing any of the cell-pointer movement keys immediately collapses the selection, reducing it to just the cell with cell pointer.

Extend that cell selection

If holding the Shift key as you move the cell pointer is too tiring, you can place Excel in Extend mode by pressing (and promptly releasing) F8 before you press any cell-pointer movement key. Excel displays the EXT (for extend) indicator on the status bar — your sign that the program will select all the cells that you move the cell pointer through (just as though you were holding down the Shift key).

When you've highlighted all the cells you want in the cell range, press F8 again to turn off Extend mode. The EXT indicator disappears from the status bar and then you can once again move the cell pointer with the keyboard without highlighting everything in your path.

AutoSelect keyboard style

For the keyboard equivalent of AutoSelect with the mouse (see "Selecting the cells in a table of data, courtesy of AutoSelect earlier in this chapter"), you combine the use of the F8, (Extend key) or the Shift key with the Ctrl+arrow keys or End+arrow keys to zip the cell pointer from one end of a block to the other, merrily selecting all the cells in its path as it goes.

To select an entire table of data with a keyboard version of AutoSelect, you follow these steps:

1. **Position the cell pointer in the first cell.**

    That's the one in the upper-left corner of the table.

2. **Press F8 (or hold the Shift key), and then press Ctrl→ (or End,→ if you prefer) to extend the cell selection to the cells in the columns on the right.**

3. **Then press Ctrl+↓ (or End,↓ if you prefer) to extend the selection to the cells in the rows below.**

Keep in mind that the directions in the above steps are arbitrary — you can just as well press Ctrl↓ (or End,↓) before you press Ctrl+→ (or End,→). Just be sure (if you're using the Shift key instead of F8) that you don't let up on the Shift key until after you finish performing these two directional maneuvers. Also, if you pressed F8 to get the program into Extend mode, don't forget to press this key again to get out of Extend mode once the table cells are all selected (or you'll end up selecting cells you don't want included when you next move the cell pointer).

Nonadjacent cell selections with the keyboard

Selecting more than one cell range is a little more complicated with the keyboard than it is with the mouse. When using the keyboard, you alternate between anchoring the cell pointer and moving the cell pointer to select the cell range, unanchoring the cell pointer and repositioning it at the beginning of the next range. To unanchor the cell pointer so that you can move it into position for selecting another range, press Shift+F8. This puts you in Add mode, in which you can move to the first cell of the next range without selecting any more cells. Excel lets you know that the cell pointer is unanchored by displaying the ADD indicator on the status bar.

To select more than one cell range using the keyboard, you follow these general steps:

1. **Move the cell pointer to the first cell of the first cell range you want to select.**

2. **Press F8 to get into Extend mode.**

   Move the cell pointer to select all the cells in the first cell range. Alternatively, hold the Shift key as you move the cell pointer.

3. **Press Shift+F8 to switch to Add mode.**

   The ADD indicator appears in the status bar.

4. **Move the cell pointer to the first cell of the next nonadjacent range you want to select.**

5. **Press F8 again to get back into Extend mode and then move the cell pointer to select all the cells in this new range.**

6. **If you still have other nonadjacent ranges to select, repeat steps 3, 4, and 5 until you have selected and added all the cell ranges you want to use.**

Cell selections à la Go To

If you want to select a really big cell range that would take a long time to select by pressing various cell-pointer movement keys, use the Go To feature to extend the range to a far distant cell. All you gotta do is follow this pair of steps:

1. **Start by positioning the cell pointer in the first cell of the range; then press F8 to anchor the cell pointer and get Excel into Extend mode.**

2. **Press F5 to open the Go To dialog box, type the address of the last cell in the range (the cell kitty-corner from the first cell), and then press Enter.**

Because Excel is in Extend mode at the time you use Go To to jump to another cell, the program not only moves the cell pointer to the designated cell address but selects all the intervening cells as well. After selecting the range of cells with the Go To feature, don't forget to press F8 (the Extend key) again to prevent the program from messing up your selection by adding on more cells the next time you move the cell pointer.

Trimming Your Tables with AutoFormat

Here's a formatting technique that doesn't require you to do any prior cell selecting. (Kinda figures, doesn't it?) In fact, the AutoFormat feature is so automatic that, to use it, the cell pointer just has to be somewhere within the table of data prior to your choosing the AutoFormat command on the Format pull-down menu.

As soon as you open the AutoFormat dialog box, Excel automatically selects all the cells in the table. (You get a rude message in an alert box if you choose the command when the cell pointer isn't within the confines of the table or in one of the cells directly bordering the table.)

After you open the AutoFormat dialog box, you can make short work of formatting the selected table by choosing one of the 16 built-in table formats. Here's how:

1. **Click a format in the Table Format list box to see a preview of its formats in the Sample area.**

   This sample should give you an idea of what kind of formatting is included in a particular table format and how it makes the table look. (Unfortunately, Excel can't display a miniature of your table in the Sample area.)

2. **Continue selecting formats from the list box in this manner to preview other table formats until you find the one you want to use.**

3. **Click the OK button or press Enter to lose the AutoFormat dialog box and apply the selected format to the table in the worksheet.**

When you're familiar enough with the table formats to know which one you want to use, you can save time by double-clicking the desired format in the Table Format list box to both close the AutoFormat dialog box and apply the formatting to the selected table.

If you ever goof up and select a table format that you just absolutely hate once you see it in the worksheet, choose the Undo AutoFormat command from the Edit menu (or press Ctrl+Z) before you do anything else; Excel restores the table to its previous state (for more on getting yourself out of a jam with the Undo feature, see Chapter 4). If you decide later on that you don't want any of the automatic table formatting, you can get rid of all of it (even when it's too late to use Undo) by opening the AutoFormat dialog box and choosing None in the Table Format list box (located at the very bottom of the list) before you choose OK or press Enter.

Each of the built-in table formats offered by AutoFormat is nothing more than a particular combination of various kinds of cell and data formatting that Excel applies to the cell selection in a single operation. (Boy, does this ever save time!) Each one enhances the headings and values in the table in a slightly different way.

Figure 3-5 shows the first quarter 1996 sales table for Mother Goose Enterprises (introduced in Chapter 2) just before the Simple table format is selected in the AutoFormat dialog box. Figure 3-6 shows the sales table with the Simple table format applied to it. Notice that, not only did AutoFormat bold the worksheet title and headings in rows 1 and 2 and draw borderlines to separate these headings from the rest of the table data, but it also centered the title *Mother Goose Enterprises — 1996 Sales* over columns A through E and the headings in cells B2 through E2. Note, however, that the Simple table format does nothing to spruce up the dollar amounts in the table.

Figure 3-7 shows the table after reopening the AutoFormat dialog box and, this time, choosing the 3D Effects 2 table format for the same cell range. As you can see, after selecting this table format, Excel increased the width of column A to contain the entire worksheet title, *Mother Goose Enterprises — 1996 Sales* in cell A1. This kind of column sizing is known as *best-fit* (somewhat misapplied in this case) and is accomplished with the AutoFit feature. To rectify this little boo-boo, you simply narrow column A until it's just wide enough to display all of the company names in rows 3 through 9 of column A and let the worksheet title in cell A1 once again overhang columns B through E as it naturally wants to do. (For information on how to widen and narrow columns, both manually and with the AutoFit feature, see "Calibrating Columns," later in this chapter.)

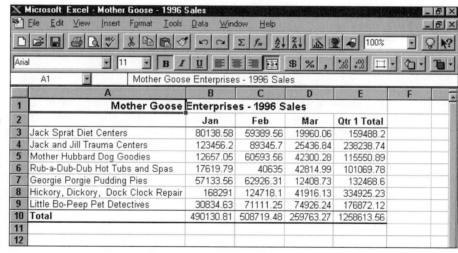

Figure 3-5:
Using
AutoFormat
to select the
Simple table
format for
the Mother
Goose
Enterprises
first quarter
sales table.

Figure 3-6:
Mother's
first quarter
sales table
in the
Simple table
format.

The 3D Effects 2 AutoFormat is not the only table format that uses AutoFit to apply this type of *best-fit* to all the selected columns (and therefore can give you a really wide first column if your table has a long title in the first cell like the ones shown in Figure 3-5 through 3-7). You also get this best-fit-which-is-not situation — shown in Figure 3-7 — if you choose the Classic 2; Financial 1, 2, or 3; Accounting 1; Colorful 3; List 1 or 2; or 3D Effects 1 table formats. All the others prefer to center long titles in the first cell across all the columns in the table (which can give you the problem illustrated in Figure 3-6!).

Figure 3-7:
Mother's
first quarter
sales tables
in the 3D
Effects 2
table format.

Festooning Your Cells with the Formatting Toolbar

Some worksheets require a lighter touch than the AutoFormat feature offers. For example, you may have a table where the only emphasis you want to add is to make the column headings bold at the top of the table and to underline the row of totals at the bottom (done by drawing a borderline along the bottom of the cells).

With the tools on the Formatting toolbar, which appears right below the Standard toolbar, you can accomplish most data and cell formatting without ever venturing into the shortcut menus, let alone (heaven forbid) opening up the pull-down menus.

You can use the tools on the Formatting toolbar to assign new fonts and number formats to cells, change the alignment of their contents, or add borders, patterns, and colors to them. (See Table 1-3 in Chapter 1 for a complete rundown on the use of each of these tools).

Transient toolbars

Normally, the Standard and Formatting toolbars appear at the top of the Excel program window (right below the menu bar) in a stationary position politely referred to as being in a *docked* position (*beached* is more like it). Although

Excel automatically docks these toolbars at the top of the screen, you are free to move them (as well as any other toolbars that you open — see Chapter 13 for details on using and customizing other toolbars) around by dragging them (kicking and screaming) into new positions.

When you drag the Standard or Formatting toolbar down from its perch and into the work area containing the open workbook, the toolbar then appears in a separate little window like the one containing the Formatting toolbar shown in Figure 3-8. Such toolbars-in-a-window are referred to as *floating toolbars* because they float like clouds above the open workbook below (how poetic!). And not only can you move these little dears but you can resize them as well:

- ✔ You can move a floating toolbar into new positions over the worksheet document by dragging it by its tiny title bar.

- ✔ You can resize a floating toolbar by dragging any one of its sides (wait until the mouse pointer changes to a double-headed arrow before you start dragging).

- ✔ As you drag a side of the floating toolbar, the outline of the toolbar assumes a new shape to accommodate the tools in a prescribed tool arrangement. When the toolbar outline assumes the shape you want, release the mouse button, and Excel redraws the toolbar.

- ✔ To close a floating toolbar when you no longer want it in the document window, click the close box (the small box in the upper-left corner of the toolbar window).

When dragging a toolbar, be sure that you're clicking the space between or around the toolbar buttons. Otherwise, should you just happen to get part of one of the buttons when you click to relocate the toolbar, Excel will perform whatever command is assigned to the button instead of letting you carry the toolbar away.

Toolbar docking maneuvers

Let's face it, sometimes a floating toolbar can be a real pain because you're constantly having to move it out of the way as you add to and edit your worksheet data. To get a toolbar out of the way so it no longer obscures any of the worksheet cells, you can simply dock it.

There are four docking stations in Excel: the top of the screen above the formula bar, the very left edge of the screen, the very right edge of the screen, or the bottom of the screen right above the status bar. Figure 3-9 shows the Formatting toolbar after docking it at the bottom of the work area.

Figure 3-8:
The Formatting toolbar floating above the workbook.

Figure 3-9:
The Formatting toolbar docked at the bottom of the work area.

To dock a floating toolbar in one of these four areas, drag it by the title bar as far to the side of the window as possible and release the mouse button when the outline of the bar assumes a shape that accommodates a single column (when docking left or right) or a single row (when docking top or bottom). Toolbars you dock on the left or right of the document window reorient their tools so that they run vertically down the toolbar.

Excel won't let you dock the Standard or Formatting toolbar on the left or right side of the screen because both of these toolbars contain drop-down list boxes that can't be reoriented with the toolbar (so that their contents pop out to the left or right of the tool). This restriction on docking on the left or right side of the screen also applies to the Drawing, Chart, and WorkGroup toolbars due to their inclusion of tools that use drop-down list boxes.

Sometimes, after docking a toolbar, the active document window loses one or the other of the scroll bars. To get the missing scroll bar back, click the document Maximize button to max out the current document. If you're working with an empty workbook (like Book1), you can properly size the document window and restore the scroll bars by closing the workbook with the Close command on the File menu and then opening a new workbook in its place by clicking on the New tool on the Standard toolbar (the very first tool). When Excel opens the new workbook (Book2), the document window fits nicely (with all the scroll bars intact) and reflects your current toolbar-docking arrangement.

Using the Format Cells Dialog Box

Excel's Cells command on the Format menu (Ctrl+1 for short) makes it a snap to apply a whole rash of different kinds of formatting to a cell selection. The Format Cells dialog box that this command calls up contains six tabs: Number, Alignment, Font, Border, Patterns, and Protection. In this chapter, I show you how to use the Number, Alignment, Font, Border, and Patterns tabs in the Format Cells dialog box to assign new number formats and fonts to your cells as well as to change their alignment, borders, and patterns. For information on how and when to use the options on the Protection tab, see Chapter 6.

The keystroke shortcut — Ctrl+1 — that opens the Format Cells dialog box is one worth learning (many of you will be doing almost as much formatting as you do data entry in a worksheet). Just keep in mind that the shortcut is Ctrl plus the number 1 and not the function key F1. Further, you must use the 1 key on the top row of the regular typewriter keyboard, not the 1 located on your numeric keypad. Pressing Ctrl plus the 1 on the numeric keypad doesn't work any better than pressing Ctrl+F1.

Getting to know the number formats

As Chapter 2 explains, how you enter values into a worksheet determines the type of number format they get. Here are some examples:

- ✔ If you enter a financial value complete with the dollar sign and two decimal places, Excel assigns a Currency number format to the cell along with the entry.

- ✔ If you enter a value representing a percentage as a whole number followed by the percent sign without any decimal places, Excel assigns to the cell the Percentage number format that follows this pattern along with the entry.

- ✔ If you enter a date (remember that dates are values too) that follows one of the built-in Excel number formats like 02/19/96 or 19-Feb-96, the program assigns a Date number format that follows the pattern of the date along with a special value representing the date.

Although it's fine to format values in this manner as you go along (and even necessary in the case of dates), you don't have to do it this way. You can always assign a number format to a group of values before or after you enter them. And, in fact, formatting numbers after you enter them is often the most efficient way to go because it's just a two-step procedure:

1. **Select all the cells containing the values that need dressing up.**

2. **Select the number format you want to use either from the Formatting toolbar or the Format Cells dialog box.**

   Many times, you can use one of the tools on the Formatting toolbar — if not, you can select a number format from the Number tab in the Format Cells dialog box (Ctrl+1).

Even if you're a really good typist and prefer (thank you very much) to enter each value exactly as you want it to appear in the worksheet, you'll still have to resort to using number formats to make the values that are calculated by formulas match the others you've entered. This is because Excel applies a General number format (which the Format Cells dialog box explains as, "General format cells have no specific number format.") to all the values it calculates as well as any you enter that don't exactly follow one of the other Excel number formats. The biggest problem with the General format is that it has the nasty habit of dropping all leading and trailing zeros from the entries. This makes it very hard to line up numbers in a column on their decimal points.

Figure 3-10 shows this sad state of affairs. The figure shows a sample worksheet with the first-quarter 1996 sales figures for Mother Goose Enterprises before any of the values have been formatted. Notice how the columns of monthly sales figures zig and zag? This is the fault of Excel's General number format; the only cure is to format the values with another more uniform number format.

Currying your cells with the Currency Style

Given the financial nature of most worksheets, you probably use the Currency format more than any other. This is a really easy format to apply because the Formatting toolbar contains a Currency Style tool that adds a dollar sign, commas between thousands of dollars, and two decimal places to any values in a selected range. If any of the values in the cell selection are negative, this Currency format displays them in parentheses (the way accountants like them) and displays them in red on a color monitor (the way governments like them).

In Figure 3-11, only the cells containing totals are selected for the Currency format (cell ranges E3:E10 and B10:D10). This cell selection was then formatted with the Currency format by simply clicking the Currency Style button on the Formatting toolbar (the one with the $ icon, naturally).

Note: Although you could put all the figures in the table into the Currency format to line up the decimal points, this would result in a superabundance of dollar signs in a fairly small table. In this example, I've decided that only the monthly and quarterly totals should be formatted à la Currency.

Figure 3-11:
The totals in
the Mother
Goose
Enterprises
sales table
after
clicking the
Currency
Style button.

Format overflow!

You may be wondering if I've lost it altogether, if Excel lost it altogether, or a combination of the two has occurred. Somehow, we must have here a failure to communicate (maybe just a bum screen shot) because there's no way that the #######s showing in cell ranges E3:E10 and B10:D10 in Figure 3-11 resemble anything close to numbers using the Currency format!

Well, if you carefully reread the caption for Figure 3-11, you'll see that all I'm claiming here is that this is how the totals appear in the Mother Goose Enterprises sales table after clicking the Currency Style button on the Formatting toolbar. In fact, the appearance of strings of pound signs where nicely formatted dollar totals should be merely indicates that applying the Currency format added so much to the display of the value that Excel can no longer display them within the current column widths.

These blasted #######s appear in cells whenever any number format you use (not just the Currency format) adds more junk onto the values than can be displayed within the current column width. Be aware that these #######s will replace perfectly fine-looking formatted numbers if you go ahead and narrow the column too much. Of course, should this happen to you, you now know that you simply turn around and widen the column to get your numbers back!

To get rid of the pound signs and bring back the prettied-up values, you simply have to widen the columns. Figure 3-12 shows you the Mother Goose Enterprises sales table after widening columns B through E (to find out how to widen columns yourself, jump ahead to "Calibrating Columns," later in this chapter). As you can see, not only are the numbers all there, but they're also all sporting dollar signs, commas, and two decimal places.

Currying your cells with the Comma Style

The Comma format offers a good alternative to the Currency format. Like Currency, the Comma format inserts commas in larger numbers to separate thousands, hundred thousands, millions, and, well, you get the idea.

This format also displays two decimal places and puts negative values in parentheses and in red (on a color monitor). What it doesn't display is dollar signs. This makes it perfect for formatting tables where it's obvious that you're dealing with dollars and cents or for larger values that have nothing to do with money.

Figure 3-12:
The totals formatted as currency after widening columns B through E.

	A	B	C	D	E	F	G	H
1	Mother Goose Enterprises - 1996 Sales							
2		Jan	Feb	Mar	Qtr 1 Total			
3	Jack Sprat	80138.58	59389.56	19960.06	$ 159,488.20			
4	Jack and J	123456.2	89345.7	25436.84	$ 238,238.74			
5	Mother Hu	12657.05	60593.56	42300.28	$ 115,550.89			
6	Rub-a-Dub	17619.79	40635	42814.99	$ 101,069.78			
7	Georgie P	57133.56	62926.31	12408.73	$ 132,468.60			
8	Hickory, D	168291	124718.1	41916.13	$ 334,925.23			
9	Little Bo-P	30834.63	71111.25	74926.24	$ 176,872.12			
10	Total	$490,130.81	$508,719.48	$259,763.27	$1,258,613.56			
11								
12	Month/Qtr	0.389421206	0.40419037	0.206388425				
13								
14								
15								
16								
17								

The Comma format also works well for the bulk of the values in the sample first-quarter sales worksheet. Figure 3-13 shows this table after the cells containing the monthly sales for each Mother Goose company were formatted with the Comma format. To do this, select the cell range B3:D9 and click the Comma Style button (the one with the , [comma] icon, of course) on the Formatting toolbar.

Figure 3-13 shows how the Comma format takes care of the earlier alignment problem in the quarterly sales figures. Moreover, notice how the Comma-formatted monthly sales figures align perfectly with the Currency-formatted monthly totals in row 10. If you look really closely (you might need a magnifying glass for this one), you see that these formatted values no longer abut the right edges of their cells; they've moved slightly to the left. The gap on the right between the last digit and the cell border is there to accommodate the right parenthesis in negative values, ensuring that they too align precisely on the decimal point.

Playing Around with the Percent Style

Many worksheets use percentages in the form of interest rates, growth rates, inflation rates, and so on. To insert a percentage in a cell, place the percent sign (%) after the number. To indicate an interest rate of 12 percent, for example, you enter **12%** in the cell. When you do this, Excel assigns a Percent number format and, at the same time, divides the value by 100 (that's what makes it a percentage) and places the result in the cell (0.12 in this example).

Figure 3-13:
Monthly sales figures after formatting with the Comma format.

Not all percentages in a worksheet are entered by hand in this manner. Some may be calculated by a formula and returned to their cells as raw decimal values. In such cases, you should add a Percent format to convert the calculated decimal values to percentages (done by multiplying the decimal value by 100 and adding a percent sign).

The sample first-quarter sales worksheet just happens to have some percentages calculated by formulas in row 12 that need formatting (these formulas indicate what percentage each monthly total is of the first-quarter total in cell E10). Figure 3-14 shows these values after they have been formatted with a Percent format. To accomplish this feat, you simply select the cells and click the Percent Style button on the Formatting toolbar. (Need I point out that it's the tool with % sign?)

Deciding how many decimal places

You can increase or decrease the number of decimal places used in a number entered with the Currency Style, Comma, or Percent Style tool on the Formatting toolbar simply by clicking the Increase Decimal tool or the Decrease Decimal tool also located on this toolbar (remember to click these tools while the cell range you just formatted is still selected).

Figure 3-14: Monthly to quarterly sales percentages formatted with the Percent format.

Each time you click the Increase Decimal tool (the one with the arrow pointing left), Excel adds another decimal place to the number format you applied. Figure 3-15 shows percentages in the cell range B12:D12 after I increased the number of decimal places in the Percent format from none to two (the Percent Style doesn't use any decimal places). I accomplished this by clicking the Increase Decimal tool twice in a row.

The values behind the formatting

Make no mistake about it, all that these fancy number formats do is spiff up the presentation of the values in the worksheet. Like a good illusionist, a particular number format sometimes appears to magically transform some entries, but, in reality, the entries are the same old numbers you started with. For example, suppose that a formula returns the following value:

```
25.6456
```

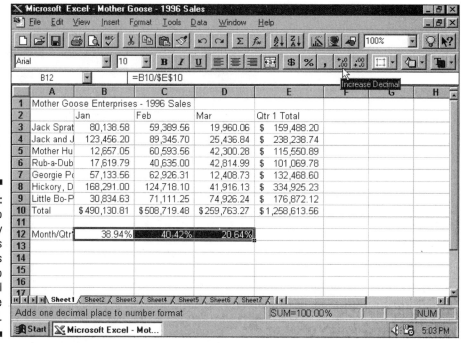

Figure 3-15:
Monthly to quarterly sales percentages after two decimal places were added.

Now suppose that you format the cell containing this value with the Currency Style tool. The value now appears as follows:

```
$25.65
```

This change may lead you to believe that Excel rounded the value up to two decimal places. In fact, the program has rounded up only the *display* of the calculated value — the cell still contains same old value of 25.6456. If you use this cell in another worksheet formula, keep in mind that Excel uses the behind-the-scenes value in its calculation, not the spiffed-up one shown in the cell.

But what if you want the values to match their formatted appearance in the worksheet? Well, Excel can do that in a single step. Be forewarned, however, that this is a one-way trip. You can convert all underlying values to the way they are displayed by selecting a single check box, but you can't return them to their previous state by deselecting the check box.

Well, because you insist on knowing this little trick anyway, here goes (just don't write and try to tell me that you weren't warned):

1. **Make sure that all the values in your worksheet are formatted with the right number of decimal places.**

   You must do this step before you convert the precision of all values in the worksheet to their displayed form.

2. **Choose the Tools menu and then select the Options command.**

3. **Click the Calculation tab to bring up the calculation options.**

4. **Choose the Precision as Displayed option under Workbook Options to put a check mark in its check box and click the OK button.**

   Excel displays the "Data will permanently lose accuracy" alert dialog box.

5. **Go ahead (live dangerously) and click the OK button or press Enter to convert all values to match their display.**

After converting all the values in a worksheet with the Precision as Displayed option, as described in the steps above, you may be wise to select the Save As command on the File pull-down menu and edit the filename in the File name edit box (maybe, by appending "as Displayed" to the current filename) before you choose the Save button or press Enter. That way, you'll still have a disk copy of the original workbook file with the values as entered and calculated by Excel that can act as a backup to your new "as Displayed" version.

Ogling the other number formats

Excel supports a whole bunch more number formats than just the Currency, Comma, and Percent formats. To use them, select the cell range (or ranges) to be formatted and select the Format Cells on the cell shortcut menu (click the secondary mouse button somewhere in the cell selection) or the Cells command on the Format menu (Ctrl+1) to open the Format Cells dialog box.

Once the Format Cells dialog box is open, you then choose the Number tab and select the desired format from the Category list box. The Number format categories — such as Date, Time, Fraction, and Special — give you further formatting choices in a Type list box. Other number formats, such as Number and Currency, have their own particular boxes that give you options for refining their formats. As you click the different formats in these list boxes, Excel shows what effect this would have on the first of the values in the current cell selection in the Sample area above. When the sample has the format you want to apply to the current cell selection, you just choose the OK button or press Enter to apply the new number format.

Sorting through the Special number formats

Excel contains a new category of number formats called Special. The Special category contains the following four number formats that may be of interest to you:

- ✔ **Zip Code:** Retains any leading zeros in the value (important in zip codes and of absolutely no importance in arithmetic computations) as in 00123.

- ✔ **Zip Code + 4:** Automatically separates the last four digits from the first five digits and retains any leading zeros as in 00123-5555.

- ✔ **Phone Number:** Automatically encloses the first three digits of the number in parentheses and separates the last four digits from the previous three with a dash as in (999) 555-1111.

- ✔ **Social Security Number:** Automatically puts dashes in the value to separate its digits into groups of three, two, and four as in 666-00-9999.

These Special number formats really come in handy when creating databases in Excel, which often deal with stuff like zip codes, telephone numbers, and sometimes even Social Security numbers (see Chapter 9 for more on creating databases).

Creating custom number formats

If none of the predefined number formats of the various types in the different categories fit your bill, you can always resort to creating a custom number of your very own design. To create custom number format, you must choose Custom as the Category in the Format Cells dialog box and then select the number format code that is closest to what you want from the Type list box and then, most often, edit this number format code in the Type edit box.

There's only one problem with doing this: Excel wasn't lying when it called them number format **codes.** All you see in the T̲ype list box when Custom is the C̲ategory is a bunch of weird-looking codes composed of lots of #s, 0s, ?s, Ds, Ms, and Ys. Rather than work yourself into a lather (or, heaven forbid, do something nerdy like trying to decipher this gibberish), make life easier and focus your attention on the Sample area above the T̲ype edit box as you select various formats from the F̲ormat Codes list box. There, Excel shows how the value in the active cell of the selected range will look in the selected format. As soon as you see what you like, go for it by clicking the OK button or pressing Enter.

In addition to choosing built-in formats by their number format codes, you can create your own custom codes by doing a little creative editing. Although you do have to use these junky number format codes (ugh) when performing this editing, you really don't have to be a rocket scientist to figure out how to do it. (Not that being a rocket scientist would hurt!)

Rather than bore you with a lot of examples of custom number formats that even a computer nerd would have trouble staying awake through, I just want to introduce you to a custom number format you might actually find quite handy in your worksheets — one that hides the display of any cell entry in the worksheet (you can continue to see the entry on the formula bar when the cell pointer is in its cell). You can then use your custom hidden format to temporarily hide certain cell ranges that you don't want printed out or visible in your worksheet on-screen.

To build the custom hidden number format, open the Format Cells dialog box (Ctrl+1), click Custom in the Category list box in the Number tab of the Format Cells dialog box, and then select General in the Type list box and replace this text with the following number format codes:

```
;;;
```

Decoding those darned number format codes

If you just have to know what some of these number format codes mean, here goes. Each number format can control how positive numbers, negative numbers, and everything else looks. These parts are divided by semicolons (any format not so divided covers all the other types of entries). The 0 is a placeholder for a digit and is filled by a zero if the value lacks a digit in that place. The # sign is a placeholder for a digit not to be filled if the value lacks a digit for that place. Ms are used for months in dates or minutes in time, Ds for days, Ys for years, Hs for hours, and Ss for seconds.

The custom hidden number format just consists of three semicolons in a row (with no spaces between them). Odd as this looks, these three semicolons tell Excel that it should display nothing for positive values, nothing for negative values, and, while you're at it, nothing for anything else in the cell.

After entering the codes in the Type edit box, click the OK button or press Enter to apply the custom format to the current cell selection. Custom formats are saved as part of the worksheet the next time you save the workbook file. (Remember, don't neglect that Save tool on the Standard toolbar!)

When you apply this hidden format to cells, the cell display disappears in the worksheet (the contents still show up on the formula bar when you select the cell). To make hidden entries reappear, simply select the hidden cells, open the Format Cells dialog box, and select one of the other visible number formats (the General format, for example) and apply it to cells.

Note that the custom number formats that you create are added to the bottom of the Type list box. This means that, when you next open the Format Cells dialog box and select Custom in the Category list box of the Number tab, you may have to scroll through the Type list box all the way to the bottom before you can locate and select the number format codes that you're responsible for adding.

Calibrating Columns

Adjusting column widths is one of those never-ending worksheet chores on a par with housekeeping chores like doing dishes or dusting. It seems that no sooner do you finish putting all the columns in order than you make a change to the worksheet (like formatting a table of figures) that requires new column-width adjustments.

Fortunately, Excel makes changing the column widths a breeze. The easiest way to adjust a column is to do a *best-fit,* using the AutoFit feature. With this method, Excel automatically determines how much to widen or narrow the column to fit the longest entry currently in the column.

Here's how to use AutoFit to get the best-fit for a column:

1. **Position the mouse pointer on the column frame, on the right border of the column that needs adjusting.**

   The mouse pointer changes to a double-headed arrow pointing left and right.

2. **Double-click the mouse button.**

   Excel widens or narrows the column width to suit the longest entry.

You can do a best-fit for more than one column at a time. Simply select all the columns that need adjusting (if the columns neighbor one another, drag through their column letters on the frame; if they don't, hold Ctrl as you click the individual column letters). Once the columns are selected, double-click any of the right borders on the frame.

As I pointed out earlier in this chapter, best-fit à la AutoFit doesn't always produce the expected results. All you have to do is AutoFit a column with a table title to become acquainted with this fact (as the 3D Effects 2 table format did in Figure 3-7). A long title that spills into several columns to the right produces an awfully wide column when you use best-fit.

When AutoFit's best-fit won't do, drag the right border of the column (on the frame) until it's the size you need rather than double-clicking it. This manual technique for calibrating the column width also works when more than one column is selected. Just be aware that all selected columns assume whatever size you make the one that you're actually dragging.

You can also set the widths of columns from the Column Width dialog box. When you use the dialog box, you enter the number of characters you want for the column width. To open this dialog box, choose the Column Width command from the column context menu (which you open by clicking on any selected column or column letter with the secondary mouse button), or choose Column on the Format menu and then choose Width on the cascading menu.

The Column Width edit box in the Column Width dialog box shows how many characters are in the standard column width in the worksheet or in the current column width if you previously adjusted it. To change the widths of all the columns you've selected in the worksheet (except those already adjusted manually or with AutoFit), enter a new value in the Column Width text box and click the OK button.

If you want Excel to size the column to best-fit, using the pull-down menus, choose Column on the Format menu and then choose AutoFit Selection on the cascading menu. Note that you can use this AutoFit Selection command to apply best-fit to a column based on just some of the cell entries. For example, say that you wanted to use best-fit to make a column just wide enough for a range of headings but not including the worksheet title (that spills over several blank columns to the right). All you have to do is select just the cells in that column that contain the headings on which the new column width should be based before you choose Column on the Format pull-down menu and then choose AutoFit Selection on the cascading menu.

If you want to return a column selection to the standard (default) column width using the pull-down menus, you simply choose Column on the Format menu and then choose Standard Width on the cascading menu. This opens the

Standard Width dialog box containing the value 8.43 in the Standard Column Width edit box (this happens to be the default width of all columns in a new worksheet). To return all the selected columns to this standard width, choose the OK button in this dialog box or simply press Enter.

Rambling rows

The story with adjusting the heights of rows is pretty much the same as that with adjusting columns, except that you do a lot less row adjusting than you do column adjusting. That's because Excel automatically changes the height of the rows to accommodate changes to their entries (such as selecting a larger font size or wrapping text in a cell — both of these techniques are coming right up). Most row-height adjustments come about when you want to increase the amount of space between a table title and the table or between a row of column headings and the table of information without actually adding a blank row (see "From top to bottom" later in this chapter for details).

To increase the height of a row, drag the bottom border of the row frame down until the row is high enough and then release the mouse button. To shorten a row, reverse this process and drag the bottom row-frame border up. To use AutoFit to create a best-fit for the entries in a row, you double-click the bottom row frame border.

As with columns, you can also adjust the height of selected rows with a dialog box. To open the Row Height dialog box, choose the Row Height command from the row context menu (opened by clicking on any selected row or row number with the secondary mouse button) or choose Row on the Format menu followed by the Height command. To set a new row height for the selected row (or rows), enter the number of characters in the Row Height text box and click OK (the default row height is 12.75 characters, in case you care). To return to the best-fit for a particular row, choose Row on the Format menu followed by the AutoFit command.

Now you see it, now you don't

A funny thing about narrowing columns and rows: You can get too carried away and make a column so narrow, or a row so short, that it actually disappears from the worksheet! This can actually come in handy for those times when you don't want part of the worksheet visible. For example, you may have a worksheet that contains a column listing employee salaries — required in calculating the departmental budget figures, but that you would prefer to leave off most printed reports. Rather than waste time moving the column of salary figures outside the area to be printed, you can just hide the column until after you print the report.

Hiding columns and rows, courtesy of the pull-down and context menus

Although you can hide worksheet columns and rows by just adjusting them out of existence, Excel does offer an easier method of hiding them, via the Format pull-down menu or column or row context menus. Suppose that you need to hide column B in the worksheet because it contains some irrelevant or sensitive information that you don't want printed. To hide this column, you could follow these steps:

1. **Click the letter B on the frame to select the column.**

2. **Click the Format pull-down menu to open it and then drag down to Column and over to click Hide.**

That's all there is to it — column B goes *poof!* All the information in the column disappears from the worksheet. When you hide column B, notice that the row of column letters in the frame now reads A, C, D, E, F, and so forth.

Note that you could just as well have hidden column B by clicking its column letter on the frame with the secondary mouse button and then clicking the Hide command on the column's context menu.

So now, suppose that you've printed the worksheet and need to make a change to one of the entries in column B. To unhide the column, follow these steps:

1. **Position the mouse pointer on column letter A in the frame and drag the pointer right to select both columns A and C.**

   You must drag from A to C to include hidden column B as part of the column selection — don't click with the Ctrl key or you won't get B.

2. **Click the Format pull-down menu to open it and then drag down to Column and over to click Unhide.**

Excel brings back the hidden B column and all three columns (A, B, and C) are selected. You can then click the mouse pointer on any cell in the worksheet to deselect the columns.

Note that you could also unhide column B by selecting columns A and C and then clicking either one of them with the secondary mouse button and clicking the Unhide command on the column context menu.

Hiding columns and rows with the mouse

I won't lie to you — hiding and redisplaying columns with the mouse can be *very* tricky (just ask my assistant, Carol!). It requires a degree of precision that you may not possess (especially if you've just recently started using the rodent). However, if you consider yourself a real mouse master, you can hide and unhide columns solely by dragging the mouse pointer as follows:

✔ To hide a column with the mouse, drag the column's right edge to the left until it's on top of the left edge and then release the mouse button.

✔ To hide a row with the mouse, drag the row's bottom border up until it's on top of the upper border.

As you drag a border, Excel replaces the cell address on the formula bar with the current column width or row height measurement. When the Width or Height indicator reaches 0.00, you know that it's time to release the mouse button.

Unhiding a column or row with the mouse is a reversal of the hiding process. This time, you drag the column or row border in between the nonsequential columns or rows in the opposite direction (right for columns and down for rows). The only trick to this is that you must position the mouse pointer just right on the column or row border so that the pointer doesn't just change to a double-headed arrow but changes to a double-headed arrow split in the middle. (Contrast the shapes of the split double-headed arrow pointer with the regular, old double-headed arrow pointer in Table 1-1.)

If you ever manually hide a column or row only to find that you just can't get that blasted split-bar pointer to appear so that you can drag it back into existence, don't get frantic. With columns, just drag through the first and last column or row between those that are hidden, and then choose the Unhide command on the columns or rows context menu (see the preceding section)!

Futzing with the Fonts

When you start a new worksheet, Excel assigns a uniform font and type size to all the cell entries you make. This font varies according to the printer you use — for a laser printer like the HP LaserJet or Apple LaserWriter, Excel uses a font called *Arial* in a 10-point size. Although this font is fine for normal entries, you may want to use something with a little more zing for titles and headings in the worksheet.

If you don't especially care for the standard font that Excel uses, modify it by choosing Options on the Tools menu and then selecting the General tab. When you do this, you see an option called Standard Font near the bottom of the Options dialog box. Select the new standard font from its drop-down list. If you want a different type size, choose the Size option as well and either enter the new point size for the standard font or select it from this option's drop-down list.

With the tools on the Formatting toolbars, you can make most font changes (including selecting a new font style or new font size) without having to resort to the settings on the Font tab in the Format Cells dialog box (Ctrl+1).

✔ To select a new font for a cell selection, click the drop-down button next to the Font drop-down edit box on the Formatting toolbar; then select the name of the font you want to use from the list box.

✔ If you want to change the font size, click the drop-down button next to the Font Size drop-down edit box on the Formatting toolbar; then select the new font size.

You can also add the attributes of bold, italics, underlining, or strikeout to the font you're using. The Formatting toolbar contains the Bold, Italic, and Underline buttons, which not only add these attributes to a cell selection but remove them as well. After you click one of these attribute tools, notice that the tool changes by losing the shading around its right and bottom edge and becoming a lighter shade of gray. Excel does this to make it appear as though a tool button is pushed in. When you click a "pushed-in" button to remove an attribute, Excel changes the button back to its original form so that it no longer appears pushed in.

Although you'll probably make most font changes with the toolbars, on rare occasions you may find it more convenient to make these changes from the Font tab in the Format Cells dialog box (Ctrl+1).

As you can see in Figure 3-16, this Font tab in the Format Cells dialog box brings together under one roof fonts, font styles such as bold and italics, effects like underlining and strikeout, as well as color changes. When you want to make a lot of font-related changes to a cell selection, the Font tab may be your best bet. One of the nice things about using this tab is that it contains a Preview box that shows you how your font changes appear (on-screen at least).

If you change font colors with the Color option on the Font tab in the Format Cells dialog box or with the Font Color button on the Formatting toolbar (the very last button) and then print the worksheet with a black-and-white printer, Excel renders the colors as shades of gray. The Automatic choice in the Font

Figure 3-16:
Use the Font tab in the Format Cells dialog box to make lots of font changes at one time.

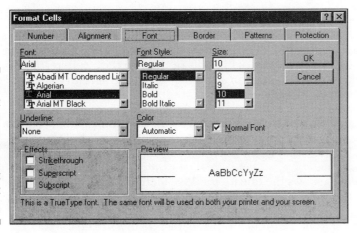

tab Color drop-down list box picks up the color assigned in Windows as the window text color. This color is black unless you changed it on the Appearance tab of the Display Properties dialog box in Windows 95. (For help on this, please see *Windows 95 For Dummies* from IDG Books Worldwide, Inc. and tell Andy that Greg sent ya!).

Altering the Alignment

The alignment assigned to cell entries when you first make them is simply a function of the type of entry it is: All text entries are left-aligned, and all values are right-aligned. You can, however, alter this standard arrangement any time it suits you.

The Formatting toolbar contains three normal alignment tools: the Align Left, Center, and Align Right buttons. These buttons align the current cell selection exactly as you expect them to. After the Right Align button, you find a special alignment tool called Center Across Columns.

Despite its rather strange name, you'll want to get to know this button. You can use it to center a worksheet title across the entire width of a table in seconds (or faster, depending upon your machine). Figures 3-17 and 3-18 show how you can use this tool. In Figure 3-17, notice that the title for the 1996 sales worksheet is entered in cell A1. Because it's a long text entry, it spills over to the empty cell to the right (B1). To center this title over the table (which extends from column A through E), select the cell range A1:E1 (the width of the table) and then click the Center Across Columns button on the Formatting toolbar. Figure 3-18 shows the result. Now the title is properly centered over the table.

From top to bottom

Left, right, and *center* alignment all refer to the placement of a text entry in relation to the left and right cell borders. You can also align entries in relation to the top and bottom borders of their cells. Normally, all entries are vertically aligned with the bottom of the cells (as though they were resting on the very bottom of the cell). You can also vertically center an entry in its cell or align it with the top of its cell.

To change the vertical alignment of a cell selection, open the Format Cells dialog box (Ctrl+1), and then choose the Alignment tab (shown in Figure 3-19) and click the Top, Center, Bottom, or Justify radio button.

Figure 3-20 shows the title for the 1996 Mother Goose Enterprises sales worksheet after it was centered vertically in its cell. (This text entry was previously centered across the cell range A1:E1; the height of row 1 was increased from the normal 12.75 characters to 33.75 characters.)

Figure 3-17: Centering the worksheet title over a table with the Center Across Columns button.

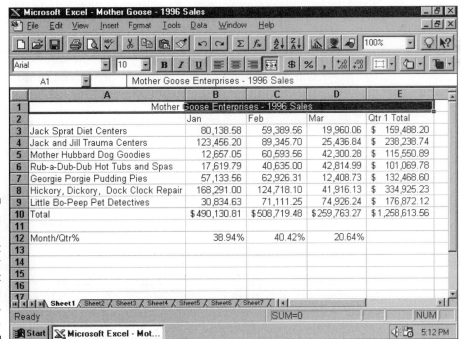

Figure 3-18: The worksheet title after centering it across columns A through E.

Figure 3-19:
Changing
the vertical
alignment
with the
options on
the
Alignment
tab of the
Format Cells
dialog box.

Tampering with how the text wraps

Traditionally, column headings in worksheet tables have been a problem because you either had to keep them really short or abbreviate them if you wanted to avoid widening all the columns more than the data warranted. You can get around this problem in Excel by using the text-wrap feature (see Figure 3-21). This figure shows a new worksheet in which the column headings containing the various Mother Goose companies use text-wrap to avoid widening the columns as much as these long company names would otherwise require.

To create the effect shown in Figure 3-21, select the cells with the column headings (the cell range B2:H2) and then click the Wrap Text check box in the Alignment tab in the Format Cells dialog box to turn on text wrap. (You can see this check box in Figure 3-19).

Text wrap breaks up the long text entries in the selection (that either spill over or are cut off) into separate lines. To accommodate more than one line in a cell, the program automatically expands the row height so that the entire wrapped-text entry is visible.

When you turn on text wrap, Excel continues to use the horizontal and vertical alignment you specified for the cell. Note that you can use any of the Horizontal alignment options including Left, Center, Right, Justify, or Center across selection. You can't, however, use the Fill option. Select the Fill radio button only when you want Excel to repeat the entry across the entire width of the cell.

If you want to wrap a text entry in its cell and have Excel justify the text with both the left and right borders of the cell, select the Justify radio button in the Alignment tab in the Format Cells dialog box.

Figure 3-20:
The table
title after
centering it
vertically
between the
top and
bottom of
row 1.

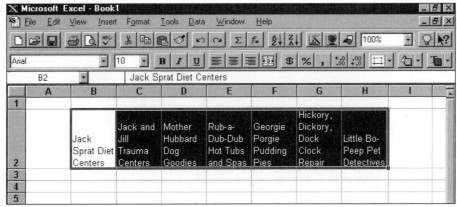

Figure 3-21:
A new
worksheet
with the
column
headings
containing
the Mother
Goose
company
names
formatted
with text
wrap.

You can break a long text entry into separate lines by positioning the insertion point in the cell entry (or on the formula bar) at the place where you want the new line to start and pressing Alt+Enter. Excel expands the row containing the cell (and the formula bar above) when it starts a new line. When you press Enter to complete the entry or edit, Excel automatically wraps the text in the cell, according to the cell's column width and the position of the line break.

Reordering the orientation

Instead of wrapping text entries in cells, you may find it more beneficial to change the orientation of the text. Figure 3-22 shows a situation where changing the orientation of the wrapped column headings works much better than just wrapping them in their normal orientation in the cells.

This example shows the same order form introduced in Figure 3-21 after switching the orientation of the column headings with the various Mother Goose companies. Notice that switching the text orientation allows their columns to be narrower than when displayed in the normal orientation.

To make this switch, you select the cell range B2:H2 and then choose the Text Orientation option in the Alignment tab of the Format Cells dialog box that has the text running up. Note that the <u>W</u>rap Text box is still selected so that the text is both rotated and wrapped (thus avoiding really long, skinny columns).

Bring on the borders!

The gridlines normally displayed in the worksheet to separate the columns and rows are just guidelines to help you keep your place as you build your spreadsheet. You can choose to print them with your data or not. To emphasize sections of the worksheet or parts of a particular table, you can add borderlines or shading to certain cells. Don't confuse the *borderlines* you add to accent a particular cell selection with the *gridlines* normally used to define cell borders in the worksheet — borders you add are printed whether or not you print the worksheet gridlines.

To better see the borders you add to the cells in a worksheet, remove the gridlines normally displayed in the worksheet as follows:

1. **Choose the <u>O</u>ptions command on the <u>T</u>ools menu, and then select the View tab.**

2. **Select the <u>G</u>ridlines option to remove the check mark from its check box.**

3. **Choose OK or press Enter.**

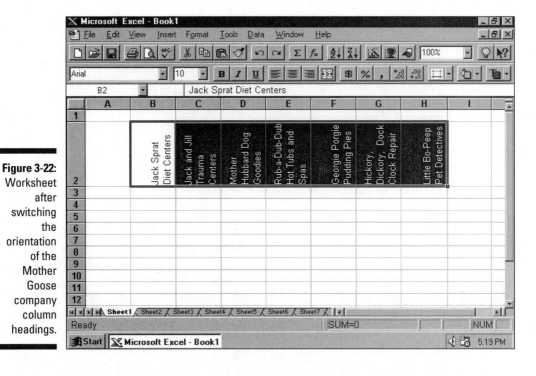

Figure 3-22:
Worksheet
after
switching
the
orientation
of the
Mother
Goose
company
column
headings.

Note that the Gridlines check box in the Options dialog box determines whether or not gridlines are displayed in the worksheet on your screen. To determine whether or not gridlines are printed as part of the worksheet printout, you choose the Page Setup command from the File menu and then select the Sheet tab and select or deselect the Gridlines check box under Print.

To add borders to a cell selection, open the Format Cells dialog box (Ctrl+1) and then choose the Border tab (shown in Figure 3-23). Select the type of line you want to use in the Style area of the dialog box and then select from the Border section of the dialog box the edge or edges you want this line applied to.

When selecting where you want the borderlines drawn, keep these things in mind:

✔ To have Excel draw borders around only the outside edges of the entire selection, choose the Outline box in the Border section.

✔ If you want borderlines to appear around all four edges of each cell in the selection, select the Left, Right, Top, and Bottom check boxes instead.

Figure 3-23:
Selecting
borders with
the Border
tab in the
Format Cells
dialog box.

When you want to add borderlines to a single cell or around the outer edge of a cell selection, you don't even have to open the Border dialog box; you can simply select the cell or cell range and then click the Border tool's drop-down list button on the Formatting toolbar and select which type of borderlines to use in the border palette that appears.

The only problem you ever have with borderlines is when you remove them from the worksheet. To get rid of borders, you must select the cell or cells that presently contain them, open the Format Cells dialog box (Ctrl+1), select the Border tab, and remove the currently used border style from each and every edge option (Outline, Left, Right, Top, and Bottom). To remove a border style from an edge, you can either press the underlined command letter, click the box in front of the Border option, or click the blank border style (the one in the lower-right corner of the Style area) in the Format Cells dialog box.

Of course, the problem you often have is figuring out which cells contain the borders you want to remove; what appears at first glance as a row of cells with borders on their bottom edges could really be a border on the top edges of the cells in the row below. If you ever try to remove borders from a cell selection only to find that they're still there, select the cells in the neighboring ranges and try deleting the borders from them as well.

Putting on new patterns

You can also add emphasis to particular sections of the worksheet or one of its tables by changing the color and/or pattern of its cells. If you're using a black-and-white printer (as all but a fortunate few of us are), you will want to restrict your color choices to light gray in the color palette. Also, you will want to restrict your use of patterns to only the very open ones with few dots when enhancing a cell selection that contains any kind of entries (otherwise, the entries will be almost impossible to read when printed).

To choose a new color and/or pattern for part of the worksheet, select the cells you want to pretty up and then open the Format Cells dialog box (Ctrl+1) and choose the Patterns tab (shown in Figure 3-24). To change the color of the cells, click the desired color in the Color palette shown under the Cell Shading heading. To change the pattern of the cells (in addition or instead), click the Pattern's drop-down list box to open an expanded color palette that contains a number of black-and-white patterns to choose from. Click the desired pattern in this expanded palette. Excel shows what your creation will look like in the worksheet in the Sample box of the Patterns tab of the Format Cells dialog box.

To remove a shading pattern from cells, select the cell range, open the Format Cells dialog box (Ctrl+1) and select the Patterns tab; then choose the None option at the top of the Color palette.

Figure 3-24: Selecting new colors and patterns with the Patterns tab in the Format Cells dialog box.

Using those fantastic floating border palettes

Just as you can add certain borders with the Border palette attached to the Border button on the Formatting toolbar, you can remove borders using this palette as well. To remove the border-lines from a cell selection with this button, choose the first border box in the Borders palette. Remember, too, that you can tear the Borders palette (like the Color and Font color palettes) off of the Formatting toolbar by dragging it completely off the toolbar, thus making it a floating palette that remains open as you work. Then, to close the floating palette later on, you click its Close button in the upper-right corner of its little-bitty window.

You can assign new colors (but not new patterns) to your cell selection from the Color palette opened with the Color button (the button second from the end) on the Formatting toolbar. Simply select the cells to be colored, click the Color tool's drop-down list button, and choose the desired color in the color palette that appears. (Remember, too, that the Color palette is one of those that you can tear off and have floating in the worksheet area.)

Although you can't select new patterns (only colors) with the Color tool, you can remove both colors and patterns assigned to a cell selection by selecting the cells and then clicking on the Color tool's drop-down list button and choosing None at the top of the color palette that appears.

If you want the text in a cell range to be a different color from the background you assign, you can change the text color from the Font Color palette opened by clicking the Font Color button on the Formatting toolbar (the very last one). Change the color of the cells' background by choosing a new color from the Color palette opened by clicking the Color button on the Formatting toolbar. To return the text to black in a cell range, select the cells and then choose Automatic at the bottom of the Font Color palette.

Showing Off in Styles

Cell styles are Excel's way of bringing together under one roof a whole lot of different kinds of formatting (including the number format, font, alignment, borders, patterns, and protection status). Excel includes six built-in cell styles that you can use in any worksheet: Comma, Comma (0), Currency, Currency (0), Normal, and Percent.

The most common of these styles is the Normal style. This is the one automatically used in formatting all cells in a new worksheet. The other five styles are used to format cell selections with different number formats.

To apply any of these built-in cell styles (or any others you create on your own) to the current cell selection, simply choose Style on the Format menu and then select a new style from the Style Name drop-down list box.

Creating new cell styles for a worksheet is as simple as falling off a log. All you do is format one of the cell entries in the worksheet to use all the formatting you want to include in the new style (including the number format, font, alignment, borders, patterns, and protection status — see Chapter 6, if you don't have a clue what that last one is or does).

Then, with the cell pointer located in the sample formatted cell, open the Style dialog box (by choosing Style on the Format menu), choose the Style Name edit box, type in the name for your new style before you choose the Add button, and choose OK or press Enter.

The next time you save the workbook, Excel saves the new style as part of the document. To apply the new style to other cells in a worksheet, simply select the cells and then open the Style dialog box and select the style name from the Style Name drop-down list box.

Styles are a great way to make custom number formats a lot easier to use in a workbook. For example, you could create a Hidden number style to use the custom number format discussed earlier in this chapter that hides all types of entries. After creating this custom number format (refer back to "Creating custom number formats" for details on how to go about doing this), apply it to a sample cell in the worksheet and then create a new style named *Hidden* in the Style dialog box and add it to the worksheet. After saving the workbook with this new style, you can thereafter apply it to other cell ranges in the worksheet right from the Style dialog box.

Follow these steps if you want to merge styles that were created for other workbooks saved on disks into the workbook you're currently creating:

1. **Open the workbook that contains the styles you want copied into the current workbook.**

2. **Choose the Window command and select the workbook that is to receive these styles.**

3. **Choose Style on the Format menu to open the Style dialog box in the workbook that is to receive a copy of the styles from the other workbook.**

4. **Choose the Merge button to open the Merge Styles dialog box and double-click the name of the workbook from which to copy the styles in the Merge Styles From list box.**

If the workbook you're currently working on contains styles (other than the standard six that are part of every new workbook) with the same names as some of those in the workbook whose styles you're copying, Excel displays an alert dialog box asking you if you want it to go ahead and merge styles that have the same name. To overwrite the styles in the current workbook whose names are the same, choose the Yes button. To merge only the styles with different names, choose the No button. To abandon the whole bloody merger of styles, choose the Cancel button.

Fooling Around with the Format Painter

Using styles to format worksheet cells is certainly the way to go when you have to apply the formatting over and over again in the workbooks you create. However, there may be times when you simply want to reuse a particular cell format and apply it to select groups of cells in a single workbook without ever bothering to create an actual style for it.

For those occasions when you feel the urge to format on the fly (so to speak), you use the Format Painter tool on the Standard toolbar (the one with the paintbrush icon right next to the Paste tool). This wonderful little tool enables you to take the formatting from a particular cell that you've fancied up and apply its formatting to other cells in the worksheet simply by selecting those cells.

To use the Format Painter to copy a cell's formatting to other worksheet cells, just follow these easy steps:

1. **Format an example cell or cell range in your workbook, selecting whatever fonts, alignment, borders, patterns, and color you want it to have.**

2. **With the cell pointer in one of the cells you just fancied up, click the Format Painter button in the Standard toolbar.**

   The mouse pointer changes from the standard thick, white cross to a thick, white cross with a paintbrush by its side, and you see a marquee around the selected cell whose formatting is to be used by the Format Painter.

3. **Drag the white-cross-plus-paintbrush pointer (the Format Painter pointer for short) through all of the cells you want to format in the same manner as the example cell you first selected.**

   As soon as you release the mouse button, Excel applies all of the formatting used in the example cell to all of the cells you just selected!

To keep the Format Painter selected so that you can format a bunch of different cell ranges with the Format Painter pointer, double-click the Format Painter button after you select the sample cell with the desired formatting. To stop formatting cells with the Format Painter pointer, you simply click the Format Painter button (it remains depressed when you double-click it) again to restore the button to its undepressed state and return the mouse pointer to its normal thick, white-cross shape.

Note that you can use the Format Painter to restore a cell range that you've gussied all up back to its boring default (General) cell format. To do this, you click an empty, previously unformatted cell in the worksheet before you click the Format Painter button and then use the Format Painter pointer to drag through the cells you want returned to the default General format.

Chapter 4

Going through Changes

● ●

In This Chapter

▶ Opening workbook files for editing

▶ Undoing your boo-boos

▶ Moving and copying with drag and drop

▶ Copying formulas

▶ Moving and copying with Cut, Copy, and Paste

▶ Deleting cell entries

▶ Deleting columns and rows from the worksheet

▶ Inserting new columns and rows in the worksheet

▶ Spell checking the worksheet

● ●

*P*icture this: You've just finished creating, formatting, and printing a major project with Excel — a workbook with your department's budget for the next fiscal year. Because you finally understand a little bit about how this thing works, you finished the job in crack time. You're actually ahead of schedule.

You turned the workbook over to your boss so that she can check the numbers. There's plenty of time for making those inevitable last-minute corrections — you're feeling on top of this situation.

Then comes the reality check — your boss brings the document back, and she's plainly agitated. "We forgot to include the estimates for the temps and our overtime hours. They've got to go right here. While you're adding them, can you move these rows of figures up and those columns over?"

As she continues to suggest improvements, your heart begins to sink. These modifications are in a different league from "let's change these column headings from bold to italics and add shading to that row of totals." Clearly, you're looking at a lot more work on this baby than you had contemplated. Even worse, you're looking at making structural changes that threaten to unravel the very fabric of your beautiful worksheet.

As the preceding fable points out, editing a worksheet in a workbook can occur on different levels:

- ✔ You can make changes that affect the contents of the cells, such as copying a row of column headings or moving a table to a new area in a particular worksheet.

- ✔ You can make changes that affect the structure of a worksheet itself, such as inserting new columns or rows (so that you can enter new data origi- nally left out) or deleting unnecessary columns or rows from an existing table so you don't leave any gaps.

- ✔ You can even make changes to the number of worksheets in a workbook (either by adding or deleting sheets).

In this chapter, you learn how to safely make all these types of changes to a workbook. As you see, the mechanics of copying and moving data or inserting and deleting rows are simple to master. It's the impact that such actions have on the worksheet that takes a little more effort to understand. Not to worry! You always have the Undo feature to fall back on for those (hopefully rare) times when you make a little tiny change that throws an entire worksheet into complete and utter chaos.

Opening the Darned Thing Up for Editing

Before you can do any damage — I mean, make any changes — to a workbook, you have to open it up in Excel. To open a workbook, you can click the Open tool on the Standard toolbar (the one second from the left with the picture of a file folder opening up), you can choose Open from the File menu, or you can even press the keystroke shortcut, Ctrl+O (or, if you prefer function keys: Ctrl+F12).

Any way you open it, Excel displays the Open dialog box similar to the one shown in Figure 4-1. Then you select the workbook file you want to work on in the list box in the middle of the Open dialog box. After clicking the filename in this list box, you can open it by choosing the Open button or pressing the Enter key. If you're handy with the mouse, double-click the workbook's filename in the list box to open it.

Opening more than one workbook at a time

If you know that you're going to edit more than one of the workbook files' sheets shown in the list box of the Open dialog box, you can select multiple files in the list box and Excel will then open all of them (in the order they're listed) when you choose the Open button or press Enter.

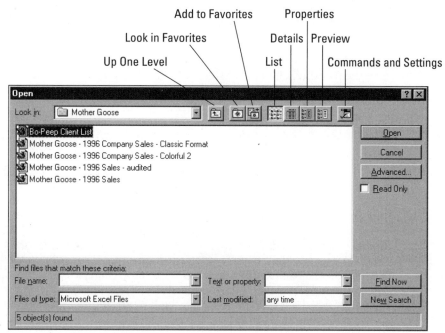

Add to Favorites   Properties
Look in Favorites   Details | Preview
Up One Level   List   Commands and Settings

Figure 4-1:
The Open
dialog box.

Remember that, in order to select multiple files all listed sequentially in the list box, you click the first filename and then hold down the Shift key as you click the last filename. To select files that are not listed sequentially, you need to hold down the Ctrl key as you click the various filenames.

After the workbook files are open in Excel, you can then switch documents by selecting their filenames from the Window pull-down menu (see Chapter 7 for detailed information on working on more than one worksheet at a time).

Opening recently edited workbooks from the File menu

If you know that the workbook you need to edit is one of those that you've had open recently, you don't even have to fool around with Open dialog box. Just open the File pull-down menu and select the filename from the bottom of the File menu (Excel keeps a running list of the last four files you opened in the program). If the workbook you want to work with is one of those shown at the bottom of the File menu, you can open it by clicking its filename in the menu or typing its number (1, 2, 3, or 4).

When you don't know where to find them

The only problem you can encounter in opening a document from the Open dialog box is locating the filename. Everything's hunky-dory as long you can see the workbook filename listed in its list box. But what about those times when a file seems to have mysteriously migrated and is now nowhere to be found in the list?

Searching the wide disk over

When you can't find the filename you're looking for in the list box, the first thing you need to do is check to make sure that you're looking in the right folder — because, if you're not, you're never going to find the missing file. To tell which folder is currently open, you check the Look in drop-down list box at the top of the Open dialog box (refer back to Figure 4-1).

If the folder that is currently open is not the one that has the workbook file you need to use, you then need to open the folder that does contain the file. In Excel, you can use the Up One Level button (see Figure 4-1) in the Open dialog box to change levels until you see the folder you want to open in the list box. To open the new folder, click its icon in the list box and then choose the Open button or press Enter (or you can just double-click its icon).

If the workbook file you want is on another disk, click the Up One Level button until My Computer appears in the Look in drop-down list box. You can then switch disks by clicking the drive icon in the list box and then choosing the Open button or pressing Enter (or you can just double-click the drive icon).

When you locate the file you want to use in the list box in the Open dialog box, you can open it by clicking its file icon and then clicking the Open button or pressing Enter (or by double-clicking the file icon).

Playing favorites

Assuming that you are successful in locating your file by going up and down the disk hierarchy as described in the preceding section, you can save yourself all this work the next time you need to open this folder to find a workbook by adding the folder to the My Favorites folder. That way, you can select and open the folder right away simply by clicking the Look in Favorites button (see Figure 4-1) and then selecting it from My Favorites.

To add a folder (or a particular file) to the My Favorites folder, you follow these steps:

1. **Select the folder or file icon the hard way (as described in the previous section) in the Open dialog box.**

2. **Click the Add to Favorites button (see Figure 4-1).**

The Desktop's connected to My Computer, My Computer's connected to my disk drives ...

Like it or not, your disk files are arranged in a strict hierarchy that starts with the Desktop at the very top and ends in the last of whatever folders are nested within other folders, within other folders, within other folders ... (ad nauseam). On the level beneath the Desktop, you have My Computer, the Network Neighborhood, and, on some computers, My Briefcase. On the level beneath My Computer, you find whatever disk drives you have attached to your system — most often, **3¹⁄₂** Floppy (A:), Hard disk (C:) and maybe

a (D:) for your CD-ROM drive. On the level below the Hard disk (C:), you find a whole bunch of folders listed in alphabetical order, containing both programs and, in some cases, document files created with your programs. Most of these folders contain files and other folders, and of course some of these folders contain other files and folders. Keep this arrangement in mind when using the Up One Level button to ascend these levels in the hierarchy.

---

3. **Choose the <u>A</u>dd Selected Item to Favorites command in the pop-up menu that's attached to the Add to Favorites button.**

    This adds the folder or file that's selected in the Open dialog list box.

After you've added a folder or a file to the My Favorites folder, you can open it in the Open dialog box by clicking the Look in Favorites button and then either double-clicking its folder or file icon or selecting it and then clicking the <u>O</u>pen button or pressing Enter.

File hide-and-seek

The Open dialog box now has a Find feature built into it that you can always use to locate a particular file within the open folder. This feature enables you to reduce your search in the Open dialog list box to just those files that fall into a specific category (like those files that you modified today or sometime this week) or just those files that contain a certain phrase or property (like they were done by a particular author or they contain a particular keyword).

When using the Find feature in the Open dialog box, you can tell Excel exactly how you want it to conduct its search.

- ✔ To have Excel restrict the files in the Open dialog list box to just those whose filenames contain certain text, select the File <u>n</u>ame drop-down list box and enter that text in its edit box.

- ✔ To have Excel include certain files with a type different from Microsoft Excel files, open the Files of <u>t</u>ype drop-down list box and select that type from the list.

✔ To have Excel restrict the files displayed in the Open list box to just those that contain a certain text or property (such as title, author, or keywords entered into a file summary — see Chapter 2 for details on adding a summary when first saving a file), choose the Text or property drop-down list box and enter the text or property in its edit box.

✔ To have Excel restrict the files displayed in the Open list box to just those that have been modified within a certain time frame, open the Last modified drop-down list box and select the time (today, last week, this week, last month, this month, or anytime).

Advanced hide-and-seek

As if the four Find drop-down list boxes for finding files by filename, file type, text or property, or date last modified weren't enough, Excel offers more searching possibilities when you click the Advanced button in the Open dialog box. Figure 4-2 shows you the Advanced Find dialog box. When you open this dialog box, you notice that whatever criteria you set up in the Open dialog box is now displayed in the Find files that match these criteria list box.

You can then use the other settings in the Define more criteria section of the Advanced Find dialog box to add more search criteria.

✔ Normally, your advanced search criteria are added onto the original criteria so that all of them must be true in order for Excel to match a file (because the And radio button is selected). If, instead, you want Excel to match a file if it meets either the original criteria *or* the new criteria you're setting up, click the Or radio button.

✔ Normally, Excel searches the filename and makes its matches according to its contents. If you want to have Excel match other properties (like the Author, Contents, Creation Date, and so on), open the Property drop-down list box and then choose the desired property in its list box.

✔ Normally, Excel just looks to see if a certain value or piece of text is included in the designated property (be it the File name, Author, or whatever). If you would rather have the program match files only when their property begins or ends with that value or text, open the Condition drop-down list box and select the begins with or the ends with option.

✔ Enter the value or text that should be matched in the Value edit box. For example, if you want to find all the files where the Contents includes the text "Jack Sprat," you enter **Jack Sprat** in this edit box. If, on the other hand, you want to find all the files where the Contents includes the number "1,250,750," you enter **1250750** in the Value edit box.

Figure 4-2:
The
Advanced
Find dialog
box.

When you're finished setting up your advanced criteria in the Define more criteria area, you can add them to the Find files that match these criteria list box by choosing the Add to List button. If you want the search to distinguish between uppercase and lowercase (when it involves text), you need to select the Match case check box to put a check mark in it.

Normally, Excel just conducts the file search in the folder that's currently listed in the Look in drop-down list box at the bottom of the Advanced Find dialog box. If you want, you can change which folders Excel will search by opening the Look in drop-down list box and selecting a different level in the file hierarchy. If you want Excel to search all folders that are contained within the folder listed in the Look in drop-down edit box, you need to select the Search subfolders check box, which puts a check mark in it. For example, if you want Excel to search the whole hard disk including all the folders (and folders within folders) on this disk, you select Hard disk (C:) in the Look in drop down list box and then select the Search subfolders check box as well.

When you have added all the advanced criteria you can think of for your search, choose the Find Now button to set Excel off hunting for the files that match all your conditions. During the search, Excel closes the Advanced File dialog box, leaving open only the Open dialog box. When the program completes the file search, it displays the results (hopefully including the workbook files you want to use) in the list box of the Open dialog box. If your search includes a lot of folders (all the folders on the hard disk or something like that), you may even have to scroll to go through all the file icons that are displayed.

Making a positive ID

Normally, Excel displays the folders and files in the Open dialog box's list box as a simple list showing the folder or file icons followed by the folder or filenames. The Open dialog box toolbar contains buttons that let you change this default list view to others that may better help you identify the file or files you want to open. These other views are especially helpful when you've conducted a file search (as described in the previous section), and Excel comes back with a list of lots of files that meet your search conditions. At that point, switching the view in the list box can help you identify which file is really the one you want to work with.

To switch the way the files are displayed in the Open dialog box's list box, you simply click any of the following buttons on the Open dialog box toolbar (see Figure 4-1):

- ✔ Click the Details button to display the file size in kilobytes, type of file, and date the file was last modified along with the file icon and filename (as shown in Figure 4-3).

- ✔ Click the Properties button to display the file summary information (see Chapter 2 for details) next to the file icon and filename when you select each file in the list (as shown in Figure 4-4).

- ✔ Click the Preview button to display a miniature preview showing the upper-left corner of the first worksheet in the workbook file next to the file icon and filename when you select each file in the list (as shown in Figure 4-5).

Save search criteria for another day

You can save the search criteria that you've gone to all of that trouble to set up so that you can reuse it later on. To save the search criteria listed in the Find files that match these criteria list box of the Advanced Find dialog box, select the Save Search button, type in a descriptive name for your search ("All files on C: with keywords 'For Eyes Only,'" or something like that), and choose OK. To reuse the search criteria later to find files in the Open dialog box, click the Commands and Settings button on the Open dialog box toolbar, select the Saved Searches command and select the name of the search from its cascading menu.

Figure 4-3:
The Open
dialog box
after
switching
the file view
to Details.

Figure 4-4:
The Open
dialog
box after
switching
the file
view to
Properties.

Figure 4-5:
The Open
dialog box
after
switching
the file
view to
Preview.

Doing stuff besides opening files

The last button on the Open dialog box toolbar is the Commands and Settings button (identified in Figure 4-1). Clicking this button (with the primary mouse button, by the way) opens the menu shown in Figure 4-6. The following commands on this menu let you make some changes to the file list in the Open dialog box as well as do stuff besides just open the selected files:

- **Open Read Only:** This command opens the files that are selected in the Open dialog box's list box in a read-only state, which means that you can look but you can't touch (actually, you can touch, you just can't save your changes). To save changes in a read-only file, you must use the Save As command on the Excel File menu and give the workbook file a new filename (see the section "Making Sure the Data's Safe and Sound," in Chapter 2).

- **Print:** This command sends the files that are selected in the Open dialog box's list box to whatever printer is selected in Windows 95. This command enables you to print a whole bunch of files without having to first open and select them in Excel (the way you normally print — see Chapter 5).

- **Properties:** This command opens the Properties dialog box for the first folder or file that is selected in the Open dialog box's list box. This enables you to change or add summary information for the file as well as look at a bunch of boring statistics about the folder or file.

- **Sorting:** This command enables you to sort the folders and files in the Open dialog box's list box. Normally, folders and files (with folders preceding files) are alphabetically sorted by name in ascending order. You can use this command to sort the folders and files alphabetically by name in descending order as well.

- ✓ **Search Subfolders:** This command acts like the Search subfolders check box (see "Advanced hide-and-seek," earlier in this chapter) in the Advanced Find dialog box. The Advanced Find dialog box includes all folders nested within the folder that's currently shown in the Look in drop-down list box during any file search that you conduct from the Open dialog box.

- ✓ **Group files by folder:** This command groups together by folder all files that meet your search criteria in the Open dialog box's list box.

- ✓ **Map Network Drive:** This command only works if you are using Excel on some kind of LAN (Local Area Network). It enables you (if you know what you're doing) to log onto somebody else's computer and have fun with all their precious files!

- ✓ **Saved Searches:** This command enables you to select a search using the search criteria that you saved with its own name in the Advanced Find dialog box (see "Save search criteria for another day," earlier in this chapter).

Figure 4-6: The Open dialog box showing the menu attached to the Commands and Settings button.

Much Ado about Undo

Before you start tearing into the workbook that you just opened, you should get to know the Undo feature and how it can put right many of the things that you could inadvertently mess up. The Undo command on the Edit menu is a regular chameleon command. If you delete the contents of a cell selection with the Clear command on this same menu, Undo changes to Undo Clear. If you move some entries to a new part of the worksheet with the Cut and Paste commands (again, found on the Edit menu), the Undo command changes to Undo Paste.

The Undo command on the Edit menu changes in response to whatever action you just took. Because it keeps changing after each action, you've got to remember to strike when the iron is hot, so to speak, by using the Undo feature to restore the worksheet to its previous state *before* you choose another command. It's imperative that you don't get going so fast that you make several changes in a row without stopping to check how each one affects the worksheet. For example, if you delete a value from a cell and then change the font in another cell and widen its column before you realize that you deleted the wrong value, you can't use the Undo feature to restore the deleted value. All you can use Undo for in this case is to restore the column to its previous width (because this was the last action you completed).

In addition to choosing Undo (in whatever guise it appears) from the Edit menu, you can also choose this command by pressing Ctrl+Z (perhaps for *unZap*) or you can click the Undo tool on the Standard toolbar (the one with the arrow curving to the left).

Undo is Redo the second time around

After choosing the Undo command (by whatever means you find most convenient), the command changes yet again — this time to a Redo command. If you delete an entry from a cell with Clear from the Edit menu and then choose Undo Clear from the Edit menu (or press Ctrl+Z or click the Undo tool on the toolbar), the next time you open the Edit menu, you see the following command at the top where Undo normally appears:

```
Redo (u) Clear Ctrl+Z
```

The (u) appears after "Redo" to remind you that U remains the command letter even though "Redo" doesn't have a U in it. When you choose the Redo command, Excel redoes the thing you just undid. Actually, this sounds more complicated than it is. It simply means that you use Undo to switch back and forth between the result of an action and the state of the worksheet just before that action until you decide how you want the worksheet (or until they turn off the lights and lock up the building).

What ya gonna do when you can't Undo?

Just when you think it is safe to begin gutting the company's most important workbook, I really feel I've got to tell you that (yikes!) Undo doesn't work all the time! Although you can undo your latest erroneous cell deletion, bad move, or unwise copy, you can't undo your latest imprudent save. (You know, like when you meant to choose Save As from the File menu to save the edited worksheet under a different document name but instead chose Save and ended up saving the changes as part of the current document.)

Unfortunately, Excel doesn't let you know when you are about to take a step from which there is no return — until it's too late. After you've gone and done the un-undoable and you open the <u>E</u>dit menu right where you expect the <u>U</u>ndo *blah, blah* command to be, it now says

```
Can't Undo
```

To add insult to injury, this extremely unhelpful command appears dimmed to indicate that you can't choose it — as though being able to choose it would change anything!

There is one exception to this rule — a time when the program gives you advance warning (which you should heed). When you choose a command that is normally undoable but currently — because you're low on memory, or the change will affect so much of the worksheet, or both — Excel knows that it can't undo the change if it goes through with it, the program displays an alert box telling you that there isn't enough memory to undo this action and asking whether you want to go ahead anyway. If you click the <u>Y</u>es button and complete the edit, just realize that you do so without any possibility of pardon. If you find out, too late, that you deleted a row of essential formulas (that you forgot about because you couldn't see them), you can't bring them back with Undo.

Doing the Old Drag-and-Drop Thing

The first editing technique you need to learn is called *drag-and-drop*. As the name implies, it's a mouse technique that you can use to pick up a cell selection and drop it into a new place on the worksheet. Although drag-and-drop is primarily a technique for moving cell entries around a worksheet, you can adapt it to copy a cell selection as well.

To use drag-and-drop to move a range of cell entries (you can only move one cell range at a time), follow these steps:

1. **Select the range as you normally would.**

2. **Position the mouse pointer on one edge of the selected range.**

   Your signal that you can start dragging the cell range to its new position in the worksheet is when the pointer changes to the arrowhead.

3. **Drag.**

   You drag by depressing and holding down the primary mouse button — usually the left one — while moving the mouse.

   As you drag, you actually move only the outline of the cell range. Drag the outline until it's positioned around the new cells in the worksheet where you want the entries to appear.

4. Release the mouse button.

The cell entries within that range reappear in the new location as soon as you release the mouse button.

Figures 4-7 and 4-8 show how you can drag-and-drop to move a cell range. In Figure 4-7, the cell range A10:E10 (containing the quarterly totals) is selected and is about to be moved to row 12 to make room for sales figures for two new companies: Simple Simon Pie Shoppes and Jack Be Nimble Candlesticks, which hadn't been acquired when this workbook was first created. In Figure 4-8, you see the Mother Goose Enterprises 1996 sales worksheet right after making this move and then selecting cell B12.

Notice in Figure 4-8 that the argument for the SUM function in cell B12 has not kept pace with the change — it continues to sum only the range B3:B9. Eventually, this range must be expanded to include cells B10 and B11, the first-quarter sales figures for the new Simple Simon Pie Shoppes and Jack Be Nimble Candlesticks (you can find out how to do this in the upcoming section, "Formulas on AutoFill").

Copies drag-and-drop style

Okay, so the preceding section explained moving a cell range with drag-and-drop. But what if you want to copy a cell range instead? For example, you need to start a new table in rows farther down the worksheet, and you want to copy the cell range with the formatted title and column headings for the new table. To copy the formatted title range in the sample worksheet, follow these steps:

1. Select the cell range.

In the case of Figures 4-7 and 4-8, that's cell range B2:E2.

2. Hold the Ctrl key as you position the mouse pointer on an edge of the selection.

The pointer changes from a thick, shaded cross to an arrowhead with a + (plus) sign to the right of it. This is your sign that drag-and-drop will *copy* the selection rather than *move* it.

3. Drag the cell-selection outline to the place where you want the copy to appear and release the mouse button.

If, when using drag-and-drop to move or copy, you position the outline of the selection so that it overlaps any part of cells that already contain entries, Excel displays an alert box with following question:

```
Replace contents of the destination cells?
```

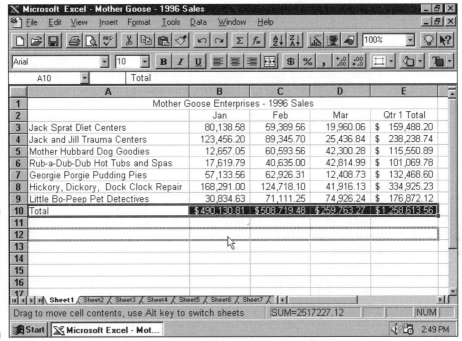

Figure 4-7:
Dragging a
selection
to its new
position
in the
worksheet.

Figure 4-8:
The
worksheet
after the
drag-and-
drop
operation.

To avoid replacing existing entries and abort the entire drag-and-drop mission, choose Cancel in this alert box. To go ahead and exterminate the little darlings, choose OK or press Enter.

Insertions courtesy of drag-and-drop

Like the Klingons of Star Trek fame, spreadsheets such as Excel never take prisoners. When you place or move a new entry into an occupied cell, the new entry completely replaces the old as though the old entry never existed in that cell.

To insert the cell range you're moving or copying within a populated region of the worksheet without wiping out existing entries, hold the Shift key as you drag the selection (if you're copying, you have to get really ambitious and hold down both the Shift and Ctrl keys at the same time!). With the Shift key depressed as you drag, instead of a rectangular outline of the cell range, you get an I-beam shape that shows where the selection will be inserted when you release the mouse button. As you move the I-beam shape, notice that it gloms on to the column and row borders as you move it. When you position the I-beam shape at the column or row border where you want the cell range to be inserted, release the mouse button. Excel inserts the cell range and repatriates the existing entries to neighboring blank cells (out of harm's way).

When inserting cells with drag-and-drop, it might be helpful to think of the I-beam shape as a pry bar that pulls apart the columns or rows along the axis of the I. Figures 4-9 and 4-10 show how to use the I-beam to move the quarterly totals in column E of the Mother Goose Enterprises 1996 sales worksheet to column B. When you drag the cell range E2:E10 to the cell range B2:B10, you can be sure that Excel will insert these totals while moving the existing columns of sales entries to the right.

Figure 4-9 shows the worksheet after I selected the cell range of quarterly totals (E2:E10), depressed *and held down* the Shift key, and dragged the I-beam shape until it rested on the border between columns A and B (between column A listing the individual Mother Goose companies and column B listing the January sales).

Notice the orientation of the I-beam shape in Figure 4-9, how the long part of the I runs with the column border. Getting the I-beam selection indicator to assume this orientation can be tricky. To prepare to drag the cell selection, position the mouse pointer on one of the long edges (either the left or right) of the selection. When you drag the selection, position the mouse pointer slightly in front of the column border (not on it).

Figure 4-9:
Dragging
the
quarterly
totals from
column E
to column
B, replacing
no existing
entries.

Figure 4-10:
Excel
inserted
the
worksheet
after the
quarterly
total
range in
column B.

But I held down the Shift key just like you said . . .

Drag-and-drop in insert mode is one of Excel's most finicky features. Sometimes, you do everything just right, and you still get the alert box indicating that Excel is about to replace existing entries instead of pushing them aside (always choose the Cancel button). Fortunately, you can insert things with the Cut and Insert Paste commands (see "Cut and Paste, digital style," later in this chapter) without worrying about which way the I-beam selection goes.

Formulas on AutoFill

Copying with drag-and-drop (by holding the Ctrl key) is useful when you need to copy a bunch of neighboring cells to a new part of the worksheet. Frequently, however, you just need to copy a single formula you've just created to a bunch of neighboring cells that need to perform the same type of calculation (such as totaling columns of figures). This type of formula copy, although quite common, can't be done with drag-and-drop. Instead, use the AutoFill feature (introduced in Chapter 2) or the Copy and Paste commands (see "Cut and Paste, digital style," later in this chapter).

Figures 4-11 and 4-12 show how you can use AutoFill to copy one formula to a range of cells. Figure 4-11 shows the Mother Goose Enterprises 1996 sales worksheet after the Simple Simon Pie Shoppes and Jack Be Nimble Candlesticks were added to the list. Remember that these companies were missing from the original worksheet, so I made room for them by moving the Totals down to row 12 (you can see this back in Figure 4-8).

Unfortunately, Excel doesn't update the sum formulas to include the new rows (the SUM function still uses B3:B9 when it should be extended to include rows 10 and 11). To make the SUM function include all the rows, position the cell pointer in cell B12 and click the AutoSum tool on the Standard toolbar. Excel suggests the new range B3:B11 for the SUM function.

Figure 4-11 shows the worksheet after I re-created the SUM formula in cell B12 with the AutoSum tool to include the expanded range. I dragged the fill handle to select the cell range C12:E12 (where this formula should be copied). Notice that I deleted the original formulas from the cell range C12:E12 in this figure to make it easier to see what's going on; normally, you just copy over the original outdated formulas and replace them with new correct copies.

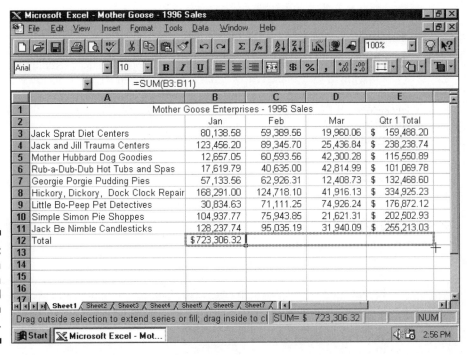

Figure 4-11:
Copying a
formula
to a cell
range with
AutoFill.

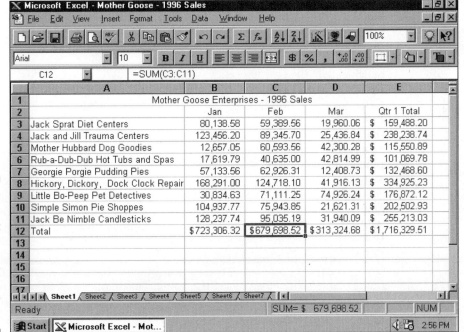

Figure 4-12:
The
worksheet
after I
copied the
formula for
totaling
monthly
sales.

Relatively speaking

Refer to Figure 4-12 to see the worksheet after the formula in a cell is copied to the cell range C12:E12 and cell C12 is active. Notice how Excel handles the copying of formulas. The original formula in cell B12 is as follows:

```
=SUM(B3:B11)
```

When the original formula is copied next door to cell C12, Excel changes the formula slightly so that it looks like this:

```
=SUM(C3:C11)
```

Excel adjusts the column reference, changing it from B to C, because I copied from left to right across the rows.

When you copy a formula to a cell range that extends down the rows, Excel adjusts the row numbers in the copied formulas rather than the column letters to suit the position of each copy. For example, cell E3 in the Mother Goose Enterprises 1996 sales worksheet contains the following formula:

```
=SUM(B3:D3)
```

When you copy this formula down to cell E4, Excel changes the copy of the formula to the following:

```
=SUM(B4:D4)
```

Excel adjusts the row reference to keep current with the new row 4 position. Because Excel adjusts the cell references in copies of a formula relative to the direction of the copying, the cell references are known as *relative cell references*.

Some things are absolutes!

All new formulas you create naturally contain relative cell references unless you say otherwise. Because most copies you make of formulas require adjustments of their cell references, you rarely have to give this arrangement a second thought. Then, every once in a while, you come across an exception that calls for limiting when and how cell references are adjusted in copies.

One of the most common of these exceptions is when you want to compare a range of different values to a single value. This happens most often when you want to compute what percentage each part is to the total. For example, in the

Mother Goose Enterprises 1996 sales worksheet, you encounter this situation in creating and copying a formula that calculates what percentage each monthly total (in the cell range B14:D14) is of the quarterly total in cell E12.

Suppose that you want to enter these formulas in row 14 of the Mother Goose Enterprises 1996 sales worksheet, starting in cell B14. The formula in cell B14 for calculating the percentage of the January-sales-to-first-quarter-total is very straightforward:

```
=B12/E12
```

This formula divides the January sales total in cell B12 by the quarterly total in E12 (what could be easier?). Look, however, at what would happen if you dragged the fill handle one cell to the right to copy this formula to cell C14:

```
=C12/F12
```

The adjustment of the first cell reference from B12 to C12 is just what the doctor ordered. However, the adjustment of the second cell reference from E12 to F12 is a disaster. You not only don't calculate what percentage the February sales in cell C12 are of the first quarter sales in E12, you also end up with one of those horrible #DIV/0! error things in cell C14.

To stop Excel from adjusting a cell reference in a formula in any copies you make, convert the cell reference from relative to absolute. You can do this by pressing the function key, F4. Excel indicates that you've made the cell reference absolute by placing dollar signs in front of the column letter and row number. For example, look at Figure 4-13. Cell B14 in this figure contains the correct formula to copy to the cell range C14:D14:

```
=B12/$E$12
```

Figure 4-14 shows the worksheet after this formula is copied to the range C14:D14 with the fill handle and cell C14 is selected. Notice that the formula bar shows that this cell contains the following formula:

```
=C12/$E$12
```

Because E12 was changed to $E$12 in the original formula, all the copies have this same absolute (non- changing) reference.

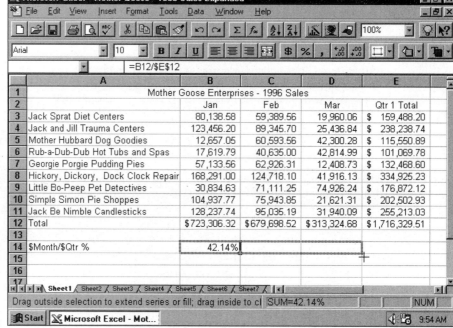

Figure 4-13:
Copying the
formula for
computing
the ratio
of monthly
to quarterly
sales with
an absolute
cell
reference.

Figure 4-14:
The work-
sheet after
copying the
formula with
the absolute
cell
reference.

If you goof up and copy a formula where one or more of the cell references should have been absolute, but you left them all relative, edit the original formula as follows:

1. **Double-click the cell with the formula or press F2 to edit it.**

2. **Position the insertion point somewhere on the reference you want to convert to absolute.**

3. **Press F4.**

4. **When you finish editing, press Enter and then copy the formula to the messed-up cell range with the fill handle.**

Cut and Paste, digital style

Instead of drag-and-drop or AutoFill, you can use the old standby Cut, Copy, and Paste commands to move or copy information in a worksheet. These commands use the Clipboard as a kind of electronic halfway house where the information you cut or copy remains until you decide to paste it somewhere. Because of this Clipboard arrangement, you can use these commands to move or copy information to any other worksheet open in Excel or even to other programs running in Windows (like a Word for Windows 95 document).

To move a cell selection with Cut and Paste, follow these steps:

1. **Select the cells you want to move.**

2. **Click the Cut button on the Standard toolbar.**

   Or, if you prefer, you can choose Cut from the cell context menu or Cut from the Edit pull-down menu.

   You can cut out all of this button-and-menu stuff and just press Ctrl+X. Whenever you choose the Cut command in Excel, the program surrounds the cell selection with a *marquee* (a dotted line that travels around the cells' outline) and displays the following message on the status bar:

   `Select destination and press ENTER or choose Paste`

3. **Move the cell pointer to, or select, the cell in the upper-left corner of the new range to which you want the information moved.**

4. **Press Enter to complete the move operation.**

   Or, if you're feeling really ambitious, click the Paste button on the Standard toolbar or choose Paste from the cell context menu or Paste from the Edit pull-down menu, or press Ctrl+V (do you think there are enough pasting alternatives in Excel?).

Notice that, when you indicate the destination range, you don't have to select a range of blank cells that matches the shape and size of the cell selection you're moving. Excel only needs to know the location of the cell in the upper-left corner of the destination range to figure out where to put the rest of the cells.

In fact, you can mess yourself up if you select more than the first cell of the destination range and the selected range doesn't exactly match the size and shape of the selection you're moving. When you press Enter, Excel displays an alert box with the following message:

```
Cut and paste areas are different shapes
```

If you choose OK to get rid of this dialog box, you have to correct the size of the destination range to successfully complete the move operation.

Copying a cell selection with the Copy and Paste commands follows an identical procedure to the one you use with the Cut and Paste commands. After selecting the range to copy, you have even more choices about how to get the information into the Clipboard. Instead of clicking the Copy button on the Standard toolbar or choosing Copy from the cell context menu or Copy from the Edit menu, you can press Ctrl+C.

"Paste it again Sam . . ."

When copying a selection with the Copy and Paste commands and the Clipboard, you can copy the information multiple times. Just make sure that instead of pressing Enter to complete the first copy operation, you click the Paste button on the Standard toolbar or choose the Paste command (from the cell context menu or the Edit menu) or press Ctrl+V.

When you use the Paste command to complete a copy operation, Excel copies the selection to the range you designated without removing the marquee from the original selection. This is your signal that you can select another destination range (either in the same or a different document).

After selecting the first cell of the next range where you want the selection copied, choose the Paste command again. You can continue in this manner, pasting the same selection to your heart's content. When you make the last copy, press Enter instead of choosing the Paste command. If you forget and choose Paste, get rid of the marquee around the original cell range by pressing the Esc key.

Note that you can only do multiple pasting jobs with the Paste command after copying stuff to the Clipboard and not after cutting stuff. This means that anytime you use the Cut and Paste commands to move something in the worksheet, you might as well as press Enter to paste because you don't accrue any more pasting benefits from choosing the Paste command.

So what's so special about Paste Special?

Normally, Excel copies all the information in the range of cells you selected: formatting as well as the formulas, text, and other values you entered. If you want, you can specify that only the entries be copied (without the formatting) or that just the formatting be copied (without the entries). You can even have Excel copy only values in a cell selection, which means that Excel copies all text entries and values entered in a cell selection but does *not* include formulas or formatting. When you paste values, all formulas in the cell selection are discarded and only the calculated values are retained — these values appear in the new cell range just as though you entered them manually.

To paste particular parts of a cell selection while discarding others, you choose the Paste Special command on the cell context menu or on the Edit pull-down menu rather than the standard Paste command (meaning that you don't get the benefit of clicking the Paste button on the Standard toolbar or using the nifty Ctrl+V keyboard shortcut). When you choose Paste Special over Paste, Excel displays the Paste Special dialog box shown in Figure 4-15. Here, you can specify which parts of the current cell selection to use by choosing the appropriate Paste radio button as follows:

- Normally, Excel chooses the All radio button in the Paste section to paste all the stuff in the cell selection (formulas, formatting, you name it).

- Choose the Formulas radio button in the Paste section to paste all the text, numbers, and formulas in the current cell selection while at the same time omitting all of the current formatting applied to their cells.

- Choose the Values radio button in the Paste section to convert formulas in the current cell selection to their calculated values.

- Choose the Formats radio button in the Paste section to paste only the formatting from the current cell selection and leave the cell entries in the dust.

- Choose the Notes radio button in the Paste section to paste only the notes that you've attached to their cells (kinda like electronic sticky notes — see Chapter 6 for details).

- Choose the All Except Borders radio button in the Paste section to paste all the stuff in the cell selection except any borders used there.

- Normally, the None radio button in the Operation section of the Paste Special dialog box is selected, indicating that Excel will perform no operation between the data entries you've cut or copied to the Clipboard and the data entries in the cell range where you paste.

- Choose the Add radio button in the Operation section to add the data you've cut or copied to the Clipboard and the data entries in the cell range where you paste.

✔ Choose the Subtract radio button in the Operation section to subtract the data you've cut or copied to the Clipboard from the data entries in the cell range where you paste.

✔ Choose the Multiply radio button in the Operation section to multiply the data you've cut or copied to the Clipboard by the data entries in the cell range where you paste.

✔ Choose the Divide radio button in the Operation section to divide the data you've cut or copied to the Clipboard by the data entries in the cell range where you paste.

✔ Choose the Skip Blanks check box when you want Excel to paste everywhere except for any empty cells in the incoming range. In other words, a blank cell cannot overwrite your current cell entries.

✔ Choose the Transpose check box when you want Excel to change the orientation of the pasted entries (for example, if the original cells' entries ran down the rows of a single column of the worksheet, the transposed pasted entries will run across the columns of a single row).

✔ Choose the Paste Link button when you're copying cell entries and you want to establish a link between copies you're pasting and the original entries so that changes to the original cells are automatically updated in the pasted copies.

Figure 4-15:
The Paste
Special
dialog box.

Let's Be Clear about Deleting Stuff

No discussion about editing in Excel would be complete without a section on getting rid of the stuff you put into cells. You can perform two kinds of deletions in a worksheet.

✔ **Clearing a cell:** just deletes or empties the cell's contents without removing the cell from the worksheet, which would alter the layout of the surrounding cells.

✔ **Deleting a cell:** gets rid of the whole kit and caboodle — cell structure along with all its contents and formatting. When you delete a cell, Excel has to shuffle the position of entries in the surrounding cells to plug up any gaps made by its demise.

Sounding the all clear!

To get rid of just the contents of a cell selection rather than delete the cells along with their contents, select the range of cells to be cleared and press Delete or choose Clear Contents from the cell context menu or Clear from the Edit menu and Contents from the Clear cascading menu.

If you want to get rid of more than just the contents of a cell selection, choose Clear on the Edit menu and then choose from among the cascading menu commands:

- Choose All to get rid of all formatting and notes as well as entries in the cell selection.

- Choose Formats to delete only the formatting from the current cell selection without touching anything else.

- Choose Notes if you only want to remove the notes in the cell selection but leave everything else behind.

Get these cells outta here!

To delete the cell selection rather than just clear out its contents, select the cell range and choose Delete from the cell context menu or Delete from the Edit menu. Excel displays the Delete dialog box shown in Figure 4-16. You use the radio button options in this dialog box to indicate how Excel should shift the cells left behind to fill in the gaps when the cells currently selected are blotted out of existence:

- Normally, the Shift Cells Left radio button is selected, meaning that Excel moves entries from neighboring columns on the right to the left to fill in gaps created when you delete the cell selection by clicking OK or pressing Enter.

- If you want Excel to move entries up from neighboring rows below, click the Shift Cells Up radio button.

- If you decide to remove all the rows in the current cell selection, click the Entire Row radio button in the Delete dialog box.

- If you decide to delete all the columns in the current cell selection, click the Entire Column radio button.

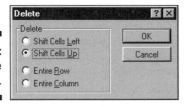

Figure 4-16:
The Delete
dialog box.

If you know ahead of time that you want to delete an entire column or row from the worksheet, you can select the column or row on the workbook window frame and then choose Delete from the column or row context menu or Delete from the Edit menu. You can remove more than one column or row at a time provided that they all neighbor one another and that you select them by dragging through their column letters or row numbers (Excel can't delete nonadjacent selections).

Deleting entire columns and rows from a worksheet is risky business unless you are sure that the columns and rows in question contain nothing of value. Remember, when you delete an entire row from the worksheet, you delete *all information from column A through IV* in that row (and you can see only a very few columns in this row). Likewise, when you delete an entire column from the worksheet, you delete *all information from row 1 through 16,384* in that column.

Kindly Step Aside . . .

For those inevitable times when you need to squeeze new entries into an already populated region of the worksheet, you can insert new cells in the area rather than go through all the trouble of moving and rearranging several individual cell ranges. To insert a new cell range, select the cells (many of which are already occupied) where you want the new cells to appear and then choose Insert on the cell context menu or the Cells command on the Insert pull-down menu. Doing either of these displays the Insert dialog box with the following radio button options:

  ✔ Choose the Shift Cells Right radio button to shift existing cells to the right to make room for the ones you want to add before choosing OK or pressing Enter.

  ✔ To instruct the program to shift existing entries down instead, use the default Shift Cells Down radio button before choosing OK or pressing Enter.

  ✔ As when you delete cells, when you insert cells with the Insert dialog box, you can insert complete rows or columns in the cell range by clicking either the Entire Row or the Entire Column radio button. You can also select the row number or column letter on the frame before you choose the Insert command.

Note that you can also insert entire columns and rows in a worksheet by choosing the Columns or Rows command on the Insert menu without having to open the Insert dialog box.

Keep in mind that, just as when you delete whole columns and rows, inserting entire columns and rows affects the entire worksheet, not just the part you see. If you don't know what's out in the hinterlands of the worksheet, you can't be sure how the insertion will impact — perhaps even sabotage — stuff (especially formulas) in the other unseen areas. I suggest that you scroll all the way out in both directions to make sure that nothing's out there.

Stamping Out Your Spelling Errors

If you're as good a speller as me, you'll be really relieved to learn that Excel has a built-in spell checker that can catch and get rid of all those embarrassing little spelling errors. With this in mind, you no longer have any excuse for putting out worksheets with typos in the titles or headings.

To check the spelling in a worksheet, choose the Spelling command from the Tools menu or click the Check Spelling tool (the one with a check mark under ABC) on the Standard toolbar or press F7.

Any way you do it, Excel begins checking the spelling of all text entries in the worksheet. When the program comes across an unknown word, it displays the Spelling dialog box, similar to the one shown in Figure 4-17.

Figure 4-17:
Checking your spelling in the Spelling dialog box.

Spelling	? X

Not in Dictionary: Feb

Change To: Feb.

Suggestions:
Feb.
Fe
Fee
Fed
Fen
Few

Ignore   Ignore All
Change   Change All
Add   Suggest

Add Words To: CUSTOM.DIC   AutoCorrect

Cell Value: Feb

☑ Always Suggest
☐ Ignore UPPERCASE   Undo Last   Cancel

Excel suggests replacements for the unknown word, with a likely replacement in the Suggestions list box appearing in the Change To list box of the Spelling dialog box. If that replacement is incorrect, you can scroll through the Suggestions list and click the correct replacement. Use the Spelling dialog box options as follows:

- ✔ To replace the word listed after the Not in Dictionary prompt with the word listed in the Change To list box, click the Change button.

- ✔ To change all occurrences of this misspelled word in the worksheet to the word listed in the Change To list box, click the Change All button.

- ✔ If you want to add the unknown word (such as your name) to a custom dictionary so that it won't be flagged when you check the spelling in the worksheet later on, click the Add button.

- ✔ If you want Excel from then on to automatically correct this spelling error with the suggestion shown in the Change To edit box (by adding the misspelling and suggestion to the AutoCorrect dialog box — see "You really AutoCorrect that for me" in Chapter 2), click the AutoCorrect button.

- ✔ If you think that the word is fine as-is, then click the Ignore button (or the Ignore All button if you don't want the spell checker to bother you with this word again).

Notice that the Excel spell checker not only flags words not found in its built-in or custom dictionary but also flags occurrences of double words in a cell entry (such as *total total*) or words with unusual capitalization (such as *NEw York* instead of *New York*).

Keep in mind that you can check the spelling of just a particular group of entries by selecting the cells before you choose Spelling from the Tools menu. Then click the Check Spelling tool in the Utility toolbar or press F7.

Chapter 5

Printing the Masterpiece

• •

In This Chapter

▶ Previewing pages before printing

▶ Using the Print button on the Standard toolbar to print the current worksheet

▶ Printing all the worksheets in a workbook

▶ Printing just some of the cells in a worksheet

▶ Changing the way the printing goes on the page

▶ Printing the whole worksheet on a single page

▶ Changing the margins for a report

▶ Adding a header and footer to a report

▶ Printing column and row headings on every page of a report

▶ Inserting page breaks in a report

▶ Printing the formulas in your worksheet

• •

Getting the data down on paper, when all is said and done, is really what spreadsheets are all about (all the talk about the "paperless" office to the contrary). All the data entry, all the formatting, all the formula checking, all the things you do to get a spreadsheet ready, is really just preparation for printing its information.

In this chapter, you find out just how easy it is to print reports with Excel for Windows 95. And you discover that, just by following a few simple guidelines, you can produce top-notch reports the first time you send the document to the printer (instead of the second, or even the third, time around).

The only trick to printing a worksheet is getting used to the paging scheme and learning how to control it. Many of the worksheets you create with Excel are not only longer than one printed page but also wider. Unlike a word processor, such as Word for Windows 95, which only pages the document vertically (because it won't let you create a document wider than the page size you're using), spreadsheet programs like Excel for Windows 95 often have to break up pages both vertically and horizontally to print a worksheet document (a kind of tiling of the print job, if you will).

When breaking a worksheet into pages, Excel first pages the document vertically down the rows in the first columns of the print area (just like a word processor). After paging the first columns, the program pages down the rows of the second set of columns in the print area. Excel pages down and then over until all the document included in the print area (which can include the entire worksheet or just sections) is paged.

When paging the worksheet, keep in mind that Excel does not break up the information within a row or column. If all the information in a row won't fit at the bottom of the page, the program moves the entire row to the following page. So, too, if all the information in a column won't fit at the right edge of the page, the program moves the entire column to a new page. (Because Excel pages down and then over, chances are that the column will not appear on the next page of the report.)

There are several ways to deal with such paging problems — and, in this chapter, you're going to be exposed to them all! Once you have these page problems under control, printing, as you shortly see, is a proverbial piece of cake.

Starting the Show with Print Preview

Do the world a favor and save a forest or two by using the Print Preview feature before you print any worksheet, section of worksheet, or entire workbook. Because of the peculiarities in paging worksheet data, you should check the page breaks for any report that requires more than one page. Print Preview mode not only shows you exactly how the worksheet data will be paged when printed but also enables you to modify the margins, change the page settings, and even go ahead and print the report when everything looks okay.

To switch to Print Preview mode, click the Print Preview button on the Standard toolbar (it's the one with the magnifying glass on the page, right next to the Print button) or choose the Print Preview command from the File menu. Excel displays all the information on the first page of the report in a separate window. Figure 5-1 shows the Print Preview window with the first page of a three-page sample report.

When Excel displays a full page in the Print Preview window, you can barely read its contents; increase the view to actual size if you need to verify some of the information. You can zoom up to 100 percent by clicking the previewed page with the magnifying-glass mouse pointer or by clicking the Zoom button at the top of the Print Preview window. Figure 5-2 shows the first page of the three-page report after you zoom in by clicking the magnifying-glass pointer in the upper-left portion of the page.

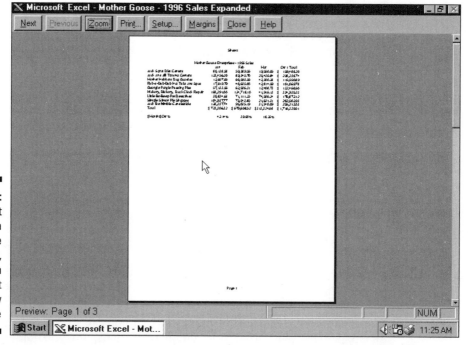

Figure 5-1:
The first
page of a
three-page
report,
shown
in Print
Preview
mode

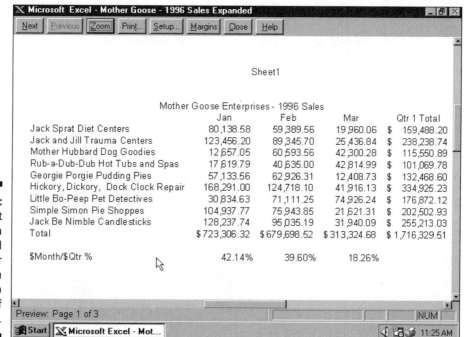

Figure 5-2:
The first
page of a
previewed
report after
zooming in
on the top
left part of
the page.

	Microsoft Excel - Mother Goose - 1996 Sales Expanded			
	Sheet1			
	Mother Goose Enterprises - 1996 Sales			
	Jan	Feb	Mar	Qtr 1 Total
Jack Sprat Diet Centers	80,138.58	59,389.56	19,960.06	$ 159,488.20
Jack and Jill Trauma Centers	123,456.20	89,345.70	25,436.84	$ 238,238.74
Mother Hubbard Dog Goodies	12,657.05	60,593.56	42,300.28	$ 115,550.89
Rub-a-Dub-Dub Hot Tubs and Spas	17,619.79	40,635.00	42,814.99	$ 101,069.78
Georgie Porgie Pudding Pies	57,133.56	62,926.31	12,408.73	$ 132,468.60
Hickory, Dickory, Dock Clock Repair	168,291.00	124,718.10	41,916.13	$ 334,925.23
Little Bo-Peep Pet Detectives	30,834.63	71,111.25	74,926.24	$ 176,872.12
Simple Simon Pie Shoppes	104,937.77	75,943.85	21,621.31	$ 202,502.93
Jack Be Nimble Candlesticks	128,237.74	95,035.19	31,940.09	$ 255,213.03
Total	$ 723,306.32	$ 679,698.52	$ 313,324.68	$ 1,716,329.51
$Month/$Qtr %		42.14%	39.60%	18.26%

After a page is enlarged to actual size, use the scroll bars to bring new parts of the page into view in the Print Preview window. If you prefer to use the keyboard, press the ↑ and ↓ keys or PgUp and PgDn to scroll up or down the page; press ← and → or Ctrl+PgUp and Ctrl+PgDn to scroll left and right.

To return to the full-page view, click the mouse pointer (in its arrowhead form) anywhere on the page or click the Zoom button at the top of the window a second time. Excel indicates the number of pages in a report on the status bar of the Print Preview window. If your report has more than one page, you can view pages that follow the one you are previewing by clicking on the Next command button at the top of the window. To review a page you've already seen, back up a page by clicking the Previous button. You can also advance to the next page by pressing the PgDn or ↓ key or move back to the previous page by pressing the PgUp or ↑ key when the page view is full-page rather than actual size.

When you finish previewing the report, you have the following options:

- ✔ If the pages look okay, you can click the Print button to display the Print dialog box and start printing the report from there (see "Printing it your way," later in this chapter).

- ✔ If you notice some paging problems that you can solve by choosing a new paper size, page order, orientation, or margins, or if you notice a problem with the header or footer in the top or bottom margin of the pages, you can click the Setup button and take care of these problems in the Page Setup dialog box.

- ✔ If you notice some problems with the margins or with the column widths and you want to adjust them in Print Preview mode, you can click the Margins button and drag the margin markers into place (see "Massaging the margins," later in this chapter for details).

- ✔ If you notice any other kind of problem, such as a typo in a heading or a wrong value in a cell, click the Close button and return to the normal worksheet document window; you cannot make any text editing changes in the Print Preview window.

- ✔ After you make corrections to the worksheet, you can print the report from the normal document window by choosing Print from the File menu. Alternatively, you can switch back to Print Preview mode to make a last-minute check and click the Print button, or use the Print button (fourth from left with the printer icon on it) on the Standard toolbar.

"The Page Stops Here . . ."

Excel automatically displays the page breaks in the normal document window after you preview the document. Page breaks appear on-screen as dotted lines between the columns and rows that will print out on different pages.

To get rid of page breaks in the document window, choose Options on the Tools menu, and then choose the View tab and clear the check mark from the Automatic Page Breaks check box, and choose OK or press Enter.

Printing it right away

As long as you want to use Excel's default print settings to print all of the cells in the current worksheet, printing in Excel for Windows 95 is a breeze. Simply click the Print tool on the Standard toolbar (the fourth tool from the left, with the printer icon). The program then prints one copy of all the information in the current worksheet, including any charts and graphics — but not including notes you added to cells. (See Chapter 8 for details about charts and graphics.)

After you click the Print tool, Excel routes the print job to the Windows 95 print queue, which acts like a middleman to send the job to the printer. While Excel is sending the print job to the print queue, Excel displays a Printing dialog box to keep you informed of its progress (such as Printing Page 2 of 3). Once this dialog box disappears, you are free to go back to work in Excel (be aware, however, that Excel will probably move like a slug until the job is actually printed). To abort the print job while it's being sent to the print queue, click the Cancel button in the Printing dialog box.

If you don't realize that you want to cancel the print job until after Excel finishes shipping it to the print queue (that is, while the Printing dialog box appears on-screen), you must open the dialog box for your printer and cancel printing from there. To cancel a print job from this dialog box, follow these steps:

1. **Click the printer icon at the far right of the Windows 95 taskbar (to the immediate left of the current time) with the secondary mouse button to open its context menu.**

   This printer icon displays the tooltip, 1 document(s) pending for *so-and-so* (for example, Greg, if I'm printing), when you position the mouse pointer over it.

2. **Choose the Open Active Printers command on the printer icon's context menu.**

   This opens the dialog box for the printer with the Excel print job in its queue (as described under the Document heading in the list box).

3. **Select the Excel print job that you want to cancel in the list box of your printer's dialog box.**

4. **Choose Cancel Printing on the Document pull-down menu.**

5. **Wait for the print job to disappear from the queue in the printer's dialog box, and then click the Close button to get rid of it and return to Excel.**

Printing it your way

Printing with the Print tool on the Standard toolbar is fine, provided that all you want is a single copy of all the information in the current worksheet. If you want more copies, more or less data (such as all the worksheets in the workbook or just a cell selection within a particular worksheet), or you need to change some of the page settings (like the size of the page or the orientation of the printing on the page), then you need to print from the Print dialog box (shown in Figure 5-3).

Figure 5-3:
The Print
dialog box.

Excel provides a number of ways to open the Print dialog box:

✔ Press Ctrl+P.

✔ Choose the Print command from the File menu.

✔ Press Ctrl+Shift+F12.

Printing in particular

Within the Print dialog box are the Print What and Page Range areas, where you can select how much of the information is printed, and the Copies area, where you can change the number of copies printed. Here's how you use these areas:

- ✔ **Selection:** Choose this radio button in the Print What section to have Excel print just the cells that are currently selected in your workbook. (Yes, you must remember to select these cells before opening the Print dialog box and choosing this radio button!)

- ✔ **Selected Sheet(s):** Excel automatically chooses this radio button and prints all of the information in whatever worksheets are selected in your workbook. Normally, this means printing just the data in the current worksheet. To print other worksheets in the workbook when this radio button is chosen, hold down Ctrl as you click the sheet's tab. To include all the sheets between two sheet tabs, click the first one, and then hold Shift as you click the second tab (Excel selects all the tabs in between).

- ✔ **Entire Workbook:** Choose this radio button in the Print What section to have Excel print all the data in each of the worksheets in your workbook.

- ✔ **Number of Copies:** To print more than one copy of the report, enter the number of copies you want to print in the Number of Copies edit box in the Copies section — or use the spinner buttons to select the required number.

- ✔ **Collate:** When you *collate* pages, you simply make separate stacks of each complete report, rather than printing all copies of page one, and then all copies of page two, and so on. To have Excel collate each copy of the report for you, choose the Collate check box in the Copies section to put a check mark in it.

- ✔ **All:** When the All radio button (found in the Page Range section) is selected, all of the pages in your document will print. Because this is the default choice, you only need to select it after you have printed only a portion of the document, using the Page(s) radio button.

- ✔ **Page(s):** Normally, Excel prints all of the pages required to produce the information in the areas of the workbook that you want printed. Sometimes, however, you may only need to reprint a page or range of pages that you've modified within this section. To reprint a single page, enter its page number in both the From and To edit boxes in the Page Range section or select these page numbers with the spinner buttons. To reprint a range of pages, put the first page number in the From edit box and the last page number in the To edit box. (Excel automatically deselects the All radio button and selects the Page(s) radio button in the Page Range section as soon as you start typing in From or To edit boxes.)

After you finish choosing new print options, you can send the job to the printer by choosing OK or pressing Enter. To use another printer that's been installed for Windows 95 (Excel lists the current printer at the top of the Print dialog box), choose the new printer in the Printer drop-down list box before you start printing.

My Page Was Setup!

As I said at the beginning of this chapter, about the only thing the slightest bit complex in printing a worksheet is figuring out how to get the pages right. Fortunately, the options in the Page Setup dialog box give you a great deal of control over what goes on which page. To open the Page Setup dialog box, choose Page Setup from the File menu or click the Setup button if the Print Preview window is open. The Page Setup dialog box contains four tabs: Page, Margins, Header/Footer, and Sheet.

The particular options offered in the Page tab of the Page Setup dialog box may vary slightly with the type of printer you use. Figure 5-4 shows the Page Setup dialog box when the Apple LaserWriter is the current printer (all the options you see here are also present when using other laser printers such as the HP LaserJet printer).

For most types of printers, the Page tab of the Page Setup dialog box includes options for changing the orientation, scaling the printing, and choosing a new paper size and print quality:

Figure 5-4:
The Page
tab of the
Page Setup
dialog box.

✔ **Orientation:** Portrait positions the paper so that the short side is on the top and bottom. Landscape positions the printing with the long side of the paper on top and bottom (see "Getting the lay of the landscape," which follows).

✔ **Adjust to:** Lets you increase or decrease the size of the printing by a set percentage (much like using the Zoom feature to zoom in and out on worksheet data on-screen). When entering values in the Adjust to text box, keep in mind that 100 percent represents normal size and that any percentage below that reduces the size of the printing (and puts more on each page), whereas any percentage above increases the size of the printing (and puts less on each page).

✔ **Fit to:** Lets you fit all of the printing on a single page (by default) or on a set number of pages wide by a set number of pages tall (see "Packing it all on one page," later in this chapter).

✔ **Paper Size:** Lets you switch to a new paper size by selecting a new size in the drop-down list box (this list contains only those paper sizes that your printer can accommodate).

✔ **Print Quality:** Some printers (like dot-matrix printers) let you change the quality of the printing depending upon whether you're producing a first rough draft or a final printout.

✔ **First Page Number:** Lets you change the starting page number when you want the first number to be higher than 1. You use this numbering option only when you're printing page numbers in the header or footer (see "From header to footer," later in this chapter).

Getting the lay of the landscape

For many printers (including most of the dot-matrix, laser, or ink-jet persuasion), the Page tab of the Page Setup dialog box includes an Orientation section for changing the printing from the more normal *portrait* (where the printing runs parallel to the short edge of the paper) to *landscape* (where the printing runs parallel to the long edge of the paper). With these types of printers, you can usually use the Adjust to or Fit to options (see " Packing it all on one page," which follows) to scale the size of the printing, making it possible to enlarge or reduce the printing by a particular percentage or to force all the information on a single page or a set number of pages.

Because many worksheets are far wider than they are tall (like budgets or sales tables that track expenditures over all 12 months), if your printer supports changing the orientation of the page, you may find that such worksheets look better if you switch the orientation from the normal portrait mode (which accommodates fewer columns on a page because the printing runs parallel to the short edge of the page) to landscape mode.

Figure 5-5 shows the Print Preview window with the first page of a report in landscape mode. For this report, Excel can get three more columns of information on this page in landscape mode than it can in portrait mode. However, because this page orientation accommodates fewer rows, the total page count for this report is increased from two pages in portrait mode to four pages in landscape mode.

Packing it all on one page

If your printer supports scaling options, you're in luck. You can always get a worksheet to fit on a single page simply by clicking the Fit to radio button. When you click this radio button, Excel figures out how much to reduce the size of the information you're printing to get it all on one page.

If you preview this one page and find that the printing is just too small to read comfortably, reopen the Page tab of the Page Setup dialog box and try changing the number of pages in the pages wide by tall text boxes (to the immediate right of the Fit to radio button). For example, instead of trying to stuff everything on one page, check out how it looks to fit the worksheet on two pages across: enter **2** in the pages wide text box and leave 1 in the pages tall text box. Alternatively, see how the worksheet looks on two pages down: Leave the 1 in the pages wide text box and enter **2** in the pages tall text box.

Figure 5-5:
A report
shown in
landscape
mode in
the Print
Preview
window.

After using the Fit to option, you may find that you don't want to scale the printing. Cancel scaling by clicking the Adjust to radio button right above the Fit to button and enter **100** in the text box.

Massaging the margins

Excel uses a standard top and bottom margin of 1 inch on each page of the report and a standard left and right margin of $^3/_4$ inch.

Frequently, you find that you can squeeze the last column or the last few rows of the worksheet data you're printing on a page just by adjusting the margins for the report. To get more columns on a page, try reducing the left and right margins. To get more rows on a page, try reducing the top and bottom margins.

You can change the margins in two ways:

  ✔ Open the Page Setup dialog box (either by choosing Page Setup on the File pull-down menu or by clicking the Setup button in the Print Preview window), and then select the Margins tab (see Figure 5-6) and enter the new settings in the Top, Bottom, Left, and Right edit boxes — or select them with the spinner buttons.

  ✔ Open the Print Preview window, click the Margins button, and drag the margin markers to their new positions (see Figure 5-7).

You can use the Center on Page options in the Margins tab of the Page Setup dialog box to center a selection of data (that takes up less than a full page) between the current margin settings. Choose the Horizontally check box to center the data between the left and right margin. Choose the Vertically check box to center the data between the top and bottom margins.

If you use the Margins button in the Print Preview window to change the margin settings, you can modify the column widths as well as the margins. (Figure 5-7 shows the margin and column markers that appear when you click the Margins button in the Print Preview window.) To change one of the margins, position the mouse pointer on the desired margin marker (the pointer shape changes to a double-headed arrow) and drag the marker in the appropriate direction. When you release the mouse button, Excel redraws the page using the new margin setting. You may gain or lose columns or rows, depending on what kind of adjustment you make. Changing the column widths is the same story: Drag the column marker to the left or right to decrease or increase the width of a particular column.

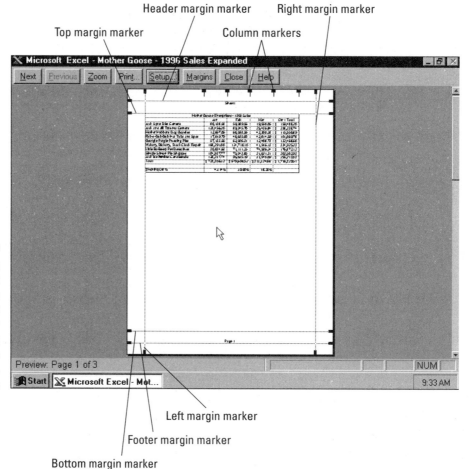

Figure 5-6:
The Margins
tab of the
Page Setup
dialog box.

Figure 5-7:
The Print
Preview
window
after
selecting
the Margins
button.

From header to footer

Headers and footers are simply standard text that appears on every page of the report. The header prints in the top margin of the page, and the footer prints — you guessed it — in the bottom margin. Both are centered vertically in the margins. Unless you specify otherwise, Excel automatically adds a header that shows the name of the worksheet you are printing (as shown on its sheet tab) and a footer that shows the current page number.

You can use a header and footer in a report to identify the document used to produce the report and display the page numbers and the date and time of printing.

Getting a standard job

To modify the headers or footers in some way, open the Header/Footer tab in the Page Setup dialog box and make your changes in the Header and/or Footer drop-down list box found there (Figure 5-8). Both the Header and Footer drop-down list boxes in this tab contain a wide number of stock pieces of information for your header and footer, including the name of the worksheet (picked up from the sheet tab — see Chapter 6 to learn how to rename a sheet tab), who prepared the worksheet (picked up from the User Name option in the General tab of the Options dialog box — see Chapter 12), the page number, the current date, the name of the workbook document, or various combinations of these pieces of information.

Figure 5-8 shows the Header/Footer tab of the Page Setup dialog box after choosing

```
Media of the Minds Confidential, 7/17/95, Page 1
```

in the Header drop-down list box (Media of the Minds is the company to which Excel is registered [this name is the same as the one listed as the registered user on the About Microsoft Excel dialog box], 7/17/95 is the current date, and Page 1 is, of course, the current page number) and also choosing

```
Page 1 of ?
```

in the Footer drop-down list box (which puts in the current page number, along with the total number of pages, in the report). You can choose this paging option in either the Header or Footer drop-down list box.

Figure 5-9 shows the first page of the report in Print Preview mode. Here, you can see the header and footer as they will print (fortunately, you can verify in the Print Preview window that the header information won't all print on top of each other as it appears in the header preview area in the Page Setup dialog box). You can also see how the Page 1 of ? works in the footer: On the first page, you see the centered footer, Page 1 of 4; on the second page, you would see the centered footer, Page 2 of 4.

Figure 5-8:
The Header/
Footer tab of
the Page
Setup dialog
box with a
header and
footer.

Figure 5-9:
The first
page of a
printed
report
showing the
header and
footer as
they will
print.

If you don't want a header or footer printed in your report, you simply open the Header/Footer tab in the Page Setup dialog box and then choose the (none) option at the very top of the He_a_der and _F_ooter drop-down list box.

Getting a custom job

Most of the time, the stock headers and footers available in the He_a_der and _F_ooter drop-down list boxes are sufficient for your report needs. Every once in a while, however, you may want to insert information not available in these list boxes or in an arrangement not offered in the stock headers and footers. For those times, you need to turn to the _C_ustom Header and C_u_stom Footer buttons in the Header/Footer tab of the Page Setup dialog box and go about creating your header or footer by inserting your own information.

Figure 5-10 shows the Header dialog box that appears when you click the _C_ustom Header button after selecting the stock header shown in Figure 5-8.

Figure 5-10: Creating a custom header in the Header dialog box.

Notice that, in the custom Header dialog box, the header is divided into three sections: _L_eft Section, _C_enter Section, and _R_ight Section. All header text you enter in the _L_eft Section of this dialog box is justified with the left margin of the report. All header text you enter in the _C_enter Section box is centered between the left and right margins, and (you guessed it) all text you enter in the _R_ight Section box is justified with the right margin of the report.

You can use the Tab key to advance from section to section in the header and to select the contents of that section, or you can press Alt plus the mnemonic letter (Alt+L for the _L_eft Section, Alt+C for the _C_enter Section, and Alt+R for the _R_ight Section). If you want to break the header text in one of the sections, press Enter to start a new line. If you want to clear the contents of a section, select the items and press Delete.

As Figure 5-10 shows, Excel puts some pretty weird codes with lots of amper-sands (&[Date] and Page &[Page]) in the center and right sections of this stock header. When creating a custom header (or footer), you too can mix weird ampersand codes with the standard text (like "For Eyes Only" and such). To insert the weird ampersand codes in a section of the header (or footer), you click the appropriate button:

- **Page button:** inserts the &[Page] code that puts in the current page number.

- **Total Page button:** inserts the &[Pages] code that puts in the total number of pages. Thus, you can have Excel display the Page 1 of 4 kind of thing by typing the word **Page** and pressing the spacebar, and then clicking the Page button, pressing the spacebar again, typing **of**, and then pressing the spacebar a third time, and, finally, pressing the Total Page button to insert Page &[Page] of &[Pages] in the custom header (or footer).

- **Date button:** inserts the &[Date] code that puts in the current date.

- **Time button:** inserts the &[Time] code that puts in the current time.

- **Filename button:** inserts the name of the workbook file.

- **Tab Name button:** inserts the &[Tab] code that puts in the name of the sheet tab.

In addition to inserting ampersand codes in the custom header (or footer), you can choose a new font, font size, or font attribute for any of its sections by clicking the Font button. When you click the Font button, Excel opens the Font dialog box where you can select a new font, font style, font size, or special effects (like strikethrough, superscript, or subscript).

When you're finished creating your custom header (or footer), choose the OK button to close the Header (or Footer) dialog box and return to the Header/Footer tab of the Page Setup dialog box (where you can see the fruits of your labor in the sample boxes).

Sorting out the sheet settings

The Sheet tab of the Page Setup dialog box (similar to the one shown in the following section in Figure 5-11) contains a variety of printing options that may come in handy from time to time:

- **Print Area:** This edit box shows you the cell range of the current print area that you've selected with the Print Area and Set Print Area commands on the File pull-down menus. Use this edit box to make changes to the range of cells that you want to print. To change the print area range, select this edit box, and then drag through the cell range in the worksheet or type in the cell references or range names (as explained in Chapter 6). Separate individual cell ranges with a comma (as in A1:G72, K50:M75) when designating nonadjacent areas.

You only use the Print <u>A</u>rea option when your workbook contains a section that you routinely need to print, and you don't want to have to keep selecting the range and then choosing the Selectio<u>n</u> radio button in the Print dialog box every blasted time you print it.

✔ **Rows to Repeat at Top:** Use this option to designate rows of a worksheet as *print titles* to be printed across the top of each page of the report (see "Putting out the print titles," which follows). Select this edit box, and then drag down the rows or enter the row references (such as 2:3).

✔ **Columns to Repeat at Left:** Use this option to designate columns of a worksheet as print titles to be printed at the left edge of each page of the report (see "Putting out the print titles," which follows). Select this edit box, and then drag across the columns or enter the column row references (such as A:B).

✔ **Gridlines:** Hides or shows the cell gridlines in the printed report. (Refer to Figure 5-5 to see the page of a report in Print Preview after removing the check mark from the <u>G</u>ridlines check box.)

✔ **Notes:** When you select this check box, Excel prints the text of any text notes attached to cells that are included in the report. Leave this check box deselected when you don't want the notes included at the end of the printout.

✔ **Draft <u>Q</u>uality:** When you select this check box, Excel doesn't print cell gridlines (regardless of the status of the <u>G</u>ridlines check box) and omits some graphics from the printout. Select this option when you want to get a fast and dirty copy of the report and are only concerned with checking the text and numbers.

✔ **<u>B</u>lack and White:** When you select this check box, Excel prints the different colors assigned to cell ranges in black and white. Select this option when you've used colors for text and graphics in a workbook on a color monitor but want to print them in monochrome on a black-and-white printer (otherwise, they become shades of gray on a black-and-white printer).

✔ **Row and Col<u>u</u>mn Headings:** When you select this check box, Excel includes the worksheet frame with the column letters and row numbers on each page of the report. Select this option when you want to be able to identify the location of the printed information (see "Letting Your Formulas All Hang Out," later in this chapter, for an example).

✔ **<u>D</u>own, then Across:** Normally, Excel selects this radio button, which tells the program to number and page a multipage report by proceeding down the rows and then across the columns to be printed.

✔ **Across, then Down:** Choose this radio button to alter the way a multipage report is numbered and paged. When you select this option, Excel proceeds to number and page across the columns and then down the rows to be printed.

Putting out the print titles

The Print Titles section of the Sheet tab of the Page Setup dialog box enables you to print particular rows and columns on each page of the report. Excel refers to such rows and columns in a printed report as *print titles*. Don't confuse print titles with the header of a report. Even though both are printed on each page, header information is printed in the top margin of the report; print titles always appear in the body of the report — at the top, in the case of rows used as print titles, and on the left, in the case of columns.

To designate print titles for a report, follow these steps:

1. **Open the Page Setup dialog box.**

   The Sheet tab of the Page Setup dialog box appears, as shown in Figure 5-11.

2. **Choose the Sheet tab.**

   To designate worksheet rows as print titles, go to 3a. To designate worksheet columns as print titles, go to 3b.

3a. **Choose the Rows to Repeat at Top text box, and then drag through the rows whose information is to appear at the top of each page in the worksheet below.**

   In the example shown in Figure 5-11, I dragged through rows 1 and 2 in column A of the Bo-Peep Pet Detectives — Client List worksheet, and the program entered the row range $1:$2 in the Rows to Repeat at Top text box.

   Note that Excel indicates the print-title rows in the worksheet by placing a dotted line (that moves like a marquee) on the border between the titles and the information in the body of the report.

3b. **Choose the Columns to Repeat at Left, then drag through the range of columns whose information is to appear at the left edge of each page of the printed report in the worksheet below.**

   Note that Excel indicates the print-title rows in the worksheet by placing a dotted line (that moves like a marquee) on the border between the titles and the information in the body of the report.

4. Choose OK or press Enter.

After you close the Page Setup dialog box, the dotted line showing the border of the row and/or column titles disappears from the worksheet.

In Figure 5-11, rows 1 and 2 containing the worksheet title and column headings for the Bo-Peep Pet Detectives clients database are designated as the print titles for the report. Figure 5-12 shows the Print Preview window with the second page of the report. In this figure, you can see how these print titles appear on all pages of the report.

Figure 5-11:
Setting the print titles for the sample report.

Figure 5-12:
The second
page of
the sample
report
showing
print titles
set in
Figure 5-11.

To clear print titles from a report if you no longer need them, open the Sheet tab of the Page Setup dialog box, and then delete the row and column ranges from the Rows to Repeat at Top and the Columns to Repeat at Left text boxes before you choose OK or press Enter.

When Ya Gonna Give Your Page a Break?

Sometimes, as you preview a report, you see that Excel split onto different pages information that you know should always appear together on the same page. If, after trying other approaches (such as changing the page size, orientation, or margins), you still can't remedy the bad page break, you can insert a manual page break to force Excel to print the information on the same page.

When inserting a manual page break, you use the top and left edges of the cell pointer to determine where the manual page break is placed. The top edge of the cell pointer determines where the page break occurs horizontally; the left edge of the cell pointer determines where the page break occurs vertically.

Figure 5-13 shows an example of a bad vertical page break that you can remedy with a manual page break. Given the page size, orientation, and margin settings for this report, Excel breaks the page between columns K and L. This break separates the sales figures for July and August, in columns J and K, from the September sales figures and the Quarter 3 Totals, in columns L and M.

To keep all the third-quarter figures on the same page, you need to insert a manual page break so that the July and August sales information in columns J and K are forced onto the page containing the September and quarterly totals in columns L and M (assuming that none of the other treatments — short of using the Fit to radio button in the Page tab — works to squeeze the information in columns L and M onto the page containing the sales information in columns J and K).

Figure 5-13 shows how you can create the vertical page break by following these steps:

1. **Position the cell pointer in cell J1.**

   Make sure that the pointer is in row 1 of column J; otherwise, Excel inserts a horizontal page break at the row as well as the vertical page break at column J.

2. **Choose Page Break from the Insert menu.**

   Excel inserts a manual vertical page break between columns I and J (see Figure 5-14). The manual page break removes the automatic page break that appeared previously between columns K and L, and forces all the third-quarter sales figures with their totals together on another page.

To remove a manual page break from a worksheet, position the cell pointer somewhere in the row below a horizontal page break or somewhere in the column to the right of a vertical page break. (Manual page breaks are indicated in the worksheet by dotted lines that are indistinguishable from automatic page breaks.) Then choose Remove Page Break from the Insert menu. (The Page Break command changes to the Remove Page Break command on the Insert menu, depending on where you place the cell pointer.) If you inserted both a vertical and a horizontal page break at the same time, you must position the cell pointer in the same cell you used to create the two page breaks in order to get rid of them both in a single operation.

Figure 5-13:
The Insert menu used to insert a manual page break between columns I and J.

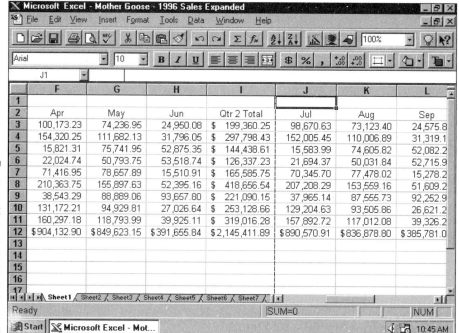

Figure 5-14:
The worksheet after you insert the manual page break between columns I and J.

Letting Your Formulas All Hang Out

One more basic printing technique you may need every once in a while is: how to print the formulas in a worksheet, instead of printing the calculated results of the formulas. You can check over a printout of the formulas in your worksheet to make sure that you haven't done anything stupid (like replace a formula with a number or use the wrong cell references in a formula) before you distribute the worksheet company-wide — which can be really embarrassing.

Before you can print a worksheet's formulas, you have to display the formulas, rather than their results, in the cells.

1. Choose the Options command on the Tools menu.

2. Choose the View tab.

3. Choose the Formulas check box to put a check mark in it.

4. Click the OK button or press Enter.

When you follow these steps, Excel displays the contents of each cell in the worksheet as they normally appear only in the formula bar or when you're editing them in the cell. Notice that value entries lose their number formatting, formulas appear in their cells (Excel widens the columns with best-fit so that the formulas appear in their entirety), and long text entries no longer spill over into neighboring blank cells.

Excel allows you to toggle between the normal cell display and the formula cell display by pressing Ctrl+~, that is, press Ctrl and the tilde key. The tilde key is the one (usually found in the upper-left corner of your keyboard) that does double-duty above the weird backward accent key, `, which is not to be confused with the apostrophe that appears on a key below the quotation mark.

After Excel displays the formulas in the worksheet, you are ready to print it as you would any other report. You can include the worksheet column letters and row numbers as headings in the printout so that, if you *do* spot an error, you can pinpoint the cell reference right away. To include the row and column headings in the printout, click the Row & Column Headings check box in the Sheet tab of the Page Setup dialog box before you send the report to the printer. Figure 5-15 shows the Print Preview window containing part of the first page of a report that prints the formulas and includes the worksheet column letters and row numbers as headings.

When you display formulas in the cells, all entries — text, values, and formulas — are left-aligned in their cells, and all formatting for the values is missing.

After you print the worksheet with the formulas, return the worksheet to normal by opening the Page Setup dialog box and choosing the View tab and then deselecting the Formulas check box before choosing OK, or pressing Enter, or just Ctrl+~.

Figure 5-15:
The first
page of a
four-page
report (in
Print
Preview
mode) that
prints the
formulas
with the
worksheet
column
and row
headings.

Part III

Getting Organized and Staying That Way

The 5th Wave · By Rich Tennant

"Hey Dad - guess how many Milk Duds fit inside your disk drive."

In this part . . .

*1*n today's business world, we all know how vital it is to stay organized — as well as how difficult it is. Needless to say, keeping straight the spreadsheets you create in Excel for Windows 95 is no less important, and in some cases, no less arduous.

Part III helps you tackle this conundrum by giving you the inside track on how to keep on top of all the stuff in every single worksheet you create or edit. Not only do you learn in Chapter 6 how to keep track of the information in one worksheet but also, in Chapter 7, how to juggle the information from one worksheet to another, and, even from one workbook to another.

Chapter 6

Oh What a Tangled Worksheet We Weave!

In This Chapter

▶ Zooming in and out on a worksheet

▶ Splitting up the workbook window into two or four panes

▶ Freezing columns and rows on-screen for worksheet titles

▶ Attaching notes to cells

▶ Naming your cells

▶ Finding and replacing stuff in your worksheet

▶ Controlling when a worksheet is recalculated

▶ Protecting your worksheets

You already know that each Excel worksheet offers an awfully big place in which to store information (and that each workbook you open offers you 16 of these babies). Because your computer monitor only lets you see a tiny bit of any of the worksheets in a workbook at any one time, the issue of keeping on top of information is not a small one (pun intended).

Although the Excel worksheet employs a coherent cell-coordinate system you can use to get anywhere in the great big worksheet, you've got to admit that this A1, B2 stuff — although highly logical — remains fairly alien to human thinking. (I mean, saying, "Go to cell IV88" just doesn't have anywhere near the same impact as saying "Go to the corner of Hollywood and Vine.") Consider for a moment how hard it is to come up with a meaningful association between the 1995 depreciation schedule and its location in the cell range AC50:AN75 so that you can remember where to find it.

In this chapter, you learn some of the more effective techniques for keeping on top of information. You learn how to change the perspective on a worksheet by zooming in and out on the information, how to split the document window into separate panes so that you can display different sections of the worksheet at the same time, and how to keep particular rows and columns on the screen at all times.

And, as if that weren't enough, you also see how to add reminders to cells with notes — assign descriptive, English-type names to cell ranges (like Hollywood_and_Vine!) — and use the Find and Replace commands to locate and, if necessary, replace entries anywhere in the worksheet. Finally, you see how to control when Excel recalculates the worksheet and how to limit where changes can be made.

Zeroing In with Zoom

So what are you gonna do now that the boss won't spring for that 21-inch monitor for your computer? All day long, it seems that you're either straining your eyes to read all the information in those little, tiny cells, or you're scrolling like mad trying to locate a table you can't seem to find today. Never fear, the Zoom feature is here. You can use Zoom like a magnifying glass to blow up part of the worksheet or shrink it down to size.

Figure 6-1 shows a blowup of an employee-roster worksheet after increasing it to 200-percent magnification (twice normal size). To blow up a worksheet like this, choose the drop-down list button for the Zoom Control tool on the Standard toolbar, and then drag up or click the 200% setting (you can also do this by choosing Zoom on the View menu and then selecting the 200% radio button in the Zoom dialog box, if you really want to go to all that trouble). One thing's for sure, you don't have to go after your glasses to read the names in those cells! The only problem with 200-percent magnification is that you can only see a few cells at one time.

Figure 6-2 shows the same worksheet, this time at 25-percent magnification (roughly one-quarter normal size). To reduce the display to this magnification, you choose the 25% setting in the drop-down list box attached to the Zoom Control tool on the Standard toolbar (unless you're just dying to open the Zoom dialog box so that you can accomplish this via its 25% radio button).

Whew! At 25 percent of normal screen size, the only thing you can be sure of is that you can't read a thing! However, notice that with this bird's-eye view, you can see at a glance how far over and down the data in this worksheet extends.

The Zoom command has five precise magnification settings (200%, 100% [normal screen magnification], 75%, 50%, and 25%). To use other percentages besides these, you have the following options:

✔ If you want to use other precise percentages in between the five preset percentages (such as 150% or 85%) or settings greater or less than the highest or lowest (such as 400% or 10%), select the edit box of the Zoom Control button on the Standard toolbar, type the new percentage, and press Enter.

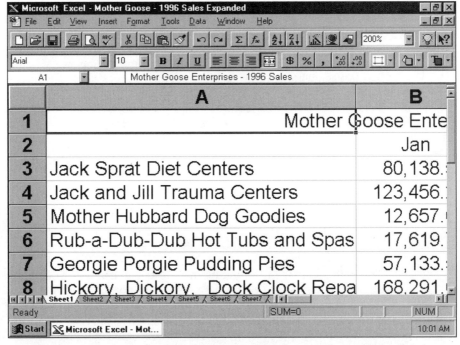

Figure 6-1: Zooming in: a sample worksheet at 200-percent magnification.

Figure 6-2: Zooming out: a sample worksheet at 25-percent magnification.

✔ If you don't know what percentage to enter in order to display a particular cell range on the screen, select the range, choose Selection in the Zoom Control drop-down list box on the Standard toolbar or open the Zoom dialog box, choose the Fit Selection radio button, and then choose OK or press Enter. Excel figures out the percentage necessary to fill up your screen with just the selected cell range.

You can use the Zoom feature to locate and move to a new cell range in the worksheet. First, select a small magnification, such as 50%. Then locate the cell range you want to move to and select one of its cells. Finally, use the Zoom feature to return the screen magnification to 100% again. When Excel returns the display to normal size, the cell you selected and its surrounding range appear on-screen.

Splitting the Difference

Although zooming in and out on the worksheet can help you get your bearings, it can't bring together two separate sections so that you can compare their data on the screen (at least not at a normal size where you can actually read the information). To manage this kind of trick, split the document window into separate panes and then scroll the worksheet in each pane so that they display the parts you want to compare.

Splitting the window is easy. Figure 6-3 shows a projected income statement for the Jack Sprat Diet Centers after splitting its worksheet window horizontally into two panes and scrolling up rows 24 through 28 in the second pane. Each pane has its own vertical scroll bar, which enables you to scroll different parts of the worksheet into view.

To split a worksheet into two (upper and lower) horizontal panes, you can drag the *split bar,* located right above the scroll arrow at the very top of the vertical scroll bar, down until the window is divided as you want it. Use the following steps:

1. **Click the vertical split bar and hold down the primary mouse button.**

   The mouse pointer changes to a double-headed arrow with a split in its middle (like the one used to display hidden rows).

2. **Drag downward until you reach the row at which you want the document window divided.**

   A gray dividing line appears in the workbook document window as you drag down, indicating where the document window will be split.

3. **Release the mouse button.**

   Excel divides the window into horizontal panes at the pointer's location and adds a vertical scroll bar to the new pane.

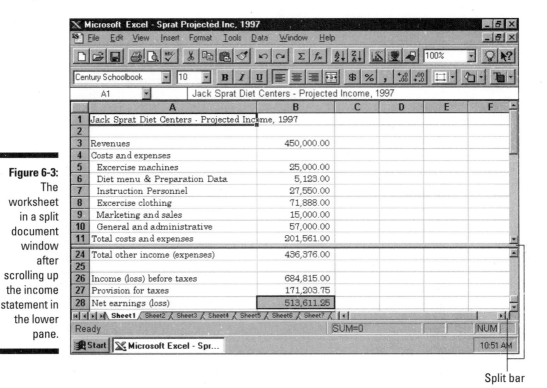

Figure 6-3:
The worksheet in a split document window after scrolling up the income statement in the lower pane.

Split bar

You can also split the document window into two vertical (left and right) panes by following these steps:

1. **Click the split bar located at the right edge of the horizontal scroll bar.**

2. **Drag to the left until you reach the column at which you want the document window divided.**

3. **Release the mouse button.**

   Excel splits the window at that column and adds a second horizontal scroll bar to the new pane.

Don't confuse the tab split bar to the left of the horizontal scroll bar with the horizontal split bar at its right. You drag the tab split bar to increase or decrease the number of sheet tabs displayed at the bottom of the workbook window; you use the horizontal split bar to divide the workbook window into two vertical panes.

Note that you can make the panes in a workbook window disappear by double-clicking anywhere on the split bar that divides the window rather than having to drag the split bar all the way to one of the edges of the window to get rid of it.

Instead of dragging split bars, you can divide a document window with the Split command on the Window menu. When you choose this command, Excel uses the position of the cell pointer to determine where to split the window into panes. The program splits the window vertically at the left edge of the pointer and horizontally along the top edge. If you want the workbook window split into just two horizontal panes, do this: Using the top of the cell pointer as the dividing line, position the cell pointer in the first column of the desired row that is displayed on your screen. If you want the workbook window split into just two vertical windows, do this: Using the left edge of the cell pointer as the dividing line, position the cell pointer in the first row of the desired column that's displayed on your screen.

When the left edge of the cell pointer is right up against the left edge of the workbook window (as it is when the pointer is in any cell in the very first column shown on-screen), the program doesn't split the window vertically — it splits the window horizontally along the top edge of the cell pointer. When the top edge of the pointer is right up against the top edge of the document window (as it is when the pointer is in a cell in the very first row displayed on-screen), the program doesn't split the window horizontally — it splits the window vertically along the left edge of the cell pointer.

If you position the cell pointer somewhere in the midst of the cells displayed on-screen when you choose Split on the Window pull-down menu, Excel splits the window into four panes along the top and left edge of the cell pointer. For example, if you position the cell pointer in cell C6 of the Mother Goose Enterprises 1996 Sales and then select Split from the Window menu, the window splits into four panes: A horizontal split occurs between rows 5 and 6, and a vertical split occurs between columns B and C (as shown in Figure 6-4).

After the window is split into panes, you can move the cell pointer into a particular pane either by clicking one of its cells or by pressing Shift+F6 (which moves the pointer to the last occupied cell or the top-left cell in each pane in the workbook window in a counterclockwise direction). To remove the panes from a window, choose Remove Split from the Window menu.

Fixed Headings Courtesy of Freeze Panes

Window panes are great for viewing different parts of the same worksheet that normally can't be seen together. You can also use window panes to freeze headings in the top rows and first columns so that the headings stay in view at all times, no matter how you scroll through the worksheet. Frozen headings are especially helpful when you work with a table that contains information that extends beyond the rows and columns shown on-screen.

Figure 6-4:
The worksheet window split into four panes with the cell pointer in cell C6.

Figure 6-5 shows just such a table. The client-list worksheet contains many more rows than you can see at one time (unless you decrease the magnification to 25% with Zoom, which makes the data too small to read). As a matter of fact, this worksheet continues down to row 34.

By splitting the document window into two horizontal panes between rows 2 and 3 and then freezing the top pane, you can keep the column headings in row 2 that identify each column of information on the screen as you scroll the worksheet up and down to review information on different employees. If you further split the window into vertical panes between columns B and C, you can keep the case numbers and last names on the screen as you scroll the worksheet left and right.

Figure 6-5 shows the employee roster after splitting the window into four panes and freezing them. To create and freeze these panes, follow these steps:

1. **Position the cell pointer in cell C3.**

2. **Choose Freeze Panes from the Window menu.**

   In this example, Excel freezes the top and left window pane above row 3 and left of column C.

When Excel sets up the frozen panes, the borders of frozen panes are represented by a single line rather than a thin bar, as is the case with unfrozen panes. (To help you see the frozen panes in Figures 6-5 through 6-7, I removed the worksheet gridlines — see Chapter 12 for information about how you can remove the display of gridlines from a particular worksheet in a workbook.)

Figure 6-6 shows what happens when you scroll the worksheet up after freezing the window panes. In this figure, I scrolled the worksheet up so that rows 24 through 34 appear under rows 1 and 2. Because the vertical pane with the worksheet title and column headings is frozen, it remains on-screen. (Normally, rows 1 and 2 would have been the first to disappear as you scrolled the worksheet up.)

Figure 6-7 shows what happens when you scroll the worksheet to the left. In this figure, I scrolled the worksheet so that columns G through L appear after columns A and B. Because the first two columns are frozen, they remain on-screen, helping you identify who belongs to what information.

To unfreeze the window panes in a worksheet, choose Unfreeze Panes from the Window menu. Choosing this command removes the window panes, indicating that Excel has unfrozen them.

Figure 6-5:
Frozen panes to keep the column headings and last names on the screen at all times.

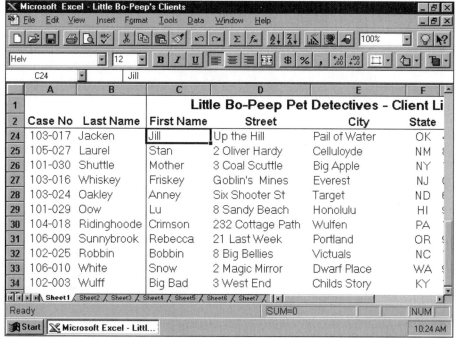

Figure 6-6:
The Bo-Peep clients list scrolled up to display the last rows in the database.

Figure 6-7:
The employee roster scrolled left to display the worksheet columns G through L.

Electronic Sticky Notes

Excel lets you add text notes to particular cells in a worksheet. *Text notes* act kind of like electronic pop-up versions of sticky notes. For example, you can add a note to yourself to verify a particular figure before printing the worksheet or to remind yourself that a particular value is only an estimate (or even to remind yourself that it's your anniversary and to pick up a little something special for your spouse on the way home!).

In addition to using notes to remind yourself of something you've done or that still remains to be done, you can also use a note to mark your current place in a large worksheet. You can then use the note's location to quickly find your starting place the next time you work with that worksheet.

To add a text note to a cell, follow these steps:

1. **Select the cell to which you want to add the note.**

2. **Choose Note on the Insert pull-down menu.**

   The Cell Note dialog box (as shown in Figure 6-8) appears with the insertion point located in the Text Note list box.

3. **Type the text of your note in the Text Note list box.**

   If you want to add notes to more than one cell, click the Add button, select the cell to which you want to add the next note, and type its text.

4. **Choose OK or press Enter when you finish adding notes.**

   Excel marks the location of notes in a cell by adding a tiny square in the upper-right corner of the cell. (This square appears in red on a color monitor.)

5. **To display the note in a cell, position the thick white-cross mouse pointer somewhere in the cell with the note indicator.**

   As long as the mouse pointer remains in the cell, Excel displays the text of the cell note in a little text box in the worksheet display, normally somewhere below the cell.

   ✔ You can always get access to all the notes that you've added to the worksheet by opening the Cell Note dialog box with the Note command on the Insert pull-down menu. All the notes in the worksheet are listed in the order in which they were created in the Notes in Sheet list box to the left.

   To browse through the notes in this dialog box (and, at the same time, select the cells that contain those notes), just click the cell note reference in the Notes in Sheet list box. (Excel displays its cell reference in the Cell edit box and its text in the Text Note list box.)

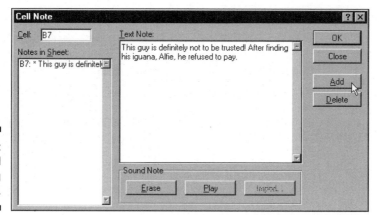

Figure 6-8:
The Cell
Note dialog
box.

✔ To edit the text of a note, click its reference in the Notes in Sheet list box, and then position the insertion point in the text displayed in the Text Note list box and make your editing changes.

✔ To delete a note from the worksheet, click its reference in the Notes in Sheet list box and then choose the Delete button. Next, choose the OK button or press Enter in the alert dialog box that appears to permanently get rid of the cell note.

When you're finished adding, browsing, editing, or deleting notes in the Cell Note dialog box, close the box by clicking the OK button or pressing Enter.

Singing cells (or "Do you hear what I hear?. . .")

If your computer is equipped with a sound card and you have a microphone that attaches to it, you can record sound notes (which are like little audio sticky notes) in cells. Just follow these steps:

1. **Open the Cell Note dialog box by choosing Note on the Insert pull-down menu.**

2. **Click the Record button to open up the Record dialog box where you record the note.**

3. **Click the Record button (the large dot) in the Record dialog box.**

4. **Say your note into the microphone.**

    Actually, you don't have to *say* anything. If you're feeling creative, you can play a few bars on your harmonica, or even whistle the theme from the *Andy Griffith Show.*

5. **Click the Stop button (the square) when you're finished recording the note.**

6. **Click the Play button in the Record dialog box.**

   This replays the note you just recorded so that you can see whether you want to save it. If you do want to save it, go on to step 7; if you don't, go back to step 2.

7. **Choose the OK button to close the Record dialog box and return to the Cell Note dialog box.**

   This adds the sound note to your cell.

In the Notes in Sheet list box of the Cell Note dialog box, Excel indicates that you have a sound note by placing an asterisk after the cell reference. To play a sound note, place your pointer on the note indicator in the cell of the worksheet, or select the sound note from the Notes in Sheet list box and then click the Play button in the Sound Note section of the Cell Note dialog box.

Dancing from note to note

If you used a note as a placeholder and want to go to that cell, first select all the cells in the worksheet that contain notes by pressing Ctrl+Shift+?, and then press Tab to move from annotated cell to annotated cell (you can press Shift+Tab to back up and revisit a previously visited annotated cell).

To remove all notes from the worksheet, first select all the cells with notes by pressing Ctrl+Shift+?, and then choose Clear on the Edit menu and Notes on the cascading menu. To remove the notes from just a particular cell selection (as opposed to all the notes in the worksheet), select the cell range as you would any other, and then choose Clear on the Edit menu followed by Notes on the cascading menu.

When printing a worksheet, you can print the notes along with the selected worksheet data by selecting the Notes check box in the Sheet tab of the Page Setup dialog box. See Chapter 5 for details on choosing what information to print.

The Cell Name Game

By assigning descriptive names to cells and cell ranges, you can go a long way towards keeping on top of the location of important information in a worksheet. Rather than trying to associate random cell coordinates with specific information, you just have to remember a name. And, best of all, after you name a cell or cell range, you can use this name with the Go To feature.

If I only had a name . . .

When assigning range names to a cell or cell range, you need to follow a few guidelines:

- ✔ Range names must begin with a letter of the alphabet, not a number. For example, instead of *96Profit*, use *Profit96*.

- ✔ Range names cannot contain spaces. Instead of a space, use the underscore (Shift+hyphen) to tie the parts of the name together. For example, instead of *Profit 96*, use *Profit_96*.

- ✔ Range names cannot correspond to cell coordinates in the worksheet. For example, you can't name a cell *Q1* because this is a valid cell coordinate. Instead, use something like *Q1_sales*.

To name a cell or cell range in a worksheet:

1. **Select the cell or cell range that you want to name.**

2. **Choose <u>N</u>ame on the <u>I</u>nsert menu; then choose <u>D</u>efine on the cascading menu.**

    Excel opens the Define Name dialog box (see Figure 6-9). The references for the selected cell or cell range appear in the <u>R</u>efers to edit box (including the sheet name followed by the absolute cell references of the range) at the bottom of the dialog box.

3. **Type the name for the selected cell or cell range in the Names in <u>W</u>orkbook edit box.**

    Refer to the bulleted list of cell-name dos and don'ts, earlier in this section.

4. **Choose OK or press Enter.**

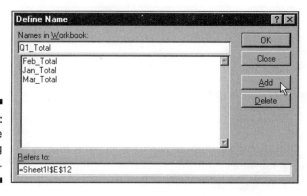

Figure 6-9:
The Define
Name dialog
box.

To select a named cell or range in a worksheet, press F5 or choose <u>G</u>o To on the <u>E</u>dit menu. The Go To dialog box appears (see Figure 6-10). Double-click the desired range name in the <u>G</u>o to list box (alternatively, select the name and choose OK or press Enter). Excel moves the cell pointer directly to the named cell. If you selected a cell range, all the cells in that range are selected.

Figure 6-10:
The Go To
dialog box.

Name that formula!

Cell names are not only a great way to identify and find cells and cell ranges in your spreadsheet but also a great way to make out the purpose of your formulas. For example, say that you have a simple formula in cell K3 that calculates the total due by multiplying the hours you worked for the client (in cell I3) by the client's hourly rate (in cell J3). Normally, this formula would be entered in cell K3 as

```
=I3*J3
```

You cell name dropper!

Instead of going to all the trouble of opening the Go To dialog box and picking out the name of the cell or cell range you want to go to, you can just use the drop-down list box on the formula bar. When you click the drop-down list box to the immediate right of the cell reference on this bar, Excel displays a list of all the cell names in the worksheet. To go to the first cell (select all the other cells, if the name refers to a multicell range), you have only to click the cell name in this list.

Note that, when you select a cell range with this formula bar drop-down list box, the name of the cell range you select on this list temporarily replaces the normal cell reference display on the formula bar.

However, if you assign the name Hours to cell I3 and the name Rate to cell J3, you could then enter the formula as

```
=Hours*Rate
```

in cell K3. I don't think there's anyone who would dispute that the formula =Hours*Rate is much easier to understand than =I3*J3.

To enter a formula using cell names rather than cell references, follow these steps (see Chapter 2 if you need to brush up on how to create formulas):

1. **Name your cells as described earlier in this section.**

   For this example, give the name Hours to cell I3 and the name Rate to cell J3.

2. **Place the cell pointer in the cell where the formula is to appear.**

   For this example, put the cell pointer in cell K3.

3. **Type = (equal sign) to start the formula.**

4. **Select the first cell referenced in the formula by selecting its cell name on the formula bar drop-down list (as described in the previous section).**

   For this example, you select cell I3 by selecting its cell name, Hours, on the drop-down list.

5. **Type the arithmetic operator used in the formula.**

   For this example, you would type * (asterisk) for multiplication (see Chapter 2 for a list of the other arithmetic operators).

6. **Select the second cell referenced in the formula by selecting its cell name on the formula bar drop-down list (as described in the previous section).**

   For this example, you select cell J3 by selecting its cell name, Rate, on the drop-down list.

7. **Click the Enter box or press Enter to complete the formula.**

   In this example, Excel enters the formula =Hours*Rate in cell K3.

Note that you can use the fill handle to copy a formula that uses cell names, rather than cell addresses, to other cells in a column or row that perform the same function (see "Formulas on AutoFill" in Chapter 4). When you copy an original formula that uses names rather than addresses, Excel automatically uses cell addresses in the copies you make, all the time adjusting their cell references as the formula requires (see "Relatively speaking" in Chapter 4).

To figure out what the copied formulas are doing, you just have to position the cell pointer in the cell containing the original formula (usually at the beginning of the row or top of the column) and read its shorthand (=Hours*Rate) on the formula bar.

"Seek and Ye Shall Find . . ."

When all else fails, you can use Excel's Find feature to locate specific information in the worksheet. When you choose Find on the Edit pull-down menu, or press Ctrl+F or Shift+F5, Excel opens the Find dialog box (see Figure 6-11). In the Find What text box, enter the text or values you want to locate and then choose the Find Next button or press Enter to start the search.

When you search for a text entry with the Find feature, be mindful of whether the text or number you enter in the Find What text box is separate in its cell or occurs as part of another word or value. For example, Figure 6-11 shows the characters "ca" in the Find What text box. Because the Find Entire Cells Only check box is not selected, Excel finds

   🖙 the field name *Ca* in *Case No* cell A2,

   🖙 the state code *CA* (for California) in cells F8, F9, and F11,

   🖙 and the *ca* that occurs in *Rebecca* in cell C31.

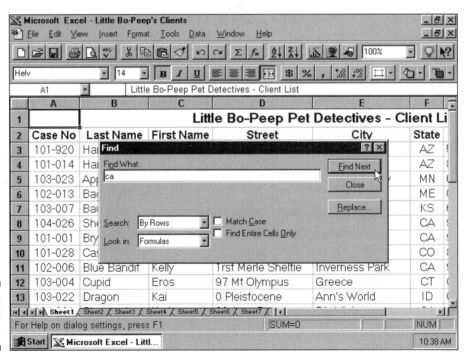

Figure 6-11: The Find dialog box.

If you checked the Find Entire Cells Only check box in the Find dialog box before starting the search, Excel would not consider the *Ca* in *Case No* or the *ca* in *Rebecca* to be a match because both of these cases have other text surrounding the text you are searching for.

When you search for text, you can also specify whether or not you want Excel to match the case you use (upper- or lowercase) when entering the search text in the Find What text box. By default, Excel ignores case differences between text in cells of your worksheet and the search text you enter in the Find What text box. To conduct case-sensitive search, you need to select the Match Case check box.

When you search for values in the worksheet, be mindful of the difference between formulas and values. For example, cell K24 of the Bo-Peep clients list (refer to Figure 6-7) contains the value $15,000. However, if you enter **15000** in the Find What dialog box and press Enter to search for this value, Excel displays an alert box with the following message:

```
Cannot find matching data
```

instead of finding the value 15000 in cell K24. This is because the value in this cell is calculated by the following formula:

```
=I24*J24
```

and nowhere in that formula does the value 15000 show up. To get Excel to find the 15000s displayed in the cells of the worksheet, you need to choose Values in the Look in drop-down list box of the Find dialog box in place of the normally used Formulas option.

If you want to restrict the search to just the text or values in the notes of the worksheet, you need to select the Notes option in this drop-down list box.

If you don't know the exact spelling of the word or name, or the precise value or formula you're searching for, you can use *wildcards,* which are symbols that stand for missing or unknown text. Use the question mark (?) to stand for a single unknown character; use the asterisk (*) to stand for any number of missing characters. Suppose that you enter the following in the Find What text box and choose the Values option in the Look in drop-down list box:

```
7*4
```

Excel stops at cells that contain the values *74, 704,* and *7,5234,* and even finds the text entry *782 4th Street.*

If you actually want to search for an asterisk in the worksheet rather than use the asterisk as a wildcard, precede it with a tilde (~), as follows:

```
~*4
```

This arrangement enables you to search the formulas in the worksheet for one that multiplies by the number 4 (remember that Excel uses the asterisk as the multiplication sign).

The following entry in the Find What text box finds cells that contain *Jan, January, June, Janet,* and so on.

```
J?n*
```

Normally, Excel searches only the current worksheet for the search text you enter. If you want the program to search all of the worksheets in the workbook, you must select all the worksheets prior to entering the search text in the Find dialog box and starting the search. To select all the worksheets in a workbook, you click one of the tabs at the bottom of the document window with the secondary mouse button and choose the Select All Sheets command on the context menu that appears. (See Chapter 7 for more on working with more than one worksheet in a workbook.)

When Excel locates a cell in the worksheet that contains the text or values you're searching for, it selects that cell while at the same time leaving the Find dialog box open (remember that you can move the Find dialog box if it obscures your view of the cell). To search for the next occurrence of the text or value, choose the Find Next button (the simplest way to do this is by pressing Enter).

Excel normally searches down the worksheet by rows. To search across the columns first, choose the By Columns option in the Search drop-down list box. To reverse the search direction and revisit previous occurrences of matching cell entries, press the Shift key as you click the Find Next button in the Find dialog box.

You Can Be Replaced!

If your purpose for finding a cell with a particular entry is so that you can change it, you can automate this process by choosing Replace instead of Find from the Edit menu (Ctrl+H). After entering the text or value you want to replace in the Find What edit box, enter the text or value you want entered as the replacement in the Replace with edit box.

When you enter replacement text, enter it exactly as you want it to appear in the cell. In other words, if you replace all occurrences of *Jan* in the worksheet with *January*, enter the following in the Replace with edit box:

January

Make sure that you use the capital J in the Replace with text box, even though you can enter the following in the Find What text box (providing you don't check the Match Case check box):

jan

After specifying what to replace and what to replace it with, you can have Excel replace occurrences in the worksheet on a case-by-case basis or globally. To replace all occurrences in a single operation, click the Replace All button.

Be careful with global search-and-replace operations; they can really mess up a worksheet in a hurry if you inadvertently replace values, parts of formulas, or characters in titles and headings that you hadn't intended to change. With this in mind, always follow one rule:

> ✔ Never undertake a global search-and-replace operation on an unsaved worksheet.

Also, verify whether or not the Find Entire Cells Only check box is selected before you begin. You can end up with a lot of unwanted replacements if you leave this check box unselected when you really only want to replace entire cell entries (rather than matching parts in cell entries).

If you do make a mess, choose the Undo Replace command on the Edit menu (Ctrl+Z) to restore the worksheet. If you don't discover the problem in time to use Undo, close the messed-up worksheet without saving the changes and open the unreplaced version you saved — thanks to reading the preceding warning!

To see each occurrence before you replace it, choose the Find Next button or press Enter. Excel selects the next cell with the text or value you entered in the Find What text box. To have the program replace the selected text, click the Replace button. To skip this occurrence, click the Find Next button to continue the search. When you finish replacing occurrences, click the Close button to close the Replace dialog box.

You Can Be So Calculating!

Locating information in a worksheet — although admittedly extremely important — is only a part of the story of keeping on top of the information in a worksheet. In really large workbooks that contain many completed worksheets, you may want to switch to manual recalculation so that you can control when the formulas in the worksheet are calculated. You need this kind of control when you find that Excel's recalculation of formulas each time you enter or change information in cells has slowed the program's response to a crawl. By holding off recalculations until you are ready to save or print the workbook, you find that you can work with Excel's worksheets without interminable delays.

To put the workbook on manual recalculation, choose Options on the Tools menu and choose the Calculation tab. Then select the Manual radio button in the Calculation area. When doing this, you probably won't want to remove the check mark from the Recalculate before Save check box below (not generally a very smart idea) so that Excel will still automatically recalculate all formulas before saving the workbook. By keeping this setting active, you are assured of saving only the most up-to-date values.

After switching to manual recalculation, Excel displays the message

`Calculate`

on the status bar whenever you make a change to the worksheet that somehow affects the current values of its formulas. Whenever you see Calculate on the status bar, this is the signal you need to bring the formulas up to date before saving the workbook (as you would before printing its worksheets).

To recalculate the formulas in a workbook when calculation is on manual, you press F9 or Ctrl+= (equal sign) or click the Calc Now (F9) button in the Calculation tab of the Options dialog box.

Excel then recalculates the formulas in all the worksheets in your workbook. If you've only made changes to the current worksheet and don't want to wait around for Excel to recalculate every other worksheet in the workbook, you can restrict the recalculation to the current worksheet by clicking the Calc Sheet button on the Calculation tab of the Options dialog box or pressing Shift+F9.

Putting On the Protection

Once you've more or less finalized a worksheet by checking out its formulas and proofing its text, you often want to guard against any unplanned changes by protecting the document.

Each cell in the worksheet can be *locked* or *unlocked*. By default, Excel locks all the cells in a worksheet so that, when you follow these steps, Excel locks the whole thing up tighter than a drum.

1. Choose Protection from the Tools menu.

2. Choose Protect Sheet on the cascading menu.

If you want to go a step further and lock all the cells in every worksheet in the workbook, choose the Protect Workbook command instead.

3. Choose OK or press Enter.

Selecting the Protect Sheet command makes it impossible to make further changes to the contents of any of the locked cells in that worksheet. Selecting the Protect Workbook command makes it impossible to make further changes to the contents of any locked cells in any worksheet in that workbook. However, because Excel automatically assigns a "locked" status to every single cell in every worksheet in every workbook, selecting the Protect Sheet or the Protect Workbook command is tantamount to protecting every single solitary cell in the whole darn worksheet (or workbook).

Excel displays an alert dialog box with the following message when you try to edit or replace an entry in a locked cell:

```
Locked cells cannot be changed
```

Usually, your intention in protecting a worksheet or an entire workbook is not to prevent *all* changes but to prevent changes in certain areas of the worksheet. For example, in a budget worksheet, you may want to protect all the cells that contain headings and formulas but allow changes in all the cells where you enter the budgeted amounts. That way, you can't inadvertently wipe out a title or formula in the worksheet simply by entering a value in the wrong column or row (not an uncommon occurrence).

To leave certain cells unlocked so that you can still change them after protecting the worksheet or workbook, follow these steps before you choose the Protect Sheet or the Protect Workbook command on the Protection cascading menu:

1. Select the cells you want to still be able to change after turning on the worksheet or workbook protection.

2. Open the Format Cells dialog box by choosing Cells on the Format menu (Ctrl+1); then choose the Protection tab.

3. Remove the check mark from the Locked check box in the Protection tab of the Format Cells dialog box; then choose OK or press Enter.

4. Turn on protection in the worksheet or workbook by choosing Protection on the Tools menu and then selecting either the Protect Sheet or the Protect Workbook command on the cascading menu and choosing OK or pressing Enter.

To remove protection from the current worksheet or workbook document so that you can once again make changes to its cells (be they locked or unlocked), choose Protection on the Tools menu and then select either the Unprotect Sheet or the Unprotect Workbook command on the cascading menu.

To make it impossible to remove protection from a document unless you know the password, enter a password in the Password (optional) text box of the Protect Sheet or Protect Workbook dialog box. Excel masks each character you enter with a tiny asterisk while you enter the password. After you choose OK, Excel makes you re-enter the password in the Confirm Password dialog box before protecting the sheet or workbook. If the password you re-enter is not identical to the first one, you get an alert box and must start the password-protecting business all over again.

Once you do get your password confirmed and put on the sheet or workbook protection, from then on, you can remove its protection only if you can reproduce the password exactly as you assigned it (including any case differences). Be very careful with passwords. If you forget the password, you cannot ever again change any locked cells and you cannot unlock any more cells in the worksheet.

Chapter 7

Maintaining Multiple Worksheets

· ·

In This Chapter

▶ Moving from sheet to sheet in your workbook

▶ Adding even more sheets to a workbook

▶ Deleting sheets from a workbook

▶ Selecting a bunch of sheets for editing as a group

▶ Naming sheet tabs something else besides Sheet1, Sheet2, and so on

▶ Putting the sheets in a different order in a workbook

▶ Displaying parts of different sheets on the same screen

▶ Copying or moving sheets from one workbook to another

▶ Creating formulas that refer to values on different worksheets in a workbook

· ·

*W*hen you're brand new to spreadsheets, you have enough trouble keeping track of a single worksheet — let alone 16 worksheets — and the very thought of working with more than one is a little more than you can take. However, as soon as you get a little experience under your belt, you find that working with more than one worksheet in a workbook is no more taxing than working with just a single worksheet.

Don't confuse the term "workbook" with "worksheet." The workbook forms the document (file) that you open and save as you work. Each workbook (file) normally contains 16 blank worksheets. These worksheets are like the loose-leaf pages in a notebook binder from which you can delete or add to as you need. To help you keep track of the worksheets in your workbook and navigate between them, Excel provides sheet tabs (Sheet1 through Sheet16) that are kinda like tab dividers in a loose-leaf notebook.

Juggling Worksheets

You need to see *how* to work with more than one worksheet in a workbook, but it's also important to know *why* you'd want to do such a crazy thing in the first place. The most common situation is, of course, when you have a bunch of worksheets that are somehow related to each other and, therefore, naturally belong together in the same workbook. For example, take the case of Mother Goose Enterprises with its different companies: Jack Sprat Diet Centers; Jack and Jill Trauma Centers; Mother Hubbard Dog Goodies; Rub-a-Dub-Dub Hot Tubs and Spas; Georgie Porgie Pudding Pies; Hickory, Dickory, & Dock Clock Repair; Little Bo-Peep Pet Detectives; Simple Simon Pie Shoppes; and Jack Be Nimble Candlesticks. To keep track of the annual sales for all these companies, you could create a workbook containing a worksheet for each of the nine different companies.

By keeping the sales figures for each company in a different sheet of the same workbook, you gain all of the following benefits:

- ✔ You can enter the stuff that's needed in all the sales worksheets (if their sheet tabs are selected) just by typing it once into the first worksheet (see "Editing en masse," later in this chapter).

- ✔ In order to help you build the worksheet for the first company's sales, you can attach *macros* to the current workbook so that they are readily available when you create the worksheets for the other companies (see Chapter 12 for details on recording macros in the current workbook).

- ✔ You can quickly compare the sales of one company to the sales of another (see "Opening Windows on Your Worksheets," later in this chapter).

- ✔ You can print all of the sales information for each store as a single report in one printing operation. (See Chapter 5 for specifics on printing an entire workbook or particular worksheets in a workbook.)

- ✔ You can easily create charts that compare certain sales data from different worksheets (see Chapter 8 for details).

- ✔ You can easily set up a summary worksheet with formulas that total the quarterly and annual sales for all nine companies (see "Worksheets that 'Cut to the Chase,'" later in this chapter).

Sliding between the sheets

Each workbook that you create contains 16 worksheets, rather predictably named Sheet1 through Sheet16. In typical Excel fashion, these names appear on tabs at the bottom of the workbook window. To go from one worksheet to another, you simply click the tab that contains the name of the sheet you want to see. Excel then brings that worksheet to the top of the stack, displaying its information in the current workbook window. You can always tell which worksheet is current because its name is displayed in bold type on the tab and its tab appears without any dividing line as an extension of the current worksheet.

The only problem with moving to a new sheet by clicking on its sheet tab occurs when the sheet tab you want to click is not visible in the workbook (because not all 16 sheet tabs are ever visible at any one time). To deal with this problem, Excel provides tab scrolling buttons (see Figure 7-1) that you can use to bring new sheet tabs into view.

✔ Click the tab scroll button with the triangle pointing right to bring the next unseen tab of the sheet on the right into view.

✔ Click the tab scroll button with the triangle pointing left to bring the next unseen tab of the sheet on the left into view.

✔ Click the tab scroll button with the triangle pointing right to the vertical bar to bring the last group of sheet tabs, including the very last tab into view.

✔ Click the tab scroll button with the triangle pointing left to the vertical bar to bring the first group of sheet tabs, including the very first tab into view.

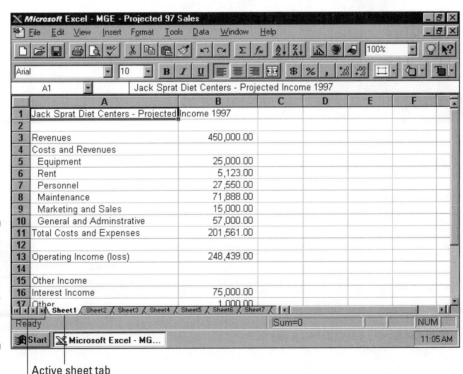

Figure 7-1:
Use the tab
scrolling
buttons to
bring new
sheet tabs
into view.

Active sheet tab

Tab scrolling buttons

Just don't forget that scrolling the sheet tab you want into view is not the same thing as *selecting* it: You still need to click the tab for the desired sheet to bring it to front of the stack.

To make it easier to find the sheet tab you want to select without having to do an inordinate amount of tab scrolling, you can drag the tab split bar (see Figure 7-2) to the right to reveal more sheet tabs (consequently making the horizontal scroll bar shorter). If you don't care at all about using the horizontal scroll bar, you can maximize the number of sheet tabs in view by actually getting rid of this scroll bar. To do this, you drag the tab split bar to the right until it's right up against the vertical split bar, which gives you a view of about 12 sheet tabs at a time (on a standard 14-inch monitor in a resolution of 640 × 480 pixels).

When you decide that you then want to restore the horizontal scroll bar to its normal length, you can either manually drag the tab split bar to the left or simply double-click it.

Figure 7-2:
Use the tab
split box to
display
more sheet
tabs by
making the
horizontal
scroll
bar shorter.

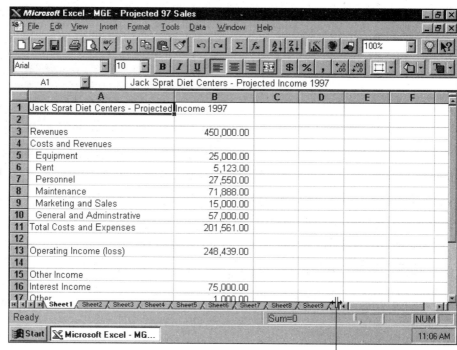

Tab split bar

Going sheet to sheet via the keyboard

You can forget all about the darned tab scrolling buttons and sheet tabs and just go back and forth through the sheets in a workbook with the keyboard. To move to the next worksheet in a workbook, press Ctrl+PgDn. To move to the previous worksheet in a workbook, press Ctrl+PgUp. The nice thing about Ctrl+PgDn and Ctrl+PgUp is that these keystroke shortcuts work whether or not the next or previous sheet tab is currently displayed in the workbook window!

Editing en masse

Each time you click a sheet tab, you select that worksheet and make it active, enabling you to make whatever changes are necessary to its cells. There are times, however, when you want to select bunches of worksheets so that you can make the same editing changes to all of them simultaneously. When multiple worksheets are selected, any editing change you make to the current worksheet, such as entering information in cells or deleting stuff from them, affects the same cells in all of the selected sheets in exactly the same way.

In other words, say you needed to set up three worksheets in a new workbook, all of which contain the names of the twelve months in row 3 starting in column B. Prior to entering January in cell B3 and then using the AutoFill handle to fill in the rest of the 11 months across row 3, you would select all three worksheets (say Sheet1, Sheet2, and Sheet3 for argument's sake). That way, Excel would insert the names of the twelve months in row 3 of all three selected worksheets just by your entering them once in the third row of the first sheet (pretty slick, huh?).

Likewise, say you have another workbook where you need to get rid of Sheet2, Sheet5, and Sheet9. Instead of clicking on Sheet2, selecting Delete Sheet on the Edit menu, and then clicking on Sheet5 and repeating the Delete Sheet command, and finally clicking on Sheet9 and repeating the command yet again, you can select all three worksheets and then zap them out of existence in one fell swoop with a single selection of the Delete Sheet command.

To select a bunch of worksheets in a workbook, you have the following choices:

- To select a group of neighboring worksheets, click the first sheet tab and then scroll the sheet tabs until you see the tab of the last worksheet you want to select. Hold the Shift key as you click the last sheet tab to select all of the tabs in between — the old shift-click method applied to worksheet tabs.

- To select a group of non-neighboring worksheets, click the first sheet tab and then hold down the Ctrl key as you click the tabs of the other sheets to be selected.

Excel shows you which worksheets are selected by turning their sheet tabs white (although only the active sheet's tab name appears in bold).

To deselect the group of worksheets when you've finished your "group editing," you simply click a nonselected (that is, gray) worksheet tab. You can also deselect all the selected worksheets by choosing the Ungroup Sheets command on any tab's shortcut menu.

Don't Short-Sheet Me!

For some of you, the 16 worksheets automatically put into each new workbook that you start are far more than you would ever, ever need (or want) to use. For others of you, a measly 16 worksheets might seldom, if ever, be sufficient for the workbooks you create (for instance, say your company operates in 20 locations, or you routinely create budgets for 30 different departments or track expenses for 40 account representatives).

Excel makes it easy to insert additional worksheets in a workbook or remove those that you don't need. To insert a new worksheet in the workbook, follow these steps:

1. **Select the tab of the sheet where you want Excel to insert the new worksheet.**

2. **Choose <u>W</u>orksheet on the <u>I</u>nsert menu or choose Insert on the tab's shortcut menu.**

3. **Choose OK in the Insert dialog box or press Enter (because Worksheet is already selected in the list box on the General tab as the type of sheet to insert).**

If you want to assign an Excel template to the new worksheet, choose the Spreadsheet Solutions tab in the Insert dialog box and then click the template to use before you choose OK (see Chapter 10 for more on using Excel templates).

To insert a bunch of new worksheets in a row in the workbook, select a group with the same number of tabs as the number of new worksheets you want to add, starting with the tab where the new worksheets are to be inserted. Next, choose <u>W</u>orksheet on the <u>I</u>nsert menu or choose Insert on the tab's shortcut menu. Finally, choose OK in the Insert dialog box or press Enter.

To delete a worksheet from the workbook

1. **Click the tab of the worksheet you want to delete.**

2. **Choose Delete Sheet on the Edit menu or choose Delete on the tab's shortcut menu.**

   Excel then displays a scary message in an alert box about how you're going to permanently delete the selected sheets.

3. **Go ahead and select the OK button or press Enter if you're really sure that you want to zap the entire sheet.**

   Just keep in mind that this is one of those situations where Undo is powerless to put things right by restoring the deleted sheet to the workbook.

To delete a bunch of worksheets from the workbook, select all the worksheets you want to delete and choose Delete Sheet on the Edit menu or choose Delete on the tab's shortcut menu. Then, if you're sure that none of the worksheets will be missed, choose OK or press Enter when the alert dialog box appears.

If you find that you're constantly having to monkey around with the number of worksheets in a workbook, either by adding new worksheets or deleting a bunch, you might want to think about changing the default number of worksheets in a workbook. To change the magic number of 16 sheets to a more realistic number for your needs, open the Options dialog box, choose the General tab, and enter a new number in the Sheets in New Workbook text box or select a new number with the spinner buttons.

A sheet by any other name . . .

Let's be honest: The sheet names that Excel comes up with for the tabs in a workbook (Sheet1 through Sheet16) are, to put it mildly, not very original — and are certainly not descriptive of their function in life! Luckily, you can easily rename a worksheet tab to whatever helps you remember what you put on the worksheet (provided that this descriptive name is no longer than 31 characters).

To rename a worksheet tab, just follow these steps:

1. **Double-click the sheet tab with the primary mouse button or choose the Rename command on the sheet tab's context menu (opened by clicking on it with the secondary mouse button).**

   This opens the Rename Sheet dialog box (similar to the one shown in Figure 7-3).

2. **Replace the current name in the Name text box with a name of your own creation.**

3. **Choose OK or press Enter.**

   Excel displays the new sheet name on its tab at the bottom of the workbook window. Figure 7-4 shows you the result of renaming Sheet1 to Sprat Diet Ctr. (for Jack Sprat Diet Centers) with the Rename Sheet dialog box.

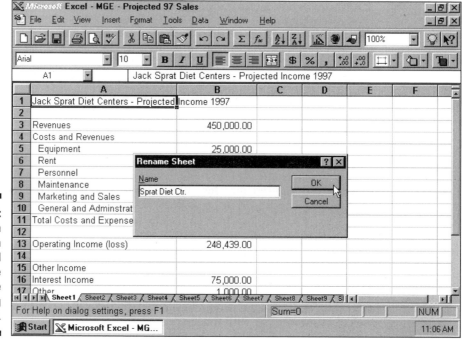

Figure 7-3:
Giving a
sheet tab a
civilized
name in the
Rename
Sheet dialog
box.

Figure 7-4:
The
workbook
after
changing
the generic
sheet name,
Sheet1, to
the more
descriptive
Sprat Diet
Ctr.

Short and sweet (sheet names)

Although Excel allows up to 31 characters (including spaces) for a sheet name, you're gonna want to keep your sheet names much briefer for two reasons:

✔ First, the longer the name, the longer the sheet tab. And the longer the sheet tab, the fewer tabs that can be displayed. And the fewer the tabs, the more tab scrolling you'll have to do to select the sheets you want to work with.

✔ Second, should you start creating formulas that use cells in different worksheets (see "To Sum Up . . .," later in this chapter, for an example of this), Excel uses the sheet name as part of the cell reference in the formula (how else could Excel keep straight the value in cell C1 on Sheet1 from the value in cell C1 on Sheet2!). Therefore, if your sheet names are long, you'll end up with unwieldy formulas in the cells and on the formula bar even when you're dealing with simple formulas that only refer to cells in a couple of different worksheets.

So remember: as a general rule, the fewer characters in a sheet name, the better.

Getting your sheets in order

Sometimes, you may find that you need to change the order in which the sheets appear in the workbook. Excel makes this possible by letting you drag the tab of the sheet you want to arrange in the workbook to the place where it should be inserted. As you drag the tab, the pointer changes to a sheet icon with an arrowhead on it, and the program marks your progress among the sheet tabs (see Figures 7-5 and 7-6 for example). When you release the mouse button, Excel reorders the worksheets in the workbook by inserting the sheet at the place where you dropped the tab off.

If you hold down the Ctrl key as you drag the tab, Excel inserts a *copy* of the worksheet at the place where you release the mouse button. You can tell that Excel is copying the sheet, rather than just moving it in the workbook, because the pointer shows a plus on the sheet icon containing the arrowhead. When you release the mouse button, Excel inserts the copy in the workbook, which is designated by the addition of (2) after the tab name. For instance, if you copy Sheet5 to another place in the workbook, the sheet tab of the copy is named Sheet5 (2). You can then rename the tab to something civilized (see "A sheet by any other name . . .," earlier in this chapter, for details).

Figure 7-5:
Reordering
the sheets in
the MGE —
Projected
1997 Sales
workbook
by dragging
the Total
Income
Sheet tab to
the front.

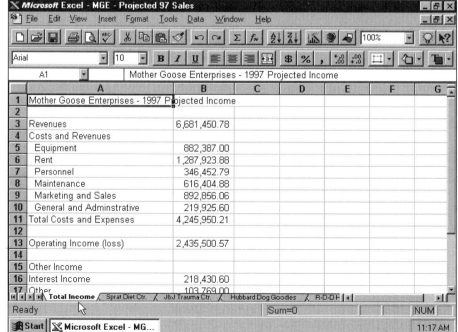

Figure 7-6:
The
workbook
after moving
the Total
Income
sheet to
the front.

Opening Windows on Your Worksheets

Just as you can split up a single worksheet into window panes so that you can view and compare different parts of that same sheet on the screen (see Chapter 6), you can split up a single workbook into worksheet windows and then arrange the windows so that you can view different parts of each worksheet on the screen.

To open up the worksheets that you want to compare in different windows, you simply insert new workbook windows (in addition to the one that Excel automatically opens when you open the workbook file itself) and then select the worksheet that you want displayed in the new window. You can accomplish this with the following steps:

1. **Choose the New Window command on the Window menu to create a second worksheet window; then click the tab of the worksheet that you want displayed in this second window (indicated by the :2 added on to the end of the filename in the title bar).**

2. **Choose the New Window command on the Window menu to create a third worksheet window; then click the tab of the worksheet that you want displayed in this third window (indicated by the :3 added on to the end of the filename in the title bar).**

3. **Continue in this manner, using the New Window command to a create a new window and then selecting the tab of the worksheet to be displayed in that window for each worksheet that you want to compare.**

4. **Choose the Arrange command on the Window menu and select one of the Arrange options (as described below); then choose OK or press Enter.**

When you open the Arrange Windows dialog box, you are presented with the following options:

✔ **The Tiled radio button:** to have Excel arrange and size the windows so that they all fit side by side on the screen in the order in which they were opened. (Figure 7-7 shows the screen after choosing the Windows of Active Workbook check box and choosing the Tiled radio button, when three worksheet windows are open.)

✔ **The Horizontal radio button:** to have Excel size the windows equally and then place them one above the other. (Figure 7-8 shows the screen after choosing the Windows of Active Workbook check box and choosing the Horizontal radio button, when three worksheet windows are open.)

Figure 7-7: Worksheet windows after arranging them with the Tiled radio button.

Figure 7-8: Worksheet windows after arranging them with the Horizontal radio button.

✔ **The Vertical radio button:** to have Excel size the windows equally and then place them next to each other. (Figure 7-9 shows the screen after choosing the Windows of Active Workbook check box and choosing the Vertical radio button, when three worksheet windows are open.)

✔ **The Cascade radio button:** to have Excel arrange and size the windows so that they overlap one another with only their title bars showing. (Figure 7-10 shows the screen after choosing the Windows of Active Workbook check box and choosing the Cascade radio button, when three worksheet windows are open).

✔ **The Windows of Active Workbook check box:** to have Excel show only the windows that you've opened in the current workbook (otherwise, the program will also display all the windows in any other workbooks you have open — yes, it is possible to open more than one workbook as well as more than one window within each open workbook, provided that your computer has enough memory and you have enough stamina to keep track of all that information).

Once the windows are placed in one arrangement or another, you can activate the one you want to use (if it's not already selected) by clicking it (in the case of the cascade arrangement, you need to click the window's title bar).

Figure 7-9:
Worksheet
windows
after
arranging
them with
the Vertical
radio button.

Figure 7-10:
Worksheet
windows
after
arranging
them with
the Cascade
radio button.

When you click a worksheet window that's been tiled or placed in the horizontal or vertical arrangement, Excel indicates that the window's selected by highlighting its title bar and adding scroll bars to the window. When you click the title bar of a worksheet window that's been placed in the cascade arrangement, the program displays the window on the top of the stack as well as highlighting its title bar and adding scroll bars.

You can temporarily zoom the window up to full size by clicking the Maximize button on the window's title bar. When you finish the work you need to do in the full-size worksheet window, return it to its previous arrangement by clicking the window's Restore button.

To select the next tiled, horizontal, or vertical window on the screen or display the next window in a cascade arrangement with the keyboard, press Ctrl+F6. To select the previous tiled, horizontal, or vertical window or display the previous window in a cascade arrangement, press Ctrl+Shift+F6. Note that these keystrokes work to select the next and previous worksheet window even when the windows are maximized in the Excel program window.

If you close one of the windows you've arranged by double-clicking on its Control-menu button, choosing Close on its Control menu, or pressing Ctrl+W, Excel does not automatically resize the other open windows to fill in the gap. Likewise, if you create another window with the New Window command, Excel does not automatically arrange it in with the others (in fact, the new window just sits on top of the other open windows).

To fill in the gap created by closing a window or to integrate a newly opened window into the current arrangement, open the Arrange Windows dialog box and click the OK button or press Enter. (The same radio button you clicked last time is still selected; if you want to choose a new arrangement, click the new radio button before you click OK.)

Don't try to close a particular worksheet window with the Close command on the File menu because you'll only succeed in closing the entire workbook file, while at the same time getting rid of all the worksheet windows you've created.

When you save your workbook, Excel saves the current window-arrangement as part of the file along with all the rest of the changes. If you don't want the current window arrangement saved, close all but one of the windows (by double-clicking their Control-menu buttons or selecting their windows and then pressing Ctrl+W); then click that last window's Maximize button and select the tab of the worksheet that you want displayed the next time you open the workbook before saving the file.

Passing Sheets in the Night

In some situations, you need to move a particular worksheet or copy it from one workbook to another. To move or copy worksheets between workbooks, you follow these steps:

1. **Open both the workbook with the worksheet(s) you want to move or copy and the workbook that is to contain the moved or copied worksheet(s).**

   Use the Open tool on the Standard toolbar or select the Open command from the File menu (Ctrl+O) to open the workbooks.

2. **Select the workbook that contains the worksheet(s) that you want to move or copy.**

   To select the workbook with the sheet(s) to be moved or copied, choose its name on the Window pull-down menu.

3. **Select the worksheet(s) you want to move or copy.**

   To select a single worksheet, click its sheet tab. To select a group of neighboring sheets, click the first tab, and then hold down Shift as you click the last tab. To select various nonadjacent sheets, click the first tab and then hold Ctrl as you click each of the other sheet tabs.

4. **Choose the Move or Copy Sheet command on the Edit menu or choose the Move or Copy command on a tab's shortcut menu.**

   Excel opens up the Move or Copy dialog box (similar to the one shown in Figure 7-11) in which you indicate whether you want to move or copy the selected sheet(s) and where to move or copy them to.

5. **Select, in the To Book drop-down list box, the name of the workbook you want to copy or move the worksheets to.**

   If you want to move or copy the selected worksheet(s) to a new workbook rather than an existing one that you have open, choose the (new book) option that appears at the very top of the To Book drop-down list box.

6. **In the Before Sheet list box, select the name of the sheet that the worksheet(s) you're about to move or copy should precede.**

7. **Choose the Create a Copy check box to copy the selected worksheet(s) to the designated workbook (rather than move them).**

8. **Choose the OK button or press Enter to complete the move or copy operation.**

Figure 7-11:
The Move or Copy dialog box where you select the workbook to move or copy the selected sheets to.

Move or Copy	? X
Move Selected Sheets	
To Book:	OK
Mother Goose - 1996 Sales Expan▾	Cancel
Before Sheet:	
Sheet1	
Sheet2	
Sheet3	
Sheet4	
Sheet5	
Sheet6	
☐ Create a Copy	

If you prefer a more direct approach, you can move or copy sheets between open workbooks by dragging their sheet tabs from one workbook window to another. Note that this method works with a bunch of sheets as well as with a single sheet; just be sure that you've selected all their sheet tabs before you begin the drag-and-drop procedure.

To drag a worksheet from one workbook to another, you must open both workbooks and then use the Arrange command in the Window menu and select an arrangement (such as Horizontal or Vertical to put the workbook windows either on top of each other or side by side). Before you close the Arrange Windows dialog box, be sure that the Windows of Active Workbook check box does *not* contain a check mark.

After arranging the workbook windows, drag the worksheet tab from one workbook to another. If you want to copy rather than move the worksheet, hold down the Ctrl key as you drag the sheet icon(s). To locate the worksheet in the new workbook, position the downward pointing triangle that moves with the sheet icon in front of the worksheet tab where it's to be inserted and then release the mouse button.

Figures 7-12 and 7-13 illustrate how easy it is to move or copy a worksheet from one workbook to another using this drag-and-drop method.

Figure 7-12: Copying the Sprat Diet Ctr. and J&J Trauma Ctr. worksheets to the Mother Goose - 1996 Sales workbook via drag-and-drop.

In Figure 7-12, you see two workbook windows: the Mother Goose - 1996 Sales Expanded workbook in the left pane and the MGE - Projected 1997 Sales workbook in the right pane (arranged with the Tiled option in the Arrange Windows dialog box). To copy the Sprat Diet Ctr. and the J&J Trauma Ctr. sheets from the Mother Goose - 1996 Sales Expanded workbook to MGE - Projected 1997 Sales workbook, you simply select both the Sprat Diet Ctr. and J&J Trauma Ctr. tabs and then hold down the Ctrl key as you click the Sprat Diet Ctr. tab and drag the sheet icons to their new position right before Sheet2 of the Mother Goose - 1996 Sales Expanded workbook.

Figure 7-13 shows the workbooks after releasing the mouse button. As you can see, Excel inserts the copy of the Sprat Diet Ctr. and the J&J Trauma Ctr. worksheets into the Mother Goose - 1996 Sales Expanded workbook at the place indicated by triangle that accompanies the sheet icon (in between Sheet1 and Sheet2 in this example).

Figure 7-13: The screen after inserting a copy of the Sprat Diet Ctr. and J&J Trauma Ctr. worksheets in between Sheet1 and Sheet2 of the Mother Goose 1996 Sales workbook.

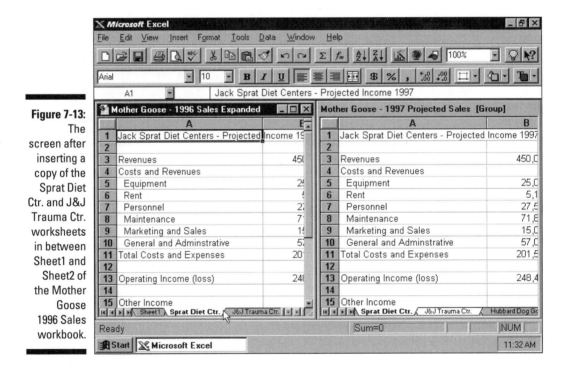

To Sum Up . . .

I now want to introduce you to the fascinating subject of creating a *summary worksheet* that recaps or totals the values stored in a bunch of other worksheets in the workbook.

The best way that I can show you how to create a summary worksheet is to walk you through the procedure of making one (entitled Total Income) for the MGE - Projected 1997 Sales workbook, which totals the projected revenue and expenses for all of the companies owned by Mother Goose Enterprises.

Because the MGE Projected 1997 Sales workbook already contains nine worksheets, each with the 1997 projected revenue and expenses for these companies, and these worksheets are all laid out in the same arrangement, creating this summary worksheet will be a breeze:

1. **I start by inserting a new worksheet in front of the other worksheets in the MGE - Projected 1997 Sales workbook and renaming its sheet tab from Sheet1 to Total Income.**

   To find out how to insert a new worksheet, refer back to "Don't Short-Sheet Me." To find out how to rename a sheet tab, refer back to "A sheet by any other name. . . ."

2. **Next, I enter the worksheet title "Mother Goose Enterprises - 1997 Projected Income" in cell A1.**

   Do this by selecting cell A1 and then typing the text.

3. **Finally, I copy the rest of the row headings for column A (containing the revenue and expense descriptions) from the Sprat Diet Ctr. worksheet to the Total Income worksheet.**

   To do this, select cell A3 in the Total Income sheet; then click the Sprat Diet Ctr. tab and select the cell range A3:A22 in this sheet before pressing Ctrl+C, clicking the Total Income tab again and pressing Enter.

Now, after widening column A to accommodate the copied row headings, I am ready to create the "master" SUM formula that totals the revenues of all nine companies in cell B3 of the Total Income sheet:

1. **I start by clicking cell B3 and then clicking the Sum tool on the Standard toolbar.**

   Excel then puts =SUM( ) in the cell with the insertion point placed between the two parentheses.

2. **Then I click the Sprat Diet Ctr. sheet tab and then its cell B3 to select the projected revenues for the Jack Sprat Diet Centers.**

   The formula bar now reads =SUM('Sprat Diet Ctr.'!B3) after selecting this cell.

3. **Next I type , (the comma starts a new argument) and then click the J&J Trauma Ctr. sheet tab followed by clicking its cell (B3) to select projected revenues for the Jack and Jill Trauma Centers.**

   The formula bar now reads =SUM('Sprat Diet Ctr.'!B3,'J&J Trauma Ctr.'!B3) after selecting this cell.

4. **I then continue on in this manner, typing a comma and then selecting cell B3 with the projected revenues for all of the other companies in the following seven sheets.**

   At the end of this procedure, the formula bar now appears with the whopping SUM formula shown on the formula bar in Figure 7-14.

5. **To complete the SUM formula in cell B3 of the Total Income worksheet, I then click the Enter box in the formula bar (I could press the Enter key as well).**

   Figure 7-14 shows you the result after using AutoFit to widen column B. As you can see in the formula bar, the master SUM formula that returns 6,681,450.78 to cell B3 of the Total Sales worksheets gets its result by summing the values in B3 in all nine of the supporting worksheets.

All that's left to do now is to use AutoFill to copy the master formula in cell B3 down to row 22 as follows:

1. **With cell B3 still selected, I drag the AutoFill handle in the lower-right corner of cell B3 down to cell B22 to copy the formula for summing the values for the nine companies down this column.**

2. **Then I delete the SUM formulas from cells B4, B12, B14, B15, and B19 (all of which contain zeros because these cells have no income or expenses to be totaled).**

In Figure 7-15, you see the first section of the final summary projected income worksheet after copying the formula created in cell B3 and deleting the formulas from the cells that should be blank (all those that came up 0 in column B).

Although this Total Income summary worksheet looks like it was a lot of work to create at first glance, it really was quite simple to put together. And the best part is that, because the values in the summary worksheet are tied by formula to the values entered in the income statement worksheet for each company, any update or correction made to these figures will be automatically reflected in the summary values in the Total Income sheet, giving you 100 percent accuracy in your totals without requiring any extra work on your part!

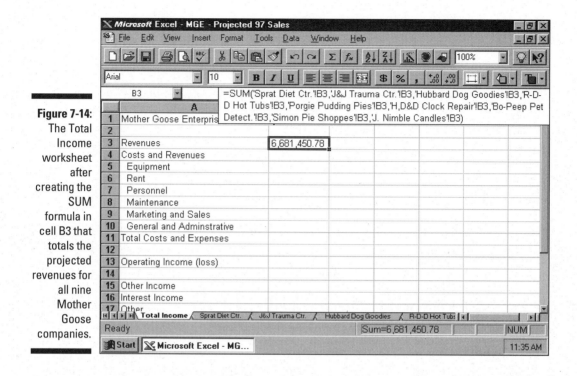

Figure 7-14: The Total Income worksheet after creating the SUM formula in cell B3 that totals the projected revenues for all nine Mother Goose companies.

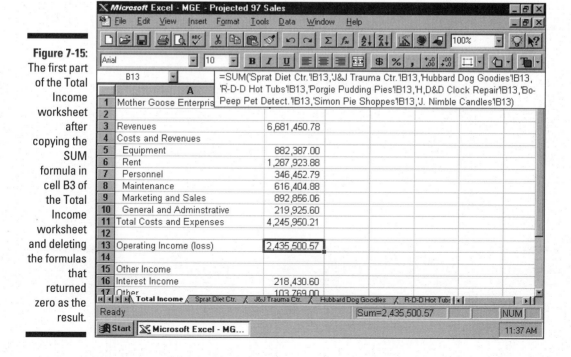

Figure 7-15: The first part of the Total Income worksheet after copying the SUM formula in cell B3 of the Total Income worksheet and deleting the formulas that returned zero as the result.

Part IV
Life beyond the Spreadsheet

The 5th Wave   **By Rich Tennant**

Bob, the laser printer repairman, finds an idle moment that costs him his sideburns.

TECHNICALLY, YOU SHOULD BE ABLE TO LIGHT YOUR CIGARETTE ON THIS THING PRETTY EASY.

In this part . . .

Don't let anybody kid you: Spreadsheets are the bread and butter of Excel for Windows 95. And for many of you, creating, editing, and printing spreadsheets is the be-all and end-all of Excel and "who could ask for anything more?" But don't get the wrong impression. Just because Excel is a wiz at spreadsheets doesn't mean that it's a one-trick pony, and just because spreadsheets may be the only thing that you churn out in your present job doesn't mean that someday you won't be moving into a job where you need to chart spreadsheet data and, who knows, even create and maintain Excel databases.

Part IV is here just in case you need to stray beyond the confines of the spreadsheet into such exotic areas as creating charts and adding graphic images or creating, sorting, and filtering databases. Between the entertaining information in Chapter 8 about making charts and the fact-filled information in Chapter 9 on working with Excel databases, you'll be more than ready should the day arise (or already be here) when you are forced to go beyond the pale of the good old Excel spreadsheet.

Chapter 8

The Simple Art of Making Charts

....

In This Chapter

▶ Creating great looking charts with the ChartWizard

▶ Changing the type of chart with the Chart toolbar

▶ Adding and formatting chart titles

▶ Creating charts on separate Chart sheets

▶ Adding a text box and arrow to a chart

▶ Formatting the chart's axes

▶ Changing the orientation of a 3-D chart

▶ Using the drawing tools to add graphics to charts and worksheets

▶ Using the Data Map feature to graphically analyze data by geographical region

▶ Printing a chart without printing the rest of the worksheet data

....

*A*s Confucius said, "A picture's worth a thousand words" (or, in our case, numbers). By adding charts to worksheets, you not only heighten interest in the otherwise boring numbers but also illustrate trends and anomalies that might not be apparent from just looking at the values alone. Because Excel makes it so easy to chart the numbers in a worksheet, you can also experiment with different types of charts until you find the one that best represents the data — in other words, the picture that best tells the particular story.

Just a word about charts before you find out how to make them in Excel. Remember your high-school algebra teacher valiantly trying to teach you how to graph equations by plotting different values on an x-axis and a y-axis on graph paper? Of course, you were probably too busy with more important things like cool cars and rock n' roll to pay too much attention to an old algebra teacher. Besides, you probably told yourself, "I'll never need this junk when I'm out on my own and get a job!"

Well, see, you just never know. It turns out that, even though Excel automates almost the entire process of charting worksheet data, you may need to be able to tell the x-axis from the y-axis, just in case Excel doesn't draw the chart the way you had in mind. To refresh your memory, the x-axis is the horizontal axis, usually located along the bottom of the chart; the y-axis is the vertical one, usually located on the left side of the chart.

In most charts that use these two axes, Excel plots the categories along the x-axis at the bottom and their relative values along the y-axis on the left. The x-axis is sometimes referred to as the *time axis* because the chart often depicts values along this axis at different time periods such as months, quarters, years, and so on.

Conjuring Up Charts with the ChartWizard

Well, that's enough background on charts. Now let's get on with the charting itself. Excel makes the process of creating a new chart in a worksheet as painless as possible with the ChartWizard. The ChartWizard walks you through a five-step procedure, at the end of which you have a complete and beautiful new chart.

Before you start the ChartWizard, first select the cell range that contains the information that you want charted. Keep in mind that, to end up with the chart you want, the information should be entered in standard table format. With the information in this format, you can select it all as a single range (see Figure 8-1).

If you create a chart that uses an x-axis and y-axis (as most do), the ChartWizard naturally uses the row of column headings in the selected table for the category labels along the x-axis. If the table has row headings, the ChartWizard uses these as the headings in the legend of the chart (if you choose to include one). The *legend* identifies each point, column, or bar in the chart that represents the values in the table.

Once you select the information to chart, follow these steps to create the chart:

1. **Click the ChartWizard tool on the Standard toolbar.**

   The ChartWizard tool is the sixth tool from the right and has a picture of a magic wand over a column chart. When you click this tool, the mouse pointer changes to a crosshair with a small column chart below and to the right.

2. **Drag the crosshair pointer through the cells in the worksheet to indicate the location and size of the finished chart.**

   To remind you that you're creating a chart, Excel displays the following message in the status bar:

   ```
   Drag in document to create a chart
   ```

Figure 8-1:
Selecting
the
information
to be
charted.

Position the crosshair at the upper-left corner of the place in the
worksheet where you want the chart; drag diagonally down until you've
drawn the outline of the chart, called a *bounding box* (as shown in Figure
8-2). Don't worry if you don't get it exactly the right size or in just the right
place — you can easily move or resize the chart after it's been created.

If you want to put the chart on a worksheet different from the one containing the selected data that you're charting, click the appropriate sheet tab
at the bottom of the document window with the crosshair pointer and
then drag it through the cells of that worksheet.

3. **When you've got the bounding box indicating the size and shape of
   the new chart where you want it in the worksheet, release the
   mouse button.**

Excel then displays the ChartWizard - Step 1 of 5 dialog box (see Figure
8-3). Notice that the outline of the shape of the finished chart no longer
appears in the worksheet, but you do see a marquee around the current
cell selection.

Figure 8-2:
Indicating
the location
and size of
the chart
in the
worksheet.

Figure 8-3:
Step 1 of 5:
Verify the
range to be
charted.

4. Verify that the current cell selection contains all the information that you want charted.

While the first ChartWizard dialog box is displayed, verify that the cell range surrounded by the marquee in your worksheet and specified in formula form (with absolute cell references) in the Range text box is correct. To modify this range (perhaps to include the row of column headings or the column of row headings), either reselect the range with the mouse or edit the cell references in the Range text box.

5. Click the Next button in the dialog box or press Enter when the selected range is correct.

Excel displays the ChartWizard - Step 2 of 5 dialog box (see Figure 8-4). Left to itself, the ChartWizard represents your data in a column chart. The Step 2 of 5 dialog box offers a wide range of chart types.

6. Select a chart type other than the default Column type if you want.

To select another chart type, click its sample chart or press the command letter associated with that chart-type name (for example, press E for a 3-D Area chart).

Figure 8-4:
Step 2 of 5:
Choose the
type of
chart you
want to use.

7. **Click the Next button or press Enter.**

   The ChartWizard - Step 3 of 5 dialog box appears (see Figure 8-5). Each chart type is available in one of many different formats. Each chart type has a default format (referred to as the *preferred format).*

8. **Choose a format for your type of chart.**

   To choose a new format, click its sample in the dialog box or type its number (type 0 if you want to choose format 10). Figure 8-5 shows the dialog box with format 6 selected as the preferred format for the column chart.

9. **Click the Next button or press Enter.**

   The ChartWizard shows you a preview of the chart in the ChartWizard - Step 4 of 5 dialog box (see Figure 8-6).

10. **Verify that Excel has charted the data correctly in the ChartWizard - Step 4 of 5 dialog box.**

    Normally, the ChartWizard makes each column of values in the selected table into a separate *data series* on the chart. The *legend* (the boxed area with samples of the colors or patterns used in the chart) identifies each data series in the chart.

Figure 8-5: Step 3 of 5: Choose the format for the type of chart you've selected.

Figure 8-6:
Step 4 of 5:
Verify that
the data is
charted
correctly.

In terms of worksheet data selected in Mother Goose 1996 first quarter
sales worksheet (shown in Figure 8-1), this means that Excel will use each
bar in the column chart to represent a different month's sales and will
cluster these sales together by the nine different companies. If you want,
you can switch the data series from columns to rows by clicking the Rows
radio button. Choosing the Rows radio button in this example would make
each bar represent the sales of one of the nine different companies and
cause them to be clustered together by month.

When the chart forms the data series by columns, the ChartWizard uses
the entries in the first column (the row headings in cell range A3:A11) to
label the x-axis (the so-called *category labels*). The ChartWizard uses the
entries in the first row (the column labels in cell range B2:D2) as the
headings in the legend.

11. **Click the Next button or press Enter.**

    The ChartWizard - Step 5 of 5 dialog box appears (see Figure 8-7).

12. **Type the titles you want into the boxes provided.**

    You can enter a title for the entire chart as well as individual titles for the
    category axis (the x-axis) and the value axis (the y-axis). You can also
    remove the legend from the chart (not recommended for any chart that
    contains more than one data series) by clicking on the No radio button.

Figure 8-7:
Step 5 of 5:
Add the
titles to the
chart.

Figure 8-7 shows the dialog box after a title for the chart was entered in the Chart Title text box. The Sample Chart area shows the title as you enter it (because of space limitations in the dialog box, the text may not wrap in the worksheet the same way it does in the Sample Chart area). If you add a title for the x-axis in the Category (X) text box, it appears right under the category labels in the chart. If you add a title for the y-axis in the Value (Y) text box, it appears to the left of the values, running up the side of the chart.

13. **Click the Finish button or press Enter to close the last ChartWizard dialog box.**

The chart you have created appears in the worksheet in the area that you selected earlier, and the Chart toolbar magically appears floating in the workbook document window. Figure 8-8 shows the column chart created for the Mother Goose Enterprises 1996 first quarter sales.

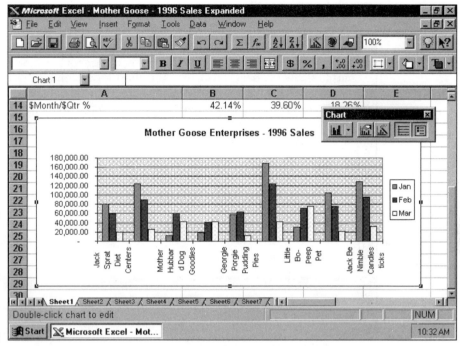

Figure 8-8:
The
completed
chart as it
appears
in the
worksheet.

You can easily move or resize the chart right after creating it because the chart is still selected. (You can always tell when a graphic object like a chart is selected because you see *selection handles* — those tiny squares — around the edges of the object.) Immediately after creating the chart, the Chart toolbar appears floating above in the workbook document window.

✔ To move the chart, position the mouse pointer somewhere inside the chart and drag the chart to a new location.

✔ To resize the chart (you may want to make it bigger if it seems distorted in any way), position the mouse pointer on one of the selection handles. When the pointer changes from the arrowhead to a double-headed arrow, drag the side or corner (depending on which handle you select) to enlarge or reduce the chart.

When the chart is properly sized and positioned in the worksheet, set the chart in place by deselecting it (simply click the mouse pointer in any cell outside the chart). As soon as you deselect the chart, the selection handles disappear, as does the Chart toolbar, from the document window. To reselect the chart (to edit, size, or move it), click anywhere on the chart with the mouse pointer.

When a Chart's Just Not Your Type!

Once you create a chart, you can use the tools on the Chart toolbar to make some changes to it. Remember that this toolbar appears whenever you select the chart in the worksheet. To change the chart type, simply click the Chart Type tool's drop-down list button and then select the new type of chart in the drop-down palette that appears (shown in Figure 8-9).

To add (or get rid of) gridlines for the major values (on the y-axis), click the Horizontal Gridlines tool. To hide or display the chart's legend, click the Legend tool.

Figure 8-9 shows the chart created in the preceding section after the chart was resized and the chart type was changed from a Column to an Area chart. Figure 8-10 shows the same chart after changing the chart type from an Area chart to a 3-D Column chart.

Figure 8-9:
The chart type changed to an Area chart.

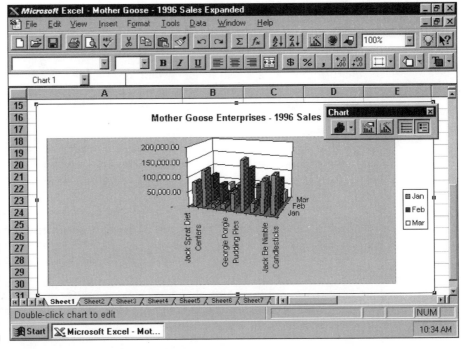

Figure 8-10:
The chart
type
changed to
a 3-D
Column
chart.

In addition to being able to change the type of chart and add or remove gridlines and the legend, you can also use the Chart toolbar to change what data Excel includes in the chart. To change the data represented in the chart, follow these steps:

1. **Click somewhere on the chart in the worksheet to select it and then click the ChartWizard tool.**

   The ChartWizard tool is located both on the Standard toolbar and on the Chart toolbar that appears as soon as you select the chart. The ChartWizard displays a ChartWizard - Step 1 of 2 dialog box that contains the Range edit box with the current cell range being charted.

2. **Change this cell range to include more or less data or labels in the worksheet.**

3. **Click the Next button.**

   The ChartWizard - Step 2 of 2 dialog box appears; it contains the same options for changing the way the data is charted as the Step 4 of 5 dialog box did when you created the chart.

4. **Change the chart options if you want.**

5. **Click the Finish button or press Enter.**

   Your changes show up immediately in the selected chart.

The fine art of spiffing up your charts

Besides changing the type of chart or adding or removing gridlines with the tools on the Chart toolbar, you may want to make changes to specific parts of the chart (for example, selecting a new font for titles or repositioning the legend). To make these kinds of changes, you must double-click the chart and then select the particular object (title, legend, plot area, and so on). When you double-click a chart, Excel selects it and displays the chart with a heavy border (shown in Figure 8-11).

Once you double-click the chart, you can select the individual parts of the chart that need formatting — like the titles, legend, x-axis, y-axis, and so on.

- To select one of these chart objects, simply click it.

- You can tell when an object is selected because selection handles appear around it. (Figure 8-11 shows the selection handles around the chart title.) With some objects, you can use the selection handles to resize or reorient the object.

- After selecting some chart objects, you can move them within the chart by positioning the arrowhead pointer in their midst and then dragging their boundary.

- To display a chart object's shortcut menu, you click the object with the secondary mouse button and then drag to the desired command on the menu or click it with the primary mouse button.

Once you select one object in the chart by clicking on it, you can cycle through and select the other objects in the chart by pressing the ↓ and ↑ keys. Pressing ↓ selects the next object; pressing ↑ selects the previous object.

All the parts of the chart that you can select in a chart window have shortcut menus attached to them. If you know that you want to select a command from the shortcut menu as soon as you select a part of the chart, you can both select the object and open the shortcut menu by clicking the chart object with the *secondary* mouse button. (You don't have to click the object with the left button to select it and then click again with the right to open the menu.)

Figure 8-11 shows the Area-chart version of the first quarter sales after double-clicking it and then selecting the chart's title and displaying its shortcut menu. To change the formatting of this title, you simply choose the Format Chart Title command in the shortcut menu. When you select this command, the Format Chart Title dialog box, similar to the one shown in Figure 8-12, appears. This dialog box has three tabs: Patterns, Font, and Alignment, each with its own options for formatting the title.

Figure 8-11:
Selecting the Format Chart Title command in the chart title's shortcut menu.

Figure 8-12:
The Format Chart Title dialog box.

✔ Select the Patterns tab (shown in Figure 8-12) and use its options to place a border or change the pattern or color within the title area.

✔ Select the Font tab and use its options to choose a new font, size, or style for the title.

✔ Select the Alignment tab and use its options to change the alignment or orientation of the title.

Note that you can move the chart title by dragging it to a new position within the chart. In addition to moving the title, you can also break the title up on several different lines. Then, if you want, you can use options in the Alignment tab of the Format Chart Title dialog box to change the alignment of the broken-up text.

To force part of the title onto a new line, click the insertion point at the place in the text where the line break is to occur. Once the insertion point is positioned in the title, press Ctrl+Enter to start a new line.

In addition to changing the way the titles appear in the chart, you can modify the way the data series, legend, and x- and y-axes appear in the chart by opening their shortcut menus and selecting the appropriate commands from them.

Telling all with a text box

Figure 8-13 shows a couple of other changes you can easily make to a chart. In this figure, you see the chart for the Mother Goose Enterprises 1996 first quarter sales (as an Area chart) after adding a text box with an arrow that points out how extraordinary the sales were for the Hickory, Dickory, & Dock Clock Repair shops in this quarter and after formatting the values on the y-axis with the Currency number format.

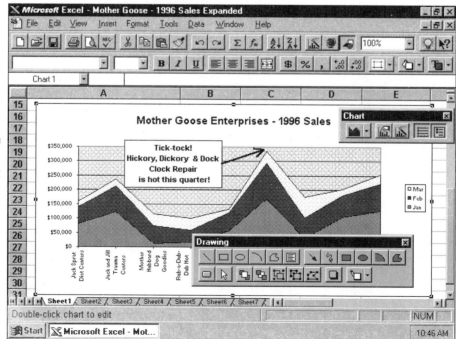

Figure 8-13:
The chart after adding a text box with an arrow and formatting the values on the y-axis with the Currency style.

To add a text box to the chart, open the Drawing toolbar (by choosing Drawing on the toolbar context menu) and click its Text Box tool (the one to the left of the Arrow tool). When you choose the Text Box tool, Excel changes the pointer to a crosshair, which you use to draw the text box either in the chart or the worksheet by dragging its outline. When you release the mouse button, the program positions the insertion point at the top of the text box, and you can then type the text you want to appear within it. The text you type appears in the text box and wraps to a new line when you reach the right edge of the text box (remember: you can press Enter when you want to force text to appear on a new line). When you've finished entering the message for your text box, click anywhere outside the box to deselect it.

After adding a text box to a chart (or worksheet), you can edit as follows:

- ✔ You can move the text box to a new location in the chart by dragging it.

- ✔ You can resize the text box by dragging the appropriate selection handle.

- ✔ Change or remove the border around the text box by choosing the Format Object command on its shortcut menu and then choosing the Patterns tab in the Format Object dialog box. To remove all borders from the text box, click the None radio button.

- ✔ To add the drop-shadow effect, click the Shadow check box in the Patterns tab of the Format Object dialog box or click the Drop Shadow tool (the one with the picture of a drop shadow on a rectangle) in the Drawing toolbar.

When creating a text box, you may want to add an arrow to point directly to the object or part of the chart you're talking about. To add an arrow, click the Arrow tool (immediately to the right of the Text Box tool) on the Drawing toolbar and then drag the crosshair from the place where the end of the arrow (the one *without* the arrowhead) is to appear to the place where the arrow starts (and the arrowhead appears) and release the mouse button.

Excel then draws a new arrow, which remains selected (with selection handles at the beginning and end of the arrow). You can then modify the arrow as follows:

- ✔ To move the arrow, drag it into position.

- ✔ To change the length of the arrow, drag one of the selection handles.

- ✔ As you change the length, you can also change the direction of the arrow by pivoting the mouse pointer around a stationary selection handle.

- ✔ If you want to change the shape of the arrowhead or the thickness of the arrow's shaft, choose the Format Object command from the arrow's context menu and make changes to the options in the Patterns tab of the Format Object dialog box.

Formatting the x- or y-axis

When charting a bunch of values, Excel isn't too careful how it formats the values that appear on the y-axis (or the x-axis when using some chart types like the 3-D Column chart or the XY Scatter chart). If you're not happy with the way the values appear on either the x- or y-axis, you can change the formatting as follows:

1. **Double-click the chart.**

2. **Click the x- or y-axis that contains the values to be formatted with the secondary mouse button.**

3. **Choose the Format Axis command on the axis context menu.**

4. **Choose the Number tab in the Format Axis dialog box; then choose the appropriate options in the Category list box and Format Codes list box.**

   For example, to select the Currency format with no decimal places, you choose Currency in the Category list box; then enter 0 in the Decimal Places edit box or select 0 with the spinner buttons.

5. **Choose the OK button or press Enter.**

As soon as you choose a new number format for a chart, Excel immediately formats all the numbers that appear along the selected axis using that format.

Vacillating values mean changing charts

As soon as you finish modifying the objects in a chart, you can deselect the chart and return to the normal worksheet and its cells by clicking the pointer anywhere outside the chart. After a chart is deselected, you can once again move the cell pointer all over the worksheet. Just keep in mind that if you use the arrow keys to move the cell pointer, the cell pointer disappears when you move to a cell in the worksheet that's hidden behind the chart (of course, if you try to select a cell covered by a chart by clicking it with the mouse pointer, you'll only succeed in selecting the chart itself).

Keep in mind that worksheet values represented graphically in the chart remain dynamically linked to the chart so that, should you make a change to one or more of the charted values in the worksheet, Excel will automatically update the chart to suit.

Changing perspectives

Figure 8-14 shows the chart in a chart window in yet another guise: this time, as a 3-D Area chart. When you select this kind of chart (as well as the 3-D Column, 3-D Line, and 3-D Surface charts), Excel draws the chart in perspective view by adding a third axis to the chart. Now you have the category (x) axis with the companies running along the bottom of the closest side, the data series (y) axis with the months running along the bottom of the other side, and the value (z) axis with the dollar amounts running up the left wall.

These three axes form a kind of open box with the category and series axes on the two sides of the floor and the values axis on the left side of the wall of the box. You can modify the view of this type of 3-D-perspective chart by rotating the box, thereby changing the viewing angles of its walls and floor.

To do this, click the chart (double-click if the chart is on a worksheet rather than a chart sheet); then select the frame of the 3-D chart by clicking one of its corners and hold down the mouse button. (If the 3-D chart is on a chart sheet, you can tell when you've clicked a corner because the word "Corners" appears on the formula bar where the current cell address usually appears.) In a second, assuming that you don't let up on the mouse button prematurely and that you have really clicked a corner of the frame and not one of the data series inside the frame, everything disappears from the 3-D chart except for the wire frame representing its orientation (see Figure 8-15).

Figure 8-14:
Sales information as 3-D Area chart in its own chart sheet.

Figure 8-15:
Modifying
the viewing
angles of the
3-D Area
chart by
rotating the
wire-frame
box.

You can then drag the corner of the wire-frame box around to reorient the entire 3-D chart. When the wire-frame box is positioned the way you want the 3-D chart, release the mouse button. Excel draws the 3-D chart using the new viewing angles. Figure 8-15 shows the wire-frame of the 3-D Area chart after rotating its lower-right corner down and around to the left before releasing the mouse button and redrawing the chart. Figure 8-16 shows you how the rotated 3-D Area chart appears after releasing the mouse button.

Notice how this change to the orientation of the 3-D Area chart causes Excel to flip the category labels with the names of the companies all the way from the lower side of the chart to its right side.

Picture This!

Charts are not the only kind of graphics you can add to a worksheet. Indeed, Excel lets you spruce up a worksheet with drawings, text boxes, and even graphic images imported from other sources, like scanned images or drawings created in other graphics programs.

Figure 8-16:
The 3-D
Area chart
after
rotating it.

To bring in a graphic image saved in its own file, like a piece of clip art, you use the Picture command on the Insert pull-down menu and select the file in the Picture dialog box. If you want to bring in a graphic image created in another program that's not saved in its own file, you select the graphic in that program and then copy it to the Clipboard (using Ctrl+C or the Copy command on the Edit menu) before returning to the Excel worksheet. When you get back to your worksheet, place the cursor where you want the picture to go and then paste the image in place (using Ctrl+V or the Paste command on the Edit pull-down menu).

Figure 8-17 shows the Mother Goose Enterprises 1996 sales worksheet after sprucing up its title with a little color (which doesn't show at all in a black-and-white book!), text formatting, and the addition of a piece of Microsoft Office clip art (this one being from a file called Account, found in the Clip art folder within the MSOffice folder). After inserting the Account graphic file in the Mother Goose worksheet, all I had to do was drag the graphic into place in the upper-left corner and size it just a little bit.

In addition to ready-made graphics or images drawn in other graphics programs, you can use the tools on the Drawing toolbar to create your own graphics within Excel. The Drawing toolbar contains all sorts of drawing tools that you can use to draw outlined or filled shapes like rectangles, squares, ovals, and circles as well as straight lines and arcs. It even includes a Freehand tool (the one with the real squiggly line) that you can use to draw free-form lines.

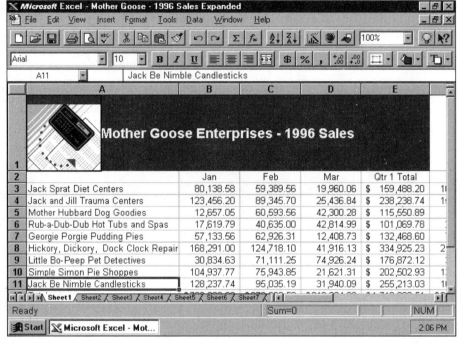

Figure 8-17:
The work-
sheet title
enhanced
with a piece
of Microsoft
Office
clip art.

One on top of the other . . .

In case you haven't noticed, graphic objects float on top of the cells of the worksheet. Most of the objects (including charts) are opaque, meaning that they hide (*without* replacing) information in the cells beneath. If you move one opaque graphic on top of another, the one on top hides the one below, just as putting one sheet of paper over another hides the information on the one below. This means that, most of the time, you should make sure that graphic objects don't overlap one another or overlap cells with worksheet information that you want to display.

Sometimes, however, you can create some interesting special effects by placing a transparent graphic object (such as a circle) in front of an opaque one. The only problem you might encounter is if the opaque object gets on top of the transparent one. If this happens, switch their positions by selecting the opaque object and then choosing Placement on the Format pull-down menu and the Send to Back command on the continuation menu. If you ever find a situation where you need to bring up a graphic that's underneath another, click this graphic and then choose Placement on the Format pull-down menu and the Bring to Front command on the continuation menu.

Sometimes you may find that you need to group several objects together so that they act as one unit (like a text box with its arrow). That way, you can move these objects or size them together in one operation. To group objects together, you need to select each object to be grouped (by clicking each one as you hold down the Shift key) and then choose Placement on the Format pull-down menu and the Group command on the continuation menu. After grouping several objects, whenever you click any part of the mega-object, every part is selected (and selection handles appear only around the perimeter of the combined object).

Should you later decide that you need to independently move or size objects that have been grouped together, you can ungroup them by selecting the grouped object and then choosing Placement on the Format pull-down menu and the Ungroup command (which replaces the Group command) on the continuation menu.

When you need to ditch the graphics

Here's something you'll want to know about the graphics you add to a worksheet: how to hide them. You see, adding graphics to a worksheet can appreciably slow down the screen response because Excel has to take the time to redraw each and every little picture in the document window whenever you scroll the view even slightly. To keep this sluggishness from driving you crazy, either hide the display of all the graphics (including charts) while you edit other things in the worksheet, or temporarily replace them with gray rectangles that continue to mark their places in the worksheet but don't take nearly as long to redraw.

To hide all the graphics or replace them with gray placeholders, choose the Options command on the Tool menu and then choose the View tab. Click the Hide All radio button under Objects to get rid of the display of all graphics entirely. Click the Show Placeholders radio button to temporarily replace the graphics with shaded rectangles. (This is the safest bet, because the placeholders give you a general idea of how changes to the cells of the worksheet impact the graphics.)

Before you print the worksheet, be sure that you redisplay the graphic objects: Open the Options dialog box, choose the View tab, and then click the Show All radio button.

Map Madness

The new Data Map feature in Excel for Windows 95 lets you represent geographical data such as sales in a particular state or foreign country or locations of different out-of-state or foreign offices in graphical form. All you have to do is enter the numbers in one column accompanied by the names of the states or countries they pertain to as row headings in the previous column (similar to the data shown selected in Figure 8-18).

After entering the geographical data in a particular worksheet, you create its data map by following these steps:

1. **Select the data to be mapped, including the row headings that identify the locations as well as all columns of values to be included.**

2. **Click the Map button on the Standard toolbar (the one with the globe right next to the ChartWizard button).**

   When you click the Map button, the mouse pointer changes to a crosshair (just like when creating a new chart with the ChartWizard). You then use this pointer to draw a bounding box that establishes the size and location of the data map.

3. **Click the crosshair at the place in the worksheet where the upper-left corner of the data map should appear and then drag down and to the right until the bounding box you've drawn is the size and shape you want for the data map; then release the mouse button.**

   Note that you don't have to be too precise with drawing the data map bounding box because you can always move and resize the data map once you've created it just as you would any other graphic object in Excel.

4. **Select the map that you want to use in the list box of the Multiple Maps Available dialog box and then choose OK or press Enter.**

   In some cases, Excel may not be able to identify a particular heading as representing geographical data in the map that you've selected. When this is the case, you have to deal with a Resolve Unknown Geographic Data dialog box, where you either change the name of the heading to something Excel recognizes or you eliminate it with the Discard button.

   After you select the map to use, Excel draws the map in the worksheet and displays the Data Map Control dialog box, which determines which data is represented and how it's represented.

   Left to its own devices, Excel chooses whatever column in the cell selection it can identify as representing values like total sales or number of employees and chooses Value Shading as the way to format these values (by representing their density with different types of gray shading and patterns).

5. **To change which columns are represented in the data map, drag the appropriate column button from the top area to the list box area in the Data Map Control dialog box.**

   To remove a column from the data map, drag its button out of the list box area until the pointer changes to the recycle bin icon and then release the mouse button.

   Each time you change which columns are included in the data map, you must wait until Excel redraws the map in the worksheet before you can make any more changes to it.

6. **To change the way a column of data is formatted in the data map, drag the desired format icon from the left area and drop it on top of the current formatting icon.**

   Each time you choose a new formatting icon for a column represented in the data map, you must wait until Excel redraws the data map using that formatting.

   When deciding on the formatting, you might want to play around with the formatting icons until you get the data map looking the way you want (different formats look better or worse depending upon how much territory the map includes).

7. **When you've got the columns that are represented in the data map formatted the way you want them, click the Close box in the Data Map Control dialog box to get rid of it.**

Even after you get rid of the Data Map Control dialog box, the data map remains selected in the worksheet and the Data Map toolbar remains displayed right below the Excel pull-down menus (as shown in Figure 8-19). You can then use the tools on this toolbar to continue to enhance your data map:

✔ **Select Objects tool** (the first button, the one with the arrowhead icon): Use this to select things in the data map like titles or map pins.

✔ **Zoom In tool** (the button with magnifying glass with a plus sign in it): Use this to make a particular part of the data map larger (and see less of the overall map).

✔ **Zoom Out tool** (the button with magnifying glass with a minus sign in it): Use this to reduce the view so that you can see more of the entire data map in the worksheet.

✔ **Grabber tool** (the button with the hand): Use this to change the way the map appears within its bounding box.

Figure 8-18:
Using the
Map tool to
create a
data map
representing
the
European
sales for
Jack Sprat
Diet Centers.

Figure 8-19:
The final
data map
showing the
location and
density
of the
European
sales of the
Jack Sprat
Diet Centers.

✔ **Map Labels** (the button with the luggage tag): Use this to label different parts of the data map, either with the geographical names (like those for the states or countries shown) or with the worksheet values entered for each place in the data map. When you click this button, Excel opens the Map Labels dialog box where you can choose between creating labels for the places on the map (Map feature names) or the labels for the values in a particular column. After you choose OK and close this dialog box, the mouse pointer changes to a crosshair pointer. Each time you pass this pointer over a part of the map, Excel displays the appropriate label (name or value) for that place. To enter that label in the data map, you need to click the place with the mouse pointer. To move the label, you need to drag the label by one of its sides.

✔ **Add Text** (the button with the letter A): Use this to add text anywhere on the data map. Note that you can edit text by choosing the Select Objects tool (see the first item in this list) and then using it to position the insertion point.

✔ **Custom Map Pin** (the button with the picture of a thumbtack): Use this to mark the data map with pins. When you first click this button, Excel opens the Custom Pin Map dialog box where you designate a name for a new custom map pin or select one of the existing map pins. When you choose OK or press Enter to close this dialog box, Excel changes the mouse pointer to a thumbtack. To add a map pin to the map (which appears as a tiny, red pushpin), simply click the place with the thumbtack mouse pointer.

 To use another symbol besides the pushpin for your map pins, choose the Select Objects tool (see the first item in this list) and click a map pin with the secondary mouse button. Then choose Format on its context menu and choose a character in the Symbol dialog box that appears.

✔ **Display Entire** (the button with the globe): Use this to redraw the data map and all its labels so that they all fit within the data map's bounding box.

✔ **Redraw Map** (the button with a paint bucket pouring paint on the globe): Use this to update the data map. Unlike with Excel charts, data maps are not automatically redrawn when you change one or more of their underlying values in the worksheet. To see your changes reflected in the data map, you need to click the Redraw Map button to have the entire data map redrawn.

✔ **Show/Hide Data Map Control** (the last button, the one with a miniature picture of the Data Map Control dialog box): Use this to display or hide the Data Map Control dialog box, from which you can change what columns are represented and how they are formatted.

When you finish enhancing your data map with the buttons on the Data Map toolbar, you still need to remember to deselect the map (by clicking outside the data map, preferably on one of the worksheet cells). When you deselect the data map, Excel automatically removes the heavy border from around the data map and hides the Data Map toolbar, thus restoring your normal screen display and making the data map appear as though it were any other chart that you had added to the worksheet.

Printing Charts Only

Sometimes, you may want to print only a particular chart in the worksheet (independent of the worksheet data it represents or any of the other stuff you've added). To do this, first make sure that the graphic objects are displayed in the worksheet (for details, see "When you need to ditch the graphics," earlier in this chapter). Then double-click the chart (to display the heavy border drawn with diagonal lines). Next, choose the Print command from the File pull-down menu (Ctrl+P) or click the Print tool on the Standard toolbar.

If you select the Print command on the File menu rather than click the Print tool, you see that the Selected Chart radio button under Print What is selected. By default, Excel prints the chart at full size on the page. This may mean that all of the chart cannot be printed on a single page — be sure to choose the Preview button to make sure that your entire map fits on one page.

If you find in Print Preview that you need to change the printed chart size or the orientation of the printing (or both), choose the Setup button in the Print Preview window. To change the orientation of the printing (or the paper size), choose the Page tab in the Page Setup dialog box and change these options. When everything looks all right in the Print Preview window, start printing the chart by choosing the Print button.

Chapter 9

How to Face a Database

In This Chapter

▶ Setting up a database in Excel

▶ Creating a data form for entering and editing records in the database

▶ Adding records via the data form

▶ Finding, editing, and deleting records through the data form

▶ Sorting records in the database

▶ Filtering records in the database so that you end up with just those you want to see

▶ Setting up custom criteria when filtering records

*T*he purpose of all the worksheet tables I've discussed up to this point in the book has been to perform essential calculations (such as to sum monthly or quarterly sales figures) and then present the information in an understandable form. But you can create another kind of worksheet table in Excel: a *database*. The purpose of a database is not so much to calculate new values but rather to store lots and lots of information in a consistent manner. For example, you can create a database that contains the names and addresses of all your clients, or you can create a database that contains all the essential facts about your employees.

Creating a database is much like creating a worksheet table. When setting up a database, you start by entering a row of column headings (technically known as *field names* in database parlance) to identify the different kinds of items you need to keep track of (such as First Name, Last Name, Street, City, State, and so on). After you enter the row of field names, you start entering the information for the database in the appropriate columns of the rows immediately below the field names.

As you proceed, notice that each column of the database contains information for a particular item you want to track in the database, such as the client's company name or an employee's telephone extension. Each column is also known as a *field* in the database. In looking back over your work, you see that each row of the database contains complete information about a particular person or thing you're keeping track of in the database, whether it's a company such as Valuerite Reality or a particular employee such as Johnny Hayseed. The individuals or entities described in the rows of the database are also known as the *records* of the database. Each record (row) contains many fields (columns).

Maintaining vast quantities of data in a tabular format is but one small part of the database story in Excel. Excel provides you with very powerful features for organizing the data as well as for displaying just the information you need. For instance, suppose that you entered the clients in a database alphabetically by company name but now want to see them listed alphabetically by company name *and* grouped by states and cities. No problem: sort the records of the database by their State, City, and then Company fields.

Or, suppose that you only want to work with clients who live in New York City and who have already established credit accounts with you. It's simple: You choose Filter on the Data menu followed by AutoFilter to add drop-down list boxes (complete with drop-down buttons) to each field name in the database. Then, to display only the records you want to see, you click the drop-down list button for the appropriate field(s) and select the entry in the drop-down list by which you want the database to be filtered (for this example, you would select New York in the City drop-down list and Yes in the Credit drop-down list). And, just like that, Excel hides all the records in your database except those containing the entries you selected (referred to as *filter criteria*). In this example, Excel displays only the records in the database where the City field contains New York and the Credit field contains Yes.

Designing the Data Form

Setting up and maintaining a database is easy with Excel's handy, built-in *data form*. You use the data form to add, delete, or edit records in the database. To create a data form for a new database, you first enter the row of column headings used as field names and one sample record in the following row (check out the client database in Figure 9-1). Then you format each field entry just as you want all subsequent entries in that column of the database to appear. Then select the two rows of cells and choose the Form command on the Data menu.

As soon as you choose the Form command on the Data menu, Excel analyzes the row of field names and entries for the first record and creates a data form that lists the field names down the left side of the form with the entries for the first record in the appropriate text boxes next to them. Figure 9-1 shows the data form for the new Little Bo-Peep Pet Detective client database; it looks kind of like a customized dialog box. The data form Excel creates includes the entries you made in the first record. The data form also contains a series of buttons on the right side that you use to add, delete, or find specific records in the database. Right above the first button (New), the data form lists the number of the record you're looking at followed by the total number of records (1 of 1 when you first create the data form).

Adding records to the database

After you create the data form with the first record, you can use the form to add the rest of the records to the database. The process is simple. When you click the New button, Excel displays a blank data form (marked New Record at the right side of the data form), which you get to fill in.

After you enter the information for the first field, press the Tab key to advance to the next field in the record.

Figure 9-1:
The data form for a new database with a row of field names followed by a row of data.

Creating a data form from field names alone

You can create a data form for a new database simply by entering a row of field names and selecting them before you choose Form on the Data menu. When you do this, Excel displays an alert dialog box indicating that no header row (that is the row with the field names for the new database) has been detected. This alert box also asks to confirm that the top row of the selection (which happens to be the only row of the selection) is the header row. Go ahead and choose OK or press Enter to create a blank data form listing all of the fields down the form in the same order as they appear across the selected row.

Creating a blank data form from field names alone is just fine provided that your database doesn't contain any calculated fields (that is, fields whose entries result from a formula's computation rather than from manual entry). If your new database will contain calculated fields, you need to build their formulas in the appropriate fields of the first record. Then select both the row of field names and the first database record with the formulas indicating how the entries are calculated before you choose Form on the Data menu. Excel knows which fields are calculated and which are not (you can tell that a field is a calculated field in the data form because Excel lists its field name but does not provide a text box for you to enter any information for it).

Whoa! Don't press the Enter key to advance to the next field in a record. If you do, you'll insert the new, incomplete, record into the database.

Continue entering information for each field and pressing Tab to go to the next field in the database.

- ✔ If you notice that you've made an error and want to edit an entry in a field you already passed, press Shift+Tab to return to that field.

- ✔ To replace the entry, just start typing.

- ✔ To edit some of the characters in the field, press ← or click the I-beam pointer in the entry to locate the insertion point; then edit the entry from there.

When entering information in a particular field, you can copy the entry made in that field for the previous record by pressing Ctrl+" (quotation mark). Press Ctrl+", for example, to carry forward the same entry in the State field of each new record when entering a series of records for people who all live in the same state.

When entering dates in a date field, use a consistent date format that Excel knows (for example, enter something like **2/19/93**). When entering zip codes that sometimes use leading zeros that you don't want to disappear from the entry (such as zip code **00102**), format the first field entry with the Special Zip Code number format (see "Sorting through the Special number formats" in Chapter 3 for details). In the case of other numbers that use leading zeros (like part numbers), you can put an ' (apostrophe) before the first 0. The apostrophe tells Excel to treat the number like a text label but doesn't show up in the database itself (the only place you can see the apostrophe is on the formula bar when the cell pointer's in the cell with the numeric entry).

Press the ↓ key when you've entered all the information for the new record. Instead of the ↓ key, you can press Enter or click the New button (see Figure 9-2). Excel inserts the new record as the last record in the database in the worksheet and displays a new blank data form in which you can enter the next record (see Figure 9-3).

When you finish adding records to the database, press the Esc key or click the Close button to close the data form. Then save the worksheet with the Save command on the File pull-down menu or click the Save tool on the Standard toolbar.

Figure 9-2: Entering information in the data form for the second record.

Figure 9-3:
The
database
after the
second
record was
entered in
the data
form.

Calculated Field Entries

When you want Excel to calculate the entries for a particular field by formula, you need to enter that formula in the correct field in the first record of the database. Then select both the row of field names and the first record when creating the data form, and Excel copies the formula for this calculated field to each new record you add with the data form.

In the Bo-Peep clients database, for example, the Total Due field in cell K3 of the first record is calculated by the formula =Hours*Rate (cell I3 with the number of case hours having been named Hours and cell J3 with the hourly rate having been named Rate). This formula then computes what the client owes by multiplying the number of case hours by the hourly rate. As you can see, Excel adds the calculated field, Total Due, to the data form but doesn't provide a text box for this field (calculated fields can't be edited). When you enter additional records to the database, Excel calculates the formula for the Total Due field. If you then redisplay the data for these records, you see the calculated value following Total Due (although you won't be able to change it).

Locating, changing, and deleting records

Once the database is underway and you're caught up with entering new records, you can start using the data form to perform routine maintenance on the database. For example, you can use the data form to locate a record you want to change and then make the edits to the particular fields. You can also use the data form to find a specific record you want to remove and then delete it from the database.

- Begin editing by positioning the cell pointer somewhere in the database (either in a cell with one of the database's field names or a cell that forms a record with a field entry).

- Locate the record you want to edit in the database by bringing up its data form (see Table 9-1 and the following two sections "Scrolling the night away!" and "Finders keepers" for hints on locating records).

- To edit the fields of the current record, move to that field by pressing Tab or Shift+Tab and replace the entry by typing a new one.

- Alternatively, press ← or → or click the I-beam cursor to reposition the insertion point and then make your edits.

- To clear a field entirely, select it and then press the Delete key.

To delete the entire record from the database, click the Delete button. Excel displays an alert box with the following dire warning:

    Displayed record will be deleted permanently

To go ahead and get rid of the record displayed in the data form, choose OK. To play it safe and keep the record intact, choose Cancel.

Please keep in mind that you *cannot* use the Undo feature to bring back a record you removed with the Delete button! Excel is definitely *not* kidding when it uses words like "deleted permanently." As a precaution, always save a backup version of the worksheet with the database before you start removing old records.

Scrolling the night away!

Once you display the data form in the worksheet by positioning the cell pointer somewhere in the database and then choosing the Form command from the Data pull-down menu, you can use the scroll bar to the right of the list of field names or various keystrokes (both summarized in Table 9-1) to move through the records in the database until you find the one you want to edit or delete.

- To move to the data form for the next record in the database: Press ↓, press Enter, or click the ↓ scroll arrow at the bottom of the scroll bar.

- To move to the data form for the previous record in the database: Press ↑, press Shift+Enter, or click the ↑ scroll arrow at the top of the scroll bar.

✔ To move to the data form for the first record in the database: Press Ctrl+↑, press Ctrl+PgUp, or drag the scroll box to the very top of the scroll bar.

✔ To move to the data form for the last record in the database: Press Ctrl+↓, press Ctrl+PgDn, or drag the scroll box to the very bottom of the scroll bar.

Table 9-1	Ways to get to a particular record
Keystrokes or Scroll Bar Technique	*Result*
Press ↓ or Enter; or click the ↓ scroll arrow or the Find Next button	Moves to the next record in the database and leaves the same field selected
Press ↑ or Shift+Enter; or click the ↑ scroll arrow or the Find Prev button	Moves to the previous record in the database and leaves the same field selected
Press PgDn	Moves forward ten records in the database
Press PgUp	Moves backward ten records in the database
Press Ctrl+↑ or Ctrl+PgUp; or drag the scroll box to the top of the scroll bar	Moves to the first record in the database
Press Ctrl+↓ or Ctrl+PgDn; or drag the scroll box to the bottom of the scroll	Moves to the last record in the database

Finders keepers

In a really large database, trying to find a particular record by moving from record to record — or even moving 10 records at a time with the scroll bar — can take all day. Rather than waste time trying to manually search for a record, you can use the Criteria button in the data form to look it up.

When you click the Criteria button, Excel clears all the field entries in the data form (and replaces the record number with the word *Criteria*) so that you can enter the criteria to search for in the blank text boxes.

For example, suppose that you need to edit Old King Cole's file status (you've finally located his missing animals!). Unfortunately, his paperwork doesn't include his case number. All you know is that currently his case is open (meaning the Status field for his record contains "Active" rather than "Closed"), and you're pretty sure that he spells his last name with a *C* instead of a *K*.

To find his record, you can at least use the information you have to narrow the search down to all the records where the last name begins with the letter *C*, and the Status field contains *Active*. To limit your search in this way, open the data form for the personnel database, click the Criteria button, and then enter the following in the text box for the Last Name field:

```
C*
```

Also enter the following in the text box for the Status field (see Figure 9-4):

```
Active
```

When you enter search criteria for records in the blank text boxes of the data form, you can use the ? (question mark) and * (asterisk) *wildcard* characters. Back in Chapter 6, I show you how to use these wildcard characters with the Find command on the Edit menu to locate cells with particular entries.

Now choose the Find Next button. Excel displays in the data form the first record in the database where the last name begins with the letter C and the Status field contains *Active*. As shown in Figure 9-5, the first record in this database that meets these criteria is for Eros Cupid. To press on and find our Old King Cole's record, choose Find Next button again. Figure 9-6 shows Old King Cole's record. Having located Cole's record, you can then edit his case status in the edit box for the Status field. When you click the Close button, Excel records his new Closed case status in the database.

Figure 9-4: The data form after Criteria was selected and the search criteria were entered in the blank field boxes.

Figure 9-5:
The first
record in the
database
that meets
the search
criteria.

Figure 9-6:
Eureka! The
king's long-
lost record
appears.

When you use the Criteria button in the data form to find records, you can include the following operators in the search criteria you enter to locate a specific record in the database:

Operator	Meaning
=	Equal to
>	Greater than
>=	Greater than or equal to
<	Less than
<=	Less than or equal to
<>	Not equal to

For example, to display only those records where a client's total due is greater than or equal to $50,000 a year, enter >=**50000** in the edit box for the Total Due field before choosing the Find Next button.

When specifying search criteria that fit a number of records, you may have to click the Find Next or Find Prev button several times to locate the record you want. If no record fits the search criteria you enter, the computer beeps at you when you click these buttons.

To change the search criteria, first clear the data form by choosing the Criteria button again and then choosing the Clear button. Then select the appropriate text boxes and clear out the old criteria before you enter the new. (You can just replace the criteria if you're using the same fields.)

To switch back to the current record without using the search criteria you enter, click the Form button (this button replaces the Criteria button as soon as you click the Criteria button).

Sorting It All Out

Every database you put together in Excel will have some kind of preferred order for maintaining and viewing the records. Depending on the database, you may want to see the records in alphabetical order by last name. In the case of a database of clients, you may want to see the records arranged alphabetically by company name. In the case of the Little Bo-Peep clients database, the preferred order is in numerical order by the case number assigned to each client when he or she hires the agency to find his or her pets.

When you initially enter records for a new database, you no doubt enter them either in the preferred order or the order in which you get a hold of their records. However you start out, as you will soon discover, you don't have the option of adding subsequent records in that preferred order. Whenever you add a new record with the New button in the data form, Excel tacks that record onto the bottom of the database by adding a new row.

This means that if you originally enter all the records in alphabetical order by company (from *Acme Pet Supplies* to *Zastrow and Sons*) and then you add the record for a new client named *Bambi's Pasta Palace,* Excel puts the new record at the bottom of the barrel, in the last row right after *Zastrow and Sons* instead of inserting it in its proper position somewhere after *Acme Pet Supplies* but definitely well ahead of Zastrow and his wonderful boys!

And this is not the only problem you can have with the order used in originally entering records. Even if the records in the database remain fairly stable, the preferred order merely represents the order you use *most* of the time. But what about those times when you need to see the records in another, special order?

For example, although you usually like to work with the clients database in numerical order by case number, you may need to see the records in alphabetical order by the client's last name to quickly locate a client and look up his or her total due in a printout. So when using the records to generate mailing labels for a mass-mailing, you want the records in zip-code order. When generating a report for your account representatives that shows which clients are in whose territory, you need the records in alphabetical order by state and maybe even city.

It seems like flexibility in the record order is exactly what's required to keep up with the different needs you have for the data. This is precisely what the Sort command offers you, once you understand how to use it.

To have Excel correctly sort the records in a database, you must specify the fields whose values determine the new order of the records (such fields being technically known as the *sorting keys* in the parlance of the database enthusiast). Further, you must specify what type of order should be created using the information in these fields. There are two possible orders: *ascending order,* in which text entries are placed in alphabetical order (A to Z) and values are placed in numerical order (from smallest to largest); and *descending order,* which is the exact reverse of alphabetical order (Z to A) and numerical order (largest to smallest).

When you sort records in a database, you can specify up to three fields on which to sort (you can also choose between ascending and descending order for each field you specify). You only need to use more than one field when the first field you use in sorting contains duplicate values and you want a say in how the records with duplicates are arranged. (If you don't specify another field to sort on, Excel just puts the records in the order in which you entered them.)

Up and down the ascending and descending sort orders

When you use the ascending sort order with a key field that contains many different kinds of entries, Excel places numbers (from smallest to largest) before text entries (in alphabetical order), followed by any logical values (TRUE and FALSE), error values, and finally, blank cells. When you use the descending sort order, Excel arranges the different entries in reverse: numbers are still first, arranged from largest to smallest; text entries go from Z to A, and the FALSE logical value precedes the TRUE logical value.

The best and most common example of when you need more than one field is when sorting a large database alphabetically in last-name order. Say you have a database that contains several people with the last name Smith, Jones, or Zastrow (as is the case when you work at Zastrow and Sons). If you specify the Last Name field as the only field to sort on (using the default ascending order), all the duplicate Smiths, Joneses, and Zastrows are placed in the order in which their records were originally entered. To better sort these duplicates, you can specify the First Name field as the second field to sort on, again using the default ascending order, (making the second field the tie-breaker), so that Ian Smith's record precedes that of Sandra Smith, and Vladimir Zastrow's record comes after that of Mikhail Zastrow.

To sort records in an Excel database, follow these steps:

1. **Position the cell pointer in the first field name of the database.**

2. **Choose the Sort command from the Data menu.**

   Excel selects all the records of the database (without including the first row of field names) and opens the Sort dialog box shown in Figure 9-7. By default, the first field name appears in the Sort By drop-down list box and the Ascending radio button is selected at the top of the Sort dialog box.

3. **Select the name of the field you first want the database records sorted by in the Sort By drop-down list box.**

   If you want the records arranged in descending order, remember also to choose the Descending radio button to the right.

4. **If the first field contains duplicates and you want to specify how these records are sorted, select a second field to sort on in the Then By drop-down list box and select between the Ascending and Descending radio buttons to its right.**

5. If necessary, specify a third field to sort the records by, using the second Then By drop-down list box, and decide on the sort order to use.

6. Choose OK or press Enter.

Excel sorts the selected records. If you see that you sorted the database on the wrong fields or in the wrong order, choose the Undo Sort command from the Edit menu or press Crl+Z to immediately restore the database records to their previous order.

Figure 9-7 shows the Sort dialog box after the Last Name field in the Bo-Peep clients database is selected as the first field to sort on and the First Name field is selected as the second field on which to sort (these being the records with duplicate entries in the Last Name field). The settings in this dialog box specify that records in the Bo-Peep clients database be sorted in alphabetical (ascending) order by last name and then first name. Figure 9-8 shows the clients database right after sorting (note how the Harveys — Allison, Chauncey, and Scott — are now arranged in the proper first name/last name alphabetical order).

Figure 9-7:
Setting up
the Sort
dialog box
to sort
records
alpha-
betically in
last-name/
first-name
order.

Figure 9-8:
The clients
database
sorted in
alphabetical
order by last
name and
then by first
name.

Sorting something besides a database

The Sort command's not just for sorting records in the database. You can use it to sort financial data or text headings in the spreadsheets you build as well. When sorting regular worksheet tables, just be sure to select all the cells with data to be sorted (and only those with the data to be sorted) before you choose Sort from the Data pull-down menu.

Also note that Excel automatically excludes the first row of the cell selection from the sort (on the assumption that this row is a header row containing field names that shouldn't be included). To include the first row of the cell selection in the sort, be sure to select the No Header Row radio button in the My List Has section before you choose the OK button to begin sorting.

You can use the Sort Ascending tool (the button with the A above the Z) or the Sort Descending tool (the button with the Z above the A) on the Standard toolbar to sort records in the database on a single field.

✔ To sort the database in ascending order by a particular field, position the cell pointer in that field's name at the very top of the database and then click the Sort Ascending button on the Standard toolbar.

✔ To sort the database in descending order by a particular field, position the cell pointer in that field's name at the very top of the database and then click the Sort Descending button on the Standard toolbar.

You AutoFilter the Database to See the Records You Want

Excel's AutoFilter feature makes it a breeze to hide everything in a database except the records you want to see. All you have to do to filter a database with this incredibly nifty feature is position the cell pointer somewhere in the database before you choose Filter on the Data menu followed by AutoFilter on the cascading menu. When you choose the AutoFilter command, Excel adds drop-down list buttons to every cell with a field name in that row (like those shown in Figure 9-9).

To filter the database to just those records that contain a particular value, you then click the appropriate field's drop-down list button to open a drop-down list box containing all of the entries made in that field and select the one you want to use as a filter. Excel then displays only those records that contain the value you selected in that field (all other records are temporarily hidden).

For example, in Figure 9-9, I filtered the Little Bo-Peep clients database to display only those records where the State field contains AZ (for Arizona) by clicking on the State's drop-down list box and then clicking on AZ in the drop-down list box. (It was as simple as that.)

Once you've filtered a database so that only the records you want to work with are displayed, you can copy those records to another part of the worksheet to the right of the database (or better yet, another worksheet in the workbook). Simply select the cells and then choose Copy from the Edit menu (Ctrl+C), move the cell pointer to the first cell where the copied records are to appear and press Enter. After copying the filtered records, you can then redisplay all the records in the database or apply a slightly different filter.

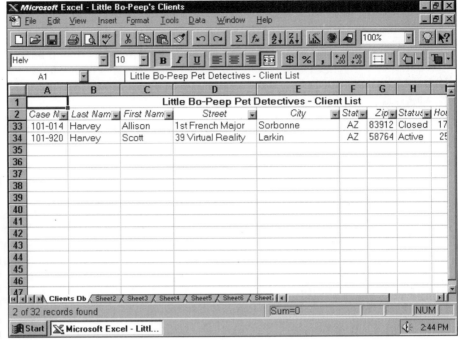

Figure 9-9:
Bo-Peep
database
after
filtering its
records to
those where
the State
is AZ.

If you find that filtering the database by selecting a single value in a field drop-down list box gives you more records than you really want to contend with, you can further filter the database by selecting another value in a second field's drop-down list box. For example, say that you select CA as the filter value in the State drop-down list box and end up with hundreds of California records still displayed in the worksheet. To reduce the number of California records to a more manageable number, you could then select a value like San Francisco in the City field's drop-down list box to further filter the database and reduce the records you have to work with on-screen. When you finish working with the San Francisco, California records, you can display another set by choosing the City's drop-down list box again and changing the filter value from San Francisco to some other city (such as Los Angeles).

When you're ready to once again display all the records in the database, choose Filter from the Data menu followed by the Show All command. You can also remove a filter from a particular field by selecting its drop-down list button and then selecting the (All) option at the top of the drop-down list.

Note that if you've only applied a single field filter to the database, choosing the (All) option is tantamount to selecting Show All command on the Data Filter cascading menu.

Viewing the top ten records

Excel for Windows 95 contains a new AutoFilter option called Top 10. You can use this option on a numerical field to show only a certain number of records (like the ones with the ten highest or lowest values in that field or those in the ten highest or lowest percent in that field). To use the Top 10 option to filter a database, follow these steps:

1. **Choose <u>F</u>ilter on the <u>D</u>ata pull-down menu and then choose Auto<u>F</u>ilter on the cascading menu.**

2. **Click the drop-down list button in the field that you want to use in filtering the database records.**

3. **Choose the (Top 10) option in the drop-down list box.**

   Excel opens the Top 10 AutoFilter dialog box, similar to the one shown in Figure 9-10.

   By default, the Top 10 AutoFilter chooses to show the top ten items in the selected field. You can, however, change these default settings before filtering the database.

4. **To show only the bottom ten records, change Top to Bottom in the drop-down list box.**

5. **To show more than the top or bottom ten records, enter the new value in the edit box that currently holds 10 or choose a new value with spinner buttons.**

6. **To show those records that fall into the top or bottom 10 (or whatever)** *percent,* **change Items to Percent in its drop-down list box.**

7. **Choose OK or press Enter to filter the database using your Top Ten settings.**

Figure 9-11 shows the Little Bo-Peep clients database after using the Top Ten option (with all its default settings) to show only those records whose Total Due values are in the top ten. David Letterman would be proud!

Getting creative with custom AutoFilters

In addition to filtering a database to records that contain a particular field entry (such as *Newark* as the City or *CA* as the State), you can create custom AutoFilters that enable you to filter the database to records that meet less-exacting criteria (such as last names starting with the letter M) or ranges of values (such as salaries between 25,000 and 35,000 a year).

Figure 9-10:
The Top Ten
AutoFilter
dialog box.

Figure 9-11:
The
database
after using
the Top Ten
AutoFilter to
show only
the records
with the ten
highest
amounts in
the Total
Due field.

To create a custom filter for a field, you click the field's drop-down list button and then choose the (Custom) option at the top of the drop-down list box — between (Top Ten) and the first field entry in the list box. When you choose the (Custom) option, Excel displays the Custom AutoFilter dialog box, similar to the one shown in Figure 9-12.

In this dialog box, you first select the operator that you want to use in the first drop-down list box (=, >, <, >=, <=, or <> — see Table 9-2 for details) and then enter the value (be it text or numbers) that should be met, exceeded, fallen below, or not found in the records of the database in the text box to the right. Note that you can select any of the entries made in that field of the database by choosing the drop-down list button and selecting the entry in the drop-down list box (much like you do when selecting an AutoFilter value in database itself).

Table 9-2	Operators used in creating custom AutoFilters		
Operator	*Meaning*	*Example*	*What It Locates in the Database*
=	Equal to	Last Name=D*	Records where the last name starts with the letter D
>	Greater than	ZIP >42500	Records where the number in the ZIP field comes after 42500
<	Less than	Salary<25000	Records where the value in the Salary field is less than 25,000 a year
>=	Greater than or equal to	Hired>=1/11/92	Records where the date in the Hired field is on or after January 11, 1992
<=	Less than or equal to	Joined<=2/15/91	Records where the date in the Joined field is on or before February 15, 1991
<>	Not equal to	State<>NY	Records where the entry in the State field is not NY (New York)

If you only want to filter records where a particular field entry matches, exceeds, falls below, or simply is not the same as the one you enter in the text box, you then choose OK or press Enter to apply this filter to the database. However, you can use the Custom AutoFilter dialog box to filter the database to records with field entries that fall within a range of values or meet either one of two criteria.

To set up a range of values, you choose the > or >= operator for the top operator and then enter or select the lowest (or first) value in the range. Then make sure that the And radio button is selected and choose < or <= as the bottom operator and enter the highest (or last) value in the range.

Figures 9-12 and 9-13 illustrate how to filter the records in the clients database so that only those records where Total Due amounts are between 25,000 and 50,000 are displayed. As shown in Figure 9-12, you set up this range of values as the filter by first selecting >= as the operator and 25000 as the lower value of the range. Then, with the And radio button selected, you choose <= as the operator and 50000 as the upper value of the range. Figure 9-13 shows the result of applying this filter to the clients database.

To set up an either/or condition in the Custom AutoFilter dialog box, you normally choose between the = (equal) and <> (unequal) operators (whichever is appropriate) and then enter or select the first value that must be met or must not be equaled. Then you select the Or radio button and choose whichever operator is appropriate and enter or select the second value that must be met or must not be equaled.

For example, if you want to filter the database so that only records where the state is WA (Washington) or OR (Oregon), you choose = as the first operator and then select or enter WA as the first entry. Next, you select the Or radio button, choose = as the second operator, and then select or enter OR as the second entry. When you then filter the database by choosing OK or pressing Enter, Excel displays only those records where either WA or OR is entered as the code in the State field.

Figure 9-12:
Custom
AutoFilter
where the
Total Due is
greater than
or equal to
25,000 and
less than or
equal to
50,000.

	D	E	F	G	H	I	J	K	L	M
1	tle Bo-Peep Pet Detectives - Client List									
2	Street	City	Stat	Zip	Status	Hour	Rate	Total Du	Pai	
6	49 Maple Syrup	Waffle	VT	05452	Active	205	125.00	$25,625	Yes	
10	3 Coal Scuttle	Big Apple	NY	10011	Active	237	125.00	$29,563	No	
11	2 Oliver Hardy	Celluloyde	NM	82128	Closed	352	125.00	$44,000	No	
12	Goblin's Mines	Everest	NJ	07639	Closed	400	125.00	$50,000	No	
14	8 Big Bellies	Victuals	NC	1076	Closed	365	100.00	$36,540	No	
15	6789 Fruitree Tr	Along The Way	MN	66017	Active	321	125.00	$40,125	Yes	
19	Very Crooked Mile	Crooked Sixpence	KY	23986	Active	300	125.00	$37,500	No	
22	60 Lucky Starr Pl	Shetland	IL	60080	Active	227	125.00	$28,313	No	
23	0 Pleistocene	Ann's World	ID	00001	Active	450	75.00	$33,765	No	
26	Sundance Kidde	Hole In Wall	CO	80477	Closed	346	75.00	$25,913	No	

Figure 9-13: The database after applying the custom AutoFilter.

10 of 32 records found

Part V
Doing a Custom Job

The 5th Wave   By Rich Tennant

"Kevin here heads our Windows software development team. Right now he's working on a spreadsheet program that's sort of a combination Excel and FrankenWolf."

In this part . . .

*I*n case you haven't noticed, one of the biggest problems with computers is how rigid they are, working for you only when you do exactly what they want you to do, right when they want you to do it. And, like it or not, software programs like Excel for Windows 95 are no different with their demanding command sequences and inflexible procedures.

Having seen how Excel for Windows 95 wants things done, I say it's high time to turn the tables and learn how to make the program work the way you want it to. To that end, Part V concentrates on all the areas that you can customize. This includes custom spreadsheets from templates in Chapter 10, changing the default settings in Chapter 11, streamlining routine procedures with macros in Chapter 12, and creating tailor-made toolbars in Chapter 13.

Chapter 10

Tearing Up the Town with Templates

● ●

In This Chapter

▶ Using templates to start a new workbook of a particular type

▶ Customizing Excel's ready-made templates for your own use

▶ Saving your own workbooks as template files

▶ Creating a template from a workbook with the Template Wizard

▶ Linking a template to a tracking database workbook with the Template Wizard

● ●

*S*preadsheet templates are special workbook files that provide you with the general formulas and formatting so that you can quickly generate specific spreadsheet examples. The great thing about Excel spreadsheet templates is that, when you open them, the program always opens a copy rather than the original template file. This enables you to make all the changes required for the specific spreadsheet you're creating, with absolutely no danger of making these changes to the original file. You can think of spreadsheet templates as the electronic equivalent of a pad of blank forms: Each time you open a template file, you get a copy that's blank except for the standard information.

Templates at Your Fingertips

The best way to become acquainted with spreadsheet templates in Excel is to look at the ready-made ones that come with Excel for Windows 95. Excel now provides you with a bunch of different types of templates called Spreadsheet Solutions designed by an outfit in Massachusetts called Village Software. (Note that if these templates are not installed on your computer, you will need to use the Excel Setup program with the Advanced option.) To use any of these Spreadsheet Solutions templates, do the following:

1. **Choose New on the File menu or press Ctrl+N to open the New dialog box.**

   Be sure not to click the New button on the Standard toolbar, because doing so opens a new, blank workbook without opening the New dialog box.

2. **Click the Spreadsheet Solutions tab in the New dialog box to display the icons for the ready-made templates (see Figure 10-1).**

3. **Click a particular template icon to display a preview of that template in the Preview area of the New dialog box.**

   In Figure 10-1, the Timecard template icon has been clicked, and you see its preview in the Preview area.

4. **To open one of the ready-made templates, either double-click its template icon or select it and then choose OK or press Enter.**

For example, Figure 10-2 shows you the screen after opening the Timecard template. Note that Excel automatically names this workbook Timecard1 so that any changes you make to this document cannot inadvertently be saved in the original Timecard template file. Notice also that the Timecard1 template workbook contains three worksheets: Customize Your Timecard, Timecard, and Personal Productivity (and that Timecard is currently selected).

Figure 10-1: Selecting the template to use in the Spreadsheet Solutions tab of the New dialog box.

Figure 10-2:
Copy of
the Time-
card tem-
plate after
opening
it in Excel.

Upon opening the Timecard template, notice that a floating toolbar called
Timecard appears in the upper-left corner of the workbook area (most of the
ready-made templates provided by Village Software open with a customized
toolbar similar to this one). This Timecard toolbar contains seven buttons:

- ✔ **Size to Screen/Return to Size** (first button on the left, top row): zooms out
  on the timecard so that its entire form appears on the screen and then
  zooms back into the normal 75% view.

- ✔ **Hide CellTips/Display CellTips** (second button from the left, top row):
  hides or redisplays the cell note indicators (those tiny red rectangles) that
  display the note's contents when you position the mouse pointer on them.

- ✔ **Document a Cell** (third button from the left, top row): opens the Cell Note
  dialog box where you can add your own notes to particular cells of the
  timecard.

- ✔ **Template Help** (fourth button from the left, top row): opens a dialog box
  with specific help on using the Timecard template.

✔ **Display Example/Remove Example** (first button on the left, bottom row): fills in the copy of the timecard with a sample record for a fictitious employee (one Annabella Dodsworth to be exact). Be sure to use this button to get rid of Annabella's sample record before you go about filling in the timecard information for your own employees.

✔ **Assign a Number** (second button from the left, bottom row): assigns a unique number to the copy of the timecard.

✔ **Capture Data in a Database** (third button from the left, bottom row): copies the timecard information.

In addition to these toolbar buttons, the Timecard worksheet contains several notes (indicated by the tiny red rectangles in various places on the form). These notes contain instructions on how to fill in different parts of the timecard. Because these buttons are actually cell-note indicators, you can display their instructions by simply positioning the mouse pointer on the red rectangle. Figure 10-3 shows the instructions associated with the Select Employee button that appeared when I positioned the mouse pointer on the note indicator (the tiny red rectangle) that's above and to the right of the button.

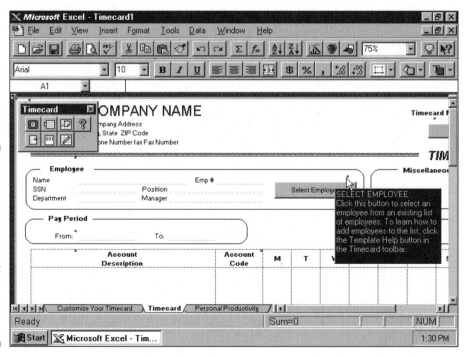

Figure 10-3:
Using CellTips to display the instructions associated with the Select Employee button in the Timecard worksheet.

Getting Village Software to do all the hard work for you

If, after using some of the ready-made templates provided by Village Software, you decide that you like the look and feel of their templates but have special template needs that aren't met by the forms they've included in Excel for Windows 95, open the Village Software template in the New dialog box. This template contains an order form for getting information about Village Software's other spreadsheet templates, complete with an 800-number you can call to get Village Software to design a completely custom spreadsheet template for you.

Customizing the Ready-Made Templates

Almost all the ready-made templates that come with Excel for Windows 95 are easy to customize for your business. When customizing these templates, you can add your company's logo, as well as its name, address, and telephone number. To customize a template, you fill this type of information in on the Customize worksheet (called Customize Your Timecard, in the case of the Timecard template). You can get this information to the worksheet either by clicking the worksheet's sheet tab or clicking the Customize button (located in the upper-right corner of the Timecard worksheet).

The Customize worksheet in the Timecard template contains three sections (Company Information, Default Timecard Information, and Formatted Information) with a bunch of different fields that you can fill in. In the Company Information part of the template (shown in Figure 10-4), you enter your company's name, address, and telephone and fax numbers.

In the Default Timecard Information section in the middle of the Customize Your Timecard sheet (shown in Figure 10-5), you can change the standard number of hours worked (from a mere 40 hours to something more realistic like 65 or 70 hours), approve overtime for the timecard template, and enable automatic and sequential shared-timecard numbering for everyone on your network (for which you must specify the path of the server where the Counter file with the shared-timecard numbers is to be located). Also, by default, Excel enables the Select Employee function, which lets you select employee information kept in a Common database, and specifies the location of the Common database and Template Wizard database (in which you can store the information you input into each timecard generated from the Timecard template).

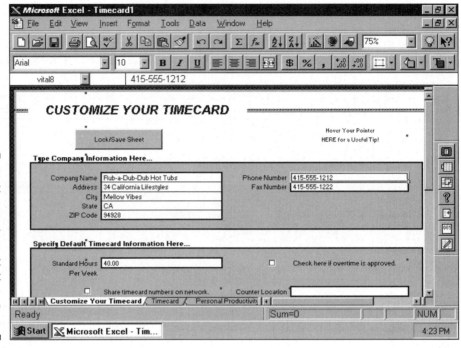

Figure 10-4:
The top part
of the
Customize
Your
Timecard
worksheet
after filling it
out for Rub-
a-Dub-Dub
Hot Tubs.

In the Formatted Information section at the bottom of the Customize Your Timecard sheet (also shown in Figure 10-5), you see the company name, address, and telephone number as it appears at the top of the Timecard worksheet. If you wish, you can change the font, font size, and style of this information by clicking the Change Plate Font button and then selecting new font stuff in the Format Cells dialog box.

Also, if you have a graphic file on your computer with your company's logo, you can use the Select Logo button to import and size this logo (so that it fits right on the square that says *Insert Logo Here*). When you click the Select Logo button, Excel opens the Picture dialog box where you select the file that contains the logo graphic. In Figure 10-5, you see the bottom part of the Customize Your Timecard sheet after selecting the Bubbles graphic (located in the Windows folder) as the logo for Rub-a-Dub-Dub Hot Tubs.

After you finish filling out the pertinent information in the Customize Your Timecard sheet, you can save this information in your own Timecard template by following these steps:

Figure 10-5:
Middle and
lower parts
of the
Customize
Your
Timecard
worksheet
after
selecting
the Bubbles
graphic
as the
company
logo for
Rub-a-Dub-
Dub Hot
Tubs.

1. **Click the Lock/Save Sheet button at the top of the Customize Your Timecard sheet to open the Lock/Save Sheet dialog box.**

   By default, Excel chooses the Lock and save Template radio button in this dialog box. Don't fool with this setting by selecting the Lock but don't save radio button unless your intention is *not* to save your customization changes at this time (which, if this is the case, why the heck are you reading these steps on how to save your customized Timecard?!).

2. **Choose the OK button or press Enter.**

   Excel opens the Save Template dialog box (similar to the one shown in Figure 10-6).

3. **Replace the temporary filename, Timecard1, by typing in the real name for your company's timecard template (something sensible like Rub-a-Dub-Dub Timecard) in the File name edit box.**

4. **Choose the Save button or press Enter.**

   When Excel finishes saving your customized template, it displays a Timecard dialog box indicating that the template has been saved in the Templates folder in the MSOffice folder. It also indicates to you that, in order to begin creating timecards from this template, you should close the current Timecard1 file and then choose <u>N</u>ew on the <u>F</u>ile menu or press Ctrl+N and select the template in the New dialog box (see "Tailored timecards thanks to the customized Timecard template," that follows, for details).

5. **Choose the OK button in the Timecard dialog box or press Enter.**

6. **Choose <u>C</u>lose on the <u>F</u>ile menu to close the Timecard1 file.**

7. **Select the <u>N</u>o button to discard your changes (now safely saved in your customized template file) when asked to save changes in the Timecard1.xlt file (the xlt stands for Excel Template).**

Customizing the other ready-made templates, like the Invoice or Purchase Order templates, for your use is very similar to customizing the Timecard template as outlined above. Simply choose the <u>N</u>ew command on the <u>F</u>ile menu (or Ctrl+N) and then open the ready-made template from the Spreadsheet Solutions tab of the New dialog box. Choose the Customize Your *Such n' Such* sheet tab in the workbook (*Such n' Such* being the actual name of a template like Invoice or Purchase Order) or click the Customize button in the template sheet. Fill in the pertinent blanks in the Customize Your *Such n' Such* worksheet; then click the Lock/Save Sheet button. After you give your customized template a new name, close the template workbook you just modified without saving your changes.

Figure 10-6:
Saving the customized Timecard template in the MSOffice Templates folder.

Tailored timecards thanks to the customized Timecard template

When you use the Lock/Save Sheet button in the Customize Your Timecard worksheet, Excel saves your customized template file in the Templates folder stored inside the MSOffice folder on your hard disk. This is, of course, of no earth-shattering importance — except for the fact that spreadsheet template files that are stored in this particular folder just happen to magically appear in the General tab of the New dialog box (making them really easy to use).

Figure 10-7 shows you the New dialog box (opened with Ctrl+N) after creating and saving the customized Timecard template, Rub-a-Dub-Dub Timecard. Notice that the General tab now contains the Rub-a-Dub-... Timecard template icon (you don't see the second "Dub" in the filename unless you switch the view to List or Details). When you click this template icon, the New dialog box shows you a preview of the Rub-a-Dub-Dub Hot Tubs timecard (Bubbles logo and all). To open a copy of this template and fill out an actual timecard for one of the employees, you simply double-click this template icon (or you can choose the OK button after selecting the icon).

Figure 10-8 shows you the Excel screen after doing just that. As you can see in this figure, Excel opens a copy (and not the original) Rub-a-Dub-Dub Timecard (named, appropriately enough, Rub-a-Dub-Dub Timecard1). You can fill in this copy of the original timecard template and then save its information with a new filename and/or in a new location (by choosing Save As on the File menu).

Opening the real McCoy

Normally, it's just great that Excel opens a copy of a template file rather than the original so that you can't possibly mess the original up. But what about those rare occasions when you need to make some modifications to the original template file itself, like when the company moves to a new address, changes the telephone number, or even, heaven forbid, adopts a new logo? How do you get Excel to open the real template file rather than a crummy copy?

Easy, just remember to hold down the Shift key when you double-click the template's file icon in the Open dialog box (and I do mean Open dialog box and *not* the New dialog box). If double-clicking an icon to open a file is against your religion, you can open the original template file by selecting its template icon in the Open dialog box and then holding down the Shift key as you click the Open button or press Enter (which just happens to be another way of saying "hold down both Shift and Enter after selecting the template icon").

Figure 10-7:
Opening a
copy of the
customized
Timecard
template
from the
General tab
of the New
dialog box.

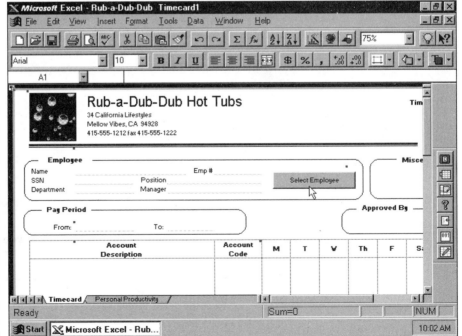

Figure 10-8:
A copy of
the custom
Rub-a-
Dub-Dub
timecard
opened in
Excel after
docking the
Timecard
toolbar on
the right
side of the
screen.

Culling employee info from the Common database

Both the Timecard and Sales Quote templates created by Village Software contain Select Employee buttons that you can use to automatically fill in the Employee sections of these forms simply by selecting the appropriate person in the Select Employee dialog box (see Figure 10-9). However, before you can use these buttons to get anything more than some dummy employees (by which I mean example database records created by Village Software — not necessarily fans of this computer-book series) into your customized timecard and sales quote workbooks, you need to customize the database that they both use by following these steps:

1. **Choose Open on the File menu or click the Open button on the Standard toolbar.**

2. **Click the Up One Level button in the Open dialog box (refer back to Chapter 4 if I started talking nonsense to you) until you see Hard disk (C:) in the Look in edit box.**

3. **Double-click the MSOffice folder to open it.**

   If you aren't using Microsoft Office for Windows 95, you won't see this folder, so proceed to step 4.

4. **Double-click the Excel folder to open it.**

5. **Double-click the Library folder to open it.**

6. **Double-click the Common file icon to open this workbook.**

The Common workbook contains two worksheets: Employee Info and Product and Service Catalog (the Product and Service Catalog information is used by the Sales Quote template to fill in the Product/Service Name edit box via a drop-down list button), each with its own database. Each database contains a heading, a row of field names (in bold), and a few dummy records.

To replace the dummy records in the Employee Info database with your own employee information, follow these steps:

1. **Click the Employee Info sheet tab to make the Employee Info sheet current.**

2. **Position the cell pointer somewhere in the sample employee records or the row of field names.**

3. **Choose Form on the Data pull-down menu to bring up the Employee Info data form with the first sample record.**

4. **Replace the sample records and add new records for your own employees as needed until you've got everybody entered.**

   (Refer back to Chapter 9 if you need help in dealing with the data form).

5. **Close the Employee Info data form, and then save your changes to the Common database by choosing Save on the File menu (Ctrl+S) or by clicking the Save button on the Standard toolbar.**

After customizing the Common database, you can then use its information to save yourself a bunch of typing when creating timecards with your customized Timecard template. Simply open a copy of the template (as described in the previous section), and then click the Select Employee button in the copy of the timecard. Excel opens a Select Employee dialog box similar to the one shown in Figure 10-9 (except that it will contain a list of the employees you put into the Employee Info database by following the preceding steps) where you can select the employee by double-clicking his or her name in the list box or clicking the name and then clicking OK or pressing Enter.

After you select the employee in this manner, Excel uses the person's record in the Common database to fill in the Name, Emp #, SSN, Position, Department, and Manager blanks in the Employee section of the timecard (or sales quote, if you opened a copy of the customized Sales Quote template).

Figure 10-10 shows you the result in a copy of the Rub-a-Dub-Dub Timecard template after selecting Cantnav Deboot in the Select Employee database.

Saving timecard data in a database

After you finish filling in an employee's timecard from a copy of your customized Timecard template, you can save the data as a record in a database by clicking the Capture Data in a Database button in the Timecard toolbar. When you click this button, Excel opens a Create and Interact with Database dialog box with two radio buttons: Create a new Template Database and Update existing Database (the default choice). To have Excel save the data in an existing database called Timedb, just choose OK or press Enter. Excel then displays the Template File - Save to Database dialog box. This dialog box contains two radio buttons of its own: Create a new record (the default choice) and Continue with updating. To save your timecard data in the Timedb database, be sure to leave the Create a new record radio button selected when you choose OK or press Enter.

Figure 10-9:
Getting employee information for Rub-a-Dub-Dub Timecard1 from the Common database via the Select an Employee dialog box.

Figure 10-10:
Rub-a-Dub-Dub Timecard1 after copying the employee information for Cantnav Deboot from the Common database.

Creating a new database for the timecard data

If you want, you can store the timecard data in another (existing) database besides the default Timedb database provided by Excel. To store the timecard data in your own database, you choose the Create a new Template Database radio button in the Create and Interact with Database dialog box before you choose OK or press Enter. When you do this, Excel opens the Template Wizard dialog box that steps you through the process of selecting a different database in which to store the data and even allows you to indicate into which cells specific timecard data is to be stored (for specific information on using the Template Wizard, see "Conjuring Up Templates with the Template Wizard," later in this chapter).

Saving the timecard workbook and updating the database

When you go to save the timecard workbook — with the Save command on the File menu, the Save button on the Standard toolbar, or by choosing the Save As command on the File menu (as you would to rename the timecard workbook and/or save it in a different folder) — Excel first displays the Template File - Save to Database dialog box before saving the workbook on disk.

If you haven't previously used the Capture Data in a Database button in the Timecard, this dialog box only contains two radio buttons: Create a new record (the default choice) and Continue with updating. However, if you have already saved the timecard data in a database with the Capture Data in a Database button, this Template File - Save to Database dialog box contains three radio buttons: Update the existing record (the default choice), Create a new record, and Continue without updating.

If you've made some changes to the timecard between now and the time you used the Capture Data in a Database button, leave the Update the existing record radio button selected when you choose OK or press Enter. Otherwise, choose the Continue with updating radio button before choosing OK or pressing Enter (you'd only use the Create a new record radio button in the very rare case when you want a timecard entered twice in the Timedb database).

Turning Workbooks into Templates

Although the template files supplied by Village Software provide you a quick and easy way to start using templates in your work, you are by no means limited to this collection. Any workbook that you create in Excel for Windows 95 can be turned into a template for generating future spreadsheets, all in a matter of minutes.

To give you an idea of how easy it is to convert a working spreadsheet into a template, look at Figure 10-11. This figure shows the first worksheet in a workbook called RDD Invoice 1003. This invoice workbook is an actual spreadsheet that's being modified over and over again to generate the invoices for Rub-a-Dub-Dub Hot Tubs. The only problem with modifying a working spreadsheet to create new invoices is that you have to remember to save all changes in a new file (otherwise, you corrupt the previous invoice file). Rather than run the risk of messing up one invoice when creating the next one, you're much better off converting a copy of the spreadsheet into a template file.

Figure 10-12 shows you the same RDD Invoice 1003 workbook after removing all the entries that are specific to the invoice for the Brothers Grimm Estate. These entries include the bill-to information, the date, invoice number, and, of course, the item numbers and quantities purchased. This does not include the underlying formulas that look up the item numbers in the Price List database and return the price and description to the invoice. Nor does it include the formulas that calculate the amount, subtotal, tax, and total amount due.

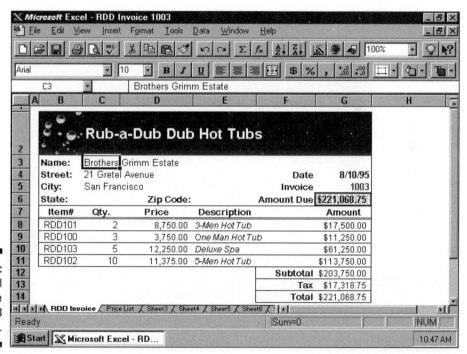

Figure 10-11:
The original
RDD Invoice
1003
workbook.

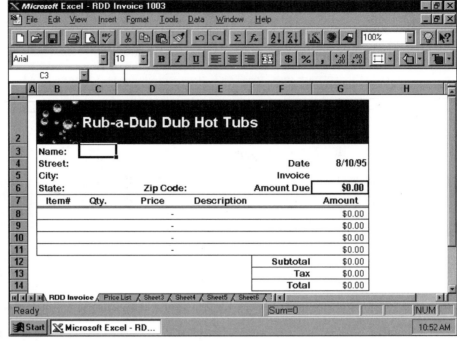

Figure 10-12:
RDD Invoice
1003 work-
book after
removing
all but
the formulas
and standard
text.

Once the RDD Invoice 1003 contains only the generic information and formulas needed in every Rub-a-Dub-Dub invoice, you are ready to save this denuded version of the workbook as a template file. To do this, you follow these steps:

1. Choose Save As on the File menu.

2. In the Save As dialog box, enter the name for the new template in the File name edit box.

3. Choose Template as the file type in the Save as type drop-down list box.

As soon as you change the type from Worksheet to Template in the Save as type drop-down list box, Excel switches to the Templates folder (see Figure 10-13).

4. Choose the Save button or press Enter.

After saving the generic form of your workbook as a template file, you can open copies of the template by selecting its file icon in the General tab of the Open dialog box.

Figure 10-14 shows a copy of the Rub-a-Dub-Dub invoice template (RDD Invoice Template1) filled out for the Sleeping Beauty Health Spas. This workbook was

Figure 10-13:
Saving the
RDD Invoice
Template in
the Save As
dialog box.

created by selecting the RDD Invoice Template file in the General tab of the
Excel Open dialog box and then filling in the bill to, date, invoice number, item
number, and quantity sold. All that remains is to save this invoice with a new
filename using the Save As command on the File menu!

Conjuring Up Templates with the Template Wizard

The Template Wizard with Data Tracking (more commonly known as just the
plain old Template Wizard) is a new Excel for Windows 95 add-in program that
enables you to create a template from an existing workbook and then link
particular cells in that template to particular fields in a new database. Because
this program is an add-in, you may not automatically find the Template Wizard
command on the Data pull-down menu. If you don't see this command on the
Data menu, you need to choose Add-Ins on the Tools pull-down menu, and then
choose the Template Wizard with Data Tracking check box in the Add-Ins
Available list box. (If this check-box option doesn't appear in the list box, this
means that the Template Wizard wasn't installed with Excel for Windows 95 and
that you need to install it — or con somebody into installing it for you.)

Figure 10-14:
Using the
RDD Invoice
Template to
create
Invoice 1004
for Sleeping
Beauty
Health Spas.

Before you can use the Template Wizard, you must create the workbook that is to be used in the creation of the new template. After creating the workbook, but before using the Template Wizard, you should remove all the specific data and use the Save As command on the File menu to save the generic form of the workbook under a new filename (see "Turning Workbooks into Templates," earlier in this chapter, for more on getting a working spreadsheet ready for templatehood).

When you have the Template Wizard add-in installed and the generic form of the workbook to be converted into a template open in Excel, you take the following steps:

1. **Choose Template Wizard on the Data menu to open the Template Wizard - Step 1 of 5 dialog box (similar to one shown in Figure 10-15).**

   In the Step 1 of 5 dialog box, Excel puts the name of the current workbook in the Select the name of the workbook you want to create a template from edit box and suggests that the same filename (minus the xls extension) be used for the template in the Templates folder inside the MSOffice folder.

Figure 10-15:
Designating
the work-
book to be
converted
and the
template
filename
in the
Template
Wizard -
Step 1 of 5
dialog box.

2. **If necessary, change the name for the template in the Type a name for the template edit box, and then choose the Next button or press Enter to open the Template Wizard - Step 2 of 5 dialog box (similar to one shown in Figure 10-16).**

   In the Step 2 of 5 dialog box, the program selects Microsoft Excel Workbook as the type of database you want the Template Wizard to create and suggests a filename for the workbook that adds the word "Database" to the current filename.

Figure 10-16:
Designating
the type,
location,
and name of
the tracking
database
in the
Template
Wizard -
Step 2 of 5
dialog box.

3. **If necessary, change the filename and/or location of the file in the Type the location and name of the database edit box and then choose the Next button or press Enter to open the Template Wizard - Step 3 of 5 dialog box (similar to one shown in Figure 10-17).**

In the Step 3 of 5 dialog box, you select the cells that are to be used as fields in the tracking database in the first column and, if necessary, edit their field names in the second column.

Figure 10-17: Selecting the cells in the work-book to be linked to the tracking database in the Template Wizard - Step 3 of 5 dialog box.

4. **Click the first cell in the workbook whose data you want to appear in the first field of the database (move the Step 3 of 5 dialog box by its title bar, if you can't see the cell).**

When you click a cell in the workbook, Excel puts its cell address (with absolute cell references) in the Cell edit box in the Step 3 of 5 dialog box.

5. **Press Tab to enter the field name in the second column and move the insertion point into the cell space for the No. 2 cell.**

Excel fills the first Field Name space with whatever heading it can associate with the first cell reference in the Cell edit box to its left. If the program doesn't properly identify the heading, you'll need to go back and edit the name in this Field Name box.

6. **Press Tab to move the insertion point to the No. 3 cell edit box.**

Repeat steps 4 and 5, selecting the next cell to be used and, if necessary, editing its field name until you've identified all the cells in the workbook whose data is to be copied to individual fields of a single record.

7. **Choose the Next button or press Enter to open the Template Wizard - Step 4 of 5 dialog box (similar to one shown in Figure 10-18).**

Figure 10-18: Adding information from existing workbooks to the database in the Template Wizard - Step 4 of 5 dialog box.

In the Step 4 of 5 dialog box, you can have Excel copy data from other existing workbooks into the new tracking database by selecting the Yes, include radio button. To use this option, the other workbooks must use the same layout as the workbook you're converting to a template (otherwise you get a lot of garbage in your tracking database). If you don't have any other workbooks whose data needs to be added to the tracking database, leave the No, skip it radio button selected.

If you select the Yes, include radio button before you choose the Next button, Excel rewrites the Step 4 of 5 dialog box (similar to the one shown in Figure 10-19). Choose the Select button and then choose all the files to be converted in the Select files to convert dialog box and choose the Open button.

When you return to the Step 4 of 5 dialog box, all the files you've selected appear in the Files to convert list box. To preview how the workbook's data will appear in the database record, click the filename in the Files to convert list box, and then choose the Preview button or press Enter.

Figure 10-19:
Selecting
other
workbooks
to be linked
to the
tracking
database in
the redrawn
Template
Wizard -
Step 4 of 5
dialog box.

8. **Choose the Yes, include radio button if you have other workbooks whose data should be copied into the tracking database; then choose Next.**

   Select and preview the other workbooks to be linked in the redrawn Step 4 of 5 dialog box before you choose Next again to open the Template Wizard - Step 5 of 5 dialog box (similar to one shown in Figure 10-20). If you don't have other workbooks to be linked, leave the No, skip it radio button selected and just choose the Next button or press Enter to open the Step 5 of 5 dialog box.

   In the Step 5 of 5 dialog box, Excel shows you the name and location of the template and the tracking database that the Template Wizard has created for you. If you are on a network and want each workbook generated from the new template automatically e-mailed to other people, click the Add Routing Slip button before you choose the Finish button.

9. **Choose the Finish button or press Enter to finish creating the template and tracking database and to close the Template Wizard.**

After you create your template and tracking database with the Template Wizard, each time you save a new workbook generated from the template, Excel displays the Template File - Save to Database dialog box, where you can create a new record in the linked database using the worksheet data by choosing OK or just pressing Enter.

Figure 10-20:
Displaying
the names
of the
template
and tracking
database
in the
Template
Wizard -
Step 5 of 5
dialog box.

Chapter 11

Stating Your Preferences

● ●

In This Chapter

▶ Changing the way stuff is displayed on-screen

▶ Customizing general settings

▶ Customizing the colors displayed on a color monitor

● ●

*E*ach time you open a new workbook, Excel for Windows 95 makes a whole bunch of assumptions about how you want the spreadsheet and chart information you enter into it to appear on-screen and in print. These assumptions may or may not fit the way you work and the kinds of spreadsheets and charts you need to create.

In this chapter, you get a quick rundown on how to change the default or *preference* settings in the Options dialog box. This is the biggest dialog box in Excel, with a billion tabs (ten actually), which explains why it takes so long to open. From the Options dialog box, you can see what things appear on-screen and how they appear, as well as when and how Excel calculates worksheets.

Nothing in this chapter is critical to your being able to operate Excel. Just know that if you find yourself futzing with the same setting over and over again in most of the workbooks you create, then it's high time to get into the Options dialog box and modify that setting so that you won't end up wasting anymore time tinkering with the same setting in future workbooks.

Varying the View Options

Excel gives you a lot of control over what appears on-screen and how it looks. The options for controlling the appearance of the Excel program and workbook windows mostly show up on the View tab of the Options dialog box. In addition, you can customize the cell-reference style, the menus used, the number of worksheets to a new workbook, and the font that each new workbook uses — all in the General tab of the Options dialog box (discussed in the next section, "Fooling Around with the General Options").

Figure 11-1 shows the options on the View tab of the Options dialog box. To open this dialog box, choose Options on the Tools menu, then choose the View tab. The View tab contains a mess of check boxes that turn on and off the display of various elements in both the Excel program window and a particular workbook document window. As you would expect, all the options that have check marks in their check boxes are turned on, whereas all the options with empty check boxes are turned off.

Figure 11-1:
The View tab in the Options dialog box.

The check-box options in the Show area of this dialog box control which elements are displayed in the Excel program window:

- **Formula Bar:** to hide or show the formula bar right below the Formatting toolbar at the top of the program window (see Chapter 2).

- **Status Bar:** to hide or show the status bar at the bottom of the program window (see Chapter 1).

- **Note Indicator:** to hide or show a little red dot in the upper-right corner of a cell that contains a note (see Chapter 6).

- **Info Window:** to hide or show a separate window, displaying information about the contents of whatever cell is current in your worksheet.

The check-box options in the Window Options area of the View tab determine whether or not a number of elements in the current worksheet are displayed. Keep in mind that turning off a particular element in the current worksheet does not turn it off in any other worksheet in that workbook. All of the following option settings are saved as part of your worksheet when you save the work-book except for the Automatic Page Breaks option (which always reverts to the default of being hidden):

- ✔ **Automatic Page Breaks:** to hide or show the page breaks that Excel puts in the worksheet when you print it or look at it in Print Preview mode.

- ✔ **Formulas:** to switch between showing the formulas in the cells of your worksheet and showing the calculated values (the normal state of affairs). When you select this check box, Excel also automatically widens all the columns and left-aligns all of the information in the cells.

- ✔ **Gridlines:** to hide or show the column and row separators that define the cells in your worksheet. Note that you can also change the color of the gridlines (when they're displayed, of course) by choosing a new color in the color palette that appears when you click the Color drop-down list button (I find that navy blue is rather fetching).

- ✔ **Row & Column Headers:** to hide or show the row of column letters at the top of the worksheet and the column of row numbers at the left.

- ✔ **Outline Symbols:** to hide or show all the various symbols that appear when you outline a worksheet table (something you only do with really large tables so that you can collapse the table to its essentials by hiding all but particular levels) or when you use the Subtotals feature to calculate subtotals, totals, and grand totals for certain fields in a database.

- ✔ **Zero Values:** to hide or display entries of zero in the worksheet. Deselect this check box if you want to suppress the display of all zeros in a worksheet (as you might in a worksheet template if you don't want to see all those zeros in a new worksheet generated from the template).

- ✔ **Horizontal Scroll Bar:** to hide or display the horizontal scroll bar to the right of the worksheet tabs at the bottom of the workbook document window. When you hide the horizontal scroll bar and leave the sheet tabs displayed (see Sheet Tabs below), Excel fills the area normally reserved for the horizontal scroll bar with more sheet tabs. Note that this option affects the display of every worksheet in your workbook.

- ✔ **Vertical Scroll Bar:** to hide or display the vertical scroll bar on the right side of the workbook document window. This option also affects the display of every worksheet in your workbook.

- ✔ **Sheet Tabs:** to hide or display the tabs that enable you to activate the various worksheets in your workbook. Note that, when you remove the display of the sheet tabs, you can still use Ctrl+PgDn and Ctrl+PgUp to move between worksheets. However, without the tabs, you won't know which worksheet you're looking at unless you can recognize the sheet from its data alone.

Chapter 8 introduces the Objects radio buttons in the View tab of the Options dialog box. Remember that these settings determine how graphic objects (including charts and other types of graphics) are displayed in the worksheet. To speed up the screen response time when making editing changes, you can replace the detailed display of graphic objects with placeholders (shaded rectangles) by clicking on the Show Placeholders radio button. To hide the graphic objects altogether, select the Hide All radio button instead. When you finish editing and are again ready to display the charts and graphics in a worksheet, click the Show All radio button.

Fooling Around with the General Options

The General tab in the Options dialog box (shown in Figure 11-2) contains a number of program-setting options that you might want to change (if not right away, then after working with Excel for Windows 95 a little more). Of special interest to some might be the Sheets in New Workbook option that sets the number of blank worksheets in each new workbook (you might never ever need 16 and want to choose a more realistic number: hey, like 3, or maybe, if you're feeling wild, 4); the Standard Font option that sets the font used in every cell of a new workbook; and the Default File Location that determines which directory Excel automatically chooses when you try to open or save a workbook document.

Figure 11-2:
The General
tab in the
Options
dialog box.

✔ **Reference Style:** This box contains the A1 and R1C1 radio buttons. The A1 style (kinda sounds like a steak sauce) is the reference style you know from this book and the one that Excel normally uses. The R1C1 style is this creepy alternative in which each column is numbered just like the rows, and the row (that's the R part) reference number precedes the column (that's the C part) reference number. In this system, the cell you know and love as B2 would be cell R2C2. (Hey, wasn't that the name of that vacuum-cleaner-like droid in *Star Wars?!*)

✔ **Recently Used File List:** When you select this check box, Excel lists the last four documents you opened (in order from most recently used to least recently used) at the bottom of the File menu. You can then open any of these four files simply by selecting its name (or number) after you open the File menu.

✔ **Microsoft Excel 4.0 Menus:** When you select this check box, the program gives you a blast from the past by resetting the pull-down menus to the way they appeared in Excel 4.0 (the major difference being the use of separate Formula, Data, and Macro menus whose items are relocated on other menus in Excel for Windows 95). Don't put a check mark in this box and then expect to make sense out of the instructions and steps in this book — this option is intended for old Excel 4.0 hands who just can't make the transition to the new menu system.

✔ **Ignore Other Applications:** When this check box contains a check mark, Excel ignores requests made from other programs using DDE (which stands for Dynamic Data Exchange, as if you care). This is of interest only if you are using data created with other programs in your Excel workbooks (in which case, you definitely want leave this check box alone).

✔ **Reset TipWizard:** Normally, the TipWizard (that's the tool with the light bulb that glows yellow when it's got a hot tip for you) shows you a particular tip only once during a work session and will not display that tip again in subsequent work sessions unless you perform the action related to that tip three more times. You select this check box when you want to reset the TipWizard to clear its memory of which tips it's already shown you. This enables Excel to once again display tips you've already seen immediately after you perform the related action a single time.

✔ **Prompt for File Properties:** Normally, Excel does not display a Properties dialog box where you can enter summary information about the subject of the workbook as well as key words that you later use when searching for the file. That can all change if you put a check mark in this check box. Note that if you don't use this option (or purposely ignore it) when saving a workbook and then later decide that you want to add a summary to your workbook, you can still do so by choosing the Properties command on the File menu when the workbook is active.

✔ **Sheets in New Workbook:** Normally, Excel puts 16 blank worksheets in each new workbook you open. If you're never in a million years gonna use that many worksheets, you can select this option and reduce the number. On the other hand, you could also use this option to increase the number of worksheets in a new workbook if you find that you're routinely using more than 16 sheets, and you're getting tired of having to use the Worksheet command on the Insert menu (see Chapter 7 for more information on manually inserting and removing worksheets from a workbook).

✔ **Standard Font** and **Size:** Use these options to change the font and/or font size that Excel automatically assigns to all the cells in a new workbook. If you have a favorite font you like to see in most of the worksheets you create (and Arial ain't it), this is the way to select your font of choice rather than having to call upon the Font tool on the Formatting toolbar all the time (see Chapter 3).

✔ **Default File Location:** If you don't specify a directory for this option when you first start Excel, the program looks for each workbook that you try to open or puts each new workbook that you save in a folder named My Documents on your hard disk. Use this option to select another folder as the repository of your precious documents by entering the path name of the folder (such as **C:\Greg\Excel Stuff**). Note that this folder must exist prior to using this option (it can't be one that you intend to create but just haven't gotten around to yet). Remember that you can create a new folder at the time you first save a new workbook by clicking the Create New Folder button on the Save As dialog box toolbar.

✔ **Alternate Startup File Location:** Normally, Excel opens any document that you put in the special Startup folder called XLStart whenever you start Excel. If you don't feel that one Startup folder is enough, you can use this option to specify another one. Again, this folder must already exist before you can designate it as your alternate startup location by entering its path in this edit box.

✔ **User Name:** In my copy of Excel, this is usually Greg Harvey (unless I'm using my nom de plume, I.M. Shakes Peer), but it will differ in your copy unless you happen to go by the same name or alias. If you want to change your user name to Greg Harvey or I.M. Shakes Peer, this is where you do it.

Changing Those Crazy Color Palettes

If you're fortunate enough to have a color monitor on your computer, you can spruce up the on-screen appearance of a document by applying various colors to different parts of worksheets or charts. Excel lets you choose from a palette of 56 predefined colors; you can apply these colors to specific cells, cell borders, fonts, or graphic objects (such as a particular data series in a chart or a text box or an arrow).

✔ To apply a new color to a cell selection or a selected graphic object, click the Color tool on the Formatting toolbar (the one with the paint bucket) and select the color you want to apply from the pop-up palette of 56 colors.

✔ To change the color of the font Excel uses in a cell selection or for a selected graphic object (such as a chart title or text box), choose the Font Color tool on the Formatting toolbar (the one with T partially hidden by a red square) and select the color you want to apply in the pop-up palette of 56 colors.

✔ To change the color of the borders of a cell or cell selection, open the Format Cells dialog box (Ctrl+1); then select the Border tab and choose the Color option or click its drop-down list button to display the palette of 56 colors from which you can select the one you want to assign to the borders of the selected cells.

If none of the 56 predefined colors exactly suits your artistic tastes, you can customize colors on the palette. Although you can't place additional colors on the palette, you can change any or all of the predefined colors, depending on how ambitious you want to get.

To customize a color on the palette, follow these steps:

1. **Choose the Color tab in the Options dialog box (shown in Figure 11-3).**

2. **Select the color you want to modify in any of the areas: Standard Colors, Chart Fills, Chart Lines, or Other Colors.**

3. **Select the Modify button.**

Figure 11-3:
The Color tab in the Options dialog box.

When you choose <u>M</u>odify, Excel opens the Color Picker dialog box (shown in Figure 11-4) where you can modify the selected color. If you know something about color theory, you can modify the color by adjusting its hue (H<u>u</u>e), saturation (<u>S</u>at), and luminosity (<u>L</u>um), or its red (<u>R</u>ed), green (<u>G</u>reen), and blue (<u>B</u>lue) content.

Figure 11-4:
The Color
Picker
dialog box.

If you, like me, don't have the foggiest idea what to do with these individual settings, you can still customize the color by dragging the crosshair around the color square or the triangle up and down the color bar on the right.

✔ When you drag the crosshair, you change the color's hue and saturation.

✔ When you drag the triangle up and down the color bar, you change the color's luminosity as well as its mixture of red, green, and blue.

As you change the color settings, check how the color will appear by looking at the Color/Solid rectangle in the Color Picker dialog box. When you've got the color just the way you want it, choose OK or press Enter to close the Color Picker dialog box and return to the Color Palette dialog box. The custom color now appears in this dialog box.

To customize other colors in the palette, select them and repeat this modification process. To restore the predefined colors to Excel, click the <u>R</u>eset button in the Color tab.

After you customize the colors for a particular workbook, you can then copy your colors to another workbook (saving you all the time and effort of modifying each color individually again). To do this, follow these instructions:

1. **Open the workbook with the customized palette.**

2. **Using the Window pull-down menu, switch to the workbook to which you want to copy the palette.**

3. **Open the Color tab in the Options dialog box in the second workbook.**

4. **From the drop-down list box, choose Copy Colors.**

5. **Select the name of the workbook with the custom colors you want copied.**

   Excel modifies the colors in the Color tab of the Options dialog box to match the ones in the workbook you selected.

6. **To use these colors in the new workbook, close the Options dialog box by choosing OK or pressing Enter.**

Editing the Edit Options

The Edit tab of the Options dialog box (shown in Figure 11-5) contains options that determine how editing works. As you notice when you first select the Edit tab, most of these check-box options are already turned on for you.

Figure 11-5:
The Edit tab
of the
Options
dialog box.

- ✔ **Edit Directly in Cell:** If you deselect this option, you can't do any more editing within the cell. Instead, you have to edit the cell's contents on the formula bar after either double-clicking the cell or selecting it and then pressing F2.

- ✔ **Allow Cell Drag and Drop:** If you deselect this option, you can no longer use the drag-and-drop method to copy or move cells around a worksheet, from worksheet to worksheet within a workbook, or from workbook to workbook.

- ✔ **Alert before Overwriting Cells:** If you deselect this option (which I really don't recommend), Excel no longer warns you when a drag-and-drop operation is about to obliterate stuff that you've already entered in the worksheet.

- ✔ **Move Selection after Enter** and **Direction:** If you deselect this option, Excel no longer moves the cell pointer when you press the Enter key to complete a cell entry. If you still want Enter to complete an entry and move the cell pointer but don't want it to move to the next cell down, leave the Move Selection after Enter check box selected and choose a new direction (Right, Up, or Left) in the Direction drop-down list box.

- ✔ **Fixed Decimal** and **Places:** Select this option only when you want to set all values in the worksheet to the decimal precision indicated in the associated edit box (see "The values behind the formatting" in Chapter 3 for more information). When selecting this check box, you can modify the number of decimal places from the default of 2 by entering the new value in the edit box or using the spinner buttons.

- ✔ **Cut, Copy, and Sort Objects with Cells:** Deselect this editing option only when you don't want graphic objects (like text boxes, arrows, and imported images) to move around when you cut, copy, or sort the cells underneath them.

- ✔ **Ask to Update Automatic Links:** Deselect this option when you don't want Excel to bother you before going ahead and updating links between formulas in different workbooks.

- ✔ **Animate Insertion and Deletion:** Select this option when you want Excel to animate the process of making room for insertions or the process of pulling up and over cells to close gaps in the worksheet when making deletions.

- ✔ **Enable AutoComplete for Cell Values:** Deselect this option if you find that the AutoComplete feature gets in your way when entering columns of data in a worksheet (see "You really AutoCorrect that for me" in Chapter 2 for information on what the heck AutoComplete is, let alone what it does).

The Very Model of a Module General

The Module General tab of the Options dialog box is only of interest to some of you more cosmopolitan types because it contains the International settings that determine what character Excel uses as the list separator as well as how it displays Number, Currency, and Date/Time formats in the worksheet (along with some dorky options that determine how you code Visual Basic commands on Macro sheets — whew?!).

By default, the Language/Country option on the Module General tab (shown in Figure 11-6) is set to English/United States. If you happen to be creating spreadsheets for some foreign, English-speaking clients or offices, you can change this setting in the Language/Country drop-down list box. The choices on this drop-down list include a variety of English-speaking countries from Australia to the United Kingdom. When you choose a new language/country option in this list box, the Module General tab shows you what effect your choice will have on the list separator and the Number, Currency, and Date/Time formats in your worksheet.

Figure 11-6:
The Module
General tab
of the
Options
dialog box.

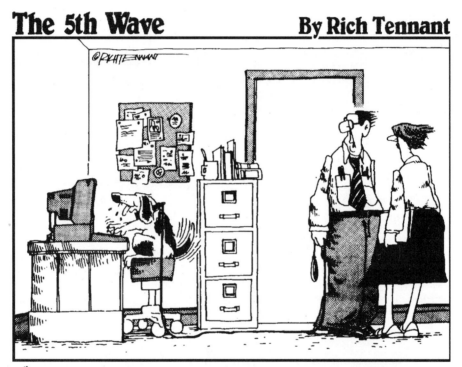

The 5th Wave   By Rich Tennant

"NAAAH - HE'S NOT THAT SMART. HE WON'T BACK UP HIS HARD DISK, FORGETS TO CONSISTENTLY NAME HIS FILES, AND DROOLS ALL OVER THE KEYBOARD."

Chapter 12

Macros Like Your Mom Used to Make

● ●

In This Chapter

▶ Recording macros that perform common tasks

▶ Playing your macros

▶ Editing macros

▶ Adding macros to Excel toolbars

● ●

*M*acros! Just hearing the word can be enough to make you want to head for the hills. But rather than think of this term as so much techno-babble, keep in mind that "macro" is short for "macro instruction" and that the word "macro" refers to the BIG picture. A *macro* (at least, at the level of this book) is nothing more than a way to record the actions you take to get a particular task done (such as to enter a company name in a worksheet, save and print a worksheet, or format row headings) and have Excel play those actions back for you.

Using a macro to perform a routine task instead of doing it by hand has some definite advantages. First, Excel can execute the commands involved much faster than you can (no matter how good you are at the keyboard or how familiar you are with Excel). Also, Excel performs the task flawlessly each and every time (because the macro plays back your actions exactly as recorded, you only have to worry that you record them correctly). Besides, you can even streamline the playback process by assigning keystroke shortcuts to your favorite macros, essentially reducing common tasks that otherwise require quite a few steps to just two keystrokes.

Recording Macros

The process of recording a macro is surprisingly straightforward:

1. **Open the Record New Macro dialog box to turn on the macro recorder by choosing Tools⇨Record Macro⇨Record New Macro.**

2. **Name the macro and (optionally) assign it a keystroke shortcut and/or assign it to the Tools pull-down menu.**

3. **Perform the sequence of actions you want recorded in the macro just as you normally do in Excel.**

   You can choose commands from the pull-down or shortcut menus, click tools in the toolbars, or use shortcut keystrokes.

4. **Turn off the macro recorder when you're finished by clicking the Stop Macro tool that appears in its own toolbar as soon as you start recording.**

   You can also turn off the macro recorder by choosing Tools⇨Record Macro⇨Stop Recording.

5. **Perform the task anytime you want simply by double-clicking the macro name in the Macro dialog box (opened by choosing Tools⇨Macro) or by selecting the macro name and then choosing the Run button.**

   Alternately, if you bothered to assign a keystroke shortcut to the macro or to assign the macro to the Tools menu when you recorded it, you can run the macro by pressing the keystroke shortcut or by selecting the macro on the Tools pull-down menu.

You'll be happy to know that, when recording your actions, Excel doesn't record mistakes (don't you wish everyone else was so forgiving?). In other words, if you're entering the heading "January" in the macro and you type **Janaury** by mistake and then correct your error, Excel does not record your pressing of the Backspace key to delete the characters "aury" and then typing **uary**. The only thing the macro records is the final, corrected result of **January**!

To record your actions, Excel for Windows 95 uses a language called *Visual Basic* (a language, by the way, that you don't need to know diddley about in order to create and use *simple* macros — the only kind you're going to get involved with in this book). Visual Basic commands are recorded in a separate module sheet (a *module sheet* is just a fancy name for a worksheet that doesn't use cells and therefore looks more like a typical page on a word processor screen).

Recording macros in good old Excel 4.0 style!

Although Excel for Windows 95 *prefers* recording macros in the new fangled Visual Basic language (instead of the good old standby macro language we all knew and loved in Excel 4.0 and earlier versions), this doesn't mean that the program has now adopted an "Only Visual Basic Spoken Here!" attitude. Indeed, Excel for Windows 95 not only runs existing macros in Visual Basic language, but it continues to record new macros in the "obsolete" language should you desire it.

To record a macro in the Excel 4.0 language, you choose the Options button in the Record New Macro dialog box; then choose the MS Excel 4.0 Macro radio button under Language before you start recording the new macro. Excel then records all your actions in the old, familiar macro language, which you can find in a Macro1 worksheet appended to the end of the current workbook.

Personally Speaking

Excel automatically assumes that you want to record your macro as part of the current workbook. Recording the macro as part of the workbook means that you can only run the macro when this workbook is open. You may want to have access to some of the macros that you create any old time you're using Excel, regardless of whether or not the workbook that happened to be current when you originally recorded the macro is now open or whether or not you're creating a new workbook or editing an existing one.

To record a macro so that it's universally available for use anytime, anywhere in Excel, you must record the macro in your personal macro workbook rather than in the current workbook. Because your personal macro workbook is automatically opened whenever you start up Excel (although it remains hidden at all times), you can run any of its macros no matter what workbook or workbooks are open at the time.

To record a macro in the personal macro workbook

1. **Choose Tools⇨Record Macro⇨Record New Macro to open the Record New Macro dialog box.**

2. **Choose the Options button in the Record New Macro dialog box.**

3. **Choose the Personal Macro Workbook radio button under Store in.**

4. **Start recording the new macro.**

Taking a look at your personal macro workbook

Excel doesn't actually create a personal macro workbook for you until you take the trouble to record your first macro in that location (no sense creating something you're never gonna use). After creating your first macro(s) in the personal macro workbook, you also have to save your changes in this file called PERSONAL.XLS (though you don't see the .XLS in Excel for Windows 95 displays), which is located in the XLStart Startup folder when you save this workbook upon exiting the program.

After creating and saving your first macro in the personal macro workbook, you can thereafter make this mysterious workbook visible (letting you take a gander at its contents) by choosing the Unhide command on the Window menu and selecting Personal in the Unhide dialog box. After you finish scratching your head over all those strange Visual Basic commands in the macros in the Module1 sheet of this workbook (which is the only sheet that this workbook happens to contain), be sure to hide the workbook once again by choosing Hide on the Window menu (otherwise, you'll have to look at those Visual Basic macro commands each and every time you fire up Excel — not a particularly pleasant thought!).

A Macro a Day

The best way to get a feel for how easy it is to record and play back a simple macro is to follow along with the steps for creating a couple of them. The first sample macro enters and formats a company name in a cell. In these steps, you turn on the macro to record as you enter the company name, such as **Mother Goose Enterprises,** and change the font to 18-point Broadway-WP. If you're actually following along at your computer as you read these steps, be sure to adapt the basic macro so that it enters the name of *your* company in the font and type size *you* want to use.

The very first thing you need is a place in which to perform the actions you're going to have Excel record in the macro. For this example, open a new worksheet (although you can also use a blank cell in an existing worksheet). Then follow these steps:

1. **Position the pointer in the cell where you want to enter the company name.**

   For this example, position the pointer in cell A1 in a blank worksheet in the current workbook. If necessary, choose a new blank worksheet by clicking the next sheet tab or pressing Ctrl+PgDn.

2. **Choose Tools⇨Record Macro⇨Record New Macro.**

   The Record New Macro dialog box, similar to the one shown in Figure 12-1, appears.

Record Macro tool

Figure 12-1:
The Record
New Macro
dialog box
with Visual
Basic
toolbar
above.

If the Visual Basic toolbar is displayed (shown above the Record New Macro dialog box in Figure 12-1), you can also open the Record New Macro dialog box by clicking the Record Macro tool (the one with the red dot).

3. **Replace the temporary macro name, Macro1, in the Macro Name text box with a more descriptive macro name of your own.**

When naming a macro, follow the same guidelines as when naming ranges (see Chapter 6); that is, start the name with a letter (not a number), don't use spaces (tie the parts of the name together with an underscore created by pressing Shift+hyphen), and don't use weird punctuation in the name.

For this example, in place of Macro1, type **Company_Name**.

4. **If you want to, edit or annotate the macro description in the Description text box that appears beneath the Macro Name text box.**

This is a good place to describe briefly the purpose of the macro you're creating. (You *do* know what this thing is supposed to do, don't you? Enter the name of your company, that's what.)

5. **Choose the Options button to expand the Record New Macro dialog box (as shown in Figure 12-2) if you want to assign the macro to the Tools pull-down menu, assign a shortcut key to run the macro, store the macro in your personal macro workbook (so that you can use it anywhere, anytime), or record the macro actions in the old-fashioned macro sheet in the Excel 4.0 macro language rather than a module sheet in Visual Basic.**

   If none of these macro options holds any appeal, skip to step 10.

6. **(Optional) To be able to play your macro, select it on the Tools pull-down menu by choosing Menu Item from the Tools Menu in the Assign to area; then type the name of the command that will play this macro.**

   Be sure to type the name of the command exactly as you want it to appear on the Tools menu in the text box below. For example, to be able to choose the command "Company Name" at the bottom of the Tools menu to enter the company name with this macro, you would select this text box and then type **Company Name** in its text box (Figure 12-2).

7. **(Optional) To assign a shortcut key to play your macro, choose Shortcut Key in the Assign to area to select it and then enter a letter from A to z (in upper- or lowercase) or a number between 0 and 9 in its text box below.**

   The number or letter you enter is the key you use (in combination with the Ctrl key) to run the macro. Try to avoid using letters already assigned to standard Excel shortcuts (such as Ctrl+P for displaying the Print dialog box or Ctrl+S to save a workbook). See the tables in Chapter 20, "Top Ten Thousand Keystroke Shortcuts" for a complete list of existing Excel keyboard shortcuts.

   For this example, you could enter the letter n as the shortcut key so that you can insert the company name by pressing Ctrl+n.

8. **(Optional) To store your macro in your personal macro workbook, choose the Personal Macro Workbook radio button under Store in.**

   If you want to save the macro in a module in a brand new workbook (which you can save later after recording the macro) rather than in either the current workbook (in which you will perform the actions recorded in the new macro) or in your personal macro workbook, and then choose the New Workbook radio button instead.

9. **(Optional) To save the macro in the old Excel 4.0 macro language rather than in the cool new Visual Basic language, choose the MS Excel 4.0 Macro radio button under Language.**

   Figure 12-2 shows the expanded Record New Macro dialog box just before the dialog box was closed to record the macro. As you can see, the Tools menu item will be called Company_Name and the shortcut keystroke will be Ctrl+n (for name). Also, because the company name is so often added to new workbooks, the Personal Macro Workbook radio button is selected so that this macro is available any time you're using Excel.

Figure 12-2:
The expanded Record New Macro dialog box for the Company_ Name macro.

10. **Choose OK or press Enter to start recording your macro.**

    The Record Macro dialog box closes, and Excel shows you that the macro recorder is turned on by displaying the message, "Recording," on the status line.

11. **Perform the task you want to record.**

    For the Company_Name sample macro, you enter the company name in cell A1. Next, select the new font (Broadway WP in this case) from the Font tool drop-down list box and the font size (18 points) from the Size tool drop-down list box.

12. **When you've finished recording all the actions you want your macro to perform, turn off the macro recorder by clicking the Stop Macro button either in its own toolbar (shown in Figure 12-3) or in the Visual Basic toolbar (if that's displayed) or by choosing the Record Macro command on the Tools pull-down menu followed by the Stop Recording command on the cascading menu.**

    As soon as you stop recording a macro, the Recording message disappears from the status bar.

Figure 12-3:
Turning off
the macro
recorder by
clicking the
Stop tool.

It's playback time!

After you turn off the macro recorder, you are ready to test the macro. If your macro enters new text or deletes some text as part of its actions, be very careful where you test it out. Be sure that the cell pointer is in a part of the worksheet where existing cell entries won't be trashed when you play back the macro. When you're ready to test the macro, you can do any of the following:

✔ The easiest way to play back a macro is to press the shortcut keystrokes (Ctrl+n for the sample Company_Name macro), assuming that you assigned a shortcut to your macro.

✔ You can select the macro name from the bottom of the Tools pull-down menu (Company Name for the sample macro) assuming that you assigned the macro to the Tools menu. Note that Excel does not assign a mnemonic letter (you know, the one with the underlining that you can type to select it) to a macro added as a Tools menu item.

✔ You can choose Macro on the Tools menu, and then double-click the macro's name in the Macro dialog box or select the name and choose the Run button (this method works for any macro whether or not it has shortcut keys or is assigned to the Tools pull-down menu).

If, when you play back the macro, you find it running amok in your worksheet, press Esc to stop the macro prematurely. Excel displays a macro error dialog box indicating the point at which the macro was interrupted. Click the H<u>a</u>lt button in this dialog box to shut the macro down.

Where Excel saves your macro depends on how you created the macro in the first place:

- ✔ If you created the macro as part of the current workbook, Excel places the macro in a module sheet (called Module1) that is appended to the end of the workbook.

- ✔ If you created the macro as part of the personal macro workbook, Excel places the macro in a hidden workbook called PERSONAL.XLS (although the .XLS part doesn't show in Excel for Windows 95 displays).

- ✔ If you saved the macro as part of a new workbook, Excel puts the macro in a module sheet (Module1) appended to a new workbook (and given a temporary filename like Book1, Book2, or whatever the next available number is).

When you save the current workbook or the new workbook, the macros in its module sheets are saved as part of the files. In the case of the hidden Personal macro workbook, when you exit Excel, the program asks whether you want to save changes to this macro workbook. Be sure to select the <u>Y</u>es button so that you can still use the macros you've placed there the next time you work in Excel.

A macro for all months

The second sample macro enters the 12 months of the year (from January to December) across a single row of a worksheet. This macro enters the names of the months, makes them bold and italic, and then widens their columns with the best-fit feature.

As with the first macro, first find a place in a worksheet where you can enter and format the names. For this macro, you can select a new worksheet in your workbook or use a region of an existing worksheet that has 12 unused columns so that existing cell entries don't skew how wide the best-fit feature makes the columns. (You want the length of the name of the month to determine how wide to make each column.)

Figure 12-4 shows the Record New Macro dialog box for this macro. Its name, appropriately enough, is Months_of_the_Year, its shortcut keystroke is Ctrl+m, and its menu item name is 12 Months.

Figure 12-4:
The Record
New Macro
dialog box
for the
Months_of_
the_Year
macro.

To create this macro (or one like it), follow these steps:

1. **Position the cell pointer in cell A1 and choose Tools⇨Record Macro⇨Record New Macro.**

2. **Type** Months_of_the_Year **in the Macro Name text box in the Record New Macro dialog box and, if you wish, enter a description of the macro in the Description list box.**

3. **(Optional) Click the Options button to expand the Record New Macro dialog box, enter a name in the Menu Item on Tools Menu text box, select the Shortcut Key check box and enter a letter in its text box, indicate where to locate the macro in the Store in area and in which language to record the macro in the Language area.**

4. **Enter January in cell A1 and then use the AutoFill handle to select through cell L1.**

   You didn't think you were going to have type out all those months, did you?

5. **Click the Bold and Italic tools on the Formatting toolbar.**

   This step adds these enhancements to the entries (the cell range A1:L1 with the month names is still selected).

6. **Select the range of columns containing the months (columns A through L) and double-click the right border of one of the columns to widen the columns with best-fit.**

7. **Select the first cell, A1, to deselect the cell range with the names of the months.**

8. Click the Stop Macro button either in its own toolbar or in the Visual Basic toolbar (if that's displayed) or by choosing the Record Macro command on the Tools pull-down menu followed by the Stop Recording command on the cascading menu to stop recording.

After turning off the macro recorder, you are ready to test your Months_of_the_Year macro. To adequately test the macro, use some new columns to the right. For example, I tested this macro on the virgin columns N through Y in Sheet2 by placing the cell pointer in cell N1 and then pressing Ctrl+m.

If you play this macro where I did, you get a rather rude Macro Error dialog box indicating that

```
Run-time error '1004,'
AutoFill method of Range of class failed
```

occurred (is that English?!). This Macro Error dialog box gives you a choice between ending the macro playback right there with the End button, debugging the macro (yeah, right!) with the Debug button, or going to the offending Visual Basic command in its Module sheet with the Goto button. All this because I didn't play this macro when the cell pointer was in cell A1, where it was recorded.

Relative macro recording

What, you may ask, causes the Months_of_the_Year macro to screw up so that it displays a Macro Error dialog box with the Run-time error '1004' when you play it back from cell N1? Chapter 4 explains the differences between copying a formula with *relative cell references* and one with *absolute cell references*. In that chapter, I explain that Excel adjusts cell references in copies of a formula unless you take steps to convert them to *absolute* (or unchanging) references.

When recording macros, just the opposite is true: When you select a cell range (or a range of columns in this case), Excel records the cell references as absolute references rather than relative ones. This is the reason that the Months_of_the_Year macro only works properly when you run it with the cell pointer in cell A1. It keeps wanting to apply AutoFill to the cell range A1:L1 when cell A1 is the active cell. When cell A1 isn't active, the Visual Basic AutoFill command can't be completed, and you end up with this lovely

```
Run-time error '1004,'
AutoFill method of Range of class failed
```

message in a Macro Error dialog box.

Re-recording a macro

To change the Months_of_the_Year macro so that it works correctly from any cell in the worksheet and not just in cell A1, you have to re-record it, this time using relative cell references. To do this, follow these steps:

1. **Open up a new worksheet where you can perform the actions to be recorded.**

2. **Choose the Tools⇨Record Macro⇨Record New Macro.**

3. **Set up the Record New Macro dialog box the same way you did when you first created the macro and then choose OK or press Enter.**

4. **Choose the Yes button when Excel prompts whether you want to overwrite the existing keystroke assignments and, later on, the macro itself.**

5. **Choose Tools⇨Record Macro⇨Use Relative Reference before you start recording the macro steps.**

6. **Perform all the actions to be re-recorded (typing** January, **using AutoFill to generate the rest of the months, applying bold and italics to the cell range, and then selecting their columns and adjusting their widths with best-fit).**

7. **Click the Stop Macro button either in its own toolbar or in the Visual Basic toolbar (if that's displayed) or by choosing the Record Macro command on the Tools pull-down menu followed by the Stop Recording command on the cascading menu to stop recording.**

   This time, Excel records the command for AutoFilling the months of the year with relative column references so that the AutoFilling is always relative to the cell where the macro enters January.

After stopping the macro, test it in a new worksheet, starting in a cell other than cell A1. Now, no matter where you position the cell pointer when you run the macro, Excel is able to fill in the names of the months with AutoFill without so much as a Run-time error '1,' let alone '1004'!

Chapter 13

Button Up That Toolbar!

In This Chapter

▶ Customizing the built-in toolbars in Excel

▶ Creating you own toolbars

▶ Assigning macros to blank buttons on a toolbar

▶ Assigning your own pictures to the buttons on a toolbar

*A*ll of the preceding chapters have shown you how to use the tools on the various built-in toolbars exactly as they are configured when they come with Excel. In this chapter, you can find out how to customize the toolbars so that they contain only the tools you need — and how to create toolbars of your own.

As you will soon discover if you read this chapter, the tools found on the built-in toolbars represent just a small part of the total number of tools supplied with Excel. You can add unused tools to any of the existing toolbars or combine them to create new toolbars of your own design.

Not only can you customize Excel toolbars by creating new combinations of various built-in tools, but you can also customize toolbars by assigning the macros that you've recorded (see Chapter 12 for details) to any of the unassigned tools that come with Excel. Further, if none of the pictures used on the unassigned tools suits the function of the macro that you're adding to a toolbar, you can use a graphic created in another program (such as a clip-art image or one that you create yourself with another graphics program).

Toolbars — Now You See 'em, Now You Don't

As you discovered in previous chapters, if not in practice, Excel comes with a set of several built-in toolbars. Each toolbar consists of a group of tools that the program designers thought would be most helpful in getting particular tasks done. As you know, the Standard and Formatting toolbars that are automatically displayed at the top of the screen when you start Excel contain a wide variety of tools useful for creating, formatting, and printing documents.

Although the arrangements on most of the built-in toolbars may satisfy your needs, it's easy to modify the arrangement of any of them. For example, if there are tools you seldom or never use, you can replace them with ones more useful for the type of work you do. If you use a tool quite often but are not happy with its position in the toolbar — or even the toolbar it's on — you can move it to a more convenient position.

You determine which toolbars are displayed on-screen as well as modify their contents from the Toolbars dialog box (shown in Figure 13-1). To display the Toolbars dialog box, you choose Toolbars on the View menu or choose the Toolbars command on one of the toolbar context menus.

Figure 13-1:
The
Toolbars
dialog box.

To display a toolbar in the Excel program window from the Toolbars dialog box (remember that you can also do this by choosing the toolbar's name on a toolbar shortcut menu), you click its particular check box in the <u>T</u>oolbars list box. Likewise, you can hide any of the displayed toolbars by removing the check mark from its check box.

Across the bottom of the Toolbars dialog box, you see three check boxes whose settings affect all the toolbars displayed in Excel:

- ✔ **C<u>o</u>lor Toolbars:** Remove the check mark from this check box when you're using Excel on a monochrome monitor, such as a monochrome laptop.

- ✔ **<u>L</u>arge Buttons:** Normally, Excel uses small buttons to display the tools on the toolbars. Select this check box to increase the size of the buttons (this is especially helpful when you're running Excel on a computer with a really small screen, such as a laptop).

- ✔ **<u>S</u>how ToolTips:** Normally, Excel shows you the name of each tool on a toolbar when you position the mouse pointer on the button without clicking the mouse button. (Microsoft refers to these descriptions as ToolTips.) If you no longer need to see the name of each tool, you can remove the ToolTips display by deselecting this check box.

To modify the contents of a particular toolbar from the Toolbars dialog box, you must either already have that toolbar displayed on-screen, or you must select it in the Toolbars dialog box. You can select a toolbar in the Toolbars dialog box either by selecting its check box or clicking its name in the <u>T</u>oolbars list box. Remember that you can select as many toolbars as you want in this list box, should you feel up to modifying more than one toolbar at a time.

Customizing the Built-In Toolbars

After selecting the toolbar(s) that you want to modify that aren't already displayed on-screen, you choose the <u>C</u>ustomize button to display the Customize dialog box (shown in Figure 13-2).

If the toolbar you want to edit is already displayed on the screen, you can open the Customize dialog box directly without having to first open the Toolbars dialog box. Simply click the toolbar with the secondary mouse button and then choose the Customize command on the toolbar's context menu.

Figure 13-2:
The
Customize
dialog box.

Adding buttons from the Customize dialog box

When you open the Customize dialog box, Excel displays a Categories list box with all the groups of buttons available (File through Custom) followed by a Buttons list box that actually displays the button icons included in each group. To display a new group of buttons in the Buttons list box, you need only click its category name in the Categories list box. Once the Customize dialog box displays the buttons for a particular category, you can then select individual buttons just as you would any graphic object in a worksheet window.

To add one of the buttons shown in the Buttons list box to one of the toolbars displayed on the Excel screen, you drag the button from the Customize toolbar to its new position on the toolbar and release the mouse button.

Note that you can always find out what a particular button does by clicking its icon in the Buttons section. When you click a button icon in the Buttons area, Excel displays a short description of that button's function in the Description area at the bottom of the Customize dialog box.

Removing buttons from a toolbar

When the Customize dialog box is open, you can not only add new buttons to a displayed toolbar, but also get rid of existing buttons by literally dragging them off the toolbar. To junk a button that you don't need, select it on the toolbar and then drag the button's outline until it's off the toolbar before you release the mouse button. As soon as you release the mouse button, the toolbar button disappears and Excel closes up the gap on the toolbar.

Playing musical chairs with buttons

When customizing a toolbar, you may only want to reposition the buttons or move or copy them to one of the other toolbars that are displayed.

- ✔ To reposition a button on the same toolbar, drag it until it is positioned slightly in front of the button it is to precede and release the mouse button.

- ✔ To move a button to a different toolbar, drag it to the desired position on the new toolbar and then release the mouse button.

- ✔ To copy a button to a different toolbar, hold down the Ctrl key as you drag the button to the new toolbar (you see a small plus sign next to the arrowhead pointer, just as you do when copying a cell selection with the drag-and-drop feature).

What a bunch of spaced-out buttons!

You may have noticed how buttons on various built-in toolbars are grouped together with little spaces before and after the group of buttons. You too can group various buttons when customizing a toolbar.

To insert a space on the left or right side of a button to separate it from other buttons, drag the button slightly in the opposite direction of where you want the space to appear (to the right to insert a space on its left side, and to the left to insert a space on its right side) and release the mouse button. Excel inserts a space before or after the button you just dragged.

To delete a space in front of or after a button so that the button abuts — or touches — the one next to it, drag the button in the appropriate direction until it touches or slightly overlaps the neighboring button and then release the mouse button. Excel redraws the toolbar to remove the space from the button you just dragged.

It's not my default!

Sometimes, you may make changes to a built-in toolbar and then decide that you don't want to keep those changes. No matter what wild changes you make to a built-in toolbar, you can always restore the toolbar to its original form by opening the Toolbars dialog box (by choosing the Toolbars on the View menu or choosing the Toolbars command on a toolbar shortcut menu) and then selecting the toolbar's name in the Toolbar list box and choosing the Reset button.

Designing Your Own Toolbars

You are by no means limited to the built-in toolbars that come with Excel. You can create your own toolbars to combine any of the available buttons: those that are used in the built-in toolbars as well as those that are not.

To create a toolbar of your very own, follow these steps:

1. **Choose View⇨ Toolbars or select the Toolbars command on a toolbar context menu to open the Toolbars dialog box.**

2. **Enter a name for the new toolbar in the Toolbar Name text box.**

3. **Select the New command button.**

   The Customize dialog box opens and a small toolbar dialog box appears in the upper-left corner of the document window. Use the toolbar dialog box to add the tools to the new toolbar.

4. **Choose the category containing the first button you want to add to the new toolbar from the Categories list box.**

5. **Drag the button from the Buttons area in the Customize dialog box to the tiny toolbar dialog box in the upper-left corner of the document window; then release the mouse button.**

6. **Repeat steps 4 and 5 until you have added all the buttons you want to the new toolbar.**

   Once the buttons are on the new toolbar, you can rearrange and space them out as you want.

7. **Select the Close button or press Enter to close the Customize dialog box.**

As you add buttons to the new toolbar, Excel automatically widens the toolbar dialog box. When the dialog box is wide enough, the name you assigned to the toolbar appears in the title bar. If the toolbar dialog box starts running into the Customize dialog box, just drag the new toolbar down by its title bar until it's entirely clear of the Customize dialog box.

You can also create a new toolbar simply by dragging a tool from the Customize dialog box to somewhere in the document window and releasing the mouse button. Excel creates a new toolbar dialog box for the tool and assigns a name (like Toolbar1) to the toolbar. You can then add more tools to the new toolbar. Unfortunately, when you create a toolbar in this manner, you can't rename the toolbar later to give it a more descriptive title.

Figures 13-3 through 13-5 show the process of creating a new toolbar (called, modestly enough, Greg's Cool Tools). Figure 13-3 shows the Toolbars dialog box after I entered the catchy name for the new toolbar. Figure 13-4 shows the new toolbar after I clicked on the New button on the Toolbars dialog box. This action adds a blank toolbar dialog box and activates the Customize dialog box. Figure 13-5 shows Greg's Cool Tools toolbar after I've added buttons for setting the print area in a worksheet, inserting a new worksheet in a workbook, applying the table format last used to a cell range, erasing a cell range, erasing only the formatting from a cell range, pasting only the formatting from a copied cell, and pasting only the values from a copied cell.

Figure 13-3: Naming the new Greg's Cool Tools toolbar.

Figure 13-4:
The new
Greg's Cool
Tools
toolbar
before the
cool tools
were added.

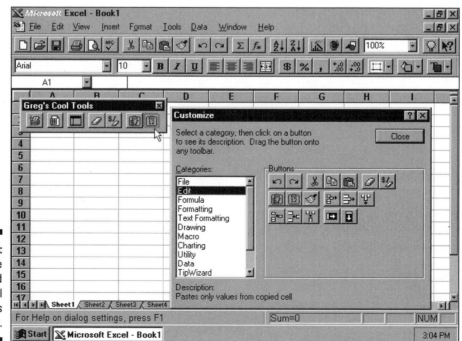

Figure 13-5:
The
completed
Greg's Cool
Tools
toolbar.

After creating a new toolbar, you can display, hide, move, resize, and dock it just like you do any of the built-in toolbars. If you don't want to keep a toolbar you've created, delete it by opening the Toolbars dialog box and selecting the toolbar name in the Toolbars list box. As soon as you select the name of a toolbar that you created, Excel replaces the Reset button with a Delete button (the program won't let you delete any built-in toolbars). When you click Delete, Excel displays an alert dialog box, in which you confirm the deletion by choosing OK or pressing Enter.

Adding buttons that play macros

As I hinted earlier in this chapter, you can assign macros that you've recorded (covered back in Chapter 12) to tools and then place these tools on toolbars (either on one of the built-ins or on one of your own creations). That way, you can play back a macro by clicking its button. This is particularly helpful when you've assigned all 26 letters (A through Z) and 10 numbers (0 through 9) as shortcut keystrokes in a particular macro sheet.

Excel has a variety of blank tools in the Custom category (shown in Figure 13-6) to which you can assign macros. Unfortunately, these buttons use a mixed bag of pictures, many of which you will be hard put to associate with the function of a macro. Come on, what's a happy-face macro supposed to do, anyway?!

Figure 13-6: The Customize dialog box with the Custom buttons.

To assign a macro to a custom button, follow these steps:

1. **If the macro you want to assign to a tool is attached to a particular workbook rather than in your personal macro workbook, make sure that the workbook is open. If the workbook is not open, you need to open it with the Open tool on the Standard toolbar or the Open command on the File menu.**

   Remember, Excel opens the personal macro workbook each time you start the program, making its macros available anywhere and anytime in the program. Macros saved as part of a particular workbook, however, are only available when that workbook is open.

2. **Display the toolbar to which you want to add the macro, if it isn't already on-screen.**

3. **Open the Customize dialog box by choosing the Customize command on a toolbar context menu.**

4. **Select the Custom category in the Categories list box.**

   Excel displays the Custom buttons shown in Figure 13-6.

5. **Drag one of the Custom buttons in the Buttons area to the desired position on your toolbar; then release the mouse button.**

   Excel opens the Assign Macro dialog box (see Figure 13-7).

6. **Select or record the macro that you want to assign to the tool.**

   To assign an existing macro to the selected tool, double-click the macro name in the Macro Name/Reference list box or select the macro name and choose OK or press Enter.

   To record a new macro for the tool, click the Record button and record a macro just as you would record any other (see Chapter 12).

7. **Repeat steps 5 and 6 for every macro you want to assign to a custom button.**

8. **Click the Close button or press Enter to close the Customize dialog box.**

Cute as a button

Fortunately, you aren't stuck with customized tools that have pictures of smiley faces, hearts, and coffee mugs. You can copy an image from another button or, if you're an artiste, you can use the Button Editor to create your image.

To paste a picture from one button to another, follow these steps:

1. **Open the Customize dialog box by choosing the Customize command on a toolbar shortcut menu.**

Figure 13-7:
The Assign
Macro
dialog box.

2. **Select the button that you want to copy in the Buttons area of the Customize dialog box.**

3. **Choose Copy Button Image on the Edit pull-down menu.**

4. **Select the custom tool in the toolbar whose image you want to replace with the one that you just copied.**

5. **Choose Edit⇨Paste Button Image or choose the Paste Button Image command on the toolbar shortcut menu.**

That's all there is to it. Excel replaces the face of the selected tool with the picture stored in the Clipboard.

If you'd prefer to create your own masterpiece rather than steal one of the existing button images (which may already be associated with a particular action if it appears on another toolbar that you use), you can edit an image with the new Button Editor. To open the Button Editor (shown in Figure 13-8), you open the Customize dialog box and then choose the tool whose image you want to edit and select the Edit Button Image command on the toolbar's context menu.

To then edit the button's icon, you click the color you want to use and then click the squares (called pixels) in the Picture area to paint with the color. If you make a mistake, you can click the pixel a second time to restore it to its original color. If you want to draw a picture from scratch rather than edit the one you selected, you need to choose the Clear button before you start drawing. If you want to erase part of the image, you click the Erase box in the Colors area and then click the pixels you want to erase in the picture.

Figure 13-8 shows my artwork after editing that silly Happy Face icon in the Button Editor so that it looks more like my dog Spike. Figure 13-9 shows my custom toolbar after replacing the Happy Face button in with Spike's button.

Figure 13-8:
Customizing the Happy Face icon in the Button Editor.

Figure 13-9:
Greg's Cool
Tools
custom
toolbar after
adding the
edited
custom
icon.

Part VI

From the Home Office in Foster City...

The 5th Wave — By Rich Tennant

KEG SOFTWARE

"YEAH, I STARTED THE COMPANY RIGHT AFTER I GRADUATED FROM COLLEGE. HOW'D YOU GUESS?"

In this part . . .

Finally, you come to the fun part of Excel for Windows 95, the so-called Part of Tens, where the chapters all consist of lists with the top ten Excel tips on this, that, and everything in between. In homage to David Letterman, you'll find a chapter on the top ten new features in Excel for Windows 95, top ten things in Excel that always trip you up, top ten ways to impress your boss, top ten fun things to do with Excel on a network, as well as the top ten thousand (or so it seems) keystroke shortcuts included in this baby. And, in homage to Cecil B. deMille, Moses, and a much higher power, we've even included a chapter with the Ten Commandments of Excel for Windows 95, that although not written in stone, when followed faithfully are guaranteed to give you heavenly results.

Chapter 14

Top Ten New Features in Excel for Windows 95

● ●

*1*f you're looking for a quick rundown on what's new in Excel for Windows 95, look no further! Here it is, my official Top Ten New Features list. Just a cursory glance down the list tells you that the thrust of the new features is auto this n' that, such n' such tips, and so n' so Wizards.

And just in case you're interested in more than just a cursory feature description, I've included a cross reference with chapter and verse to the place in this book where I cover the feature in more detail.

10. **AutoCalculate:** This status bar feature gives you a running total of all the values in whatever cells in the worksheet are selected (see "You AutoCalculate my totals" in Chapter 1).

9. **AutoComplete:** This data-entry feature completes cell entries in a column with a previously used entry whenever you begin a new entry with the same first character (see "I'm just not complete without you" in Chapter 2).

8. **AutoCorrect:** This feature automatically fixes typos or spells out acronyms by matching a list of typos or abbreviations to a list of text replacements (see "You really AutoCorrect that for me" in Chapter 2).

7. **Answer Wizard:** This Help feature attempts to give you a list of relevant help topics based on your asking, in English, how something is done in Excel (see "Asking the Answer Wizard" in Chapter 1).

6. **ScrollTips:** This new scroll bar feature indicates the column letter or row number that will appear in the upper left corner of the worksheet when you stop scrolling by releasing the mouse button (see "Calling up new columns with the horizontal scroll bar" and "Raising up new rows with the vertical scroll bar" in Chapter 1).

5. **CellTips:** This new note feature displays the contents of a cell note whenever you position the mouse pointer long enough on its note indicator (see "Electronic Sticky Notes" in Chapter 6).

4. **Expanded Drag and Drop:** In the past, you could only copy or move sheets between workbooks with Drag and Drop a single sheet at a time. With the new, expanded Drag and Drop, you can copy or move as many sheets as you want in a single operation (see "Passing Sheets in the Night" in Chapter 7).

3. **Data Map:** This new charting feature lets you display geographically-related data in graphical form by using a series of maps supplied with Excel (see "Map Madness" in Chapter 8).

2. **AutoFilter with Top 10:** This addition to the AutoFilter feature lets you quickly display the records in an Excel database with the top ten highest or lowest entries in particular fields (see "Viewing the top ten records" in Chapter 9).

1. **Template Wizard:** The Template Wizard guides you through the process of converting a workbook into a template file and linking the template with a database so that entries made in workbooks generated from the template are automatically stored in that database (see "Conjuring Up Templates with the Template Wizard" in Chapter 10).

Chapter 15

Top Ten Beginner Basics

*f these ten items are all you ever really master in Excel for Windows 95, you'll still be way ahead of the competition. When all is said and done, this top ten list lays out all of the fundamental skills required to successfully use Excel for Windows 95:

10. To start Excel from the Windows 95 taskbar, click the Start button, choose Programs on the Start menu, and then choose Microsoft Excel on the Programs continuation menu.

9. If you're using Microsoft Office for Windows 95, you can open a workbook at the same time you start Excel for Windows 95, click the Start button, and then choose Open Office Document at the top of the Start menu. Then open the folder with the Excel workbook in the Open dialog box and double-click the workbook's icon. (To find out more about Microsoft Office for Windows 95, check out *Microsoft Office For Windows 95 For Dummies.*)

   If you don't have Microsoft Office for Windows, locate the Excel workbook with Explorer or My Computer and then double-click its icon.

8. To locate a part of a worksheet that you cannot see on-screen, use the scroll bars at the right and bottom of the workbook window to bring new parts of the worksheet into view. When scrolling, the CellTips indicator on the scroll bar shows the letter of the column or the number of the row that will appear in the upper left corner of the worksheet upon releasing the mouse button.

7. To start a new workbook (containing 16 blank worksheets), choose the New Workbook tool on the Standard toolbar (or choose New on the File menu or press Ctrl+N). To insert a new worksheet in a workbook (should you need more than 16), choose Worksheet on the Insert menu or press Shift+F11.

6. To activate an open workbook and display it on-screen (in front of any others you have open), open the Window pull-down menu and select the name or number of the workbook you want. To locate a particular worksheet in the active workbook, click that worksheet's sheet tab at the bottom of the workbook document window. To display more sheet tabs, click the sheet scrolling arrows on the left side of the bottom of the workbook window.

5. To enter stuff in a worksheet, select the cell where the information should appear; then begin typing. When you're finished, click the Enter button on the formula bar or press Tab, Enter, or one of the arrow keys.

4. To edit the stuff you've already entered into a cell, double-click the cell or position the cell pointer in the cell and press F2. Excel then locates the insertion point at the end of the cell entry. When you've finished correcting the entry, click the Enter button on the formula bar or press Tab or Enter.

3. To choose one of the many commands on the pull-down menus, click the menu name (on the menu bar) to open the menu, and then click the command name on the pull-down menu. To choose a command on a context menu, click the object (cell, sheet tab, toolbar, chart, and so on) with the secondary mouse button.

2. To save a copy of your workbook on disk the first time around, choose Save or Save As on the File menu (or click the Save button on the Standard toolbar or press Ctrl+S); then designate the drive and folder directory where the file should be located in the Save in drop-down list box and replace the temporary BOOK1.XLS filename in the File name edit box with your own filename (up to 255 characters long, including spaces!). To save changes to the workbook thereafter, click the Save tool on the Standard toolbar (or choose Save on the File menu or press Ctrl+S or Shift+F12).

1. To exit Excel when you're done working with the program, choose the Exit command from the File menu or click the program's close box or press Alt+F4. If the workbook you have open contains unsaved changes, Excel asks whether you want to save the workbook before closing Excel and returning to Windows 95. Before you shut off your computer, be sure to use the Shut down command on the Start menu to shut down Windows 95.

Chapter 16

The Ten Commandments of Excel for Windows 95

● ●

*I*n working with Excel for Windows 95, you discover certain *dos* and *don'ts* that, if followed religiously, can make using this program just heavenly. Lo and behold, the following Excel ten commandments contain just such precepts for eternal Excel bliss:

10. Thou shalt commit thy work to disk by saving thy changes often (File⇨Save or Ctrl+S). If thou findest that thou tendeth to be lax in the saving of thy work, then shalt thou engage thy AutoSave add-in (Tools⇨Add-Ins⇨AutoSave) and have thy program automatically save thy work for thee at a set time interval.

9. Thou shalt nameth thy workbooks when saving them the first time with filenames of no more than twelve score and fifteen characters (255), including spaces and all manner of weird signs and symbols. So, too, shalt thou mark well into which folder thou savest thy file lest thou thinkest in error that thy workbook be lost when next thou hast need of it.

8. Thou shalt not spread wide the data in thy worksheet, but rather shalt thou gather together thy tables and avoideth skipping columns and rows unless this be necessary to make thy data intelligible. All this shalt thou do in order that thou mightest conserve the memory of thy computer.

7. Thou shalt begin all thy Excel formulas with = (equal) as the sign of computation. If, however, ye be formerly of the Lotus 1-2-3 tribe, thou shalt haveth special dispensation and canst commence thy formulas with the + sign and thy functions with the @ sign.

6. Thou shalt select thy cells before thou bringeth any Excel command to bear upon them, just as surely as thou doest sow before thou reapest.

5. Thou shalt useth the Undo feature (Edit⇨Undo or Ctrl+Z), immediately upon committing any transgression in thy worksheet so that thou mayest clean up thy mess. In no wise shalt thou chooseth another command in Excel before thou hast called upon Undo to restoreth thy worksheet to its former state.

4. Thou shalt not delete, neither shalt thou insert, columns and rows in a worksheet lest thou hath first verified that no part as yet uncovered of thy worksheet will thereby be wiped out nor otherwise displaced.

3. Thou shalt not print thy worksheet lest thou hath first previewed the printing (File⇨Print Preview) and art satisfied that all of thy pages are upright in the sight of the printer.

2. Thou shalt changeth the manner of recalculation of thy workbooks from automatic to manual (Tools⇨Options⇨Calculation tab⇨Manual) when thy workbook grows so great in size that Excel sloweth down to a camel crawl whenever thou doest anything in any one of its worksheets. Woe to thee, however, should thou also removest the check mark from the Recalculate before Save check box when thou setteth up manual calculation or should thou ignorest the Calculate message on the status bar and not presseth the Calculate Now key (F9) before such time as thou mayest print any of thy workbook data.

1. Thou shalt protecteth thy completed workbooks and all of its worksheets from corruption and inequities at the hands of others (Tools⇨Protection⇨Protect Sheet or Protect Workbook). And if thou be brazen enough to addeth a password to thy workbook protection, beware lest thou forgeteth thy password in any part. For verily I say unto to you, on the day that thou knowest not thy password, that day shalt be the last upon which thou lookest upon thy workbook in any wise.

Chapter 17

Top Ten Things in Excel That Can Trip You Up

● ●

*T*he following "welcome warnings" point out the most common pitfalls that get beginning Excel users. Avoid them like the plague and, I promise, you'll be a lot happier using Excel:

10. Remember that Excel for Windows 95 automatically adds the file extension .XLS to whatever filename you assign to your workbook when you first save it (this file extension indicates that the file contains Excel worksheets). So, when you first save and name a workbook, you don't ever have to bother typing the .XLS at the end of the filename. Also, when you edit a filename in the Save As dialog box, you can leave the .XLS extension in the File name edit box if you wish, but when replacing an existing filename with a completely new filename, you never have to add this .XLS extension as part of the name you enter.

9. If you introduce a space into an otherwise completely numeric entry, Excel categorizes the entry as text (indicated by its alignment at the left edge of the cell). If you feed that entry into a formula, the text classification completely throws off the answer because text entries are treated like zeros (0) in a formula.

8. When nesting parentheses in a formula, pair them properly so that you have a right parenthesis for every left parenthesis in the formula. If you do not include a right parenthesis for every left one, Excel displays an alert dialog box with the message "Parentheses do not match" when you try to enter the formula. After you close this dialog box, Excel goes right back to the formula bar, where you can insert the missing parenthesis and press Enter to correct the unbalanced condition. By the way, Excel always highlights matched parentheses.

7. You can re-enter edited cell contents by clicking the Enter box on the formula bar or pressing Tab or Enter, but you can't use the arrow keys. When you are editing a cell entry, the arrow keys only move the insertion point through the entry.

6. Be sure that you don't press one of the arrow keys to complete a cell entry within a preselected cell range instead of clicking the Enter box or pressing Enter. Pressing an arrow key deselects the range of cells when Excel moves the cell pointer.

5. The Undo command on the Edit menu changes in response to whatever action you just took. Because it keeps changing after each action, you've got to remember to strike when the iron is hot, so to speak, by using the Undo feature to restore the worksheet to its previous state *before* you choose another command.

4. Deleting entire columns and rows from a worksheet is risky business unless you are sure that the columns and rows in question contain nothing of value. Remember, when you delete an entire row from the worksheet, you delete *all information from column A through IV* in that row (and you can see only a very few columns in this row). Likewise, when you delete an entire column from the worksheet, you delete *all information from row 1 through 16,384* in that column.

3. Be careful with global search-and-replace operations; they can really mess up a worksheet in a hurry if you inadvertently replace values, parts of formulas, or characters in titles and headings that you hadn't intended to change. As a precaution, *never undertake a global search-and-replace operation on an unsaved worksheet.*

   Also, verify whether or not the Find Entire Cells Only check box is selected before you begin. You can end up with a lot of unwanted replacements if you leave this check box unselected when you really only want to replace entire cell entries (rather than matching parts in cell entries). If you do make a mess, choose the Undo Replace command on the Edit menu (Ctrl+Z) to restore the worksheet. If you don't discover the problem in time to use Undo, close the messed-up worksheet without saving the changes and open the unreplaced version that you saved — thanks to reading this warning!

2. To make it impossible to remove protection from a particular worksheet in a workbook or an entire workbook and all its worksheets unless you know the password, enter a password in the Password (Optional) text box of the Protect Sheet or Protect Workbook dialog box (Tools⇨Protection⇨Protect Sheet or Protect Workbook). Excel masks each character you type in this text box with an asterisk. After you choose OK, Excel makes you re-enter the password before protecting the worksheet or workbook. From then on, you can remove protection from the worksheet or workbook only if you can reproduce the password exactly as you assigned it (including any case differences). Be very careful with passwords. If you forget the password, you cannot change any locked cells and you cannot unlock anymore cells in the particular worksheet, or in the case of a workbook any of its worksheets!

1. You *cannot* use the Undo feature to bring back a database record you removed with the Delete button in the data form! Excel is definitely *not* kidding when it uses words like "deleted permanently." As a precaution, always save a backup version of the worksheet with the database before you start removing old records.

Chapter 18
Top Ten Ways to Impress the Boss

*T*he ten little tips contained in this chapter are worth their weight in Intel's Pentium chips (gold is out this season). Please keep them in mind as you work with Excel. After all, who wants computing to be any harder than it has to be?

10. Watch the TipWizard tool on the Standard toolbar. When the lightbulb turns yellow, you know that Excel has some tidbits of wisdom to dispense to you based on the things you were just doing in the workbook. Click the TipWizard to display a box of tips above the formula bar, complete with scroll arrows enabling you to peruse the list at your leisure. When you've taken in about as many tips as you can stand, click the TipWizard tool a second time to make the box of tips disappear.

9. Name any often-used cell range in a worksheet (Insert⇨Name⇨Define) and then use its name to move to it, select its cells, or print it. Remember, you can press the Go To key (F5) and then select the range name in the Go To dialog box. When you choose OK, Excel not only moves you to the first cell in that range but selects all its cells as well.

8. Don't waste all day scrolling through a seemingly endless table of data. Instead, use the Ctrl+arrow key (or End, then arrow key) combination to jump from one edge of the table to another edge or to jump from the edge of one table to another.

7. If you find yourself continually entering the same list of items over and over again in new worksheets, create a custom list of items and then enter the entire list by typing just the first item in the series and then dragging out the rest of the series with the AutoFill handle (see "Creating custom lists for AutoFill" in Chapter 2 for a refresher course on how to create a custom series).

6. Lose the graphics in a workbook worksheet by replacing them on-screen with placeholders (Tools⇨Options⇨View⇨Show Placeholders) when you find that Excel just can't keep up with your movements in a particular worksheet. Screen response time is greatly improved by this trick — just don't forget to put the graphics back before you print the worksheet, or you'll end up with shaded rectangles where the pictures ought to be!

5. When making editing and formatting changes in your Excel workbooks, don't overlook the context menus attached to the things that need fixing (opened by clicking the secondary mouse button). This can save a lot of time that you would otherwise waste searching the menus on the menu bar to find the editing or formatting command you need. Also, don't forget how much time you can save by using the tools on the Standard and Formatting toolbars to get things done!

4. Before making changes to an unfamiliar worksheet, use the Zoom Control button on the Standard toolbar to zoom out to 50% or 25% so that you can get a good idea of how the information is laid out. When inserting or deleting cells in an unfamiliar worksheet, resist the temptation to insert or remove entire columns and rows, which can damage unseen tables of data. Instead, just insert or cut out the cell ranges in the region you're working in — you know, think globally, but act locally!

3. To maximize the number of worksheet cells displayed on-screen at one time without having to resort to changing the magnification with the Zoom feature, choose View⇔Full Screen. This makes the formula bar, the Standard and Formatting toolbars, and the status bar all go away, leaving only the pull-down menus and scroll bars in addition to the cells in the current worksheet (giving you a view of 25 full rows rather than the normal 17). When you're ready to return to the normal (rather cramped) screen display, click the Full Screen button in the floating Full toolbar (which automatically appears whenever you choose View⇔Full Screen) or, if this toolbar is hidden, choose View⇔Full Screen a second time.

2. Give yourself a break and record a macro for doing those little tasks that you end up doing over and over and over again (choose Tools⇔Record Macro⇔Record New Macro). Using macros to get things done not only alleviates the boredom but also frees you up to do truly important things (like playing another game of Hearts or Minesweeper).

1. Name each worksheet that you use in a workbook with some intelligible English name like Invoice or Price List (by double-clicking the sheet tab and entering a new name in the Rename Sheet dialog box) rather than leaving them with their normally indecipherable names like Sheet1 and Sheet2. That way, you not only know which sheets in your workbook you've already used but you also have a fair idea of what they contain and when you should select them.

Chapter 19

Top Ten Fun Things to Do with Excel for Windows 95 on a Network

•••

*I*f you use Excel for Windows 95 on a Local Area Network, you can do some neat communication and file-sharing stuff with your pals on the network, especially those who are in the same workgroup as you. Just a quick look-see at the following top-ten list should give you some good ideas for sharing the work you strive so hard to create in Excel for Windows 95 (and I'll bet you thought the network was only good for playing a good game of Hearts with your coworkers!).

10. In the Windows 95 Explorer, you can use the Map Network Drive button to connect to the hard disk of the computer that contains Excel workbook and template files that you need to share. If you want Windows 95 to re-establish this connection each time you logon to your computer, make sure to choose the Reconnect at logon check box when you map the network drive.

9. After mapping a network drive in the Windows 95 Explorer, you can create and place on the desktop of your computer a shortcut that opens the folder on that network drive and contains the Excel workbook and template files that you need to share.

8. In the Windows 95 Explorer, you can activate file sharing for whatever folders contain Excel documents that other people on the network need access to. To do this, choose Sharing on the folder icon's context menu; then click the Sharing tab, choose the Shared As radio button, and set the Access Type: Read-Only, Full, or Depends on Password. If you choose the Depends on Password option, you can set a password for being able to open the file (a Read-Only Password) as well as one for being able to make changes to the file (a Full Access Password).

7. You can give all the users on the network access to an Excel workbook that needs to be kept up-to-date by a number of different users on the network (such as expense reports or a customer database) by using the Shared Lists command on the File menu and then selecting the Allow Multi-User Editing check box on the Editing tab. Then save the workbook in a shared folder (as described in the third Fun Thing to Do with Excel for Windows 95 on a Network).

6. You and your coworkers on the network can simultaneously edit a workbook that's been saved as a shared list, and Excel will keep the data up-to-date. Keep in mind, however, that, although you can add and sort data as well as insert new columns and rows in the sheets of the workbook, you cannot change the cell formatting or edit formulas in the worksheets.

5. When you save your changes to a workbook that's been saved as a shared list, Excel saves your changes along with those made by everybody else who accessed the shared list. If certain entries in the workbook are in conflict with each other (that is, if you both tried to update the same cell in a worksheet), you get an alert box asking you which edit to accept. You can review a listing of the conflicts and their resolutions pertaining to the workbook by choosing File⇨Shared Lists and then selecting the Show Conflict History check box on the Edit tab.

4. You can check to see who else is working on the workbook that's been saved as a shared list in cases of an updating conflict (see the fifth Fun Thing to Do with Excel for Windows 95 on a Network) by choosing the Shared Lists command on the File menu and then selecting the Status tab. This tab lists all the people who currently have the workbook open, along with the date and time that they opened the file.

3. You can e-mail a copy of a workbook file to other users on the network by opening the file and then choosing the Send command on the File menu. If prompted, indicate the messaging profile in the Profile Name drop-down list box of the Choose Profile dialog box, and then choose OK to open the Microsoft Exchange dialog box where you indicate the recipient(s), any people to be cc'd, and add any message you want to accompany the Excel file. After adding this information, send the file either by clicking the Send button on the Microsoft Exchange's Standard toolbar, pressing Ctrl+Enter, or choosing File⇨Send.

2. You can e-mail a copy of a workbook file so that it is routed to one recipient after another (so that each one can see the comments and changes made by the previous user) by choosing Add Routing Slip on the File menu. If prompted, indicate the messaging profile in the Profile Name drop-down list box of the Choose Profile dialog box, and then choose OK to open the Microsoft Exchange dialog box where you select the recipients the file is to be routed to in the order in which it is to be sent. Then, to send the workbook file to the first person on the route list, choose the Route button.

1. You can have a routing slip (see the preceding Fun Thing to Do) automatically added to any workbook that you generate from a template created with the Template Wizard by choosing the Adding Routing Slip button in the Template Wizard–Step 5 of 5 dialog box (see "Conjuring Up Templates with the Template Wizard" in Chapter 10 for details).

Chapter 20

Top Ten Thousand Keystroke Shortcuts

● ●

*I*f you like using keystroke shortcuts on your computer, have I got great news for you — Excel is loaded with them. There are keystroke shortcuts for doing just about everything you'd probably be tempted to do with the program. In the tables in this chapter, I've brought together the most popular of these keystroke shortcuts and arranged them according to what kind of work they do.

For Getting Online Help	
Press	*To*
F1	Open the Excel Help window
Shift+F1	Get context-sensitive Excel Help

For Moving through the Worksheet	
Press	*To*
Arrow keys (↑, ↓, ←, →)	Move up, down, left, right one cell
Home	Move to the beginning of the row
PgUp	Move up one screenful
PgDn	Move down one screenful
Ctrl+Home	Move to the first cell in the worksheet (A1)
Ctrl+End	Move to the last active cell of the worksheet
Ctrl+Arrow key	Move to the edge of a data block

For Selecting Cells in the Worksheet

Press	*To*
Shift+Spacebar	Select the entire row
Ctrl+Spacebar	Select the entire column
Ctrl+Shift+Spacebar or Ctrl+A	Select the entire worksheet
Shift+Home	Extend the selection to the beginning of the current row

For Moving around a Cell Selection

Press	*To*
Enter	Move the cell pointer down one cell in the selection when there's more than one row, or move one cell to the right when the selection consists of only one row
Shift+Enter	Move the cell pointer up one cell in the selection when there's more than one row, or move one cell to the left when the selection consists of only one row
Tab	Move the cell pointer one cell to the right in the selection when there's more than one column, or move one cell down when the selection has only one column
Shift+Tab	Move the cell pointer one cell to the left in the selection when there's more than one column, or move one cell up when the selection has only one column
Ctrl+. (period)	Move to the next corner of the current cell range
Shift+Backspace	Collapse the cell selection to just the active cell

For Sizing a Workbook or Moving through Its Sheets

Press	*To*
Ctrl+PgDn	Move to the next sheet in the workbook
Ctrl+PgUp	Move to the previous sheet in the workbook
Ctrl+F9	Minimize the workbook
Ctrl+F10	Maximize the workbook

For Formatting a Cell Selection	
Press	***To***
Ctrl+Shift+~	Apply the General number format to the cell selection
Ctrl+Shift+$	Apply the currency format with two decimal places to the cell selection
Ctrl+Shift+%	Apply the percentage format with no decimal places to the cell selection
Ctrl+Shift+^	Apply the scientific (exponential) number format with two decimal places to the cell selection
Ctrl+Shift+#	Apply the date format with the day, month, and year to the cell selection (as in 27-Oct-95)
Ctrl+Shift+@	Apply the time format with the hour, minute, and AM or PM to the cell selection (as in 12:05 PM)
Ctrl+Shift+&	Apply an outline border to the cell selection
Ctrl+Shift+_ (underscore)	Get rid of all borders in the cell selection
Ctrl+1	Display Format Cells dialog box
Ctrl+B	Apply or get rid of bold in the cell selection
Ctrl+I	Apply or get rid of italics in the cell selection
Ctrl+U	Apply or get rid of underlining in the cell selection
Ctrl+5	Apply or get rid of strikeout in the cell selection
Ctrl+9	Hide selected rows
Ctrl+Shift+((left parenthesis)	Show all hidden rows
Ctrl+0 (zero)	Hide selected columns
Ctrl+Shift+) (right parenthesis)	Show all hidden columns

For Editing a Worksheet	
Press	**To**
Enter	Carry out your action
Esc	Cancel a command or close the displayed dialog box
F4	Repeat your last action
Ctrl+Z	Undo your last command or action
Ctrl+Shift++ (plus sign)	Display the Insert dialog box to insert new cells, columns, or rows in the worksheet
Ctrl+− (minus sign)	Display the Delete dialog box to delete cells, columns, or rows from the worksheet
Delete	Clear the contents of your cell selection
Ctrl+X	Cut the selection to the Clipboard
Ctrl+C	Copy the selection to the Clipboard
Ctrl+V	Paste the contents of the Clipboard
Shift+F2	Display the Cell Note dialog box
Ctrl+F2	Switch between the Info window (with information about the active cell) and the active document window
F3	Display the Paste Name dialog box so that you can paste a range name into a formula
Shift+F3	Display the Function Wizard dialog box so that you can paste a function and its arguments into a formula
Ctrl+F3	Display the Define Name dialog box so that you can assign a range name to the cell selection
Ctrl+= (equal sign) or F9	Recalculate the formulas in all open worksheets
Shift+F9	Recalculate the formulas in just the active worksheet
Alt+= (equal sign)	Create a sum formula (same as clicking the AutoSum tool on the Standard toolbar)
Ctrl+8	Toggle the outline symbols on and off or, if no outline exists, display an alert dialog box prompting you to create an outline
F7	Check spelling
Ctrl+F	Find
Ctrl+H	Replace

For Editing an Entry in the Cell	
Press	*To*
F2	Activate the formula bar and position the insertion point at the end of the current entry
Ctrl+; (semicolon)	Insert the current date in the cell
Ctrl+Shift+; (semicolon)	Insert the current time in the cell (same as Ctrl+:)
Ctrl+' (apostrophe)	Copy the formula from the cell above the active cell
Ctrl+Shift+' (apostrophe)	Copy the value from the cell above the active cell
Ctrl+Enter	Enter the contents of the formula bar in all cells in the current selection
Arrow key (↑, ↓, ←, →)	Move the insertion point one character up, down, left, or right
Home	Move the insertion point to the beginning of the formula bar
Alt+Enter	Insert a new line in the cell entry
Backspace	Delete the preceding character when editing a cell or clear the entry in the current cell and put Excel in Enter mode
Ctrl+Shift+Delete	Delete the text to the end of the line when editing a cell

For Opening, Saving, and Printing Excel Workbooks	
Press	*To*
F11	Create a column chart from the current cell selection in a new chart sheet in the workbook
Ctrl+F12	Display the Open dialog box so that you can open an existing Excel workbook file
Ctrl+F11	Open a new macro sheet in the workbook
Alt+Shift+F2 or Shift+F12	Save the active file with the Save command on the File menu
Alt+F2 or F12	Save the active file with the Save As command on the File menu
Ctrl+P	Open the Print dialog box

Glossary

. . . .

absolute cell reference

A cell reference that Excel cannot automatically adjust. If you're about to copy a formula and you want to prevent Excel from adjusting one or more of the cell references (the program has a tendency to change the column and row reference in copies), make the cell references absolute. Absolute cell references are indicated by a dollar sign (yes, a $) in front of the column letter and the row number — $K$11, for example. You can convert a relative reference to an absolute reference by pressing the F4 key. See also *relative cell reference*.

active

The program window, workbook window, worksheet window, or dialog box currently in use. The color of the title bar of an active window or dialog box is different from the color of a nonactive window's title bars. When several document windows are displayed, you can activate an inactive window by clicking it.

arguments

Not what you have with your spouse but rather the values you give to a worksheet function to compute. Arguments are enclosed in parentheses and separated from one another by commas. See also *function.*

AutoCalculate

Refers to the area of the status bar that automatically indicates the sum of the values in any cell selection (see "You AutoCalculate my totals" in Chapter 1 for details).

borders

The different types of lines Excel can draw around the edges of each cell or the outside edge of a bunch of cells. Excel offers a wide variety of different line styles and colors for this purpose.

cell

The basic building block of plant and animal life and also of the Excel worksheet. The *worksheet cell* is a block formed by the intersections of column and row gridlines displayed in the worksheet. All worksheet data is stored in cells. Each cell is identified by the letter of its column and the number of its row, the so-called *cell reference*.

cell pointer

A heavy outline that indicates which cell in the worksheet is selected. You must move the cell pointer to a particular cell before you can enter or edit information in that cell.

cell range

A bunch of cells that are all right next to each other. To select a range of cells with the mouse, you simply point at the beginning of the range, click the mouse button, and drag through the cells. See also **nonadjacent selection.**

cell reference

Identifies the location of a cell in the worksheet. Normally, the cell reference consists of the column letter followed by the row number. (For example, "B3" indicates the cell in the second column and third row of the worksheet.) When you place the cell pointer in a cell, Excel displays its cell reference at the beginning of the formula bar. See also **relative cell reference** and **absolute cell reference.**

chart

Also known as a *graph*. This is a graphic representation of a set of values stored in a worksheet. You can create a chart right on a worksheet, where it is saved and printed along with the worksheet data. You can also display a chart in its own chart window, where you can edit its contents or print it independently of the worksheet data. (Such a chart is called, appropriately enough, a *chart sheet.*)

check box

Turns an option on or off in a dialog box. If the check box is selected, the option is turned on. If the check box is blank, the option is turned off. The nice thing about check boxes is that you can select more than one of the multiple options presented as a group. See also **radio button.**

click

The simplest mouse technique. You press and immediately release the mouse button. See also **double-click.**

Clipboard

The Windows equivalent of a hand-held clipboard to which you attach papers and information you need to work with. The Windows 95 Clipboard is a special area of memory, a holding place, where text and graphics can be stored to await further action. You can paste the contents of the Clipboard into any open Excel document (or any document in other Windows programs). The contents of the Clipboard are automatically replaced as soon as you cut or copy new information there (whether in Excel or some other program).

command button

A dialog-box button that initiates an action. The default command button is indicated by a dotted rectangle and a darker border. A button with an ellipsis (. . .) opens another dialog box or window. Frequently, after you choose options in the dialog box, you click the OK or Cancel command button.

context menus

Also known as *shortcut menus*, these menus are attached to certain things on the screen — namely, the toolbar, worksheet cell, or parts of a chart that are open in a chart window. These menus contain quick lists of command options related to the object they're attached to. You must use the mouse to open a shortcut menu and choose its commands by clicking the object with the right mouse button.

Control menu

A standard pull-down menu attached to all Windows programs and Excel workbook icons in the upper-left corner of their windows. This menu contains commands that open, close, maximize, minimize, or restore a window or dialog box. You can display a Control menu by clicking the program or workbook icon.

database

A tool for organizing, managing, and retrieving large amounts of information. A database is created right on a worksheet. The first row of the database contains column headings called *field names,* which identify each item of information you are tracking (such as First Name, Last Name, City, and the like). Below the field names, you enter the information you want to store for each field (column) of each record (row). See also *field* and *record.*

default

Don't be alarmed; we're not talking blame here. A *default* is a setting, value, or response that Excel automatically provides unless you choose something else. Some defaults can be changed and rearranged.

dialog box

A box containing various options that appears when you select Excel commands followed by an ellipsis (. . .). The options in a dialog box are presented in groups of buttons and boxes. (Oh, boy!) Many dialog boxes in Excel contain different tabs (see *tab*) that you click to bring up a different set of options. A dialog box can also display warnings and messages. Each dialog box contains a title bar and a Control menu but has no menu bar. You can move a dialog box around the active document window by dragging its title bar.

docking

Has nothing at all to do with the space shuttle. Docking in Excel refers to dragging one of the toolbars to a stationary position along the perimeter of the Excel window with the mouse. See also **toolbar.**

document

See **workbook.**

double-click

To click the mouse button twice in rapid succession. Double-clicking opens things like a program or a workbook. You can double-click to close things, too.

drag and drop

A really direct way to move stuff around on a worksheet. Select the cell or range (bunch) of cells you want to move, position the pointer on one of its edges, and then press and hold the primary mouse button. The pointer assumes the shape of an arrowhead pointing up toward the left. Hold the mouse button as you move the mouse and drag the outline of the selection to the new location. When you get where you're going, let it all go.

drop-down list box

A text box that displays the currently selected option, accompanied by an arrow button. When you click the associated arrow button, a list box with other options that you can choose from drops down (or sometimes pops up) from the text box. To select a new option from this list and close the drop-down list box, click the option.

edit box

Also known as a text box. The area in a dialog box where you type a new selection or edit the current one.

error value

A value Excel displays in a cell when it cannot calculate the formula for that cell. Error values start with a number sign (#) and end with an exclamation point (!), and they have various capitalized informative words in the middle. An example is #DIV/0!, which appears when you try to divide by zero.

field

A column in an Excel database that tracks just one type of item (like a city, state, zip code, and so on). See also **database** and **record.**

file

Any workbook document saved to a computer disk. See also ***workbook.***

font

Shapes for characters — typeface. Fonts have a point size, weight, and style, such as Helvetica Modern 20-point bold italic. You can pick and choose the fonts used to display information in an Excel worksheet and change their settings at any time.

footer

Information you specify to be printed in the bottom margin of each page of a printed report. See also ***header.***

formula

Ready for some math anxiety? A sequence of values, cell references, names, functions, or operators that is contained in a cell and produces a new value from existing values. In other words, a mathematical expression. Formulas in Excel always begin with an equal sign (=).

formula bar

Sound like a high-energy treat? Well, it is . . . sort of. Located at the top of the Excel window under the menu bar, the formula bar displays the contents of the current cell (in the case of formulas, this means that you see the formula rather than the calculated result, which shows up in the cell itself). You can also use the formula bar to enter or edit values and formulas in a cell or chart. When activated, the formula bar displays a Cancel box, Enter box, and Function Wizard button between the current cell reference on the left and the place where the cell contents appear on the right. Click the Enter box or press the Enter key to complete an entry or edit. Click the Cancel button or press Esc to leave the contents of the formula bar unchanged.

function

(Let's see, I know what *dysfunction* is. . . .) A function simplifies and shortens lengthy calculations. Functions have built-in formulas that use a series of values called *arguments* to perform the specified operations and return the results. The easiest way to enter a function in a cell is with the Function Wizard, which walks you through the entry of the function's arguments. The Function Wizard tool uses the icon with the *fx* on it and appears as buttons on both the Standard toolbar and the formula bar. See also ***arguments.***

graphics object

Any of the various shapes or graphics images (including charts) that you can bring into the sheets in your workbook document. All graphics objects remain in a separate layer on top of the cells in the sheet so that they can be selected, moved, resized, and formatted independently of the other information stored in the sheet.

header

Information you specify to be printed in the top margin of each page of a printed report. See also *footer.*

I-beam cursor

The I-beam shape (looks just like the end of a girder or a capital letter I) that the mouse pointer assumes when you position it in a place on-screen where you can enter or edit text. Click the I-beam cursor in the formula bar or a text box in a dialog box, for example, to place the insertion point where you want to add or delete text. When you double-click a cell, Excel positions the insertion point exactly where you clicked. If you press F2, Excel positions the insertion point at the end of the entry in that cell: You can then click the I-beam cursor in the cell entry to reposition the insertion point for editing. See also *insertion point.*

insertion point

The blinking vertical bar that indicates your current location in the text. The insertion point shows where the next character you type will appear or the next one you delete will disappear. See also *I-beam cursor.*

list box

A boxed area in a dialog box that displays a list of choices you can choose from. When a list is too long for all the choices to be displayed, the list box has a scroll bar you can use to bring new options into view. Most list boxes are already open and have the list on display. Those that you must open by clicking an arrow button are called *drop-down list boxes.*

macro

A sequence of frequently performed, repetitive tasks and calculations that you record. At the touch of a couple keystrokes, Excel can play back the steps in the macro much faster than is humanly possible.

marquee

Those moving dotted lights around the movie stars' names, right? Well, a *marquee* exists in Excel in a slightly toned-down version. It's the moving dotted line around a selection that shows what information is selected when you move or copy data with the Cut, Copy, and Paste commands on the Edit menu.

Maximize button

The center button of the three on the right side of the title bar on the less-than-full-size Excel program or workbook window. When you click the Maximize button, the workbook or program window expands to full size and fills the screen. See also **Minimize button** and **Restore button.**

menu

A vertical list of commands that can be applied to the active window or application. Also known as a *pull-down menu,* because the menu opens down from the menu bar when you select the menu name. When an option is currently unavailable on a pull-down menu, the option is dimmed. See also **context menus.**

menu bar

The row at the top of a program window that contains the names of the menu items available for the active document window.

message box

Also known as an *alert box.* This is a type of dialog box that appears when Excel gives you information, a warning, or an error message, or when it asks for confirmation before carrying out a command.

Minimize button

The first of the three buttons on the right side of the title bar in the Excel program or workbook window. When you click a Minimize button in a workbook window, the window shrinks to an icon at the bottom of the Excel screen. When you click the Minimize button in the Excel program window, the Excel window shrinks to a button on the Windows 95 taskbar. See also **Maximize button** and **Restore button.**

mode indicators

The information on the right side of the status bar (the row at the bottom of the screen) that tells you what keyboard modes are currently active. Some examples are ADD, NUM, and CAPS.

mouse pointer

Indicates your position on-screen as you move the mouse on the desk. The mouse pointer assumes various forms to indicate a change in the action when you use different features: the *arrowhead* when you point, select, or drag; the *I-beam* when you place the insertion point in text; the *double-headed arrow* when you drag to adjust row height or column width; and the *hourglass* when you need to wait.

nonadjacent selection

Also called a *discontiguous selection* (is that any better?). A nonadjacent selection is one composed of various cells and cell ranges that don't all touch each other. To accomplish this feat, click the first cell or click and drag through the first range; then hold down Ctrl as you click or drag through the remaining cells or ranges you want to select. See also *cell range.*

notes (text and sound)

Comments you attach to a particular worksheet cell to remind yourself of something important (or trivial) about the cell's contents. You can display text notes in the worksheet by positioning the mouse pointer on the cell note indicator. If your computer is wired for sound, you can record sound notes to be played back directly through your computer's speaker for all the world to hear.

pane

A part of a divided worksheet window. You can display different parts of the same worksheet together on one window in different panes. Horizontal and vertical split bars are involved with creating and sizing.

paste

Yum, yum, remember kindergarten? Alas, in the computer age, paste means to transfer the cut or copied contents of the Clipboard into a document, either in the cell with the cell pointer or in a line of text at the location of the insertion point.

pointing

Babies do it, politicians do it, and so can you. *Pointing* also means selecting a cell or cell range as you enter a formula in the formula bar to automatically record cell references.

primary mouse button

Politically correct name for the mouse button that used to be known as the left mouse button (on the two-button mouse commonly used with IBM compatibles). This is the button that you use to click pull-down menus, cells, charts, or whatever. If you're right-handed and you keep the mouse on the right side of your keyboard, the primary mouse button continues to be the left button. If, however, you are left-handed, have switched the mouse button functions, and keep the mouse on the left side of the keyboard, the right mouse button becomes the primary mouse button. In both cases, we are talking about the inmost button closest to the keyboard. Calling this button the primary button (rather than the inmost button) calls attention to the fact that, in Excel, you use the secondary mouse button mainly to open context menus. See also *secondary mouse button* and *context menus.*

radio button

When it's selected, a radio button in a dialog box looks like an old-fashioned radio push button (because it has dot in the middle). Radio buttons are used for dialog box items that contain mutually exclusive options. This means that you can select only one of the options at a time (only one can have the dot in the middle). See also **check box.**

range

Also called a *cell range.* A range is a bunch of neighboring cells that form some type of solid block when selected with the mouse or the keyboard.

record

A single row in a database that defines one entity (like an employee, a client, or a sales transaction). See also **database** and **field**.

relative cell reference

The normal cell reference (like A2) that is automatically adjusted when you copy formulas that refer to the cell. Row references are adjusted when you copy up or down; column references are adjusted when you copy to the left or right. See also **absolute cell reference** and **cell reference.**

Restore button

The center of the three buttons on the right side of the title bar when the Excel program window or a workbook window is displayed full-size on the screen. Mouse users can click the Restore button to shrink a window or return a window to the size and location it had before being zoomed to full size. See also **Maximize button** and **Minimize button.**

scroll bar

The vertical or horizontal bar in the active document window and in some list boxes. Use a scroll bar to move rapidly through a document or list by clicking the scroll arrows or dragging the slider box.

secondary mouse button

Politically correct name for what used to be known as the right mouse button. This is the button that you use to click various screen objects in Excel to display its shortcut (or *context*) menu. If you're right-handed and you keep the mouse on the right side of your keyboard, the secondary mouse button continues to be the right button. If, however, you are left-handed, have switched the mouse button functions, and keep the mouse on the left side of the keyboard, the left mouse button becomes the secondary mouse button. In both cases, we are talking about the outermost button furthest from the keyboard. Calling this button the secondary button (rather than the outermost button) calls attention to the fact that, in Excel, you use the primary mouse button much more often than the secondary mouse button. See also ***primary mouse button*** and ***context menus***.

selection

The chosen element, such as a cell, cell range, nonadjacent selection, file, directory, dialog box option, graphics object, or text. To select an element, highlight it by dragging the mouse or pressing keystroke shortcuts. You normally select an element before choosing the actions you want to apply to that element.

sheet tabs

The tabs that appear at the bottom of each workbook window. To select a new sheet (worksheet, chart, and so on) in your workbook, you click its tab. To display new sheet tabs, you use the tab scrolling buttons. Excel indicates which sheet is the active one by displaying the sheet name in bold on its tab. To rename sheet tabs (which are normally given names such as Sheet1, Sheet2, and so on), double-click a tab and enter the new name in the Rename Sheet dialog box; then select OK or press Enter. See also ***tab***.

size box

The little square box in the lower-right corner of a workbook window that is neither minimized nor maximized with the scrolling arrows pointing to it. Use the size box to manually adjust the size of any open document window by dragging it until the window is the size and shape you want.

spreadsheet

A type of computer program that enables you to develop and perform all sorts of calculations between the text and values stored in a document. Most spreadsheet programs like Excel also include charting and database capabilities. *Spreadsheet* is also commonly used as an alternative term for *worksheet* — so see also ***worksheet.***

status bar

The line at the bottom of the Excel window. The status bar displays messages, such as Ready, or a short description of the menu option you have chosen, and it indicates any active modes, such as CAPS or NUM when you press the Caps Lock or Num Lock key.

style

If you've got it, flaunt it. Also known to some of us as a group of formatting instructions, all bundled together, that you can apply to the cells in a worksheet. Use styles to save time and keep things consistent. Styles can deal with the number format, font, alignment, border, patterns, and protection of the cells.

tab

You find tabs in two places in Excel: on some larger dialog boxes, such as the Format Cells or Options dialog boxes, and attached to the bottom of each worksheet in a workbook. In the case of dialog box tabs, you simply click a tab to display its set of options on the top of all the others in the dialog box. In the case of sheet tabs, you click a tab to display its sheet on top of all the others in, the workbook. See also **dialog box** and **sheet tabs**.

title bar

The top bar of a program window, workbook window, or dialog box that contains its title. You can move an active window or dialog box around the screen by dragging its title bar.

toolbar

A series of related tools (buttons with icons) that you simply click to perform common tasks such as opening, saving, or printing a document. Excel comes with several built-in toolbars that you can use as-is or customize. You can create toolbars of your own design, using predefined tools or blank tools to which you assign macros. You can display them in their own little dialog boxes that float around the active document window; you can also dock them along the perimeter of the screen. See also **docking.**

window

A framed area on-screen that contains the program (called a *program window*) or the workbook (called a *workbook window*) that you're working with. The Excel program window typically contains a title bar, Control menu, menu bar, Standard toolbar, open document windows (with the active one on top), and status bar. The program and workbook windows can be resized and moved around the screen as needed.

workbook

An Excel file containing multiple, related sheets such as worksheets, charts, and macro sheets. When you start a new workbook, Excel automatically puts 16 blank worksheets in it (named Sheet1 through Sheet16) and gives the workbook a temporary name (such as Book1, Book2, and so on). You can then add or remove worksheets as needed as well as add chart and or module/macro sheets as needed. When you save the workbook, you can then give the workbook a permanent filename. See also **chart**, **file**, and **worksheet**.

worksheet

Also called a *spreadsheet.* This is the primary document for recording, analyzing, and calculating data. The Excel worksheet is organized in a series of 256 columns and 16,384 rows, making for a heck of a lot of cells, and each new workbook you open contains 16 blank worksheets. See also **workbook.**

Index

• *Symbols* •

: (colon)
 in cell ranges, 44
, (comma)
 entering currency values, 63
 in large numbers, 115–116
( ) (parentheses)
 entering negative values, 63
 order of operations, 71–72
. (period)
 entering decimal values, 63
.. (periods)
 in cell ranges, 44
' (apostrophe)
 retaining leading zeros, 271
* (asterisk)
 in formulas, 68–69
 masking passwords, 216
 wildcard character, 211, 275
@ (at sign)
 in functions, 44
^ (carat)
 in formulas, 68–69
$ (dollar sign)
 displaying, 115
 entering currency values, 63
= (equal sign)
 AutoFilter operator, 286
 in formulas, 43, 68–69
 in functions, 44, 85
 search operator, 277
! (exclamation point)
 in error messages, 72–73
>= (greater than or equal sign)
 AutoFilter operator, 286
 search operator, 277
> (greater than sign)
 AutoFilter operator, 286
 search operator, 277

<= (less than or equal sign)
 AutoFilter operator, 286
 search operator, 277
< (less than sign)
 AutoFilter operator, 286
 search operator, 277
- (minus sign)
 entering negative values, 63
 in formulas, 68–69
<>= (not equal sign)
 AutoFilter operator, 286
 search operator, 277
(number sign)
 in error messages, 72–73
% (percent sign)
 in cell values, 116–117
+ (plus sign)
 in formulas, 43, 68–69
(pound sign)
 cells filled with, 114–115
? (question mark)
 in error messages, 72–73
 wildcard, 211
 wildcard character, 275
" (quotation mark)
 copying database records, 270
/ (slash)
 activating menus, 42
 in formulas, 68–69
~ (tilde)
 displaying formulas, 191
 searching for asterisks, 212

• *A* •

A1 cell reference system, 15
absolute cell references, 160
 defined, 373
Across, then Down button, 185
 illustration, 187

active, defined, 373
Add Text tool, 265
adding machine data entry style, 65–67
addition
  in formulas, 68–69
  SUM function, 88–91
  when pasting from Clipboard, 163
Adjust to button, 176–177
Advanced Find dialog box, 145
Alert Before Overwriting Cells check
    box, 324
alert boxes, 49
Align Left tool, 29
Align Right tool, 29
All button, 174–175
Allow Cell Drag and Drop check box, 324
Alternate Startup File Location field, 320
Animate Insertion and Deletion check
    box, 324
animating deletion/insertion, 324
Answer Wizard, 51–53
apostrophe (')
  retaining leading zeros, 271
arguments
  defined, 373
  of functions, 85
Arrange Windows dialog box, 227–229
arrays, 14
arrow and question mark pointer, 24
arrowhead pointer, 24
arrows, adding to text box, 255
ascending sort order, 278–279, 282
Ask to Update Automatic Links check
    box, 324
Assign a Number button, 294
Assign Macro dialog box, 349
asterisk (*), 211
  in formulas, 68–69
  masking passwords, 216
  wildcard character, 275
at sign (@)
  in functions, 44
AutoCalculate
  defined, 373
  illustration, 35

AutoComplete, 77–78
AutoCorrect, 73–75
AutoFill
  copying cell contents, 81–82
  copying formulas, 156–157
  custom lists, 82–83
  filling a cell range, 78–81
  handle, 79
  illustration, 80, 157
AutoFilter
  customizing, 284–287
  filtering databases, 282–283
  operators, 286
  top ten records, 284
AutoFilter dialog box, 285
AutoFit, 122–124
AutoFormat, 105–108
automatic completion
  enabling/disabling, 324
Automatic Page Breaks check box, 317
AutoSelect
  illustration, 101–102
  keyboard equivalent, 103–104
AutoSum, 88–91
  on Standard toolbar, 28

● *B* ●

best-fit column sizes, 106, 122–124
Black and White check box, 185
  illustration, 187
black cross pointer, 24
blanks in numeric values, 361
block moves, 39
Bold tool, 29, 127
Border palette tool, 135
borders, defined, 373
Borders tool, 30
buttons
  Across, then Down, 185, 187
  adding to toolbars, 342
  Adjust to, 176–177
  All, 174–175
  Assign a Number, 294
  assigning macros to, 347–348

Capture Data in a Database, 294
Cascade, 229
 copying, 343
 copying pictures, 348–349
 creating, 344–347
 creating pictures, 349–351
 Date, 183–184
 in dialog boxes, 48
 Display Example/Remove Example, 294
 Document a Cell, 293
 Down, then Across, 185, 187
 enlarging, 341
 Entire Workbook, 174–175
 Filename, 183–184
 Fit to, 176–177
 Hide CellTips/Display CellTips, 293
 Horizontal, 227
 Minimize, illustration, 26
 moving, 343
 Orientation, 176–177
 Page, 184
 Pages, 174–175
 rearranging, 343
 removing, 343
 Restore, illustration, 26
 restoring defaults, 344
 Select Employee, illustration, 293
 Selected Sheet(s), 174–175
 Selection, 174–175
 Size to Screen/Return to Size, 293
 spacing, 343
 Tab Name, 183–184
 Template Help, 293
 Tiled, 227
 Time, 183–184
 Total Page, 183–184
 Vertical, 229

● C ●

calculating values automatically, 34
Capture Data in a Database button, 294
carat (^)
 in formulas, 68–69

Cascade button, 229
cascading worksheets, 229–230
case sensitivity
 functions, 85
 searching a workbook, 211
cell borders, 132–134
 colors, 321
cell information windows
 hiding/showing, 316
Cell Note dialog box, 204–206
cell pointer
 compared to mouse pointers, 24
 defined, 374
 illustration, 15
 moving with Enter key, 59
  illustration, 66
 moving with keys, 37–38
cell ranges
 copying, 152–154
 defined, 374
 dragging and dropping, 151–156
 filling, 78–81
  with dates, 335–337
 inserting, 154–156, 166–167
 moving, 151–152
 naming, 206–208, 363
 printing, 185
 selecting, 98
 summing, 88–91
cell references, defined, 374
cells
 absolute addresses, 158–161
 active, 98
 aligning contents, 128–130
 background color, 134–135
 background pattern, 134–135
 blank, omitting from cut and paste, 164
 borderlines, 132–134
 borders, omitting from cut and paste, 163
 clearing, 164–165
 color, 135
 compared to word processor pages, 17
 confirmation before dropping, 324

cells *(continued)*
  copying
    with cut and paste, 161–164
    data, 84–85, 156–157
    formats, 137–138
    formats without data, 163
  current, 14
  defined, 373
  deleting, 76, 164–166
  deselecting, 100
  displayed *vs.* actual contents, 118–119
  editing, 75–77
    enabling/disabling, 324
  entering values, 66
  filling a range, 78–81
  formatting, 97, 108–111
  gridlines, 132–134
  insert mode, 76
  inserting, 155, 166–167
  inserting data, 76
  linking entries, 164
  moving objects with, 324
  moving with cut and paste, 161–162
  naming, 206–208
  numbers in a worksheet, 14–16
  overtype mode, 76
  pointing to, 69–71
  relative addresses, 158
  rotating, 132, 164
  selecting
    before acting on, 359
    AutoSelect method, 101–102
    for formulas, 69–71
    Go To method, 105
    groups, 98–99
    keyboard method, 103–105
    with mouse, 99–100
    multiple blocks, 104–105
    nonadjacent, 100, 104–105
    point-and-click method, 99
    ranges, 98–99
    tables, 101–104
  setting to same precision, 324
  shading, 135
  sizing columns, 122–124

sizing rows, 124
summing, 90–91
summing a range, 88–91
text
  color, 136
  orientation, 132
  wrapping, 130–132
viewing contents of, 30
Center Across Columns tool, 29
Center tool, 29
centering titles across columns, 129
chart sheets, 31
Chart Title dialog box, 252–254
Chart toolbar, 251–254
charts
  bounding box, 243
  category labels, 247
  changing data, 251
  changing type, 250
  changing when values change, 256
  choosing format, 245–246
  choosing type, 245
  clip art, 260
  data series, 246
  defined, 374
  formatting, 252–254
  graphic images, 259–261
  gridlines, 250
  labels, 247
  legends, 243, 246, 250
  location, 244
  moving, 249
  moving objects in, 252
  perspectives, 256–258
  positioning, 242–243
  previewing, 246–247
  resizing, 249
  rotating, 256–259
  selecting data, 243
  selecting objects, 252
  selection handles, 249
  shortcut menus, 252
  sizing, 242–244
  text boxes, 254–255
  3-D, 251, 256–258

titles, 247–248, 252–254
verifying data range, 244
See also maps
ChartWizard
chart format, 246
chart type, 245
labels, 247
positioning a chart, 242–243
previewing a chart, 246
sizing a chart, 242–243
on Standard toolbar, 28
titles, 247
check boxes, 47–48
defined, 374
click, defined, 374
clip art
See graphic images
Clipboard
copying cells, 162
defined, 374
moving cells, 161–162
separating data from format, 163
on Standard toolbar, 27
Close button, illustration, 26
Collate check box, 174–175
colon (:)
in cell ranges, 44
color palette, customizing, 321–323
Color Picker dialog box, 322
Color tab, 320–323
Color tool, 30
Color Toolbars check box, 341
color
cell background, 134–135
cell borders, 321
cell selections, 321
Color tool, 30
customizing, 321–323
fonts, 127–128, 321
gridlines, 317
monochrome *vs.* color monitors, 341
printing in black and white, 185
text, 30, 50, 136
column headers, hiding/showing, 317

Column Width dialog box, 123–124
columns
deleting, 360, 362
disappearing, 124
hiding, 124–126
labeling, 16
selecting, 100
Columns to Repeat at Left field, 185
illustration, 187
comma (,)
entering currency values, 63
in large numbers, 115–116
Comma number format, 115–116
See also Currency number format
Comma Style tool, 29
command buttons
defined, 375
in dialog boxes, 48
command letters, 41, 49
Commands and Settings button, 141, 148
Commands and Settings menu, 148–149
illustration, 149
Common database, 301–302
computer memory, conserving, 57, 359
context menus
accessing, 44
defined, 375
illustration, 45
on workbook objects, 40–41, 364
Control menu
defined, 375
illustration, 32
Copy tool, 27
country settings, 325
crossed double-headed arrow pointer, 24
currency, international settings, 325
Currency number format, 112–115
See also Comma number format
Currency Style tool, 29
current cell reference, 15
Custom Map Pin tool, 265
custom number formats, 120–121
Customize dialog box
assigning macros to buttons, 347–348
customizing toolbars, 341–342

Cut, Copy, and Sort Objects with Cells
    check box, 324
cut and paste, 161–164
Cut tool, 27

• *D* •

data entry
  canceling, 59
  currency values, 63
  date values, 62, 67–68
  decimal values, 63
  fractions, 63
  guidelines for, 56–59
  negative values, 63
  percentages, 64
  positive values, 63
  time values, 62, 67
data forms, 268–272
Data Map, 262–266
Data Map Control dialog box, 265
Data Map toolbar, 263–266
data types, 60
databases
  adding records, 269–272
  calculated fields, 272
  copying previous record, 270
  dates, 271–272
  defined, 375
  deleting records, 273
  editing records, 273
  filtering, 268, 282–283, 285, 287–288
  leading zeros, 271–272
  locating records, 273–277
  searching, 275–276
  sorting, 277–282
  techniques for searching, 274
  viewing top ten records, 284
  zip codes, 271–272
Date button, 183–184
date format, 112
  international settings, 325
date values, Macintosh style, 67
DDE requests, ignoring, 319

decimal places
  changing, 118
  fixing, 64–65
  setting, 117–118
decimal points
  adding automatically, 64
  aligning on, 112–113
  automatically adding, 66
Decrease Decimal tool, 29
default, defined, 375
Default File Location field, 320
Define Name dialog box, 207
Delete dialog box, 166
descending sort order, 278–279, 282
dialog boxes
  Advanced Find, 145
  Arrange Windows, 227–229
  Assign Macro, 349
  AutoFilter, 285
  Cell Note, 204–206
  Chart Title, 252–254
  check boxes, 47–48
  Color Picker, 322
  Color tab, Options, 321
  Column Width, 123–124
  command buttons, 48
  command letters, 49
  Customize, 341–342, 347
  Data Map Control, 265
  Define Name, 207
  defined, 375
  Delete, 166
  drop-down list boxes, 47
  edit boxes, 47
  Edit tab, Options, 323
  Find, 210–212
  Format Cells
    cell borders, 134–135
    changing fonts, 127
    Comma number format, 115–116
    Currency number format, 112–114
    custom number formats, 120–121
    date format, 112
    decimal places, 117–118
    displayed *vs.* actual values, 118

format overflow, 114–115
  illustration, 127, 134–135
  keystroke shortcut, 111
  number formats, 112
  Percent number format, 116–117
  percentage, 112
  phone numbers, 120
  rounding, 119
  social security numbers, 120
  Special number format, 120–122
  zip codes, 120
Format Chart Title, 253
Go To, 208
Header, 183–184
Insert, 166–167
keyboard selection, 49
list boxes, 47
Move or Copy, 232
moving, 48
New, 292
Open, 141, 147–149
Options
  Color tab, 320–323
  Edit tab, 324
  General tab, 319–320
  illustration, 47
  Module General tab, 325
  View tab, 315–318
Page Setup
  footers, 181–184
  headers, 181–184
  illustration, 176
  margins, 179–180
  sheet settings, 184–185
parts of, 47–48
Paste Special, 163–164
Print, 174–175
radio buttons, 48
Record New Macro, 328, 331, 333, 336
Save As, 46, 93
Select an Employee, 303
sizing, 48
Sort, 280
Spelling, 167
spinner buttons, 48

tabs, 47
  Toolbars, 340–341
dimmed menu items, 42
Direction list, 324
directory, setting default, 320
Display Entire tool, 265
Display Example/Remove Example
  button, 294
#DIV/0! message, 73
dividing by zero, 73
division
  in formulas, 68–69
  when pasting from Clipboard, 163
docking
  defined, 376
  toolbars, 108–111
document, defined, 376
Document a Cell button, 293
dollar sign ($)
  displaying, 115
  entering currency values, 63
double-click, defined, 376
double-headed arrow pointer, 24
Down, then Across button, 185
  illustration, 187
Draft Quality check box, 185
  illustration, 187
drag-and-drop
  copying cells, 152–154
  defined, 376
  enabling/disabling, 324
  inserting cells, 154–156
  moving cells, 151–152
Drawing tool, 28
Drawing toolbar, 255, 259–260
drop-down lists
  defined, 376
  in dialog boxes, 47

• **E** •

edit boxes, 47
  defined, 376
Edit Directly in Cell check box, 324
Edit tab, 323–324
e-mail, 366

Enable AutoComplete for Cell Values
    check box, 324
enlarging windows
    See maximizing windows
Enter key
    defining action of, 324
    moving cell pointer, 59
        illustration, 66
Entire Workbook button, 174–175
equal sign (=)
    AutoFilter operator, 286
    in formulas, 43, 68–69
    in functions, 44, 85
    search operator, 277
error values, 72–73
    defined, 376
Excel
    exiting, 53
    uses for, 12
Excel for Windows 95
    AnswerWizard, 51–53
    AutoComplete, 77–78
    AutoCorrect, 74
    AutoFilter option, 284
    Data Map, 262–266
    Excel shortcut, 20–21
    Explorer, 19–20
    Find, 143
    long filenames, 92
    Microsoft Office shortcut bar, 18
    My Favorites folder, 142
    opening at startup, 21–22
    opening Excel at startup, 21–22
    Special number formats, 120
    Spreadsheet Solutions, 291–294
    Start menu, 19
    starting
        from Microsoft Office shortcut bar, 18
        from task bar, 357
    top ten new features, 355–356
exclamation point (!)
    in error messages, 72–73
exiting Excel, 358
Explorer, 19–20

exponentiation, in formulas, 68–69
EXT indicator, 103
Extend mode, 103

• F •

fields
    database, 268
    defined, 376
Filename button, 183–184
filename extensions
    added automatically, 361
    hidden, 92
filenames, long, 92
files
    defined, 377
    displaying information about, 145–148
    finding, 147–148
    grouping by folder, 149
    opening as read-only, 148
    organization of, 143
    printing, 148
    searching subfolders, 149
    sharing on a network, 365–366
    sorting, 148
    summary information, 148
    See also workbooks
fill handle, 24
filling a range of cells, 78–81
    with dates, 335–337
filter criteria, 268
Find, Options dialog box, 143
Find dialog box, 210–212
First Page Number field, 176–177
Fit to button, 176–177
Fixed Decimal Places check box, 324
Fixed Decimal setting, 64–65
floating toolbars, 109
folders, sorting, 148
Font Color tool, 30
Font Size tool, 29
Font tool, 29
fonts
    bold, 127
    changing, 127

color, 127–128
colors, 321
defined, 377
italic, 127
selecting default, 320
strikeout, 127
underlined, 127
footers
defined, 377
in reports, 182
Format Cells dialog box
cell borders, 134–135
changing fonts, 127
Comma number format, 115–116
Currency number format, 113–114
decimal places, 117–118
displayed *vs.* actual values, 118
format overflow, 114–115
illustration, 127, 134–135
keystroke shortcut, 111
number formats, 112
Percent number format, 116–117
rounding, 119
Special number format, 120–122
Format Chart Title dialog box, 253
format overflow, 114–115
Format Painter, 27, 137–138
Formatting toolbar
emphasizing text, 127
formatting cells, 108–111
illustration, 26, 110
removing, 364
summary of tools, 29–30
formula bar
defined, 377
described, 30
editing cell contents, 77
hiding/showing, 316
illustration, 26
removing, 364
Formula Bar check box, 316
formulas
addition, 68–69
cell names in, 208–209
converting to values, 163

copying, 156–157
creating, 28
defined, 377
division, 68–69
entering, 70
exponentiation, 68–69
Lotus 1-2-3 style, 42–44, 359
multiplication, 68–69
naming, 208–209
printing, 191–192
selecting cells for, 69–71
subtraction, 68–69
switching to calculated values, 317
Formulas check box, 317
frozen panes, 202–203
functions
creating with Function Wizard, 86–88
defined, 377
syntax, 85–86
Function Wizard
illustration, 86–89
on Standard toolbar, 28

• *G* •

General tab, 319–320
illustration, 318
glossary terms, 50
Go To dialog box, 40
illustration, 208
Grabber tool, 263
graphic images, charts, 259–261
graphics objects
defined, 378
hiding, 363
greater than or equal sign (>=)
AutoFilter operator, 286
search operator, 277
greater than sign (>)
AutoFilter operator, 286
search operator, 277
gridlines
color, 317
hiding/showing, 317
Gridlines check box, 185, 317
illustration, 187

• H •

header, report, 182
  defined, 378
Header dialog box, 183–184
help
  colored text, 50
  online, 49–50
  underlined text, 50
  See also Answer Wizard
  See also TipWizard
  See also ToolTips
help pointer, 24
Help tool, 28, 50
Hide CellTips/Display CellTips button, 293
hierarchy of files, 143
Horizontal button, 227
horizontal scroll bar
  hiding/showing, 317
  illustration, 26
Horizontal Scroll Bar check box, 317
horizontal worksheets, 227–228
hue, 322

• 1 •

I-beam pointer, 24
  defined, 378
icons, customizing, 350–351
Ignore Other Applications check box, 319
Increase Decimal tool, 29
Info Window check box, 316
Insert dialog box, 166–167
insertion point, defined, 378
international settings, 325
invoices, creating from a template,
    305–308
Italic tool, 29, 127

• J •

jump terms, 50

• K •

keystroke shortcuts
  dialog box selection, 49
  editing cells, 76–77, 371
  editing worksheets, 369–370
  formatting cell selections, 369
  moving around selected cells, 368
  moving cell pointer with, 38
  moving through worksheets, 367–368
  online help, 367
  opening context menus, 46
  opening Format Cells dialog box, 111
  opening workbooks, 371
  printing workbooks, 371
  saving workbooks, 371
  scrolling sheet to sheet, 221
  selecting cells, 367–368
  sizing a workbook, 368

• L •

labels
  See text
landscape page orientation, 177–178
language settings, 325
Large Buttons check box, 341
legends, 242, 246, 250
less than or equal sign (<=)
  AutoFilter operator, 286
  search operator, 277
less than sign (<)
  AutoFilter operator, 286
  search operator, 277
lightbulb icon
  changes color/intensity, 53
links, confirmation before updating, 324
list boxes
  defined, 378
  in dialog boxes, 47
lists
  automatic generation, 363
  creating with AutoFill, 82–83
long filenames, 92
Lotus 1-2-3
  Excel equivalents, 42–44, 359
luminosity, 322

• *M* •

Macintosh computers
  date values, 67
macro recorder, 334
macro sheets, 31
macros
  absolute cell references, 337
  assigning to toolbar buttons, 347–348
  defined, 378
  personal macro workbook, 329
  playing back, 334–335
  recording, 328
  relative cell references, 337
  re-recording, 338
  Run-time error 1004 message, 337
  samples
    entering a company name, 330–335
    filling a range with dates, 335–337
  saving, 329
magnifying
  See zooming
manual recalculation, 360
Map Labels tool, 265
Map Network Drive command, 149
Map tool, 28
maps
  creating, 262–266
  labels, 265
  manually redrawing, 265
  moving objects, 263
  printing chart data only, 266
  pushpins, 265
  selecting objects, 263
  text, 265
  viewing entire, 265
  zooming, 263
margins, 180
marquee, defined, 378
Maximize button, defined, 379
maximizing windows, 26, 379
menu bar, 25–26
menus
  choosing commands, 358
  defined, 379
  using Excel 4.0 style, 319

message bar, defined, 379
Microsoft Excel 4.0 Menus check box, 319
Microsoft Office shortcut bar, 18
Minimize button
  illustration, 26
minimizing windows, 26, 379
minus sign (-)
  entering negative values, 63
  in formulas, 68–69
mode indicators, defined, 379
Module General tab, 325
module sheets, 328
monitors
  monochrome *vs.* color, 341
mouse pointers, 23–24
  defined, 379
Move or Copy dialog box, 232
Move Selection after Enter check box, 324
multiplication
  in formulas, 68–69
  when pasting from Clipboard, 163
My Favorites folder, 142

• *N* •

#NAME? message, 73
nested parentheses, 72, 361
networks, sharing files, 365–366
New dialog box, 292
New Workbook tool, 27
nonadjacent selection
  defined, 380
  by keyboard, 104–105
  by mouse, 100
not equal sign (<>=)
  AutoFilter operator, 286
  search operator, 277
Note Indicator check box, 316
note indicators
  hiding/showing, 316
notes
  See sound notes
  See text notes
Notes check box, 185
  illustration, 187

#NULL! message, 73
Num Lock indicator, 35
#NUM! message, 73
number formats
  Comma, 115–116
  Currency, 112–115
  custom, 120–121
  international settings, 325
  Percent, 112, 116–117
  Special, 120–122
Number of Copies field, 174–175
number sign (#)
  in error messages, 72–73
numeric keypad, entering data with, 35,
    65–67

• *O* •

Open dialog box, illustration, 141, 147–149
Open Read Only command, 148–149
Open tool, 27
Options dialog box
  Automatic Page Breaks box, 317
  Color tab, 320–323
  Edit tab, 324
  Formula Bar box, 316
  Formulas box, 317
  General tab, 319–320
  Gridlines, 317
  Horizontal Scroll Bar box, 317
  illustration, 47
  Info Window box, 316
  Module General tab, 325
  Note Indicator box, 316
  Outline Symbols box, 317
  Row & Column Headers box, 317
  Sheet Tabs box, 317
  Status Bar box, 316
  Vertical Scroll Bar box, 317
  View tab, 315–318
  Zero Values, 317
order of operations, mathematics, 71–72
Orientation button, 176–177
outline symbols, hiding/showing, 317
Outline Symbols check box, 317

• *P* •

page breaks
  hiding/showing, 317
  illustration, 190
  screen appearance, 173
Page button, 184
Page Setup dialog box
  Adjust to button, 176–177
  Black and White check box, 185
  Columns to Repeat at Left field, 185
  Down, then Across button, 185
  Draft Quality check box, 185
  First Page Number field, 176–177
  Fit to button, 176–177
  Gridlines check box, 185
  headers and footers, 182
  illustration, 176, 180, 182
  margins, 180
  Notes check box, 185
  Orientation button, 176–177
  Paper Size list box, 176–177
  Print Area box, 184–185
  Print Quality list box, 176–177
  Row and Column Headings check
      box, 185
  Rows to Repeat at Top field, 185
  sheet settings, 184–186
Pages button, 174–175
pane, defined, 380
Paper Size list box, 176–177
parentheses (( ))
  entering negative values, 63
  order of operations, 71–72
passwords
  creating, 216
  forgetting, 360, 362
  masking, 216
paste, defined, 380
Paste Special dialog box, 163–164
Paste tool, 27
Percent number format, 112, 116
  illustration, 117
percent sign (%)
  in cell values, 116–117

Percent Style tool, 29
percentages, 112, 116–117
period (.)
  entering decimal values, 63
periods (..)
  in cell ranges, 44
PERSONAL.XLS file, 330
phone numbers, 120
Places list, 324
plus sign (+)
  in formulas, 43, 68–69
pointing, defined, 380
portrait page orientation, 177–178
pound sign (#)
  cells filled with, 114–115
preferences, setting, 315–325
primary mouse button, defined, 380
Print Area check box, 184–185
  illustration, 187
Print command, 148–149
Print dialog box, 174–175
Print Preview, 170–172
Print Preview tool, 27
Print Preview window, 180
Print Quality list box, 176–177
Print tool, 27
printing
  cell ranges, 185
  centering on a page, 179–180
  chart data only, 266
  colors in black and white, 185
  files, 148
  footers, 181–184
  formulas, 191–192
  gridlines, 185
  headers, 181–184
  inserting current date, 183–184
  inserting current time, 183–184
  inserting workbook name, 183–184
  margins, 179–180
  multiple copies, 174–176
  numbering pages, 183–186
  page breaks, 188–190
  page orientation, 176–177
  page settings, 174–176

  paper size, 176–177
  previewing, 360
  print quality, 176–177, 185
  row and column headings, 185
  scaling output, 176–179
  selecting cells for, 174–176, 185
  from Standard toolbar, 27, 173–174
  starting page number, 176–177
  text notes, 185
  titles, 185–188
  workbooks
    keystroke shortcut, 371
printing, previewing, 360
program window bars, 26
program window buttons, 26
Prompt for File Properties check box, 319
Properties command, 148–149
Properties dialog box
  hiding/showing, 319
pull-down menus, 41–42

• **Q** •

question mark (?)
  in error messages, 72–73
  wildcard character, 211, 275
question mark pointer, 50
quotation mark (")
  copying database records, 270

• **R** •

R1C1 cell reference system, 15
radio buttons
  defined, 381
  See also buttons
ranges
  defined, 381
  See also cell ranges
Recently Used File List check box, 319
recently-used file list
  hiding/showing, 319
record, defined, 381
Record New Macro dialog box, 328
  illustration, 331, 333, 336
records, 268

Redo command, 150
Redraw Map tool, 265
#REF! message, 73
reference style, selecting, 319
Reference Style check box, 319
relative cell reference, defined, 381
Repeat tool, 28
Reset TipWizard check box, 319
Restore, illustration button, 26
Restore button
  defined, 381
  illustration, 26
restoring windows, 26
rotating
  cells, 132, 164
  charts, 256–259
  text, 132–133
rounding, 119
Row & Column Headers check box, 317
Row & Column Headings check box, 185
  illustration, 187
row headers, hiding/showing, 317
rows
  deleting, 360, 362
  disappearing, 124
  hiding, 124–126
  selecting, 100
Rows to Repeat at Top field, 185
  illustration, 187

• *S* •

saturation, 322
Save tool, 27
Save As dialog box, 46, 93
Saved Searches command, 149
scaling
  See zooming
scroll bar
  defined, 381
  missing, 111
  removing, 220
scrolling buttons, 219
Search Subfolders command, 149

search-and-replace operations, 362
secondary mouse button, defined, 381–382
Select an Employee dialog box, 303
Select Employee button
  illustration, 294
Select Objects tool, 263
Selected Sheet(s) button, 174–175
selection, defined, 382
Selection button, 174–175
sequential series, 81
sheet tabs
  defined, 382
  hiding, 317
  illustration, 26
  renaming, 223–225
  scrolling, 219
  scrolling worksheets, 33–34
  showing, 219–220, 317
  turned white, 222
Sheet Tabs check box, 317
Sheets in New Workbook list, 320
shortcut menus
  See context menus
Show ToolTips check box, 341
Show/Hide Data Map Control tool, 265
shrinking windows
  See minimizing windows
size box, defined, 382
Size list, 320
Size to Screen/Return to Size button, 293
sizing buttons, 25, 32
slash (/)
  activating menus, 42
  in formulas, 68–69
slow screen response, 261
Social Security numbers, 120
Sort Ascending tool, 28, 282
Sort Descending tool, 28, 282
Sort dialog box, 280
Sorting command, 148–149
sorting keys, 278
sound notes, 205–206
  defined, 380
Special number formats, 120

spell checking
 after the fact, 167–168
 during text entry, 73–75
Spelling dialog box, 167
Spelling tool, 27
spinner buttons, 48
split bar, 198
split double-headed arrow pointer, 24
splitting windows, 199, 201
Spreadsheet Solutions, 291–294
spreadsheets
 defined, 382
 vs. worksheets, 13
Standard Font list, 320
Standard toolbar
 Help tool, 50
 illustration, 26
 removing, 364
 sorting a database, 282
 summary of tools, 27–28
Start menu, 19
startup file
 selecting an alternate, 320
status bar
 defined, 382
 hiding/showing, 316
 illustration, 26
 removing, 364
Status Bar check box, 316
sticky notes
 See text notes
styles
 defined, 382
 formatting numbers, 136–137
subtraction
 in formulas, 68–69
 when pasting from Clipboard, 163
SUM function, 88–91
summary worksheets, 235–237

● T ●

Tab Name button, 183–184
tab split bar, 220

tables
 data entry, 83–85
 error correction, 106
 formatting, 105–108
 jumping across, 363
 moving in, 39
 sizing columns, 106–107
 3D effects, 106–108
 undoing changes, 106
tabs
 defined, 383
 in dialog boxes, 47
Template Help button, 293
templates
 creating from workbooks, 304–308
 creating with TemplateWizard, 308–313
 customizing, 295–298
 ready-made, 291–294
 timecard, 299–304
 using, 291–294
Template Wizard, 309–313
ten-key data entry, 65–67
text
 aligning, 29, 130–131
 bold, 29
 in a cell, 58
 centering across columns, 29
 color, 30, 50, 136
 cutoff, 60–61
 disappearing, 60–61
 italic, 29
 maps, 265
 rotating, 132–133
 spilling across cells, 60–61
 underlined, 29, 50
 wrapping, 130–132
 as zero value, 62
text boxes, 254–255
text notes
 adding, 204–205
 cutting and pasting, 163
 defined, 380
 finding, 206
 printing, 185
 removing, 206

3-D area chart, 257
3-D chart, 251
  rotating, 258–259
tilde (~)
  displaying formulas, 191
  searching for asterisks, 212
Tiled button, 227
tiled worksheets, 227–228
Time button, 183–184
time formats, international settings, 325
Timecard template
  customized, 300
  filling, 303
  illustration, 293
Timecard toolbar, 293–294
Timecard worksheet notes, 294
Timecard worksheets
  customizing, 296–298
timecards
  adding cell notes, 293
  data from common database, 301–302
  help, 293
  hiding/showing cell note indicators, 293
  hiding/showing example data, 294
  numbering, 294
  saving, 294, 302–304
  template, 299–304
  zooming, 293
TipWizard, 363
  resetting, 319
  on Standard toolbar, 28
title bars
  defined, 383
  illustration, 26
titles, report, 187–188
toolbar context menu, 45
toolbars
  adding buttons, 342
  assigning macros to, 347–348
  Chart, 250–2541
  copying button pictures, 348–349
  copying buttons, 343
  creating, 344–347
  creating button pictures, 349–351
  custom, 345–346
  Data Map, 263–266
  defined, 383
  docking, 108–111
  Drawing, 255, 259–260
  floating, 109
  Formatting
    emphasizing text, 127
    formatting cells, 108–111
    removing, 364
    summary of tools, 29–30
  hiding/showing, 340–341
  moving buttons, 343
  rearranging buttons, 343
  removing buttons, 343
  restoring defaults, 344
  spacing buttons, 343
  Standard, 28, 50, 282
    removing, 364
  Timecard, 293–294
Toolbars dialog box, 340–341
ToolTips, hiding/showing, 341
Total Page button, 183–184
typing data into cells, 57–59

• *U* •

Underline tool, 29, 127
Undo AutoFormat command, 106
Undo command
  database restriction, 273, 362
  undoing actions, 149–150, 359
Undo Replace command, 212–213
Undo tool, 28
user name, changing, 320
User Name field, 320

• *V* •

#VALUE!, message, 73
Vertical button, 229
vertical scroll bar
  hiding/showing, 317
  illustration, 26
Vertical Scroll Bar check box, 317

vertical worksheets, 229
View tab, 315–318

• *W* •

white cross pointer, 24
wildcards
  * (asterisk), 275
  ? (question mark), 211, 275
  asterisk (*), 275
  database search, 275
  question mark (?), 211, 275
window, defined, 383
Windows 95 taskbar, 26
Windows of Active Worksheet check
    box, 229
workbook window
  AutoCalculate, 34
  illustration, 26
  moving, 26, 33
  scrolling, 36–37
  sheet tabs, 33–34
  sheets, 33–34
  sizing, 26, 31–32
  status bar, 34
workbooks
  aligning text, 29
  bold text, 29
  cell borders, 30
  cell color, 30
  centering text across columns, 29
  charts, 28
  commas, in large numbers, 29
  conserving computer memory, 359
  copying to Clipboard, 27
  creating formulas, 28
  cutting to Clipboard, 27
  decimal places, 29
  defined, 383
  descriptive information, 93
  drawing, 28
  e-mailing, 366
  finding
    with Advanced Find, 144–145
    by browsing, 142

    with Find, 142
    from My Favorite folder, 142
    on a network, 149
    reusing search criteria, 149
    saving search criteria, 146
  font changes, 29
  frozen headings, 200–203
  frozen panes, 202
  going directly to a cell, 40
  help for, 28
  italic text, 29
  locking, 214–215
  manual recalculation, 213–214
  maps, 28
  moving in, 37–40
  naming, 359
  number of worksheets in, 16
  opening, 27
    active, 357
    multiple, 140–141
    recently edited, 141
    when Excel starts, 357
  painting formats, 27
  passwords, 216
  pasting from Clipboard, 27
  print preview, 27
  printing
    centering on a page, 179–180
    colors in black and white, 185
    first page number, 176–177
    footers, 181–184
    formulas, 191–192
    gridlines, 185
    headers, 181–184
    inserting current date, 183–184
    inserting current time, 183–184
    inserting workbook name, 183–184
    margins, 179–180
    multiple copies, 174–176
    numbering pages, 183–186
    page breaks, 188–190
    page orientation, 176–177
    page settings, 174–176
    paper size, 176–177

workbooks, printing *(continued)*
   print quality, 176–177, 185
   row and column headings, 185
   scaling output, 176–179
   selecting cells for, 174–176, 185
   from Standard toolbar, 27, 173–174
   text notes, 185
   titles, 185–188
  renaming, 92
  repeating last action, 28
  saving, 27, 93, 358–359
  saving to a file, 91–94
  searching, 210–212
  searching and replacing, 212–213
  sorting, 28
  spell check, 27
  splitting windows, 198–200
  starting new, 357
  summary information, 93–94
  summing a list of values, 28
  text color, 30
  underlined text, 29
  undoing actions, 28
  unlocking, 214–215
  vs. worksheets, 217
  window panes, 198–200
  zooming, 28, 170–172, 196–198
  See also files
worksheet cell context menu, 45
worksheets
  assigning a template to, 222
  cascading, 230
  changing default number of, 223
  converting to a template, 305–307
  copying, 233–234
  copying across workbooks
   with dialog box, 231–232
   by dragging and dropping, 233–234
  data entry, 358
  defined, 383
  deleting, 222–223
  editing data, 358
  illustration, 13
  inserting, 222–223, 225

  list of recently used, 229
  maximizing display size, 364
  moving between, 218–221
  multiple, 218
  naming, 364
  number of cells, 14–16
  out of space, 57
  propagating changes across, 221
  saving space, 57
  scrolling between, 219–220
  scrolling within, 357
  selecting multiple, 221
  sorting, 225–226, 281
  summary, 235–237
  vs. workbooks, 217
  in windows, 227–231

• X •

x-axis, formatting, 256

• Y •

y-axis, formatting, 256

• Z •

zero values, hiding/showing, 317
Zero Values check box, 317
zip codes, 120
Zoom Control tool, 28
Zoom In tool, 263
Zoom Out tool, 263
zooming
  print preview, 170–172
  worksheets, 197, 364

The Internet For Macs® For Dummies® 2nd Edition	by Charles Seiter	ISBN: 1-56884-371-2	$19.99 USA/$26.99 Canada
The Internet For Macs® For Dummies® Starter Kit	by Charles Seiter	ISBN: 1-56884-244-9	$29.99 USA/$39.99 Canada
The Internet For Macs® For Dummies® Starter Kit Bestseller Edition	by Charles Seiter	ISBN: 1-56884-245-7	$39.99 USA/$54.99 Canada
The Internet For Windows® For Dummies® Starter Kit	by John R. Levine & Margaret Levine Young	ISBN: 1-56884-237-6	$34.99 USA/$44.99 Canada
The Internet For Windows® For Dummies® Starter Kit, Bestseller Edition	by John R. Levine & Margaret Levine Young	ISBN: 1-56884-246-5	$39.99 USA/$54.99 Canada

MACINTOSH

Mac® Programming For Dummies®	by Dan Parks Sydow	ISBN: 1-56884-173-6	$19.95 USA/$26.95 Canada
Macintosh® System 7.5 For Dummies®	by Bob LeVitus	ISBN: 1-56884-197-3	$19.95 USA/$26.95 Canada
MORE Macs® For Dummies®	by David Pogue	ISBN: 1-56884-087-X	$19.95 USA/$26.95 Canada
PageMaker 5 For Macs® For Dummies®	by Galen Gruman & Deke McClelland	ISBN: 1-56884-178-7	$19.95 USA/$26.95 Canada
QuarkXPress 3.3 For Dummies®	by Galen Gruman & Barbara Assadi	ISBN: 1-56884-217-1	$19.99 USA/$26.99 Canada
Upgrading and Fixing Macs® For Dummies®	by Kearney Rietmann & Frank Higgins	ISBN: 1-56884-189-2	$19.95 USA/$26.95 Canada

MULTIMEDIA

Multimedia & CD-ROMs For Dummies® 2nd Edition	by Andy Rathbone	ISBN: 1-56884-907-9	$19.99 USA/$26.99 Canada
Multimedia & CD-ROMs For Dummies® Interactive Multimedia Value Pack, 2nd Edition	by Andy Rathbone	ISBN: 1-56884-909-5	$29.99 USA/$39.99 Canada

OPERATING SYSTEMS:

DOS

MORE DOS For Dummies®	by Dan Gookin	ISBN: 1-56884-046-2	$19.95 USA/$26.95 Canada
OS/2® Warp For Dummies® 2nd Edition	by Andy Rathbone	ISBN: 1-56884-205-8	$19.99 USA/$26.99 Canada

UNIX

MORE UNIX® For Dummies®	by John R. Levine & Margaret Levine Young	ISBN: 1-56884-361-5	$19.99 USA/$26.99 Canada
UNIX® For Dummies®	by John R. Levine & Margaret Levine Young	ISBN: 1-878058-58-4	$19.95 USA/$26.95 Canada

WINDOWS

MORE Windows® For Dummies® 2nd Edition	by Andy Rathbone	ISBN: 1-56884-048-9	$19.95 USA/$26.95 Canada
Windows® 95 For Dummies®	by Andy Rathbone	ISBN: 1-56884-240-6	$19.99 USA/$26.99 Canada

PCS/HARDWARE

Illustrated Computer Dictionary For Dummies® 2nd Edition	by Dan Gookin & Wallace Wang	ISBN: 1-56884-218-X	$12.95 USA/$16.95 Canada
Upgrading and Fixing PCs For Dummies® 2nd Edition	by Andy Rathbone	ISBN: 1-56884-903-6	$19.99 USA/$26.99 Canada

PRESENTATION/AUTOCAD

AutoCAD For Dummies®	by Bud Smith	ISBN: 1-56884-191-4	$19.95 USA/$26.95 Canada
PowerPoint 4 For Windows® For Dummies®	by Doug Lowe	ISBN: 1-56884-161-2	$16.99 USA/$22.99 Canada

PROGRAMMING

Borland C++ For Dummies®	by Michael Hyman	ISBN: 1-56884-162-0	$19.95 USA/$26.95 Canada
C For Dummies® Volume 1	by Dan Gookin	ISBN: 1-878058-78-9	$19.95 USA/$26.95 Canada
C++ For Dummies®	by Stephen R. Davis	ISBN: 1-56884-163-9	$19.95 USA/$26.95 Canada
Delphi Programming For Dummies®	by Neil Rubenking	ISBN: 1-56884-200-7	$19.99 USA/$26.99 Canada
Mac® Programming For Dummies®	by Dan Parks Sydow	ISBN: 1-56884-173-6	$19.95 USA/$26.95 Canada
PowerBuilder 4 Programming For Dummies®	by Ted Coombs & Jason Coombs	ISBN: 1-56884-325-9	$19.99 USA/$26.99 Canada
QBasic Programming For Dummies®	by Douglas Hergert	ISBN: 1-56884-093-4	$19.95 USA/$26.95 Canada
Visual Basic 3 For Dummies®	by Wallace Wang	ISBN: 1-56884-076-4	$19.95 USA/$26.95 Canada
Visual Basic "X" For Dummies®	by Wallace Wang	ISBN: 1-56884-230-9	$19.99 USA/$26.99 Canada
Visual C++ 2 For Dummies®	by Michael Hyman & Bob Arnson	ISBN: 1-56884-328-3	$19.99 USA/$26.99 Canada
Windows® 95 Programming For Dummies®	by S. Randy Davis	ISBN: 1-56884-327-5	$19.99 USA/$26.99 Canada

SPREADSHEET

1-2-3 For Dummies®	by Greg Harvey	ISBN: 1-878058-60-6	$16.95 USA/$22.95 Canada
1-2-3 For Windows® 5 For Dummies® 2nd Edition	by John Walkenbach	ISBN: 1-56884-216-3	$16.95 USA/$22.95 Canada
Excel 5 For Macs® For Dummies®	by Greg Harvey	ISBN: 1-56884-186-8	$19.95 USA/$26.95 Canada
Excel For Dummies® 2nd Edition	by Greg Harvey	ISBN: 1-56884-050-0	$16.95 USA/$22.95 Canada
MORE 1-2-3 For DOS For Dummies®	by John Weingarten	ISBN: 1-56884-224-4	$19.99 USA/$26.99 Canada
MORE Excel 5 For Windows® For Dummies®	by Greg Harvey	ISBN: 1-56884-207-4	$19.95 USA/$26.95 Canada
Quattro Pro 6 For Windows® For Dummies®	by John Walkenbach	ISBN: 1-56884-174-4	$19.95 USA/$26.95 Canada
Quattro Pro For DOS For Dummies®	by John Walkenbach	ISBN: 1-56884-023-3	$16.95 USA/$22.95 Canada

UTILITIES

Norton Utilities 8 For Dummies®	by Beth Slick	ISBN: 1-56884-166-3	$19.95 USA/$26.95 Canada

VCRS/CAMCORDERS

VCRs & Camcorders For Dummies™	by Gordon McComb & Andy Rathbone	ISBN: 1-56884-229-5	$14.99 USA/$20.99 Canada

WORD PROCESSING

Ami Pro For Dummies®	by Jim Meade	ISBN: 1-56884-049-7	$19.95 USA/$26.95 Canada
MORE Word For Windows® 6 For Dummies®	by Doug Lowe	ISBN: 1-56884-165-5	$19.95 USA/$26.95 Canada
MORE WordPerfect® 6 For Windows® For Dummies®	by Margaret Levine Young & David C. Kay	ISBN: 1-56884-206-6	$19.95 USA/$26.95 Canada
MORE WordPerfect® 6 For DOS For Dummies®	by Wallace Wang, edited by Dan Gookin	ISBN: 1-56884-047-0	$19.95 USA/$26.95 Canada
Word 6 For Macs® For Dummies®	by Dan Gookin	ISBN: 1-56884-190-6	$19.95 USA/$26.95 Canada
Word For Windows® 6 For Dummies®	by Dan Gookin	ISBN: 1-56884-075-6	$16.95 USA/$22.95 Canada
Word For Windows® For Dummies®	by Dan Gookin & Ray Werner	ISBN: 1-878058-86-X	$16.95 USA/$22.95 Canada
WordPerfect® 6 For DOS For Dummies®	by Dan Gookin	ISBN: 1-878058-77-0	$16.95 USA/$22.95 Canada
WordPerfect® 6.1 For Windows® For Dummies® 2nd Edition	by Margaret Levine Young & David Kay	ISBN: 1-56884-243-0	$16.95 USA/$22.95 Canada
WordPerfect® For Dummies®	by Dan Gookin	ISBN: 1-878058-52-5	$16.95 USA/$22.95 Canada

FOR DUMMIES
BOOK SERIES
FROM IDG

DUMMIES PRESS™ QUICK REFERENCES

IDG BOOKS
WORLDWIDE

Fun, Fast, & Cheap!™

9/19/95

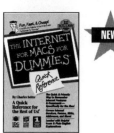

The Internet For Macs® For Dummies® Quick Reference
by Charles Seiter

ISBN:1-56884-967-2
$9.99 USA/$12.99 Canada

Windows® 95 For Dummies® Quick Reference
by Greg Harvey

ISBN: 1-56884-964-8
$9.99 USA/$12.99 Canada

Photoshop 3 For Macs® For Dummies® Quick Reference
by Deke McClelland

ISBN: 1-56884-968-0
$9.99 USA/$12.99 Canada

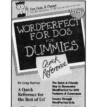

WordPerfect® For DOS For Dummies® Quick Reference
by Greg Harvey

ISBN: 1-56884-009-8
$8.95 USA/$12.95 Canada

Title	Author	ISBN	Price
DATABASE			
Access 2 For Dummies® Quick Reference	by Stuart J. Stuple	ISBN: 1-56884-167-1	$8.95 USA/$11.95 Canada
dBASE 5 For DOS For Dummies® Quick Reference	by Barrie Sosinsky	ISBN: 1-56884-954-0	$9.99 USA/$12.99 Canada
dBASE 5 For Windows® For Dummies® Quick Reference	by Stuart J. Stuple	ISBN: 1-56884-953-2	$9.99 USA/$12.99 Canada
Paradox 5 For Windows® For Dummies® Quick Reference	by Scott Palmer	ISBN: 1-56884-960-5	$9.99 USA/$12.99 Canada
DESKTOP PUBLISHING/ILLUSTRATION/GRAPHICS			
CorelDRAW! 5 For Dummies® Quick Reference	by Raymond E. Werner	ISBN: 1-56884-952-4	$9.99 USA/$12.99 Canada
Harvard Graphics For Windows® For Dummies® Quick Reference	by Raymond E. Werner	ISBN: 1-56884-962-1	$9.99 USA/$12.99 Canada
Photoshop 3 For Macs® For Dummies® Quick Reference	by Deke McClelland	ISBN: 1-56884-968-0	$9.99 USA/$12.99 Canada
FINANCE/PERSONAL FINANCE			
Quicken 4 For Windows® For Dummies® Quick Reference	by Stephen L. Nelson	ISBN: 1-56884-950-8	$9.95 USA/$12.95 Canada
GROUPWARE/INTEGRATED			
Microsoft® Office 4 For Windows® For Dummies® Quick Reference	by Doug Lowe	ISBN: 1-56884-958-3	$9.99 USA/$12.99 Canada
Microsoft® Works 3 For Windows® For Dummies® Quick Reference	by Michael Partington	ISBN: 1-56884-959-1	$9.99 USA/$12.99 Canada
INTERNET/COMMUNICATIONS/NETWORKING			
The Internet For Dummies® Quick Reference	by John R. Levine & Margaret Levine Young	ISBN: 1-56884-168-X	$8.95 USA/$11.95 Canada
MACINTOSH			
Macintosh® System 7.5 For Dummies® Quick Reference	by Stuart J. Stuple	ISBN: 1-56884-956-7	$9.99 USA/$12.99 Canada
OPERATING SYSTEMS:			
DOS			
DOS For Dummies® Quick Reference	by Greg Harvey	ISBN: 1-56884-007-1	$8.95 USA/$11.95 Canada
UNIX			
UNIX® For Dummies® Quick Reference	By John R. Levine & Margaret Levine Young	ISBN: 1-56884-094-2	$8.95 USA/$11.95 Canada
WINDOWS			
Windows® 3.1 For Dummies® Quick Reference, 2nd Edition	by Greg Harvey	ISBN: 1-56884-951-6	$8.95 USA/$11.95 Canada
PCs/HARDWARE			
Memory Management For Dummies® Quick Reference	Doug Lowe	ISBN: 1-56884-362-3	$9.99 USA/$12.99 Canada
PRESENTATION/AUTOCAD			
AutoCAD For Dummies® Quick Reference	by Ellen Finkelstein	ISBN: 1-56884-198-1	$9.95 USA/$12.95 Canada
SPREADSHEET			
1-2-3 For Dummies® Quick Reference	by John Walkenbach	ISBN: 1-56884-027-6	$8.95 USA/$11.95 Canada
1-2-3 For Windows® 5 For Dummies® Quick Reference	by John Walkenbach	ISBN: 1-56884-957-5	$9.95 USA/$12.95 Canada
Excel For Windows® For Dummies® Quick Reference, 2nd Edition	by John Walkenbach	ISBN: 1-56884-096-9	$8.95 USA/$11.95 Canada
Quattro Pro 6 For Windows® For Dummies® Quick Reference	by Stuart J. Stuple	ISBN: 1-56884-172-8	$9.95 USA/$12.95 Canada
WORD PROCESSING			
Word For Windows® 6 For Dummies® Quick Reference	by George Lynch	ISBN: 1-56884-095-0	$8.95 USA/$11.95 Canada
Word For Windows® For Dummies® Quick Reference	by George Lynch	ISBN: 1-56884-029-2	$8.95 USA/$11.95 Canada
WordPerfect® 6.1 For Windows® For Dummies® Quick Reference, 2nd Edition	by Greg Harvey	ISBN: 1-56884-966-4	$9.99 USA/$12.99/Canada

For scholastic requests & educational orders please call Educational Sales at 1. 800. 434. 2086

FOR MORE INFO OR TO ORDER, PLEASE CALL ▶ 800. 762. 2974

For volume discounts & special orders please call Tony Real, Special Sales, at 415. 655. 3048

9/19/95

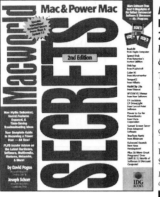

Macworld® Mac® & Power Mac SECRETS™, 2nd Edition
by David Pogue & Joseph Schorr

This is the definitive Mac reference for those who want to become power users! Includes three disks with 9MB of software!

WINNERS 1994-95 TECHNICAL PUBLICATIONS AND ART COMPETITIONS OF THE SOCIETY FOR TECHNICAL COMMUNICATION

ISBN: 1-56884-175-2
$39.95 USA/$54.95 Canada

Includes 3 disks chock full of software.

NEWBRIDGE BOOK CLUB SELECTION

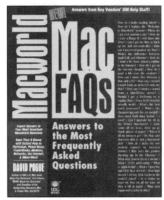

Macworld® Mac® FAQs™
by David Pogue

Written by the hottest Macintosh author around, David Pogue, *Macworld Mac FAQs* gives users the ultimate Mac reference. Hundreds of Mac questions and answers side-by-side, right at your fingertips, and organized into six easy-to-reference sections with lots of sidebars and diagrams.

ISBN: 1-56884-480-8
$19.99 USA/$26.99 Canada

Macworld® System 7.5 Bible, 3rd Edition
by Lon Poole

ISBN: 1-56884-098-5
$29.95 USA/$39.95 Canada

NATIONAL BESTSELLER!

Macworld® ClarisWorks 3.0 Companion, 3rd Edition
by Steven A. Schwartz

ISBN: 1-56884-481-6
$24.99 USA/$34.99 Canada

NATIONAL BESTSELLER!

Macworld® Complete Mac® Handbook Plus Interactive CD, 3rd Edition
by Jim Heid

ISBN: 1-56884-192-2
$39.95 USA/$54.95 Canada

Includes an interactive CD-ROM.

BMUG SPRING 1995 CHOICE PRODUCT

NEWBRIDGE BOOK CLUB SELECTION

Macworld® Ultimate Mac® CD-ROM
by Jim Heid

ISBN: 1-56884-477-8
$19.99 USA/$26.99 Canada

CD-ROM includes version 2.0 of QuickTime, and over 65 MB of the best shareware, freeware, fonts, sounds, and more!

Macworld® Networking Bible, 2nd Edition
by Dave Kosiur & Joel M. Snyder

ISBN: 1-56884-194-9
$29.95 USA/$39.95 Canada

XI WINNER

Macworld® Photoshop 3 Bible, 2nd Edition
by Deke McClelland

ISBN: 1-56884-158-2
$39.95 USA/$54.95 Canada

Includes stunning CD-ROM with add-ons, digitized photos and more.

WINNERS 1994-95 TECHNICAL PUBLICATIONS AND ART COMPETITIONS OF THE SOCIETY FOR TECHNICAL COMMUNICATION

NEW!

Macworld® Photoshop 2.5 Bible
by Deke McClelland

ISBN: 1-56884-022-5
$29.95 USA/$39.95 Canada

NATIONAL BESTSELLER!

Macworld® FreeHand 4 Bible
by Deke McClelland

ISBN: 1-56884-170-1
$29.95 USA/$39.95 Canada

Macworld® Illustrator 5.0/5.5 Bible
by Ted Alspach

ISBN: 1-56884-097-7
$39.95 USA/$54.95 Canada

Includes CD-ROM with QuickTime tutorials.

Mac is a registered trademark of Apple Computer. Macworld is a registered trademark of International Data Group, Inc. ----SECRETS, and ----FAQs are trademarks under exclusive license to IDG Books Worldwide, Inc., from International Data Group, Inc.

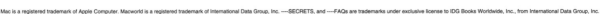

For scholastic requests & educational orders please call Educational Sales, at 1. 800. 434. 2086

FOR MORE INFO OR TO ORDER, PLEASE CALL ▶ 800. 762. 2974

For volume discounts & special orders please call Tony Real, Special Sales, at 415. 655. 3048

Order Center: **(800) 762-2974** *(8 a.m.–6 p.m., EST, weekdays)*

Quantity	ISBN	Title	Price	Total

Shipping & Handling Charges

	Description	First book	Each additional book	Total
Domestic	Normal	$4.50	$1.50	$
	Two Day Air	$8.50	$2.50	$
	Overnight	$18.00	$3.00	$
International	Surface	$8.00	$8.00	$
	Airmail	$16.00	$16.00	$
	DHL Air	$17.00	$17.00	$

*For large quantities call for shipping & handling charges.
**Prices are subject to change without notice.

Ship to:

Name _____

Company _____

Address _____

City/State/Zip _____

Daytime Phone _____

Payment: ☐ Check to IDG Books Worldwide (US Funds Only)

☐ VISA   ☐ MasterCard   ☐ American Express

Card # _____ Expires _____

Signature _____

Subtotal _____

CA residents add
applicable sales tax _____

IN, MA, and MD
residents add
5% sales tax _____

IL residents add
6.25% sales tax_____

RI residents add
7% sales tax_____

TX residents add
8.25% sales tax_____

Shipping_____

Total _____

Please send this order form to:

IDG Books Worldwide, Inc.
7260 Shadeland Station, Suite 100
Indianapolis, IN 46256

Allow up to 3 weeks for delivery.
Thank you!

IDG BOOKS WORLDWIDE REGISTRATION CARD

RETURN THIS
REGISTRATION CARD
FOR FREE CATALOG

Title of this book: Excel For Windows 95 For Dummies

My overall rating of this book: ❏ Very good [1]   ❏ Good [2]   ❏ Satisfactory [3]   ❏ Fair [4]   ❏ Poor [5]

How I first heard about this book:

❏ Found in bookstore; name: [6]   ❏ Book review: [7]

❏ Advertisement: [8]   ❏ Catalog: [9]

❏ Word of mouth; heard about book from friend, co-worker, etc.: [10]   ❏ Other: [11]

What I liked most about this book:

What I would change, add, delete, etc., in future editions of this book:

Other comments:

Number of computer books I purchase in a year: ❏ 1 [12]   ❏ 2-5 [13]   ❏ 6-10 [14]   ❏ More than 10 [15]

I would characterize my computer skills as: ❏ Beginner [16] ❏ Intermediate [17] ❏ Advanced [18] ❏ Professional [19]

I use ❏ DOS [20] ❏ Windows [21] ❏ OS/2 [22] ❏ Unix [23] ❏ Macintosh [24] ❏ Other: [25]_____
                                                                                    (please specify)

I would be interested in new books on the following subjects:

(please check all that apply, and use the spaces provided to identify specific software)

❏ Word processing: [26]   ❏ Spreadsheets: [27]

❏ Data bases: [28]   ❏ Desktop publishing: [29]

❏ File Utilities: [30]   ❏ Money management: [31]

❏ Networking: [32]   ❏ Programming languages: [33]

❏ Other: [34]

I use a PC at (please check all that apply): ❏ home [35] ❏ work [36] ❏ school [37] ❏ other: [38] _____

The disks I prefer to use are ❏ 5.25 [39] ❏ 3.5 [40] ❏ other: [41]_____

I have a CD ROM: ❏ yes [42]   ❏ no [43]

I plan to buy or upgrade computer hardware this year: ❏ yes [44]   ❏ no [45]

I plan to buy or upgrade computer software this year: ❏ yes [46]   ❏ no [47]

Name: _____ Business title: [48] _____ Type of Business: [49] _____

Address (❏ home [50] ❏ work [51]/Company name: _____)

Street/Suite# _____

City [52]/State [53]/Zipcode [54]: _____   Country [55] _____

❏ **I liked this book!** You may quote me by name in future
   IDG Books Worldwide promotional materials.

My daytime phone number is _____

**IDG
BOOKS**

THE WORLD OF
COMPUTER
KNOWLEDGE

YES!

Please keep me informed about IDG's World of Computer Knowledge.
Send me the latest IDG Books catalog.

NO POSTAGE
NECESSARY
IF MAILED
IN THE
UNITED STATES

BUSINESS REPLY MAIL

FIRST CLASS MAIL   PERMIT NO. 2605   FOSTER CITY, CALIFORNIA

IDG Books Worldwide
919 E Hillsdale Blvd, STE 400
Foster City, CA 94404-9691